CISA Exam Prep Objective Matrix

— winter 87

CISA Job Practice Area 1: IS Audit Process (Approximately 10% of Exam)

Task	Page
Develop and implement a risk-based IS audit strategy for the organization in compliance with IS audit standards, guidelines and best practices.	32
Plan specific audits to ensure that IT and business systems are protected and controlled.	24
Conduct audits in accordance with IS audit standards, guidelines and best practices to meet planned audit objectives.	27
Communicate emerging issues, potential risks, and audit results to key stakeholders.	50
Advise on the implementation of risk management and control practices within the organization, while maintaining independence.	39

Knowledge Statement	Page
Knowledge of ISACA IS Auditing Standards, Guidelines and Procedures and Code of Professional Ethics	27
Knowledge of IS auditing practices and techniques	27
Knowledge of techniques to gather information and preserve evidence (e.g., observation, inquiry, interview, CAATs, electronic media)	39
Knowledge of the evidence life cycle (e.g., the collection, protection, chain of custody)	39
Knowledge of control objectives and controls related to IS (e.g., CobiT)	36
Knowledge of risk assessment in an audit context	35
Knowledge of audit planning and management techniques	24
Knowledge of reporting and communication techniques (e.g., facilitation, negotiation, conflict resolution)	39
Knowledge of control ...	
Knowledge ...	

CISA Job Practice Area 2: IT Governance (Appr...

Task	Page
Evaluate the effectiveness of IT governance structure to ensure adequate board control over the decisions, directions, and performance of IT so that it supports the organization's strategies and objectives.	67
Evaluate IT organizational structure and human resources (personnel) management to ensure that they support the organization's strategies and objectives.	88
Evaluate the IT strategy and the process for its development, approval, implementation, and maintenance to ensure that it supports the organization's strategies and objectives.	67
Evaluate the organization's IT policies, standards, and procedures; and the processes for their development, approval, implementation, and maintenance to ensure that they support the IT strategy and comply with regulatory and legal requirements.	74

Knowledge ...	
Knowledge of the purpose of IT strategies, policies, standards and procedures for an organization and the essential elements of each	74
Knowledge of IT governance frameworks	67
Knowledge of the processes for the development, implementation and maintenance of IT strategies, policies, standards and procedures (for example, protection of information assets, business continuity and disaster recovery, systems and infrastructure lifecycle management, IT service delivery and support)	74
Knowledge of quality management strategies and policies	95
Knowledge of organizational structure, roles and responsibilities related to the use and management of IT	99

Continues on Following Page

CISA Job Practice Area 2: (Continued)

Task (continued)	Page	Knowledge Statement (continued)	Page
Evaluate management practices to ensure compliance with the organization's IT strategy, policies, standards, and procedures.	74	Knowledge of generally accepted international IT standards and guidelines	74
Evaluate IT resource investment, use, and allocation practices to ensure alignment with the organization's strategies and objectives.	72	Knowledge of enterprise IT architecture and its implications for setting long-term strategic directions	72
Evaluate IT contracting strategies and policies, and contract management practices to ensure that they support the organization's strategies and objectives.	93	Knowledge of risk management methodologies and tools	79
		Knowledge of the use of control frameworks (e.g., CobiT, COSO, ISO 17799)	95
Evaluate risk management practices to ensure that the organization's IT related risks are properly managed.	79	Knowledge of the use of maturity and process improvement models (e.g., CMM, CobiT)	95
		Knowledge of contracting strategies, processes and contract management practices	93
Evaluate monitoring and assurance practices to ensure that the board and executive management receive sufficient and timely information about IT performance.	67	Knowledge of practices for monitoring and reporting of IT performance (e.g., balanced scorecards, key performance indicators [KPI])	71
		Knowledge of relevant legislative and regulatory issues (e.g., privacy, intellectual property, corporate governance requirements)	67
		Knowledge of IT human resources (personnel) management	88
		Knowledge of IT resource investment and allocation practices (e.g., portfolio management return on investment (ROI))	71

CISA Job Practice Area 3: Systems and Infrastructure Lifecycle Management (Approximately 16% of Exam)

Task	Page	Knowledge Statement	Page
Evaluate the business case for the proposed system development/acquisition to ensure that it meets the organization's business goals.	130	Knowledge of benefits management practices, (e.g., feasibility studies, business cases)	130
Evaluate the project management framework and project governance practices to ensure that business objectives are achieved in a cost-effective manner while managing risks to the organization.	120	Knowledge of project governance mechanisms (e.g., steering committee, project oversight board)	117
		Knowledge of project management practices, tools, and control frameworks	117
Perform reviews to ensure that a project is progressing in accordance with project plans, is adequately supported by documentation and status reporting is accurate.	120	Knowledge of risk management practices applied to projects	176
		Knowledge of project success criteria and risks	121
Evaluate proposed control mechanisms for systems and/or infrastructure during specification, development/acquisition, and testing to ensure that they will provide safeguards and comply with the organization's policies and other requirements.	130	Knowledge of configuration, change and re-lease management in relation to development and maintenance of systems and/or infrastructure	146
		Knowledge of control objectives and tech-niques that ensure the completeness, accuracy, validity, and authorization of transactions and data within IT systems applications	158

CISA Job Practice Area 3: (Continued)

Task (continued)	Page	Knowledge Statement (continued)	Page
Evaluate the processes by which systems and/or infrastructure are developed/acquired and tested to ensure that the deliverables meet the organization's objectives.	168	Knowledge of enterprise architecture related to data, applications, and technology (e.g., distributed applications, web-based applications, web services, *n*-tier applications)	178
Evaluate the readiness of the system and/or infrastructure for implementation and migration into production.	130	Knowledge of requirements analysis and management practices (e.g., requirements verification, traceability, gap analysis)	130
Perform post-implementation review of systems and/or infrastructure to ensure that they meet the organization's objectives and are subject to effective internal control.	176	Knowledge of acquisition and contract management processes (e.g., evaluation of vendors, preparation of contracts, vendor management, escrow)	130
Perform periodic reviews of systems and/or infrastructure to ensure that they continue to meet the organization's objectives and are subject to effective internal control.	168	Knowledge of system development methodologies and tools and an understanding of their strengths and weaknesses (e.g., agile development practices, prototyping, rapid application development [RAD], object-oriented design techniques)	142
Evaluate the process by which systems and/or infrastructure are maintained to ensure the continued support of the organization's objectives and are subject to effective internal control.	146	Knowledge of quality assurance methods	130
		Knowledge of the management of testing processes (e.g., test strategies, test plans, test environments, entry and exit criteria)	130
Evaluate the process by which systems and/or infrastructure are disposed of to ensure that they comply with the organization's policies and procedures.	130	Knowledge of data conversion tools, techniques, and procedures	130
		Knowledge of system and/or infrastructure disposal procedures	130
		Knowledge of software and hardware certification and accreditation practices	130
		Knowledge of post-implementation review objectives and methods (e.g., project closure, benefits realization, performance measurement)	130
		Knowledge of system migration and infrastructure deployment practices	130

CISA Job Practice Area 4: IT Service Delivery and Support (Approximately 14% of Exam)

Task	Page	Knowledge Statement	Page
Evaluate service level management practices to ensure that the level of service from internal and external service providers is defined and managed.	198	Knowledge of service level management practices	198
Evaluate operations management to ensure that IT support functions effectively meet business needs.	198	Knowledge of operations management best practices (e.g., workload scheduling, network services management, preventive maintenance)	198
Evaluate data administration practices to ensure the integrity and optimization of databases.	221	Knowledge of systems performance monitoring processes, tools, and techniques (e.g., network analyzers, system utilization reports, load balancing)	274

Continues on Following Page

CISA Job Practice Area 4: (Continued)

Task (continued)	Page	Knowledge Statement (continued)	Page
Evaluate the use of capacity and performance monitoring tools and techniques to ensure that IT services meet the organization's objectives.	244	Knowledge of the functionality of hardware and network components (e.g., routers, switches, firewalls, peripherals)	242
Evaluate change, configuration, and release management practices to ensure that changes made to the organization's production environment are adequately controlled and documented.	198	Knowledge of database administration practices	221
		Knowledge of the functionality of system software including operating systems, utilities, and database management systems	221
Evaluate problem and incident management practices to ensure that incidents, problems, or errors are recorded, analyzed, and resolved in a timely manner.	274	Knowledge of capacity planning and monitoring techniques	198
Evaluate the functionality of the IT infrastructure (e.g., network components, hardware, system software) to ensure that it supports the organization's objectives.	209	Knowledge of processes for managing scheduled and emergency changes to the production systems and/or infrastructure including change, configuration, release, and patch management practices	198
		Knowledge of incident/problem management practices (e.g., help desk, escalation procedures, tracking)	198
		Knowledge of software licensing and inventory practices	221
		Knowledge of system resiliency tools and techniques (e.g., fault tolerant hardware, elimination of single point of failure, clustering)	209

CISA Job Practice Area 5: Protection of Information Assets (Approximately 31% of Exam)

Task	Page	Knowledge Statement	Page
Evaluate the design, implementation, and monitoring of logical access controls to ensure the confidentiality, integrity, availability and authorized use of information assets.	337	Knowledge of the techniques for the design, implementation and monitoring of security (e.g., threat and risk assessment, sensitivity analysis, privacy impact assessment)	294
Evaluate network infrastructure security to ensure confidentiality, integrity, availability and authorized use of the network and the information transmitted.	293	Knowledge of logical access controls for the identification, authentication, and restriction of users to authorized functions and data (e.g., dynamic passwords, challenge/response, menus, profiles)	303
Evaluate the design, implementation, and monitoring of environmental controls to prevent or minimize loss.	364	Knowledge of logical access security architectures (e.g., single sign-on, user identification strategies, identity management)	303
Evaluate the design, implementation, and monitoring of physical access controls to ensure that information assets are adequately safeguarded.	364	Knowledge of attack methods and techniques (e.g., hacking, spoofing, Trojan horses, denial of service, spamming)	313
Evaluate the processes and procedures used to store, retrieve, transport, and dispose of confidential information assets.	312	Knowledge of processes related to monitoring and responding to security incidents (e.g., escalation procedures, emergency incident response team)	330

CISA Job Practice Area 5: (Continued)

Knowledge Statement (continued)	Page
Knowledge of network and Internet security devices, protocols, and techniques (e.g., SSL, SET, VPN, NAT)	340
Knowledge of intrusion detection systems and firewall configuration, implementation, operation, and maintenance	319
Knowledge of encryption algorithm techniques (e.g., AES, RSA)	340
Knowledge of public key infrastructure (PKI) components (e.g., certification authorities, registration authorities) and digital signature techniques	340
Knowledge of virus detection tools and control techniques	329
Knowledge of security testing and assessment tools (e.g., penetration testing, vulnerability scanning)	337
Knowledge of environmental protection practices and devices (e.g., fire suppression, cooling systems, water sensors)	381
Knowledge of physical security systems and practices (e.g., biometrics, access cards, cipher locks, tokens)	303
Knowledge of data classification schemes (e.g., public, confidential, private, and sensitive data)	389
Knowledge of voice communications security (e.g., voice over IP)	328
Knowledge of the processes and procedures used to store, retrieve, transport, and dispose of confidential information assets	312
Knowledge of controls and risks associated with the use of portable and wireless devices (e.g., PDAs, USB devices, Bluetooth devices)	319

Continues on Following Page

CISA Job Practice Area 6: Business Continuity and Disaster Recovery (Approximately 14% of Exam)

Task	Page
Evaluate the adequacy of backup and restore provisions to ensure the availability of information required to resume processing.	432
Evaluate the organization's disaster recovery plan to ensure that it enables the recovery of IT processing capabilities in the event of a disaster.	436
Evaluate the organization's business continuity plan to ensure its ability to continue essential business operations during the period of an IT disruption.	436

Knowledge Statement	Page
Knowledge of data backup, storage, maintenance, retention and restoration processes, and practices	431
Knowledge of regulatory, legal, contractual, and insurance issues related to business continuity and disaster recovery	406
Knowledge of business impact analysis (BIA)	411
Knowledge of the development and maintenance of the business continuity and disaster recovery plans	419
Knowledge of business continuity and disaster recovery testing approaches and methods	421
Knowledge of human resources management practices as related to business continuity and disaster recovery (e.g., evacuation planning, response teams)	421
Knowledge of processes used to invoke the business continuity and disaster recovery plans	421
Knowledge of types of alternate processing sites and methods used to monitor the contractual agreements (e.g., hot sites, warm sites, cold sites)	425

CISA

Michael Gregg

CISA Exam Prep

ISBN-10: 0-7897-3573-3

ISBN-13: 978-0-7897-3573-7

Library of Congress Cataloging-In-Progress data

       Library of Congress Cataloging-in-Publication Data

Gregg, Michael (Michael C.)

  CISA exam prep / Michael Gregg.

    p. cm.

  Includes index.

  ISBN 978-0-7897-3573-7 (pbk.) 1. Information Systems Audit and Control Association—Examinations—Study guides. 2. Electronic data processing personnel—Certification—Study guides. 3. Electronic data processing departments—Auditing—Examinations—Study guides. 4. Management information systems—Auditing—Examinations—Study guides. I. Title. II. Title: Certified Information Systems Auditor exam prep.

  QA76.3.G75268 2007

  658.4'03—dc22

                      2007012694

Printed in the United States of America

First Printing: April 2007

10 09 08 07   4 3 2 1

Trademarks

Warning and Disclaimer

Bulk Sales

Que Publishing offers excellent discounts on this book when ordered in quantity for bulk purchases or special sales. For more information, please contact

U.S. Corporate and Government Sales
1-800-382-3419
corpsales@pearsontechgroup.com

For sales outside the U.S., please contact

International Sales
international@pearsoned.com

Associate Publisher
Dave Dusthimer

Acquisitions Editor
Betsy Brown

Senior Development Editor
Christopher Cleveland

Managing Editor
Patrick Kanouse

Project Editor
Seth Kerney

Copy Editor
Krista Hansing

Indexer
Tim Wright

Proofreader
Debbie Williams

Technical Editors
Donald Glass
Shawn Merdinger

Publishing Coordinator
Vanessa Evans

Multimedia Developer
Dan Scherf

Book Designer
Gary Adair

Page Layout
Bronkella Publishing LLC

Contents at a Glance

Table of Contents

Part I: IT Governance and the Audit Process

Chapter 1:

The Audit Process **21**

Part III: IT Service Delivery and Support

Chapter 5:
Information Systems Hardware and Architecture 195

Part IV: Protection of Information Assets

Chapter 7:

About the Author

As the founder and president of Superior Solutions, Inc., a Houston-based IT security consulting and auditing firm, **Michael Gregg** has more than 15 years of experience in information security and risk management. He holds two associate's degrees, a bachelor's degree, and a master's degree. Some of the certifications he holds include the following: CISA, CISSP, MCSE, CTT+, A+, N+, Security+, CNA, CCNA, CIW Security Analyst, CCE, CEH, CHFI, CEI, DCNP, ES Dragon IDS, ES Advanced Dragon IDS, and TICSA.

Michael not only has experience in performing security audits and assessments, but he also is the co-author of *Inside Network Security Assessment: Guarding Your IT Infrastructure* (ISBN 0672328097, Sams, 2005). Other publications he has authored include the *CISSP Exam Cram 2* (ISBN 078973446X, Que, 2005) and the *Certified Ethical Hacker Exam Prep 2* (ISBN 0789735318, Que, 2006). Michael is a site expert for TechTarget.com websites, including SearchSMB.com and SearchNetworking.com; he also serves on their editorial advisory board. His articles have been published on IT websites including CertMag.com, CramSession.com, and GoCertify.com. Michael has created security audit and assessment course material for various companies and universities. Although audits and assessments are where he spends the bulk of his time, teaching and contributing to the written body of IT security knowledge is how Michael believes he can give something back to the community that has given him so much.

He is a member of the American College of Forensic Examiners and of the Texas Association for Educational Technology. When not working, Michael enjoys traveling and restoring muscle cars.

Dedication

To Christine, thank you for your love and support through all the long hours that such a project entails. Thank you for all your help and for supporting my dreams and ambitions.

Acknowledgments

I would like to again acknowledge Christine, Betty, Curly, Gen, Alice, and all my family. A special thanks to everyone at Que. It has been a great pleasure to have worked with you on four different books.

We Want to Hear from You!

As the reader of this book, *you* are our most important critic and commentator. We value your opinion and want to know what we're doing right, what we could do better, what areas you'd like to see us publish in, and any other words of wisdom you're willing to pass our way.

As an editor for Que Publishing, I welcome your comments. You can email or write me directly to let me know what you did or didn't like about this book—as well as what we can do to make our books better.

Please note that I cannot help you with technical problems related to the topic of this book. We do have a User Services group, however, where I will forward specific technical questions related to the book.

When you write, please be sure to include this book's title and author as well as your name, email address, and phone number. I will carefully review your comments and share them with the author and editors who worked on the book.

Email: feedback@quepublishing.com

Mail: Betsy Brown
Acquisitions Editor
Que Publishing
800 East 96th Street
Indianapolis, IN 46240 USA

Reader Services

Visit our website and register this book at www.examcram.com/register for convenient access to any updates, downloads, or errata that might be available for this book.

Introduction

Welcome! Whether this is your first Exam Prep series book or your fifteenth, you will find information here that will help ensure your success as you pursue knowledge, experience, and certification. This introduction explains the Information Systems Audit and Control Association (ISACA) certification program and discusses the way this Exam Prep book can help you prepare for the Certified Information Systems Auditor (CISA) exam. In particular, this introduction discusses the basics of ISACA certification exams and describes the test-taking environment and test-taking strategies. Chapters 1–9 are designed to help you study and prepare for the exam. Next, a Fast Facts section provides a high-level overview of exam objectives; finally, you'll find a full-length exam at the end of the book to give you a reasonable assessment of your knowledge. This book also provides the answers and explanations to the practice exam so you can go back and review why you missed specific questions or better understand the rationale of specific questions. If you read this book, study the material, and review the practice test, you will have a good chance of passing the actual exam.

How This Book Helps You

Exam Prep books are designed to help you understand and appreciate the subjects and materials you need to pass the ISACA CISA certification exam. The Exam Prep series is aimed strictly at test preparation and review. You will not learn the intricate details about everything there is to know about a specific topic because the assumption is that you have either on-the-job experience or coursework in the past that makes you eligible as a CISA certification candidate. This book is designed to present you with the material and topics you are likely to find on the actual test. We've worked to bring together as much information as possible about the CISA exam.

With this in mind, you still should make sure you are fully prepared for the exam and also have the subsequent skills that an employer might ask you to perform with such a certification. This might mean that in addition to reading the book, you also attend classroom training, gain hands-on practice auditing systems, or read one or more complementary texts, including the award-winning certification preparation series from Que Publishing. We recommend that you supplement your study program with visits to http://www.examcram.com to receive additional practice questions, get advice, and track the CISA program.

About the CISA Exam

The Information Systems Audit and Control Association (ISACA) developed the Certified Information Systems Auditor (CISA) program in 1978 to accomplish the following goals:

▶ Develop and maintain a testing instrument that can be used to evaluate an individual's competency in conducting information systems audits

▶ Provide a mechanism for motivating systems auditors to maintain their competencies and monitoring the success of the maintenance programs

▶ Aid top management in developing a sound information systems audit function by providing criteria for personnel selection and development

The CISA program is designed to assess and certify individuals in the IS audit, control, or security profession who demonstrate exceptional skills judgment and proficiency in IS audit control and security practices.

More than 50,000 professionals have earned the certification since its creation, and it is widely recognized as the premier information systems auditing certification.

This number is sure to grow as the U.S. Department of Defense (DoD) 8570.01-M *Information Assurance Workforce Improvement Program* manual names ISACA's Certified Information Systems Auditor (CISA) and Certified Information Security Manager (CISM) certifications among those approved for DoD information assurance (IA) professionals. This IT-based directive requires up to 80,000 professionals to earn one of 13 certifications offered by five organizations.

CISA Exam Objectives

The CISA exam is divided into six job practice areas, each of which is weighted differently. Table I.1 lists and describes the different job practice areas and provides the percentage of the exam pulled from each area.

TABLE I.1   CISA Exam Job Practice Areas and Breakdown

Job Practice Area	Title	Description	Percentage of Exam
Area 1	IS Audit Process	The IS Audit Process job practice area describes the IS audit services in accordance with IS audit standards, guidelines, and best practices. These services are provided to assist the organization in ensuring that its information technology and business systems are protected and controlled.	10%

TABLE I.1 *Continued*

Job Practice Area	Title	Description	Percentage of Exam
Area 2	IT Governance	The IT Governance job practice area describes the assurance controls that the organization has in place, such as structure, policies, accountability, mechanisms, and monitoring to control the practices of IT.	15%
Area 3	Systems and Infrastructure Lifecycle	The Systems and Infrastructure Lifecycle job practice area describes controls used to meet organizational objectives in the development/acquisition, testing, implementation, maintenance, and disposal of information systems and infrastructure.	16%
Area 4	IT Service Delivery and Support	The IT Service Delivery and Support job practice area discusses the practices used to ensure the delivery of the level of services required to meet the organization's objectives in providing assurance to IT service management.	14%
Area 5	Protection of Information Assets	The Protection of Information Assets job practice area ensures the confidentiality, integrity, and availability of information assets by means of the security architecture (policies, standards, procedures, and related controls).	31%
Area 6	Business Continuity and Disaster Recovery	The Business Continuity job practice area takes into consideration IT and critical business services. Disaster Recovery describes the controls used to reduce the impact of a disruption and minimize these events to ensure a timely resumption of IT services.	14%

You can review a complete breakdown of the CISA exam objectives at http://www.isaca.org/ Template.cfm?Section=Content_Areas&Template=/ContentManagement/ContentDisplay. cfm&ContentID=20418.

How to Prepare for the Exam

The CISA exam is somewhat difficult to prepare for because it is so broad in scope. It is also challenging because it asks indirect questions that require strong cognitive skills. The exam format is also something that most test takers are not familiar with—it is paper-based, not computerized, and is presented as 200 multiple-choice questions prepared in booklet form. Individuals attempting the exam are required to fill in the bubble on the basic Scantron-type answer sheet.

Don't think that this is an exam that you can adequately prepare for by simply memorizing terms and definitions. The questions presented by the CISA exam require you to analyze facts from various domains and knowledge points. Synthesizing this information requires giving thought and analysis to various factors in concluding what is the best answer from several possible answers. Having passed exams such as the CISM, CISSP, SCNP, CCSE, and others will help when analyzing questions and related material.

Additional Exam-Preparation Resources

Because the scope of the exam is so broad, it would not be hard to spend months or even years preparing for the exam. Although it would be helpful to read the hundreds of books that some might recommend preparing for the exam, this is not always feasible. This points to one of the reasons this book was created. However, those preparing for the exam have other resources available as well. Your decisions to use these materials will be driven largely on a case-by-case basis: Some individuals have many years of experience in many domains, whereas others may have focused on only one or two and have little knowledge in the other CISA domains. Some of the additional resources available include the following:

▶ *The CISA Review Manual*—This book is available at http://www.isaca.org. The official review manual is for students to review the type of content that can be found on the exam. Although this is a good supplementary resource, do not expect it to provide 100% coverage of what is needed for the exam.

▶ **The CISA Review Questions and Answers CD-ROM**—This good—yet expensive—resource offers practice questions for review. Although it will give you some additional questions that are of the same structure as those on the actual exam, do not expect to see much overlap between these questions and the real exam. This resource is also available at http://www.isaca.org.

▶ **Instructor-led training**—Instructor-led training is another option for those preparing for the exam. Some ISACA chapters provide review seminars to help those preparing for the exam. These sessions are generally reasonably priced. Just keep in mind that although ISACA provides the overall template for the review sessions, the individual chapters have the final say on how these are delivered. It's also worth noting that a volunteer instructor provides the instruction, so the quality, presentation skills, and amount of time the instructor has spent preparing for the class will vary.

Other professional training organizations also offer CISA training. The author of this book works for one such company, Superior Solutions, Inc. As president of the company, he has led the development of its CISA training material and often teaches the class. This specialized curriculum focuses on the core essentials of IT audit and IT governance best practices. Superior Solutions, Inc., provides these classes throughout the world. If you feel that you need more than an exam guide and are looking for instructor-led training, take a moment to look over the Superior Solutions, Inc., course offerings at http://www.thesolutionfirm.com.

Practice Tests

You do not need to know much about practice tests other than that they are a worthwhile expense, for three reasons:

▶ They help you diagnose areas of weakness.

▶ They help you get used to the format of questions.

▶ They help you determine when you are ready to take the exam.

This book contains questions at the end of each chapter and also includes a full-length practice test. ISACA is one source for additional practice questions, and many other companies provide CISA certification practice tests (of course, their quality is an unknown factor).

What This Book Does

This book is designed to point you to the topics and subjects that the CISA exam will cover. The book is designed to be used early on, well before the test, to give you insight on how comprehensive your knowledge is of the various topics. This might be enough for some readers; others might then need to research some material to get a deeper understanding of a specific topic. For example, you might read about CobiT and realize that you have very little knowledge about this framework, and then visit http://www.isaca.org to read more about the subject.

This book is also designed to be used as a final review. Perhaps you have attended a review seminar or instructor-led training but would like one more review before attempting the exam. In that case, this book distills the various topics for you, giving you a complete review of each in as few pages as possible. Exam Alerts, bullet points, study review points, and chapter reviews will all help build that level of confidence and knowledge needed to pass the exam on the first try.

As the author of this book, I developed the material from my experience teaching many students around the world, from my review of the official guide, from personal knowledge of the material, and from a battery of third-party test tools and websites. Apart from the actual logical step-by-step learning progression of the chapters themselves, this book—and all *Exam Prep* books—uses elements such as Exam Alerts, tips, notes, and practice questions to make the information easier to read and absorb.

Most people seeking certification use multiple sources of information. Check out the links at the end of each chapter to get more information about subjects with which you might not have as much experience. Practice tests can help indicate when you are ready. You can also find a variety of security and audit books that deal with many of the other topics, discussed in much greater detail. Don't forget that many individuals have described the CISA exam as being very challenging! Some ISACA chapters report only a 60–70 percent first-time pass rate. The CISA exam assumes that you already have a strong background in information system auditing and controls. This book helps you fill in the gaps.

What This Book Does Not Do

Now that you know what this book provides, it is only fair to cover what the book does not do. Primarily, this book will not teach you all you need to know about auditing systems and controls. The book is also not designed to be an introduction to computer technology. This book focuses on what you need to know to prepare for and pass the CISA exam.

The targeted reader for this book is someone seeking CISA certification. However, it should be noted that an *Exam Prep* book is an easily readable rapid presentation of facts. Therefore, an *Exam Prep* book is also extremely useful as a quick-reference manual.

Contacting the Author

The goal of this book is to provide you with the best prep possible. I am interested in any feedback you would like to share about the book. I would like to know any ideas you have on how it could be improved. Hopefully this book provides you with the tools you need to pass the CISA exam. You can contact me at the following email address:

info@thesolutionfirm.com

Finally, thank you for selecting my book; I hope you like it. If you have a moment, please email and let me know what you thought your chances of passing the test were before you read the book and after you read the book. Most of all, I would love to hear that you passed the exam. It always feels good to share personal successes with others. Good luck!

About the Book

This book is organized by individual exam objectives; it covers every objective you need to know for the CISA exam. We have attempted to present the objectives in an order that is as close as possible to that listed by ISACA. However, we have not hesitated to reorganize them where needed to make the material as easy as possible for you to learn. Some job practice areas of content are much larger than others, so we have broken them up into digestible elements. The list shown here outlines the basic structure of the chapters as they map to the CISA areas of knowledge:

- ▶ Part I: The Audit Process
  - ▶ Chapter 1: The Audit Process
- ▶ Part II: IT Governance
  - ▶ Chapter 2: IT Governance
- ▶ Part III: System and Infrastructure Lifecycle Management
  - ▶ Chapter 3: Lifecycle Management
  - ▶ Chapter 4: System Infrastructure Control
- ▶ Part IV: IT Service Delivery and Support
  - ▶ Chapter 5: Information Systems Hardware and Architecture
  - ▶ Chapter 6: Information Systems Used for IT Delivery and Support
- ▶ Part V: Protection of Information Assets
  - ▶ Chapter 7: Protection of Logical Assets
  - ▶ Chapter 8: Physical Security
- ▶ Part VI: Business Continuity and Disaster Recovery
  - ▶ Chapter 9: Business Continuity and Disaster Recovery

We have also attempted to make the information accessible in the following ways:

- ▶ The Exam Objectives Reference element of the book gives the full list of job practice areas and tasks and knowledge statements.

- ▶ Each chapter begins with a list of the tasks and knowledge statements to be covered.

- ▶ Each chapter also begins with an outline that provides you with an overview of the material and the page numbers where particular topics can be found.

- ▶ The tasks and knowledge statements are repeated where the material most directly relevant to it is covered.

Instructional Features

This book has been designed to provide you with multiple ways to learn and reinforce the exam material. The following are some of the helpful methods:

- ▶ **Study and Exam Preparation Tips**—You should read this section early on, to help develop study strategies. This section also provides you with valuable exam-day tips and information on exam/question formats such as adaptive tests and case study–based questions.

▶ **Objective explanations**—As mentioned previously, each chapter begins with a list of the tasks and knowledge statements (collectively referred to as objectives) covered in the chapter. In addition, immediately following each objective is an explanation of the objective, in a context that defines it meaningfully.

▶ **Study strategies**—The beginning of each chapter also includes strategies for approaching the studying and retention of the material in the chapter, particularly as it is addressed on the exam, but also in ways that will benefit you on the job.

▶ **Exam Alerts**—Exam Alerts provide specific exam-related advice. Such tips might address what material is covered (or not covered) on the exam, how it is covered, mnemonic devices, or particular quirks of that exam.

▶ **Review breaks and summaries**—Crucial information is summarized at various points in the book in lists or tables. Each chapter ends with a summary as well.

▶ **Key terms**—A list of key terms appears at the end of each chapter.

▶ **Notes**—Notes contain various kinds of useful or practical information, such as tips on technology or administrative practices, historical background on terms and technologies, or side commentary on industry issues.

▶ **Warnings**—When using sophisticated information technology, the potential for mistakes or even catastrophes because of improper application of the technology always exists. Warnings alert you to such potential problems.

▶ **"In the Field" sidebars**—These relatively extensive discussions cover material that might not be directly relevant to the exam but that is useful as reference material or in everyday practice. "In the Field" sidebars also provide useful background or contextual information that is necessary for understanding the larger topic under consideration.

▶ **Exercises**—Found at the end of the chapters in the "Apply Your Knowledge" section and in the Challenge Exercises found throughout chapters, exercises are performance-based opportunities for you to learn and assess your knowledge.

Extensive Practice Test Options

The book provides numerous opportunities for you to assess your knowledge and practice for the exam. The practice options include the following:

▶ **Exam questions**—These questions appear in the "Apply Your Knowledge" section within each chapter. You can use them to help determine what you know and what you need to review or study further. Answers and explanations for these questions are pro-vided in a separate section, titled "Answers to Exam Questions," later in each chapter.

▶ **Practice exam**—A practice exam is included in the "Final Preparation" section of the book.

Final Preparation

The Final Preparation part of the book provides three valuable tools for preparing for the exam:

▶ **Fast Facts**—This condensed version of the information contained in the book is extremely useful for last-minute review.

▶ **Practice exam**—Questions on this practice exam are written in styles similar to those used on the actual exam. You should use the practice exam to assess your readiness for the real thing.

▶ **Practice exam answers**—Use the extensive answer explanations to improve your retention and understanding of the material.

The book includes several other features, such as a section titled "Need to Know More" at the end of each chapter that directs you to additional information that can aid you in your exam preparation and your real-life work, and a glossary.

For more information about the exam or the certification process, refer to the ISACA website at http://www.isaca.org.

Final Words of Wisdom

More extensive tips are found in the "Study and Exam Prep Tips" section, but keep this advice in mind as you study:

▶ **Read all the material**—ISACA has been known to include complex wording or create questions in ways that will make the reader search for pertinent facts. This book includes additional information that is not reflected in the objectives, in an effort to give you the best possible preparation for the examination—and for your real-world experiences to come.

▶ **Complete the exercises in each chapter**—They will help you gain experience and aid in gaining real-life skills so that you can apply the knowledge learned.

▶ **Use the exam questions to assess your knowledge**—Don't just read the chapter content; use the exam questions to find out what you know and what you don't know. If you are struggling, study some more, review, and then assess your knowledge again.

▶ **Review the objectives**—Develop your own questions and examples for each objective listed. If you can develop and answer several questions for each objective, you should not find it difficult to pass the exam.

NOTE

Exam-Taking Advice Although this book is designed to prepare you to take and pass the CISA exam, there are no guarantees. Read this book, work through the questions and exercises, and when you feel confident, take the practice exam and additional exams provided in the MeasureUp test software. Your results should tell you whether you are ready for the real thing.

When taking the actual certification exam, make sure you answer all the questions before your time limit expires. Do not spend too much time on any one question. If you are unsure about the answer to a question, answer it as best as you can; then mark it for review when you have finished the rest of the questions.

Remember that the primary goal is not just to pass the exam, but to understand the material. When you understand the material, passing the exam will be much easier. Knowledge is a pyramid; to build upward, you need a solid foundation. This book and the CISA certification are designed to help you build your IT audit and IT security future.

Good luck!

Study and Exam Prep Tips

CISA

It's a rush of adrenaline during the final day before an exam. Because the CISA exam is given only twice a year—once in June and once in December—there's the underlying knowledge that there is no easy retake. For many people, thoughts in the back of their mind tell them to read just a bit more, study a little more, or practice another skill so that they can successfully get this exam out of the way.

For most of you, this will probably be the first ISACA exam you have taken.

This element of the book provides you with some general guidelines for preparing for any certification exam, including the CISA. It is organized into four sections:

- ▶ The first section addresses learning styles and how they affect preparation for the exam.

- ▶ The second section covers exam-preparation activities and general study tips.

- ▶ The third section takes an extended look at the ISACA certification exams, two of which are the CISA and CISM.

- ▶ The final section includes a number of specific tips that apply to ISACA's testing policies and how they might affect you.

Learning Styles

To best understand the nature of preparation for the test, it is important to understand learning as a process. You are probably aware of how you best learn new material. You might find that outlining works best for you, or, as a visual learner, you might need to "see" things. Or, as a person who studies kinesthetically, the hands-on approach serves you best. Whatever your learning style, solid test preparation works best when it takes place over time. Obviously, you shouldn't start studying for a certification exam the night before you take it; learning is a developmental process. Understanding learning as a process helps you focus on what you know and what you have yet to learn.

Thinking about how you learn should help you recognize that learning takes place when you are able to match new information to old. You have some previous experience with auditing or security. Now you are preparing for this certification exam. Using this book, software, and supplementary materials will not just add incrementally to what you know; as you study, the organization of your knowledge actually restructures as you integrate new information into your existing knowledge base. This leads you to a more comprehensive understanding of the tasks and concepts outlined in the objectives and of IT audit practices in general. Again, this happens as a result of a repetitive process rather than a singular event. If you keep this model of learning in mind as you prepare for the exam, you will make better decisions concerning what to study and how much more studying you need to do.

Study Tips

You can approach studying in many ways, just as you have many different types of material to study. However, the tips that follow should work well for the type of material covered on the CISA exam.

Study Strategies

Although individuals vary in the ways they learn information, some basic principles of learning apply to everyone. You should adopt some study strategies that take advantage of these principles. One of these principles is that learning can be broken into various depths. Recognition (of terms, for example) exemplifies a rather surface level of learning in which you rely on a prompt of some sort to elicit recall. Comprehension or understanding (of the concepts behind the terms, for example) represents a deeper level of learning than recognition. The ability to analyze a concept and apply your understanding of it in a new way represents further depth of learning.

Your learning strategy should enable you to know the material at a level or two deeper than mere recognition. This will help you perform well on the exam. You will know the material so thoroughly that you can go beyond the recognition-level types of questions commonly used in fact-based multiple-choice testing: You will be able to apply your knowledge to solve new problems.

Macro and Micro Study Strategies

One strategy that can lead to deep learning includes preparing an outline that covers all the objectives and subobjectives for the particular exam you are working on. Delve a bit further into the material and include a level or two of detail beyond the stated objectives and subobjectives for the exam. Then expand the outline by coming up with a statement of definition or a summary for each point in the outline.

An outline provides two approaches to studying. First, you can study the outline by focusing on the organization of the material. Work your way through the points and subpoints of your outline, with the goal of learning how they relate to one another. For example, you should understand how each of the six main job practice areas for the CISA exam is similar to and different from another. Then do the same thing with the tasks and knowledge statements; know which tasks and knowledge statements pertain to each job practice area and how they relate to one another.

Next, work through the outline, focusing on learning the details. Memorize and understand terms and their definitions, facts, rules and tactics, advantages and disadvantages, and so on. In this pass through the outline, you should attempt to learn detail rather than the big picture (the organizational information that you worked on in the first pass through the outline).

Research has shown that attempting to assimilate both types of information at the same time interferes with the overall learning process. If you separate your studying into these two approaches, you will perform better on the exam.

Active Study Strategies

The process of writing down and defining objectives, subobjectives, terms, facts, and definitions promotes a more active learning strategy than merely reading the material does. In human information-processing terms, writing forces you to engage in more active encoding of the information. Simply reading over the information leads to more passive processing. Using this study strategy, focus on writing down the items highlighted in the book—bulleted or numbered lists, exam tips, notes, warnings, and review sections, for example.

Determine whether you can apply the information you have learned by attempting to create examples and scenarios on your own. Think about how or where you could apply the concepts you are learning. Again, write down this information to process the facts and concepts in an active fashion.

The hands-on nature of the exercises at the end of each chapter provides further active learning opportunities that will reinforce concepts.

Common-Sense Strategies

Follow common-sense practices when studying: Study when you are alert, reduce or eliminate distractions, and take breaks when you become fatigued.

Pretesting Yourself

Pretesting enables you to assess how well you are learning. One of the most important aspects of learning has been called *meta-learning*. Meta-learning has to do with realizing when you know something well and when you need to study some more. In other words, you recognize how well or how poorly you have learned the material you are studying.

For most people, this can be difficult to assess. Review questions, practice questions, and practice tests are useful because they reveal objectively what you have learned and what you have not learned. Use this information to guide review and further studying. Developmental learning takes place as you cycle through studying, assessing how well you have learned, reviewing, and assessing again until you feel you are ready to take the exam.

You might have noticed the practice exam included in this book; use it as part of the learning process. The MeasureUp test-simulation software included on this book's CD-ROM also provides you with an excellent opportunity to assess your knowledge.

Set a goal for your pretesting: A reasonable goal would be to score consistently in the 90% range.

Exam Prep Tips

After you have mastered the subject matter, the final preparatory step is to understand how the exam will be presented. Make no mistake: The CISA exam challenges both your knowledge and your test-taking skills. The following sections describe the basics of exam design and the exam format, as well as provide some hints.

Preparing for the CISA exam might be somewhat different for you if this is the first paper-based noncomputerized exam you have taken in a while. This exam is unlike Microsoft, CompTIA, or Cisco exams you might have taken. Consider doing the following:

▶ **Combine your skill sets into solutions**—This exam assumes that you have a minimum of five years of professional information systems auditing, control, or security work experience. As such, this means that you have many skills to bring to the table. Applying your knowledge of information systems auditing, control, or security work can help you work through the various questions.

▶ **Delve into excruciating details**—The exam questions incorporate a great deal of information in the scenarios. Some of the information is ancillary—it will help you rule out possible issues but not necessarily resolve the answer. Many of the questions use words such as *most, least, best,* and *worst.* Some of the information simply provides you with a greater picture, as you would have in real life. Some information is key to your solution. Other times you might find that some information is shown but is not even needed to find the correct answer.

▶ **Read the questions carefully**—Consider making multiple passes. On the first pass, circle the important points of the question. Also underline nouns. If you know the answer, mark it; if not, continue with the next question and return to the marked question later. On the second pass, ensure the implied direction of the question and its subject. A common CISA question technique is to imply terminology associations that should not exist. Candidates miss these questions by misreading them. If a third pass is required, try to get down to two potential answers. Not answering a question counts against you, so take a guess, if you must.

▶ **Practice with a time limit**— Almost every certification exam has a time limit, and this one is no different. You have only four hours to complete 200 questions. Plan on using all of the allotted time. Just as a runner would not start his career in the New York City Marathon, you shouldn't start taking 200-question tests on the day of the exam. Before the exam, get used to answering 50 questions an hour. That's only a little less than one a minute. To get used to the time limits, testing yourself with a timer is a good way to accomplish this. Know how long it takes you to read scenarios and select answers.

Exam Format

The format for the CISA exam is a traditional fixed-form exam. As its name implies, the fixed-form exam presents a fixed set of questions during the exam session. Although everyone taking the test with you will be tested on the same set of questions, others might receive the questions in a different order than you do. These various tests are identical in terms of content coverage, number of questions, and allotted time, but the questions for each are in a different order.

Fixed-form exams also have fixed time limits in which you must complete them. A test candidate is given four hours to complete 200 multiple-choice questions. The exam tests the candidate's knowledge of IS audit principles and practices, as well as technical content areas. The exam covers one process and five content domains.

The score you achieve on a fixed-form exam, which is always calculated on a scale of 0 to 1,000, is based on the number of questions you answer correctly. A scaled score of 75% or above represents a passing score for the entire exam.

The exam is formatted as follows:

- ▶ The exam contains 200 questions.

- ▶ You are allowed four hours to complete the exam.

- ▶ You will be provided with an exam book and an answer sheet. After you complete the test, you must return both. Question review, including the opportunity to mark and change questions, is allowed.

Question Types

A variety of question types can appear on the CISA exam. We have attempted to cover all the types that are available at the time of this writing.

The CISA exam question is based on the idea of measuring skills or the ability to complete tasks. Therefore, most of the questions present you with a situation that includes a role, situation, or type of security function being performed. The answers indicate actions you might take to solve the problem or create proper audit techniques that would function correctly from the start. Keep this in mind as you read the questions on the exam. You will also encounter some questions that just call for you to regurgitate facts, so be prepared for a variety of types.

Despite the variety of question types that now appear in various exams, the CISA exam uses the multiple-choice question, which is the basic type of most exams. The multiple-choice question comes in two varieties:

- ▶ **Regular multiple-choice question**—Also referred to as an *alphabetic question*, a regular multiple-choice question asks you to choose one correct answer.

- ▶ **Enhanced multiple-choice question**—This is simply a regular or multiple-answer question that includes a graphic or table to which you must refer to answer the question correctly.

Examples of multiple-choice questions appear at the end of each chapter in this book.

More Exam Preparation Tips

Generic exam-preparation advice is always useful. Tips include the following:

- ▶ Become familiar with the IT audit functions. Experience is one of the keys to success on the CISA exam. Review the exercises and the Step by Steps in the book.

▶ Review the current exam requirement FAQ on the ISACA website. The documentation ISACA makes available on the web will help identify the skills needed to pass the exam.

▶ Take any of the available practice tests. We recommend the one included in this book and the ones you can create by using the MeasureUp software on this book's CD-ROM.

Tips for During the Exam Session

The following generic exam-taking advice that you've heard for years applies when you're taking any certification exam:

▶ Remember that you are not allowed to bring books, cell phones, electronic devices, or other materials into the test center.

▶ Take a deep breath and try to relax when you first sit down for your exam session. It is very important to control the pressure you might (naturally) feel when taking exams.

▶ You will be provided with scratch paper, if needed. Take a moment to write down any factual information and technical detail that you have committed to short-term memory.

▶ Carefully listen to the proctor when you arrive at the test area and are seated. You are not allowed to open the test booklet or begin any activities until the test proctors tell you to do so. Read all the information they provide you.

▶ Accept the nondisclosure agreement as part of the examination process. Complete it accurately and quickly move on.

▶ Read the exam questions carefully. Reread each question to identify all relevant details.

▶ In fixed-form exams such as this, tackle the questions in the order in which they are presented. If you find yourself spending too much time on any one question, mark it and move on.

▶ Don't rush, but also don't linger on difficult questions. The questions vary in degree of difficulty. Don't let yourself be flustered by a particularly difficult or wordy question.

▶ Remember that even if you have a proctor escort you to the bathroom, the clock will continue to run. Use your time wisely.

Tips for Fixed-Form Exams

Because a fixed exam is composed of a fixed, finite set of questions, you should add these tips to your strategy for taking a fixed-form exam:

▶ Note the time allotted and the number of questions on the exam you are taking. Make a rough calculation of how many minutes you can spend on each question, and use this figure to pace yourself through the exam. For the CISA, you must answer about one question every minute.

▶ Take advantage of the fact that you can return to and review skipped or previously answered questions. Mark the questions you can't answer confidently, noting the relative difficulty of each question. When you reach the end of the exam, return to the more difficult questions.

▶ If you have session time remaining after you complete all the questions (and if you aren't too fatigued!), review your answers. Pay particular attention to questions that seem to have a lot of detail or that require graphics.

▶ As for changing your answers, the general rule of thumb here is *don't!* If you read the question carefully and completely, and felt like you knew the right answer, you probably did. Don't second-guess yourself. As you check your answers, if one clearly stands out as incorrect, of course you should change it. But if you are at all unsure, go with your first impression.

Final Considerations

Finally, be aware of the ISACA exam policy, how long the certification is good for, and any other program limitations:

▶ Candidates may attempt the exam once every six months.

▶ ISACA recommends that CISA candidates attend a review seminar or seek additional classroom training to have a greater chance of passing the examination, although doing so is not required.

Hopefully this chapter has answered many of the questions you might have had about the exam and has helped get you primed for your studies ahead. Just remember that the purpose of this book is to help prepare you for the CISA exam and give you a base knowledge of what is needed to perform IT audits and security assessments.

IT Governance and the Audit Process

CHAPTER ONE

The Audit Process

This chapter helps you prepare for the Certified Information Systems Auditor (CISA) exam by covering the following ISACA objectives, which include understanding the role and importance of auditing standards, guidelines, and best practices. This also includes items such as these:

Tasks

Develop and implement a risk-based IS audit strategy for the organization in compliance with IS audit standards, guidelines and best practices.

Plan specific audits to ensure that IT and business systems are protected and controlled.

Conduct audits in accordance with IS audit standards, guidelines and best practices to meet planned audit objectives.

Communicate emerging issues, potential risks, and audit results to key stakeholders.

Advise on the implementation of risk management and control practices within the organization while maintaining independence.

Knowledge Statements

Knowledge of ISACA IS Auditing Standards, Guidelines and Procedures, and Code of Professional Ethics

Knowledge of IS auditing practices and techniques

Knowledge of techniques to gather information and preserve evidence (for example, observation, inquiry, interview, computer-assisted audit techniques [CAATs], electronic media)

Knowledge of the evidence lifecycle (e.g., collection, protection, chain-of-custody)

Knowledge of control objectives and controls related to IS (e.g., CobiT)

Knowledge of risk assessment in an audit context

Knowledge of audit planning and management techniques

Knowledge of reporting and communication techniques (e.g., facilitation, negotiation, conflict resolution)

Knowledge of control self-assessment (CSA)

Knowledge of continuous audit techniques

Outline

Study Strategies

This chapter addresses information you need to know about auditing and auditing standards. An auditor is responsible for examining the controls that protect information systems to determine their strength. The auditor also must not overlook any unusual items or those that appear suspicious. The following are the primary topics a CISA candidate should review for the exam:

▶ Understand audit strategies and methodologies

▶ Develop plans for audits to ensure that the organization's assets are secure

▶ Understand ISACA procedures to perform audits, approved auditing practices, and ISACA code of ethics

▶ Describe control self-assessment techniques and methods for continuous audit

▶ Describe methods to report and communicate with management and co-workers

Introduction

Greetings, and welcome to the world of information systems (IS) auditing! This first chapter will lay the groundwork for the knowledge you need to know to prepare for and pass the Certified Information Systems Auditor (CISA) exam. If you have an interest in auditing and technology, you will find much to be excited about in the world of IS auditing. IS auditors review the strength of information system controls and report their capability to protect the organization's assets.

Auditors are also responsible for leading, planning, and performing the audit. Different types of audits exist: financial audits, compliance audits, and information systems audits. The auditor also must understand auditing standards, how to perform an audit, and how to measure risk. Also, as in other fields, emerging changes are taking place in the field of auditing. One example is the control self-assessment (CSA). Each of these items is discussed in more detail in this chapter.

Issues and Challenges of the IS Auditor

Task

▶ Plan specific audits to ensure that IT and business systems are protected and controlled.

Knowledge Statement

▶ Knowledge of audit planning and management techniques

All organizations must work within a framework of laws and regulations. These rules may dictate how data is processed, handled, stored, and destroyed. Businesses are increasingly tasked with processing a growing amount of electronic information. If they fail to handle this information properly with due care and due diligence, they could be subject to legal fines, loss of public confidence, or even jail time. Companies can be held liable if personal data is disclosed to an unauthorized person.

An example of one such legislation is the Safe Harbor Act. This act prohibits the transfer of personal data to non–European Union (E.U.) nations that do not meet the European standard for privacy protection. Companies that fail to meet E.U. standards can face legal recourse, suffer a loss of public confidence, or even be blocked from doing business in the E.U. Although ISACA does not test CISA canidates on the specifics of regulatory standards, candidates should understand the framework in which their industry operates. Some of these regulatory standards include the following:

▶ **U.S. Health Insurance and Portability and Accountability Act (HIPAA)**—U.S. standards on management of health-care data

▶ **Sarbanes-Oxley Act (SOX)**—U.S. financial and accounting disclosure and accountability

▶ **Basel Accord Standard II**—European banking requirements

▶ **U.S. Federal Information Security Management Act (FISMA)**—Security standards for U.S. government systems

▶ **Committee for Sponsoring Organizations of the Treadway Commission (COSO)**—A private industry initiative to identify factors that lead to fraudulent financial reporting and to be used as a voluntary internal framework of controls

▶ **U.S. Supervisory Controls and Data Acquisition (SCADA)**—Enhanced security for automated control systems

▶ **U.S. Fair and Accurate Credit Transaction ACT of 2003 (FACTA)**—Legislation to reduce fraud and identity theft

The growing dependence of automated IT systems to store and transmit data has driven most of these rules and regulations. The auditor's role is to evaluate the design and operation of internal controls. The following describes the general process that occurs:

STEP BY STEP

1.1 Verifying Compliance with External Regulations

1. Identify the external requirements with which the company is responsible for being in compliance.

2. Review the specific laws and regulations with which the organization must be compliant.

3. Determine whether the organization considered these laws and regulations when policies and procedures were developed.

4. Determine whether identified policies and procedures adhere to external laws and requirements.

5. Determine whether the employees are adhering to specified policies and procedures or whether discrepancies exist.

EXAM ALERT

Auditing Compliance   Although exam candidates do not need to know details about individual external laws, they are expected to understand the general steps used to verify compliance.

Most organizations want to do the right thing and are interested in proper controls. They might just be overwhelmed by the day-to-day demands of business. That's why it is so important for auditors to verify compliance. This starts by developing a good audit plan, as described in the next section.

Audit Planning

The goal of the audit function is to present an independent and objective evaluation of the state of the internal controls with appropriate recommendations to mitigate any detected risks if applicable. At the highest level, the audit function requires an audit charter to establish the IS audit function. The charter defines what responsibilities senior management is delegating. The audit department should report to the audit committee. The audit department should not report to senior management directly because it might create an independence problem. Although this is the rule, you'll find audit department heads that report to senior management on day-to-day issues and concerns. The audit committee is responsible only to senior management and the board of directors; the audit committee should report findings directly to them. More specific audit plans can be developed next.

Long-term plans are considered strategic. *Strategic planning* looks at what effect management's planned long-term changes to the infrastructure will have on the security of the organization. Short-term planning is referred to as *tactical planning*. Tactical planning looks at issues the organization currently faces, such as what is to be audited during the current year. Audits don't occur in a vacuum. Auditors must take into account the company and its culture, and must understand the environment in which they will be working. Figure 1.1 shows some of the ways an auditor can work to better understand the organization.

Understanding the company is just the first step. Next, the auditor must develop a plan to help determine what type of audits should be performed.

STEP BY STEP

1.2 Audit Planning Process

1. Learn the business, review the mission statement, and understand its purpose and goals.

2. Review documentation and evaluate existing policies, procedures, and guidelines.

3. Identify threats, risks, and concerns.

4. Carry out a risk analysis.

5. Identify internal controls.

6. Define audit objectives and scope of audit.

7. Identify resources needed for the audit and assign appropriate personnel.

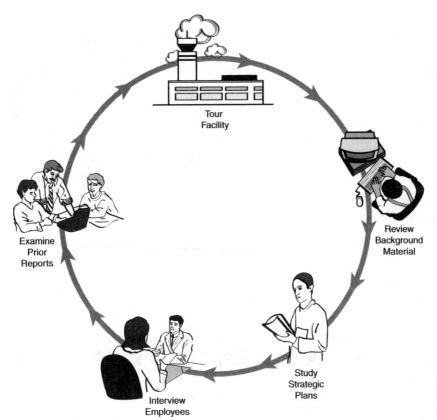

FIGURE 1.1 Ways to better understand the business.

The next section shifts the focus to some of the standards and guidelines required for auditors.

Standards and Guidelines for ISACA IS Auditors

Task

▶ Conduct audits in accordance with IS audit standards, guidelines and best practices to meet planned audit objectives.

Knowledge Statements

▶ Knowledge of ISACA IS Auditing Standards, Guidelines and Procedures, and Code of Professional Ethics

▶ Knowledge of IS auditing practices and techniques

Although you might not think of scuba diving when discussing auditing, the two are actually similar. This is because they both follow standards and guidelines. No one who has ever gone diving would consider jumping into the ocean without checking the oxygen tank or performing other basic safety checks. Auditing is similar, in that you cannot just show up at a site and announce that you are there to perform an audit. Auditing requires a specific set of skills and knowledge. As an example, an auditor must know when to perform a *compliance test* or a *substantive test*, and must understand the differences between them. Compliance tests are used to verify conformity, whereas substantive tests verify the integrity of a claim. The auditor must also understand the rules and guidelines of auditing. One way to start learning more about these rules is to review the ISACA Auditing Standards.

ISACA Standards

Standards are agreed upon principles of protocol. ISACA standards are designed and developed by the ISACA standards board. The board meets twice a year to develop ISACA standards to help advance the IS auditing profession. The term *standard* is used here to describe the category of guidance document, as shown in Table 1.1.

TABLE 1.1 Guidance Document Description

Title	Description
Standards	These documents specify requirements that are considered mandatory.
Guidelines	These documents provide guidance and require professional judgment.
Procedures	These documents provide examples of activities and procedures that an auditor can use to maintain standards.

As you can see, *standards* detail mandatory requirements, whereas *guidelines* and *procedures* offer guidance on how to maintain compliance. Standard documents begin with *S1*. Fourteen categories of standards exist:

- ► S1—Audit Charter
- ► S2—Independence
- ► S3—Professional Ethics and Standards
- ► S4—Competence
- ► S5—Planning
- ► S6—Performance of Audit Work
- ► S7—Reporting
- ► S8—Follow-Up Activities

- S9—Irregularities and Illegal Acts

- S10—IT Governance 1 September 2005

- S11—Use of Risk Assessment in Audit Planning

- S12—Audit Materiality

- S13—Using the Work of Other Experts

- S14—Audit Evidence

Guideline documents begin with *G1*. Thirty-five categories of guidelines exist:

- G1—Using the Work of Other Auditors

- G2—Audit Evidence Requirement

- G3—Use of Computer-Assisted Audit Techniques (CAATs)

- G4—Outsourcing of IS Activities to Other Organizations

- G5—Audit Charter

- G6—Materiality Concepts for Auditing Information Systems

- G7—Due Professional Care

- G8—Audit Documentation

- G9—Audit Considerations for Irregularities

- G10—Audit Sampling

- G11—Effect of Pervasive IS Controls

- G12—Organizational Relationship and Independence

- G13—Use of Risk Assessment in Audit Planning

- G14—Application Systems Review

- G15—Planning Revised

- G16—Effect of Third Parties on an Organization's IT Controls

- G17—Effect of Nonaudit Role on the IS Auditor's Independence

- G18—IT Governance

- G19—Irregularities and Illegal Acts

- G20—Reporting

- G21—Enterprise Resource Planning (ERP) Systems Review

- G22—Business-to-Consumer (B2C) E-Commerce Review
- G23—System Development Lifecycle (SDLC) Review
- G24—Internet Banking
- G25—Review of Virtual Private Networks
- G26—Business Process Reengineering (BPR) Project Reviews
- G27—Mobile Computing
- G28—Computer Forensics
- G29—Post-Implementation Review
- G30—Competence
- G31—Privacy
- G32—Business Continuity Plan (BCP) Review from IT Perspective
- G33—General Considerations on the Use of the Internet
- G34—Responsibility, Authority, and Accountability
- G35—Follow-Up Activities

Procedure documents begin with *P1* and are divided into 10 categories:

- P1—IS Risk Assessment
- P2—Digital Signatures
- P3—Intrusion Detection
- P4—Viruses and Other Malicious Code
- P5—Control Risk Self-Assessment
- P6—Firewalls
- P7—Irregularities and Illegal Acts
- P8—Security Assessment—Penetration Testing and Vulnerability Analysis
- P9—Evaluation of Management Controls over Encryption Methodologies
- P10—Business Application Change Control

You can learn more about ISACA standards by visiting http://www.isaca.org/standards. ISACA requires CISAs to comply with their auditing standards; auditors who do not comply could be subject to an investigation. Auditors are also bound to abide by legal requirements and statutory law. Such external standards of conduct place an additional level of compliance on the auditor.

EXAM ALERT

Standards, Guidelines, and Procedures CISA exam candidates are expected to understand the difference between standards, guidelines, and procedures. Standards are mandatory, guidelines provide guidance, and procedures offer "how to" information.

ISACA Code of Ethics

Auditing involves more than maintaining legal requirements. The issue of ethics also arises. Ethics go beyond legal requirements; they are defined principles and values that govern acceptable behavior. As an auditor, you must be above question at all times. You must treat clients honestly and fairly, and your actions must reflect positively on yourself, your company, and your profession. To help guide auditors in this defined level of conduct, ISACA has developed a code of professional ethics:

Members and certification holders shall:

1. *Support the implementation of, and encourage compliance with, appropriate standards, procedures and controls for information systems.*

2. *Perform their duties with due diligence and professional care, in accordance with professional standards and best practices.*

3. *Serve in the interest of stakeholders in a lawful and honest manner, while maintaining high standards of conduct and character, and not engage in acts discreditable to the profession.*

4. *Maintain the privacy and confidentiality of information obtained in the course of their duties, unless disclosure is required by legal authority. Such information shall not be used for personal benefit or released to inappropriate parties.*

5. *Maintain competency in their respective fields and agree to undertake only those activities which they can reasonably expect to complete with professional competence.*

6. *Inform appropriate parties of the results of work performed, revealing all significant facts known to them.*

7. *Support the professional education of stakeholders in enhancing their understanding of information systems security and control.*

Failure to comply with this Code of Professional Ethics can result in an investigation into a member's or certification holder's conduct and, ultimately, in disciplinary measures.

You can find the ISACA code of ethics on the ISACA website at http://tinyurl.com/2coyds.

Risk Analysis

Task

▶ Develop and implement a risk-based IS audit strategy for the organization in compliance with IS audit standards, guidelines, and best practices.

Modern networks and computerized data systems are highly complex. Individuals responsible for auditing these systems must ask, "What do I audit?" Although it might be nice to audit everything, doing so is not possible. Companies have limited funds and a finite amount of resources to be used in auditing security controls. One way to determine what to audit is to use *risk analysis*. Risk cannot be discussed in a void. When discussing risk, vulnerability and threat must also be reviewed:

▶ Risk is the potential for harm.

▶ Vulnerability is weakness in a system or process.

▶ Threat can be seen as frequency.

As an example, the *threat* of being struck by lightning is about 1 in 600,000. On a sunny day, that might not be much of a concern, but if you were standing in a thunderstorm with a metal golf club, you most certainly will have introduced a *vulnerability* and, thus, have increased your *risk* of being struck by lightning. In the world of IS auditing, the auditor must be able to identify risks and understand what controls can reduce those risks. Some common categories of risks include these:

▶ **Audit risk**—The risk that the audit report might contain a material error or that an error might exist that the auditor did not detect

▶ **Control risk**—The risk that a material error may exist that might not be detected by the system of internal controls

▶ **Business risk**—The risk that will affect the business's functional goals

▶ **Continuity risk**—The risk the business faces that might keep it from recovering from a disaster

▶ **Detection risk**—The risk that an improper test is performed that will not detect a material error

▶ **Material risk**—An unacceptable risk

▶ **Inherent risk**—The risk that a material error will occur because of weak controls or no controls

▶ **Security risk**—The risk that unauthorized access to data will result in the exposure or loss of integrity of the data

> **NOTE**
>
> **Defining Risk**   It should be noted that ISACA categorizes Inherent, Control, and Detection risk as types of Audit risk in conjuction with Overall audit risk.

These are not the only categories of risks, but they are provided to draw attention to the idea that risks come in many different forms. Risks can threaten an organization by financial, operational, or regulatory means. Auditors typically focus on high-risk, high-impact issues. The following section examines how to identify these threats.

Risk Management

Risk management follows a defined process that includes the following steps:

1. Develop a risk management team

2. Identify assets

3. Identify threats

4. Perform risk analysis

5. Perform risk mitigation

6. Monitor

The first step begins by developing a risk-management team, which is responsible for the risk-assessment process. The risk-management team needs support and funding from senior management and should be led by someone with strong project-management skills. Once established, the team can begin work on the second step, the task of identifying assets. Companies must identify assets before moving on to the next step of the risk-management process. As an example, Coca-Cola surely has some value in the original formula for Coke and must protect it. After inventorying assets, the risk-management team can move on to the third step, identifying threats. Once threats are identified, risk assessment can be performed. Risk analysts can base their assessment on dollar figures or can use nondollar values. Regardless of the method used, the idea is to rank the threats in some order to determine what requires immediate action. Some threats might have a high impact but a very low level of risk. Other threats might present a high level of risk but result in a very low impact. The idea is for the team to identify high-impact, high-risk concerns and focus on those items. As an example, a company based in Galveston, Texas would most likely consider a hurricane as a high risk, high impact item. The island has no point of land that is more than 14 feet above sea level and the Gulf of Mexico is prime area for strong storms. This same approach should be used during audits to ensure that audit time is spent on areas with the highest risks. Figure 1.2 illustrates this concept.

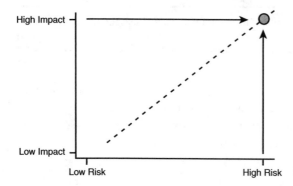

FIGURE 1.2 Analyzing risk and impact.

After identifying high-risk, high-impact concerns, the risk-management team can move on to the risk mitigation phase. Risk mitigation addresses how risks will be handled. This can be done in basically four ways:

▶ **Avoid risk**—Avoiding risk can seem like a simple alternative: You simply don't perform the activity that allows the risk to be present. In reality, many activities cannot be avoided. Even when they can be, an opportunity cost might be involved so that avoiding the risk involves missing the opportunity for profit.

▶ **Reduce risk**—Reducing risk is one of the most common methods of dealing with a risk. An example could be installing a firewall or implementing a new internal accounting control.

▶ **Accept risk**—Risk acceptance means that the organization knows about the risk but makes a conscious decision to accept the risk. Accepting risk means that the company is retaining the potential costs that are associated with the risk. As an example, a business might be considering building an e-commerce website but has determined that it will face an added risk. However, along with the risk is the potential to increase revenue.

▶ **Transfer risk**—To transfer risk is to place the risk in someone else's hands. The best example of risk transference is insurance. Although there are benefits to the approach, there are also some drawbacks. Chief among these is that insurance is an ongoing expense. In addition, it is time-consuming and costly to document and settle relatively small losses. Finally, even small payouts by the insurance company can have an adverse effect on future insurance costs.

The final phase of the risk-management process is monitoring. You can think of monitoring as a type of change management. Any time a change is made to systems or the operating environment, a reassessment should be performed to see how the changes affect a potential risk. Risk analysis is a powerful tool in the hands of the auditor because it can help identify risks and threats. It also aids the auditor in examining existing controls to determine their effectiveness and helps them focus their efforts on the area that is high risk, high impact.

Risk-Based Audits

Knowledge Statement

▶ Knowledge of risk assessment in an audit context

Understanding risk assessment can be a big help to the auditor. Audits can be designed to take a risk-based approach. A risk-based approach to auditing looks at more than just a risk; it also examines the company's practices, its tolerance for risk, and the existing internal and operational controls. Risk-based audit techniques can help pinpoint areas of high risk. The concept behind a risk-based audit approach is to determine which areas should be audited based on the perceived level of risk. These areas can then be targeted for an audit. If the decision is made to not use risk-based auditing, the alternative model is for the audit team to evaluate the organization's entire environment, which is a much more time-consuming and costly process.

You can see how this makes the risk-based audit approach much more attractive. The generalized steps of a risk-based audit are as follows:

STEP BY STEP

1.3 Risk-Based Audit Process

1. Gather information and plan:

   ▶ Understand the business

   ▶ Review audits from prior years

   ▶ Examine financial data

> ▶ Evaluate regulatory statutes

> ▶ Conduct inherent risk assessments

2. Determine internal controls and review their functionality:

> ▶ Control environment and control procedures

> ▶ Detection and control risk assessment

> ▶ Total risks

3. Perform compliance tests—Test and verify that controls are being applied.

4. Perform substantive testing—Measure the strength of the process and verify accounts.

5. Conclude the audit—Prepare the report.

The risk-based approach will look into business risks that can affect the company's bottom line. That will lead to determining which areas and processes are the most critical (from the risk point of view) for the company. The auditor must always be concerned with a level of risk that is unacceptable. Sometimes this is referred to as a *material risk*. As an auditor, anytime you see the word *material*, you should always be concerned. In auditing, the word *material* is associated with a significant level of risk that the auditor is unwilling to accept. What is material will vary because it is based on a level of judgment that includes a thorough examination of the area being audited. Even if a finding is judged not to be material, that does not mean that everything is okay. As an example, a minor error might be thought to have little effect on the security of a system, yet when this small error is combined with other small errors, a significant and material error might exist.

Auditing and the Use of Internal Controls

Knowledge Statement

> ▶ Knowledge of control objectives and controls related to IS (e.g., CobiT)

Management uses internal controls to exercise authority and effectively manage the organization. Controls typically start with high-level policy and apply to all areas of the company. CISAs are interested in IS controls because these are used to verify that IS systems are maintained in a controlled state. IS controls should protect the integrity, reliability, and accuracy of information and data. IS control objectives should also guarantee efficiency and effectiveness, protect the organization against outages, and provide for an effective incident response. As stated earlier, these controls filter down the organizational structure by means of policy and procedure. These procedures can be divided into two categories—general control and information system control.

General control procedures are established by management to provide a reasonable amount of assurance that specific objectives will be achieved. Table 1.2 describes general control procedures as well as information system control procedures, described in more detail in the text following the table.

TABLE 1.2   General Control Procedures

General Control Procedures	Information System Control Procedures
Internal accounting controls used to safeguard financial records	Procedures that provide reasonable assurance for the control of database administration
Operational controls that are focused on day-to-day activities	Business continuity and disaster-recovery procedures (BCP) that provide reasonable assurance that the organization is secure against disasters. BCP covers all critical areas of the organization and is not exclusively an IS control.
Administrative controls designed for corporate compliance	System-development methodologies and change-control procedures have been implemented to protect the organization and maintain compliance
Procedures that safeguard access and use of organizational resources	Procedures that provide reasonable assurance for the control of access to data and programs
Logical security policies designed to support proper transactions	Procedures that provide reasonable assurance for the control and management of data-processing operations
Logical security policies designed to support transactional audit trails	Procedures that provide reasonable assurance for the control of networks and communications
Security policies that address the physical control of data centers	Physical access-control procedures that provide assurance for the organization's safety

> **NOTE**
>
> **Note the Differences**   IS auditors should understand how each general control procedure correlates to an IS specific control procedure.

Information system control procedures are the second category of control. These are established by management to provide a reasonable level of assurance that specific levels of compliance will be achieved in the IS/IT area. These control procedures address such items as data processing operations, access to data and programs, networks and communication, and database administration. Controls can be preventive, detective, or corrective. Table 1.3 describes these controls in more detail. Regardless of how well controls are designed, they can provide only reasonable assurance. Using the three types of controls in conjunction with each other creates a system of checks and balances, which helps provide a greater level of assurance and ensures that processes operate in a controlled manner. Just keep in mind that no system is perfect, and controls will always be subject to error, which can be caused by breakdowns or system overrides, and can even be subjugated by employees or outsiders.

TABLE 1.3   Control Categories

Class	Function	Example
Preventive	Prevents problems before they occur Attempts to prevent problems	Access-control software that uses passwords, tokens, and/or biometrics Intrusion-prevention systems User registration process
Detective	Senses and detects problems as they occur Attempts to detect problems	Hashing algorithms Variance reports
Corrective	Reduces impact of a threat Attempts to minimize the impact of a problem	Backup procedures Backup power supplies Intrusion-detection systems

CobiT

Control Objectives for Information and Related Technology (*CobiT*) is a framework designed around four domains:

▶ Plan and organize

▶ Acquire and implement

▶ Deliver and support

▶ Monitor and evaluate

CobiT was designed for performance management and IT management. It is considered a system of best practices. CobiT was created in 1992 by the Information Systems Audit and Control Association (ISACA) and the IT Governance Institute (ITGI), which is a research arm of ISACA. CobiT (4) is focused in IT Governance, including strategic alignment, value delivery, resource management, risk management, and performance measurement. The CISA exam does not expect you to understand the inner workings of CobiT, but you should be able to understand the general framework.

CobiT is designed around 34 key controls. These are grouped into four broad domains. Each of these objectives can be found in one of these areas. As an example, the planning and organization contains 11 controls, acquisition and implementation contains six controls, delivery and support contains 13 controls, and monitoring contains four controls. The four domains are as follows:

- ▶ M1 Monitor the processes

- ▶ M2 Assess internal control adequacy

- ▶ M3 Obtain independent assurance

- ▶ M4 Provide for independent audit

Each control objective can be regarded as a separate process to which COBIT's Management Guidelines are applied.

The Audit Process

Task

- ▶ Advise on the implementation of risk management and control practices within the organization while maintaining independence.

Knowledge Statements

- ▶ Knowledge of the evidence lifecycle (for example, collection, protection, chain-of-custody)

- ▶ Knowledge of reporting and communication techniques (for example, facilitation, negotiation, conflict resolution)

- ▶ Knowledge of techniques to gather information and preserve evidence (for example, observation, inquiry, interview, computer-assisted audit techniques [CAATs], electronic media)

An audit can be defined as a planned, independent, and documented assessment to determine whether agreed-upon requirements and standards of operations are being met. Basically, it is a review of the operation and its activities. An IS audit is similar, except that it deals specifically with computerized systems used for information processing. These systems can be fully computerized or can have only elements of computerization, with other components being handled manually. The auditor is responsible for examining the computerized systems and the interfaces that exist between the computerized and manual systems. As an auditor, your job is to report the facts and report an independent review of the computerized and manual systems. As an auditor, you have a position of *fiduciary* responsibility. This means you hold a position of special trust and confidence. You are responsible for placing the interest of the organization for which you are performing the audit above your own interests and concerns. Of course, placing the company first does not mean that you lie or misrepresent the truth to help the company. Your position should be fair and balanced—you report the truth, whether it's good or bad.

Auditors must also be independent. Independence means that you are free of any connection or bias that might affect your findings. As an example, if you hold $200,000 of stock in the company and know that a negative finding will significantly reduce the value of your stock, you are not independent. External auditors are required to maintain independence at all times.

Being an Auditor Is Not Always Easy

Things have changed in the world of accounting and auditing. 2002 represented a watershed year: More than 30 companies reported auditing irregularities. Included in this list were companies such as Enron, WorldCom, and Quest Communications. These companies had used the accounting services of many of the biggest accounting and auditing firms, such as Arthur Andersen, Ernst & Young, and PricewaterhouseCoopers. Errors of such a large scale make one wonder how things could have gone so wrong.

Some accountants and auditors involved with these firms have stated that it wasn't just bad ethics. It was more about a loss of independence and a mandate to get the job done quickly. The implementation of computerized systems in the 1980s and the 1990s made the job of accounting and auditing much more complex, as the demands of instant communication pushed workers to deliver information quickly with little time for review. Without additional control, these factors helped to negatively affect the process.

The results of these scandals led to questions of oversight and the effectiveness of rule-based controls, such as Generally Approved Accounting Procedures (GAAP), and led to the passage of the 2002 Sarbanes-Oxley Act (SOX). SOX established new rules for the oversight of public companies and is divided into 11 sections. To address the problems such as those experienced in 2002, SOX addresses issues such as auditor independence and corporate governance. Although some might see SOX as a burden to business, it has helped restore a much-needed balance for control.

Independence is not the only concern the auditor must have. An auditor must also be prepared to report both good and bad findings. These findings will be tied back to the procedures and documents used to guide the audit. Within these documents, the auditor must be aware of the key distinction in wording between *recommended* and *required*. *Required* means the activity or action must be carried out; required activities are mandatory, not optional. *Recommended* actions are optional; they should be carried out but are not obligatory. As an example, a small organization might have combined several roles into one operational position yet built in compensating controls. These are just a few of the details an auditor must be concerned with. The following sections continue this discussion by looking in detail at each step of the audit process and the concerns the auditor should have at each point in the process. The next section looks at some of the types of audits a CISA might be involved in and their classification.

Audit Classification

Although the CISA primarily is concerned with the auditing of information systems, it is important to understand the other types of audits that can occur. These audits can be internal or external:

► Administrative audits—An audit that focuses on operational processes.

► Financial audits—An audit that relates to the correctness of the organization's financial statement. Financial audits typically include substantive testing.

► Forensic audits—An audit that focuses on the recovery of information that might uncover fraud or crimes committed to alter the financial figures of the organization. Information recovered from a forensic audit is typically reviewed by law enforcement.

NOTE

Chain of Custody One important issue that cannot be overlooked during a forensic audit is chain of custody. Chain of custody means that the auditor can account for who had access to the collected data, that access to the information is controlled, and that it is protected from tampering.

► **Information system audits**—An audit that is performed to verify the protection mechanisms provided by information systems and related systems. Information system audits should examine internal controls to ensure that they protect integrity, confidentiality, and assurance of data and electronic information, and that they operate efficiently.

► **Operational audits**—An audit designed to examine the internal control structure of a process or area. Examples of operational audits are those that examine application controls or logical security systems.

► **Other audits**—Other types of audits include those that examine compliance. Examples of compliance audits include the Sarbanes-Oxley, Health Insurance Portability and Accountability Act (HIPAA), or Statement on Auditing Standards (SAS) 70. These are used to verify that a service organization has been through an in-depth audit of its control activities.

EXAM ALERT

Define IS Audits Exam candidates must be able to define IS auditing and explain its function.

Audit Programs

Audit programs are the objectives, scope, and methodologies for a particular audit. Audit programs should comply with the objective of a particular project. Information systems can be audited in many different ways, including security, quality, fiduciary control, service, and capacity. The audit program should be defined so that the scope audit objective and procedures are properly defined to develop and support reliable conclusions and opinions. Testing and evaluation of system controls require the auditor to fully understand proper test procedures. Procedures for testing and evaluation can include the following:

► Auditing through observation

► Reviewing documentation

► Documenting systems and processes by means of flowcharting

► Using standard audit software controls to examine log files and data records

► Using specialized software packages to examine system parameter files

ISACA has developed a repository of audit programs and internal control questionnaires that ISACA members can use for guidance. These are available at http://tinyurl.com/2kaet5.

Audit Methodology

An *audit methodology* is a documented approach for performing the audit in a consistent and repeatable manner. The audit methodology is designed to meet audit objectives by defining the following:

► A statement of work

► A statement of scope

► A statement of audit objectives

The methodology should be approved by management and thoroughly documented so that it provides a highly repeatable process. All audit employees must be trained and must have knowledge of the methodology. Figure 1.3 illustrates an example of a typical audit process.

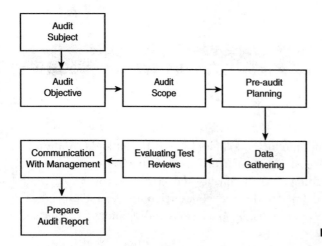

FIGURE 1.3 Audit process and steps.

Using a structured and repeatable methodology fosters the establishment of boundaries and builds confidence in the audit process. Each step of the audit process is described in greater detail here:

STEP BY STEP

1.4 Audit Methodology

1. **Audit subject**—Identify which areas are to be audited

2. **Audit objective**—Define why the audit is occurring. As an example, the objective of the audit might be to ensure that access to private information such as social security numbers is controlled.

3. **Audit scope**—Identify which specific functions or systems are to be examined.

4. **Pre-audit planning**—Identify what skills are needed for the audit, how many auditors are required, and what other resources are needed. Necessary policies or procedures should be identified, as should the plans of the audit. The plans should identify what controls will be verified and tested.

5. **Data gathering**—Identify interviewees, identify processes to be tested and verified, and obtain documents such as policies, procedures, and standards. Develop procedures to test controls.

6. **Evaluation of test results**—These will be organization specific. The objective will be to review the results.

7. **Communication with management**—Document preliminary results and communicate to management.

8. **Preparation of audit report**—The audit report is the culmination of the audit process and might include the identification of follow-up items.

An important part of the methodology is documentation. Findings, activities, and tests should be documented in work papers (WPs). WPs can be either hard copy or electronic documents. However, because they are created and stored, they must be properly dated, labeled, and detailed; clear; and self-contained. ISACA IS auditing standards and guidelines detail specifications that pertain to WPs.

Automated Work Papers

Businesses are not the only ones moving to a paperless environment. Although auditors have used word processors and spreadsheet programs for quite some time, more audit teams are moving to more advanced methods for automating work papers. Computer-assisted audit techniques (CAATs) are one example of this. CAATs are software audit tools used for statistical sampling techniques and data analysis.

Auditors are aware of the importance for the control of written work papers; these same controls must be provided for automated work papers. Controls that protect the confidentiality, integrity, and availability of electronic work papers should be applied at the same level of their paper-based counterparts. Some items to consider include these:

▶ Encryption to provide confidentiality

▶ Backup to provide availability

▶ Audit trails and controls

▶ Access controls to maintain authorized access

> **NOTE**
>
> **Confidentiality** Auditors are responsible for maintaining confidentiality of paper, electronic, and sensitive client information. Sensitive information should always be protected.

Challenge

This challenge involves placing the steps of the audit process in their proper order. As a CISA, you must know what the steps of the audit process are and what activities occur at each.

1. Place the following steps shown in Table 1.4 in order:

TABLE 1.4   Audit Methodology

Item	Step	Order
Audit report preparation	1	
Data gathering	2	
Audit scope	3	
Pre-audit planning	4	
Audit objective	5	
Communication with management	6	
Audit subject	7	
Evaluation of test results	8	

2. Next, compare your results to Table 1.5:

TABLE 1.5   Audit Methodology Results

Item	Step	Order
Audit report preparation	1	Audit subject
Data gathering	2	Audit objective

(continues)

(continued)

TABLE 1.5   Continued

Item	Step	Order
Audit scope	3	Audit scope
Preaudit planning	4	Pre-audit planning
Audit objective	5	Data gathering
Communication with management	6	Evaluation of test results
Audit subject	7	Communication with management
Evaluation of test results	8	Audit report preparation

With the steps of the audit process defined, answer the following questions:

3. At what step in the audit process should specific functions to be examined be identified?

4. At what step in the audit process do you identify follow-up review procedures?

5. At what step in the audit process do you identify the individuals to be interviewed?

The answers to steps 3, 4, and 5 are as follows:

(3) At the audit scope step is where specific functions to be examined should be identified.

(4) Follow-up review procedures should be developed at the audit report preparation step.

(5) At the data gathering step, the individuals to be interviewed should be determined.

Objectives of the Audit

The purpose of the IS audit is to evaluate the existing (and previously identified controls) that achieved pre-determined control objectives. As an example, an operational control object might be used to ensure that funds accepted on the company's e-commerce website are properly posted in the company's bank account. However, in an information system audit, the objective might be expanded to make sure that dollar amounts are entered correctly into the e-commerce website and that they match the posted price of the item being sold.

Management might give the auditor a general control objective to review during the audit, but the primary goal is to verify the confidentiality, integrity, and availability of information resources. Assuring compliance is also important. Compliance reviews are an integral part of any IT auditor job. Audited systems must meet regulatory and legal requirements while assuring compliance. The auditor can test compliance in several ways, as discussed in the following section.

Compliance Versus Substantive Testing

After an auditor has identified key control points, *compliance tests* can be performed. A compliance test verifies that the controls in the environment are operating properly. Compliance tests verify that controls work as designed and comply with the organization's policies and procedures. Compliance testing ensures that controls operate as perceived during initial review.

Substantive testing examines detail data in order to evaluate the results of operating controls. Substantive testing verifies validity and is sometimes called *transaction integrity*. Substantive testing examines the process for potential material errors. Whereas substantive testing examines details, compliance testing tests controls.

How much substantive testing is required depends on the level of internal controls and the amount of confidence that the auditor has in the operation of the internal control structure. IS audits that examine systems with a high number of internal controls that have high confidence lower the number of required substantive tests.

Sampling and Embedded Audit Modules

What happens when you cannot test an entire population or a complete batch? Sampling—it's the process of selecting items from a population of interest. The practice of sampling can give the auditor generalized results for the population as a whole. The two basic types of audit sampling are as follows:

- **Statistical sampling**—Based on probability. Every item of the population has a known chance of selection. The prominent feature of statistical sampling is its capability to measure risk and the use of quantitative assessment. The auditor quantitatively decides the sample size and confidence level.

- **Nonstatistical sampling**—Uses auditor judgment to select sample size and determine which items to select. Nonstatistical sampling is also known as judgmental sampling.

EXAM ALERT

Sampling Best Practice   When sampling is required, the most appropriate method for the auditor is to pull samples using an automated method.

Each sampling type, statistical and nonstatistical, has two subgroups of sampling techniques:

- **Variable sampling**—Variable sampling is used primarily for substantive testing. It measures characteristics of the sample population, such as dollar amounts or other units of measurement.

▶ **Attribute sampling**—Attribute sampling is used primarily for compliance testing. It records deviations by measuring the rate of occurrence that a sample has a certain attribute.

Attribute sampling can be further divided into three subcategories:

▶ **Frequency estimating sampling**—Answers the question of "how many?"

▶ **Stop-and-go sampling**—Used when it is believed that few errors exist

▶ **Discovery sampling**—Used to discover fraud or irregularities

Sampling is not the only way to insure compliance. Ongoing monitoring might be required. One ongoing monitoring method is to use *embedded audit modules*. Embedded modules are designed to be an integral part of an application and are designed to identify and report specific transactions or other information based on predetermined criteria. Identification of reportable items occurs as part of real-time processing. Reporting can be performed by means of real-time processing or online processing, or can use store-and-forward methods. *Parallel simulation* is another test technique that examines real results that are compared to those generated by the auditor. *Integrated test facilities (ITF)* use data that represents fake entities such as products, items, or departments. ITF is processed on actual production systems.

> **EXAM ALERT**
> **Compliance Testing**   Attribute sampling is the primary sampling method used for compliance testing.

Evidence

Evidence is any information the auditor obtains that can be used to aid in rendering an opinion. Evidence can be obtained from interviews, work papers, direct observation, internal documentation, compliance testing, and/or substantive testing. All evidence is not created equal; some evidence has more value and provides a higher level of confidence than other forms. Evidence the auditor obtains should be sufficient, usable, reliable, and relevant, and should achieve audit objectives effectively. This is sometimes referred to as the SURRE rule:

Sufficient

Usable

Reliable

Relevant

Effective

CISA candidates should be aware of ISACA standards for auditing 060.020 and should understand how evidence can be used to support any findings. These standards can be found at http://tinyurl.com/2sua9y.

Table 1.6 lists some basic questions to ask in determining the reliability of evidence.

TABLE 1.6   Evidence Reliability

Item	Description
Is the provider of the evidence independent?	Evidence from inside sources is not considered as reliable as evidence obtained from outside sources.
Is the evidence provider qualified?	The person providing the evidence has to have their qualifications reviewed to validate their credibility.
How objective is the evidence?	Some evidence requires considerable judgment; others (such as dollar amounts) are easy to evaluate.
When is the evidence available?	Backups, the write process, and updates can affect when and how long evidence is available.

CAUTION

Client Records   Confirmation letters that the customer provides are not as reliable as a confirmation letter from an outside source.

Auditors should observe auditees in the performance of their duties to assist in gathering evidence and understanding how procedures, job roles, and documentation match actual duties. Auditors should perform the following:

► Observe employee activity

► Examine and review actual procedures and processes

► Verify employee security awareness training and knowledge

► Examine actual reporting relationships to verify segregation of duties

Detection of Fraud

Laws relating to corporate governance require auditors, management, and others within the organization to report fraud. As an example, SAS No. 99 requires auditors to discuss the potential for a material misstatement in the financial statements due to fraud before, and during, the information-gathering process. ISACA Standard 030.020 requires auditors to practice due care throughout the audit engagement. Common law defines four general elements that must be present for fraud to exist:

- ▶ A material false statement
- ▶ Knowledge that the statement was false
- ▶ Reliance on the false statement
- ▶ Resulting damages or losses

Although strong internal controls, separation of duties, procedures, recordkeeping, and a structure of responsibility can reduce the frequency of fraud, it still can occur. Auditors should not overlook any of the following fraud indicators:

- ▶ No clear lines of authority
- ▶ A lack of documents and records
- ▶ A lack of independent checks and balances
- ▶ Nonexistent or poor separation of duties
- ▶ Few internal controls

Audit Closing

After interviewing employees, reviewing documentation, performing testing, and making personal observations, the auditor is ready to compile the information and provide their findings. These should be recorded in the audit opinion. The audit opinion is part of the auditor's report and should include the following components:

- ▶ Name of organization being audited
- ▶ Title, date, and signature
- ▶ Statement of audit objectives
- ▶ Audit scope
- ▶ Any limitations of scope
- ▶ Audience
- ▶ Standards used in the audit
- ▶ A detail of the findings
- ▶ Conclusions, reservations, and qualifications

- ▶ Suggestions for corrective actions

- ▶ Other significant events

CAUTION

Documentation   Auditors should always attempt to follow written procedures. If procedures are not followed, the auditor must keep documentation on why procedures were not followed and what the findings were.

Changes in the IS Audit Process

Task

- ▶ Communicate emerging issues, potential risks, and audit results to key stakeholders.

Knowledge Statements

- ▶ Knowledge of continuous audit techniques

- ▶ Knowledge of control self-assessment (CSA)

Changes occur in all industries, and auditing is no different. SOX is an example of a legal change that has affected audit process. Under SOX, auditors no longer can use certain common audit strategies. Not all changes are driven by laws and mandates; others occur because of advances in the field of auditing and the invention of new techniques. The following sections discuss some of these changes, including the control self-assessment, integrated auditing, and continuous auditing.

The Control Self-Assessment Process

Although the traditional approach to auditing has proven itself, it does have some problems. Primarily, this has to do with the fact that responsibility for the audit is placed on the auditors. Managers and employees might feel that it is the auditor's job to find and report problems. A *control self-assessment* (CSA) is an attempt to overcome the shortcomings of the traditional approach. According to ISACA,

> CSAs can best be defined as a methodology designed to provide assurance to stakeholders, customers, and employees that internal controls have been designed to minimize risks.

CSAs are used to verify the reliability of internal controls. Unlike in traditional auditing, some of the control monitoring responsibilities are shifted to functional areas and the workers in that area. As the functional area is directly involved and plays an important role in the design of the controls that protect critical assets, employees tend to be motivated. CSAs also tend to raise the level of control, which allows risk to be detected sooner and, consequently, reduces cost. Table 1.7 outlines the differences between traditional auditing and the CSA approach.

TABLE 1.7 CSA Attributes

CSA	Traditional
Empowers employees and gives them responsibility	Places responsibility on the auditing staff and management
Offers a method for continuous improvement	Limited by policies and rules. Does not involve functional area management or give them as much control.
Involves employees and raises their level of awareness	Offers little employee participation
Involves staff and employees, and makes them the first line of control	Decreased awareness of staff and employees of internal controls and their objectives

You might be thinking that CSA appears to be a cure for all auditing problems, but it does have some drawbacks. Some individuals have a misconception that CSAs can replace audits. This is not correct. The CSA was not designed to replace the audit function; it was designed to enhance the audit function. Some employees might also offer objections because a CSA program places an additional workload on employees. The key to making a CSA program work is to identify what processes are the most important to the department under examination.

Interviews, meetings with appropriate business unit employees, and questionnaires are some of the methods used to identify key process. CobiT can also help. Although it does not directly provide guidance on CSAs, it can be used to help identify key processes and controls.

Integrated Auditing

The concept of integrated auditing grew out of concepts first discussed in the late 1970s. The idea behind *integrated auditing* is to combine audit disciplines to more efficiently assess internal controls. One key advantage of this approach is that it enables auditors to see the bigger picture. Integrated auditing combines the operational audit function, financial audit function, and IS audit function. Integrated auditing typically involves the following:

- ▶ Key controls must be identified.
- ▶ Key controls must be reviewed and understood.
- ▶ Key controls must be tested to verify that they are supported by the IT system.
- ▶ Management controls must be tested to verify that they operate correctly.
- ▶ Control risks, design problems, and weaknesses are delivered in the audit report.

Because the various audit functions are combined, teams of auditors must possess a varied skill set. Whereas the audit focuses on business risk, integrated auditing produces a single audit report that offers comprehensive coverage.

Continuous Auditing

Changes in technology result in quicker transactions, and when coupled with items such as just in time (JIT), the need for instant information is much greater. Continuous auditing can help meet that demand. *Continuous auditing* works well for automated processes that capture, manipulate, store, and disseminate data. Research produced by the American Institute for Certified Public Accountants and Chartered Accountants of Canada found that six preconditions should be present before an organization can adopt continuous auditing:

▶ The system must have acceptable characteristics. Cost and items such as technical skill must be considered.

▶ The information system must be reliable, have existing primary controls, and collect data on the system.

▶ The information system must have a highly automated secondary control system.

▶ The auditor must be proficient in the system and information technology.

▶ The audit process must offer a reliable method for obtaining the audit procedure results.

▶ Verifiable controls of the audit reporting process must exist.

Continuous assurance can be achieved by combining the following:

▶ **Continuous auditing**—A methodology of providing assurance that enables auditors to provide written reports quickly.

▶ **Continuous monitoring**—Monitoring provided by tools, such as antivirus, used to meet fiduciary responsibilities.

Time and effort allow for the development of a continuous auditing environment. Auditors should acquire the skills needed for this methodology to meet the demands of the changing audit environment.

REVIEW BREAK

The audit process involves a number of terms and concepts that are important for the auditor to understand. Table 1.8 describes these phrases.

TABLE 1.8   Audit Process Terminology

Item	Attributes
Material	An item of significance that has real impact and affects the entity that is being audited
Inherent risk	The risk that a material error will occur because of weak controls or no controls
Control risk	The risk that internal controls will not prevent a material error
Detection risk	The risk that misstatements, or possible material errors, have occurred and were not detected
Audit risk	The risk that material errors might exist in financial reports
Discretionary	Used to describe nonmandatory items
Mandatory	Used to describe standards and other required documents

Chapter Summary

In this chapter, you learned about the foundational items needed to understand the IS audit process. The goal was to provide you with the basic knowledge to prepare you for the challenges of being an auditor and help you master the IS audit job practice area of the CISA exam. Successful auditors must have knowledge of ISACA IS auditing standards and guidelines. They must also understand that the auditor holds a valuable position in the organization and must abide by legal and ethical standards, including the ISACA Code of Professional Ethics. Auditors must also be able to evaluate and understand risks. Companies don't have unlimited funds, so it's important to identify areas of high risk and focus auditing efforts there. An effective auditor focuses on those areas and uses effective communication skills to facilitate and negotiate positive improvements to reduce material risks.

The next chapter focuses on lifecycle management and builds on what you have learned in this chapter.

Key Terms

- Attribute sampling
- Audit methodology
- Compliance test
- Continuous assurance
- Continuous auditing
- Continuous monitoring
- Control self-assessment (CSA)
- Fiduciary
- Guidelines
- Integrated auditing
- Material
- Nonstatistical sampling
- Overall audit risk
- Procedures
- Risk acceptance
- Risk analysis

- ▶ Risk avoidance
- ▶ Risk reduction
- ▶ Risk transference
- ▶ Standards
- ▶ Statistical sampling
- ▶ Substantive test
- ▶ Variable sampling

Apply Your Knowledge

This chapter introduced you to some of the aspects of the IS audit process. A large section of the chapter discussed risk. As you might remember, the risk assessment process consists of the following:

1. Develop a risk management team
2. Identify assets
3. Identify threats
4. Perform risk analysis
5. Risk mitigation
6. Monitoring

This exercise will introduce you to one way to perform the second step of the risk process, identifying assets. Although the ISACA does not test knowledge on the use of any type of applications, Exam Prep titles are designed to provide a deeper understanding of the material. This exercise looks at one tool to help the auditor with this task.

Exercises

1.1 Network Inventory

In this exercise, you look at an automated inventory tool used to audit systems and software.

Estimated Time: 15 minutes

1. You must download Network Inventory from http://www.emco.is/downloads.html. Network Inventory generates hardware and software information for Microsoft networks and also verifies software license information.

2. Once downloaded, execute the setup program as shown in Figure 1.4. Accept the license agreement and all default install settings.

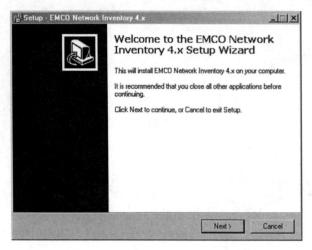

FIGURE 1.4 Network inventory setup.

3. Once installed, the program launches. Choose Evaluate because you are running the demo version of the software. Choose Enumerate LAN to have the program scan the local network and identify available systems. Allow the program several minutes to finish its enumeration. See Figure 1.5.

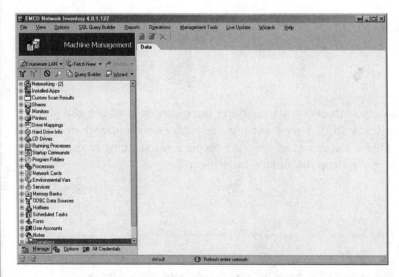

FIGURE 1.5 LAN enumeration.

4. When the enumeration has finished, from the Machine Management window, choose Installed Apps and highlight your local computer. The Data field to the right now lists all applications discovered on the local computer, as shown in Figure 1.6.

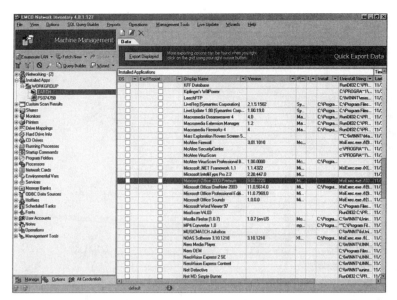

FIGURE 1.6 Installed applications.

5. As you can see, the program provides the auditor with an easy way to quickly see all programs that have been installed. To learn more about any one application, simply double-click to display information similar to that shown in Figure 1.7.

FIGURE 1.7 Application details.

6. Spend some time looking at the other types of information that Network Inventory can provide an auditor. From the Machine Management window, examine some of the other types of information the program can provide, such as processes, hotfixes, scheduled tasks, and user accounts. Figure 1.8 shows the details of a selected user account.

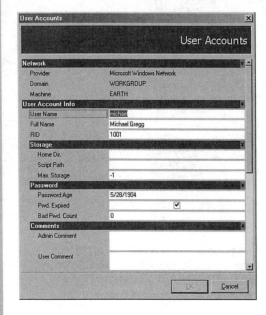

FIGURE 1.8 User account.

7. Now select Management Tools, Installed Applications, as shown in Figure 1.9.

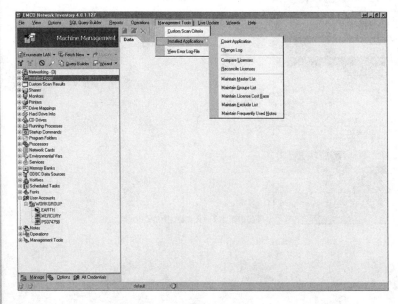

FIGURE 1.9 Installed application.

8. The Network Inventory tool counts applications, builds a database of licenses, and determines license cost base. This is a good tool to help the auditor identify and track licensed and unlicensed software installed on the company's computers and networks. Software audits are a key component of any comprehensive software asset management plan.

Exam Questions

1. Which of the following best describes integrated auditing?

   ○ **A.** Integrated auditing places internal control in the hands of management and reduces the time between the audit and the time of reporting.

   ○ **B.** Integrated auditing combines the operational audit function, the financial audit function, and the IS audit function.

   ○ **C.** Integrated auditing combines the operational audit function and the IS audit function.

   ○ **D.** Integrated auditing combines the financial audit function and the IS audit function.

2. Which type of sampling would best be used to uncover fraud or other attempts to bypass regulations?

   ○ **A.** Attribute sampling

   ○ **B.** Frequency estimating sampling

   ○ **C.** Stop-and-go sampling

   ○ **D.** Discovery sampling

3. Which of the following best describes this statement: This risk can be caused by the failure of internal controls and can result in a material error.

   ○ **A.** Audit risk

   ○ **B.** Inherent risk

   ○ **C.** Detection risk

   ○ **D.** Control risk

4. Which of the following is not one of the best techniques for gathering evidence during an audit?

   ○ **A.** Attend board meetings

   ○ **B.** Examine and review actual procedures and processes

   ○ **C.** Verify employee security awareness training and knowledge

   ○ **D.** Examine actual reporting relationships to verify segregation of duties

5. Which of the following is not an advantage of the control self-assessment (CSA)?

    ○ **A.** CSA helps provide early detection of risks.

    ○ **B.** CSA is an audit function replacement.

    ○ **C.** CSA reduces control costs.

    ○ **D.** CSA provides increased levels of assurance.

6. Which of the following is the best example of a detective control?

    ○ **A.** Intrusion-prevention systems

    ○ **B.** User registration process

    ○ **C.** Variance reports

    ○ **D.** Access-control software

7. Which of the following is the best example of a general control procedure?

    ○ **A.** Internal accounting controls used to safeguard financial records

    ○ **B.** Business continuity and disaster-recovery procedures that provide reasonable assurance that the organization is secure against disasters

    ○ **C.** Procedures that provide reasonable assurance for the control of access to data and programs

    ○ **D.** Procedures providing reasonable assurance that have been developed to control and manage data-processing operations

8. Which of the following describes a significant level of risk that the organization is unwilling to accept?

    ○ **A.** Detection risk

    ○ **B.** Material risk

    ○ **C.** Business risk

    ○ **D.** Irregularities

9. Which of the following is the most accurate description of a substantive test in which the data represents fake entities such as products, items, or departments?

    ○ **A.** Parallel tests

    ○ **B.** Integrated test facility

    ○ **C.** Embedded audit module

    ○ **D.** Test data

10. You need to review an organization's balance sheet for material transactions. Which of the following would be the best sampling technique?

   ○ **A.** Attribute sampling

   ○ **B.** Frequency estimating sampling

   ○ **C.** Stop-and-go sampling

   ○ **D.** Variable sampling

Answers to Exam Questions

1. **B.** Integrated auditing is a methodology that combines the operational audit function, the financial audit function, and the IS audit function. Therefore, answers C and D are incorrect because they do not list all three types of functions to be integrated. Answer A is incorrect because it describes the control self-assessment (CSA), which is used to verify the reliability of internal controls and places internal controls in the hands of management.

2. **D.** Discovery sampling would best be used to uncover fraud or other attempts to bypass regulations. Answer A is incorrect because attribute sampling is used to determine the rate of occurrence. Answer B is incorrect because frequency sampling is another name for attribute sampling. Both describe the same sampling technique. Answer C is incorrect because stop-and-go sampling is used when the auditor believes that only a few errors will be found in a population.

3. **D.** A control risk is the risk caused by the failure of internal controls; it can result in a material error. Answer A is incorrect because the audit risk is the amount of risk the organization is willing to accept. Answer B is incorrect because the inherent risk is the risk that can occur because of the lack of compensating controls. Combined, inherent risks can create a material risk. Answer C is incorrect because detection risk is the risk if an auditor does not design tests in such a way as to detect a material risk.

4. **A.** Attending board meetings is not one of the best ways to gather evidence during an audit. The best ways to gather evidence include observing employee activity, examining and reviewing actual procedures and processes, verifying employee security awareness training and knowledge, and examining actual reporting relationships to verify segregation of duties.

5. **B.** Answers A, C, and D are all advantages of CSA. CSA is not an audit function replacement.

6. **C.** A variance report is the best example of a detective control. Detective controls attempt to detect problems. Answers A, B, and D are incorrect because they all describe preventive controls.

7. **A.** Internal accounting controls used to safeguard financial records are an example of a general control procedure. Answers B, C, and D all describe information system control procedures.

8. **B.** The word *material* describes a significant level of risk that the auditor is unwilling to accept. Answers A, C, and D do not define the term.

9. **B.** An integrated test facility is a type of substantive test that uses data represented by fake entities such as products, items, or departments. Answer A is incorrect because a parallel test compares real results to those generated by the auditor to compare the control function. Answer C is incorrect because embedded audit modules identify and report specific transactions or other information based on predetermined criteria. Answer D is incorrect because test data uses theoretical transactions to validate program logic and control mechanisms.

10. **D.** Variable sampling would be the best sampling technique to review an organization's balance sheet for material transactions. It is also known as dollar estimation. Answer A is incorrect because attribute sampling is used to determine the rate of occurrence. Answer B is incorrect because frequency sampling is another name for attribute sampling. Both describe the same sampling technique. Answer C is incorrect because stop-and-go sampling is used when an auditor believes that only a few errors will be found in a population.

Need to Know More?

▶ The Increased Importance of Audit Controls: http://itmanagement.earthweb.com/netsys/article.php/3402561

▶ CobiT: http://en.wikipedia.org/wiki/CobiT

▶ Automated Work Papers: http://www2.bc.edu/~jerskey/wp1.pdf

▶ Audit and Fraud Detection: http://faculty.ncwc.edu/TOConnor/350/350lect05.htm

▶ Risk-Based Auditing: http://www.ffiec.gov/ffiecinfobase/booklets/audit/audit_03_risk%20ass_rb_audit.html

▶ Substantive Testing: http://www.answers.com/topic/substantive-test

▶ Computer-Assisted Audit Techniques: http://www.dor.state.ma.us/publ/pdfs/caat.pdf

▶ Control Self-Assessment: http://www.theiia.org/index.cfm?doc_id=329&bhcp=1

CHAPTER TWO

IT Governance

This chapter helps you prepare for the Certified Information Systems Auditor (CISA) exam by covering the following ISACA objectives, which includes understanding the role IT governance plays in providing assurance. The assurance structure starts at the top with senior management and continues downward through the organization. This includes items such as the following:

Tasks

Evaluate the effectiveness of IT governance structure to ensure adequate board control over the decisions, directions, and performance of IT so that it supports the organization's strategies and objectives.

Evaluate the IT organizational structure and human resources (personnel) management to ensure that they support the organization's strategies and objectives.

Evaluate the organization's IT policies, standards, and procedures; and the processes for their development, approval, implementation, and maintenance to ensure that they support the IT strategy and comply with regulatory and legal requirements.

Evaluate the IT strategy and the process for its development, approval, implementation, and maintenance to ensure that it supports the organization's strategies and objectives.

Evaluate monitoring and assurance practices to ensure that the board and executive management receive sufficient and timely information about IT performance.

Evaluate management practices to ensure compliance with the organization's IT strategy, policies, standards, and procedures.

Evaluate the IT resource investment, use, and allocation practices to ensure alignment with the organization's strategies and objectives.

Evaluate IT contracting strategies and policies, and contract management practices to ensure that they support the organization's strategies and objectives.

Evaluate the risk management practices to ensure that the organization's IT related risks are properly managed.

Knowledge Statements

Knowledge of IT governance frameworks

Knowledge of quality management strategies and policies

Knowledge of the purpose of IT strategies, policies, standards, and procedures for an organization and the essential elements of each

Knowledge of organizational structure, roles, and responsibilities related to the use and management of IT

Knowledge of generally accepted international IT standards and guidelines

Knowledge of the processes for the development, implementation, and maintenance of IT strategies, policies, standards, and procedures (e.g., protection of information assets, business continuity and disaster recovery, systems and infrastructure lifecycle management, IT service delivery and support)

Knowledge of enterprise IT architecture and its implications for setting long-term strategic directions

Knowledge of IT resource investment and allocation practices (e.g., portfolio management return on investment [ROI])

Knowledge of risk management methodologies and tools

Knowledge of the use of control frameworks (e.g., CobiT, COSO, ISO 17799)

Knowledge of the use of maturity and process improvement models (e.g., CMM, CobiT)

Knowledge of the contracting strategies, processes, and contract management practices

Knowledge of practices for monitoring and reporting of IT performance (e.g., balanced score cards, key performance indicators [KPI])

Knowledge of relevant legislative and regulatory issues (e.g., privacy, intellectual property, corporate governance requirements)

Knowledge of IT human resources (personnel) management

Outline

Study Strategies

This chapter discusses IT governance, which involves control. This control includes items that are strategic in nature. Senior management and the IT steering committee help provide the long-term vision. Control is also implemented on a more tactical level that includes personnel management, organizational change management, and segregation of duties. The following are the primary topics a CISA candidate should review for the exam:

▶ Understand the way IT governance should be structured

▶ Know the methods of risk management

▶ Describe how tools such as CobiT and the capability maturity model are used

▶ Detail proper separation of duty controls

▶ Describe good HR management practices

▶ List methods for measuring and reporting IT performance

Introduction

IT governance is a subset of corporate governance and focuses on the belief that the managers, directors, and others in charge of the organization must understand the role of IT in the organization and not treat it simply as a black box. Management must implement rules and regulations to control the IT infrastructure and develop practices to distribute responsibilities. Not only does this prevent a single person or department from shouldering responsibility, but it also sets up a framework of control. Changes in laws and new regulations, such as Sarbanes-Oxley and Basel II, have increased the need for such control.

IT governance is established by creating an IT strategy committee, developing policies and procedures, defining job roles, executing good HR practices, and performing risk assessments and periodic audits. This chapter discusses each of these topics.

Best Practices for Senior Management

Tasks

- ▶ Evaluate the effectiveness of IT governance structure to ensure adequate board control over the decisions, directions, and performance of IT so that it supports the organization's strategies and objectives.

- ▶ Evaluate the IT strategy and the process for its development, approval, implementation, and maintenance to ensure that it supports the organization's strategies and objectives.

- ▶ Evaluate monitoring and assurance practices to ensure that the board and executive management receive sufficient and timely information about IT performance.

Knowledge Statements

- ▶ Knowledge of IT governance frameworks

- ▶ Knowledge of relevant legislative and regulatory issues (e.g., privacy, intellectual property, corporate governance requirements)

Generally, *best practices* are techniques and approaches that have been proven to provide a desired result. In IT governance, best practices are designed to align IT and the organization's objectives. IT governance best practices require the company to meet two specific goals:

- ▶ **Align the goals of IT to the goals of the company**—Both must be focused on and working for the common good of the company.

- ▶ **Establish accountability**—Accountability requires that individuals be held responsible for their actions. Accountability can be seen as a pyramid of responsibility that starts with the lowest level of employees and builds itself up to top management.

The auditor is responsible for reviewing the placement of these items.

Alignment requires strategy, or the path that the company will use to move from overall policy and goals to delivery of product, accounting, and audit. Figure 2.1 depicts an example of this goal alignment.

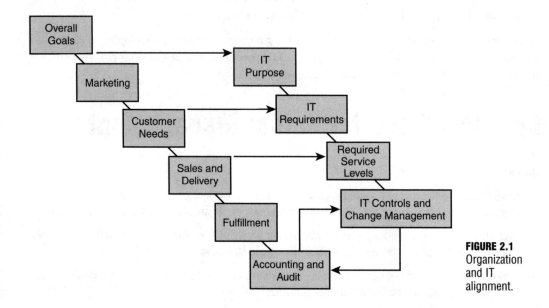

FIGURE 2.1
Organization and IT alignment.

Senior management's role in this process comes at a strategic level, not a tactical one. Consider eBay as an example. Although eBay's senior management is very concerned about merchandise being listed for the duration of an auction and about bidding and closing occurring seamlessly, they should have little concern about the operating system and platform. As long as the technology can meet the stated business goal, the choice of Windows, Linux, or UNIX should be left up to the IT department. Senior management's goal is to ensure that goals are aligned, IT is tasked with meeting those business needs, and the auditor is responsible for ensuring that controls are present and operating effectively.

Audit's Role in Governance

The primary role of an auditor in IT governance is to provide guidance and recommendations to senior management. The objective of providing this information is to improve quality and effectiveness. The first step of this process is to review the following:

- ▶ **Learn the organization**—Know the company's goals and objectives. Start by reviewing the mission statement.

- ▶ **Review the IT strategic plan**—Strategic plans provide details for the next three to five years.

- ▶ **Analyze organizational charts**—Become familiar with the roles and responsibility of individuals within the company.

- ▶ **Study job descriptions**—Job descriptions detail the level of responsibility and accountability for employees' actions.

- ▶ **Evaluate existing policies and procedures**—These documents detail the approved activities of employees.

Auditors play a big role in the success of the organization. Auditors must be independent from management and have the authority to cross over departmental boundaries. Auditors usually report governance issues to the highest level of management. Auditors must also have the proper set of skills. If individuals in-house do not have the skills required to lead the audit, an external independent third party should be hired. This situation requires careful attention. It's natural to develop relationships with those we work with. External auditors interact extensively with their clients. This can lead to problems because the level of closeness between management and external auditors might affect the results of an audit. External auditors might be too eager to please the client. Unfortunately, such an example arose in the Enron and Andersen fiasco.

Finally, both external and internal auditors can burn out as a result of staleness and repetition, and thus start to lose attention to detail, which is very important. Let's now turn our attention to the role of the steering committee.

TIP

Know Where the Audit Process Should Start   Before reviewing the organization's IT strategic plan, an auditor should understand the organization's goals and objectives.

IT Steering Committee

This committee might have more than one name: It might be referred to as an IT steering committee or an IT strategy committee. The steering committee is tasked with ensuring that the IT department is properly aligned with the goals of the business. This is accomplished by using the committee as a conduit to move information and objectives from senior business management to IT management. The committee consists of members of high-level management from within the company:

▶ **Business management**—The committee is managed by the CEO or by a personally appointed and instructed representative.

▶ **IT management**—This group is represented by the CIO or a CIO representative.

▶ **Legal**—This group is represented by an executive from the legal department.

▶ **Finance**—A representative from finance is needed to provide financial guidance.

▶ **Marketing**—A representative from marketing should also be on the committee.

▶ **Sales**—A senior manager for sales should be on the committee to make sure that the organization has the technology needed to convert shoppers into buyers.

▶ **Quality control**—Quality control ensures that consumers view products and services favorably and that products meet required standards. As such, quality control should be represented on the committee.

▶ **Research and development (R&D)**—Because R&D focuses on developing new products, this department should be represented on the committee. IT must meet the needs of new product development.

▶ **Human resources (HR)**—Managing employees is as complex as the technology needed to be successful. HR should be represented on the committee.

These represent a sampling of the department heads that might be on the IT steering committee. Figure 2.2 shows the basic organizational makeup of the committee.

Although membership might vary, the goal of the committee should be consistent. The committee is responsible for reviewing major IT projects, budgets, and plans. These duties and responsibilities should be defined in a formal charter. If an organization lacks a charter or doesn't have a steering committee, this gives clear warning that IT and business may not be closely aligned. Although the charter gives the committee the power to provide strategic guidance, it should not be involved in the day-to-day activities of the IT department. Evidence that indicates otherwise should alert auditors that the committee has strayed from its charter or that the charter is not clear on the committee's responsibilities. A steering committee is just one of three items needed to build a framework of success. The other two include performance measurement and risk management. Performance measurement, or score carding, is our next topic.

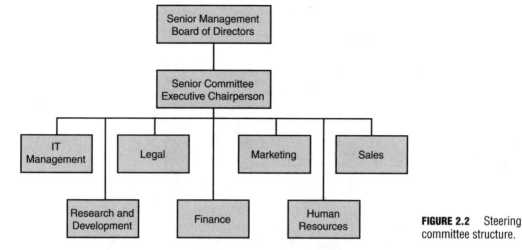

FIGURE 2.2 Steering committee structure.

Measuring Performance

Knowledge Statements

▶ Knowledge of practices for monitoring and reporting of IT performance (e.g., balanced score cards, key performance indicators [KPI])

▶ Knowledge of IT resource investment and allocation practices (e.g., portfolio management return on investment [ROI])

Measuring performance includes activities to ensure that the organization's goals are consistently being met in an effective and efficient manner. Historically, performance was measured only by financial means. In the early 1990s, Robert Kaplen and David Norton developed a new method, named the *balanced score card*. The balanced score card differs from historic measurement schemes, in that it looks at more than just the financial perspective. The balanced score card gathers input from the following four perspectives:

▶ **The customer perspective**—Includes the importance the company places on meeting customer needs. Even if financial indicators are good, poor customer ratings will eventually lead to financial decline.

▶ **Internal operations**—Includes the metrics managers use to measure how well the organization is performing and how closely its products meet customer needs.

▶ **Innovation and learning**—Includes corporate culture and its attitudes toward learning, growth, and training.

▶ **Financial evaluation**—Includes timely and accurate financial data. Typically focuses on profit and market share.

Figure 2.3 illustrates how these items balance the overall perspective.

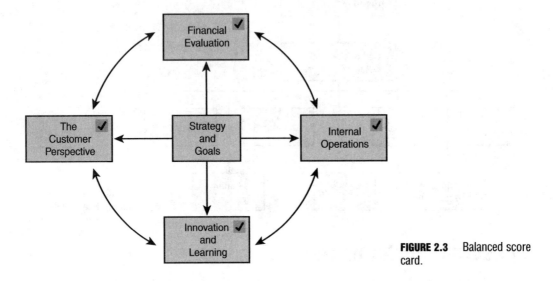

FIGURE 2.3 Balanced score card.

Use of the balanced score card at the organizational level is a good method for the steering committee to measure performance and align business strategy with IT objectives. It can be used to foster consensus among different organizational departments and groups. The information gathered by using the balanced score card should be passed down the organizational structure to supervisors, teams, and employees. Managers can use the information to further align employees' performance plans with organizational goals.

Information Security Governance

Task

▶ Evaluate the IT resource investment, use, and allocation practices to ensure alignment with the organization's strategies and objectives.

Knowledge Statement

▶ Knowledge of enterprise IT architecture and its implications for setting long-term strategic directions

Information security governance focuses on the availability of services, integrity of information, and protection of data confidentiality. Information security governance has become a much more important activity during the last decade. The growing web-ification of business and services has accelerated this trend. The Internet and global connectivity extend the company's network far beyond its traditional border. This places new demands on information security and its governance. Attacks can originate from not just inside the organization, but anywhere in the world. Failure to adequately address this important concern can have serious consequences.

One way to enhance security and governance is to implement an *enterprise architecture* (EA) plan. The EA is the practice within information technology of organizing and documenting a company's IT assets to enhance planning, management, and expansion. The primary purpose of using EA is to ensure that business strategy and IT investments are aligned. The benefit of EA is that it provides a means of traceability that extends from the highest level of business strategy down to the fundamental technology. EA has grown since John Zachman first developed it in the 1980s; companies such as Intel, BP, and the U.S. government now use this methodology.

Federal law requires government agencies to set up EA and a structure for its governance. This process is guided by Federal Enterprise Architecture (FEA) reference model. The FEA is designed to use five models:

> **Performance reference model**—A framework used to measure performance of major IT investments

> **Business reference model**—A framework used to provide an organized, hierarchical model for day-to-day business operations

> **Service component reference model**—A framework used to classify service components with respect to how they support business or performance objectives

> **Technical reference model**—A framework used to categorize the standards, specifications, and technologies that support and enable the delivery of service components and capabilities

> **Data reference model**—A framework used to provide a standard means by which data may be described, categorized, and shared

Determining Who Pays

Senior management must select a strategy to determine who will pay for the information system's services. Funding is an important topic because departments must have adequate funds to operate. Each funding option has its advantages and disadvantages. The three most common include these:

> **Shared cost**—With this method, all departments of the organization share the cost. The advantage of this method is that it is relatively easy to implement and for accounting to handle. Its disadvantage is that some departments might feel that they are paying for something they do not use.

► **Chargeback**—With this method, individual departments are directly charged for the services they use. This is a type of pay-as-you-go system. Proponents of this system believe that it shifts costs to the users of services. Those opposing the chargeback system believe that it is not that clear-cut. As an example, what if your city of 1,000 people decided to divide electrical bills evenly so that everyone pays? Many might complain, as not everyone uses the same amount of electricity. Opponents of the chargeback system make the same argument, as end users don't consume IT resources evenly.

► **Sponsor pays**—With this method, project sponsors pay all costs. Therefore, if sales asks for a new system to be implemented, sales is responsible for paying the bills. Although this gives the sponsor more control over the project, it might lead to the feeling that some departments are getting a free ride and, thus, can cause conflicts.

The Role of Strategy, Policies, Planning, and Procedures

Tasks

► Evaluate the organization's IT policies, standards, and procedures; and the processes for their development, approval, implementation, and maintenance to ensure that they support the IT strategy and comply with regulatory and legal requirements.

► Evaluate management practices to ensure compliance with the organization's IT strategy, policies, standards, and procedures.

Knowledge Statements

► Knowledge of the purpose of IT strategies, policies, standards, and procedures for an organization and the essential elements of each

► Knowledge of generally accepted international IT standards and guidelines

► Knowledge of the processes for the development, implementation, and maintenance of IT strategies, policies, standards, and procedures (for example, protection of information assets, business continuity and disaster recovery, systems and infrastructure lifecycle management, IT service delivery and support)

An auditor can learn a great deal about an organization by simply reviewing the strategic plan and examining the company's policies and procedures. These documents reflect management's view of the company. Some might even say that policies are only as good as the management team that created them. Policies should exist to cover most every aspect of organizational control because companies have legal and business requirements to establish policies and procedures.

The law dictates who is responsible and what standards must be upheld to meet minimum corporate governance requirements.

Management is responsible for dividing the company into smaller subgroups that control specific functions. Policies and procedures dictate how activities occur in each of the functional areas. One of the first steps in an audit is for the auditor to examine these critical documents. Any finding an auditor makes should be referenced back to the policy. This allows the auditor to establish a cause and specify how to rectify identified problems. Policies can be developed in either a top-down or a bottom-up method.

Policy Development

Not all policies are created in the same way. The policy process can be driven from the top or from the bottom of the organization. *Top-down policy development* means that policies are pushed down from the top of the company. The advantage of a top-down policy development approach is that it ensures that policy is aligned with the strategy of the company. What it lacks is speed. It's a time-consuming process that requires a substantial amount of time to implement. A second approach is *bottom-up policy development*. Bottom-up policy development addresses the concerns of operational employees because it starts with their input and concerns, and builds on known risk. This is faster than a top-down approach but has a huge disadvantage in that it risks the lack of senior management support.

> **EXAM ALERT**
>
> **Risk Assessment and Policy Development**   CISA exam candidates must know that a risk assessment typically drives bottom-up policy development more than top-down policy development.

No matter what the development type is, policies are designed to address specific concerns:

- ▶ **Regulatory**—Ensure that the organization's standards are in accordance with local, state, and federal laws. Industries that frequently use these documents include health care, public utilities, refining, and the federal government.

- ▶ **Advisory**—Ensure that all employees know the consequences of certain behavior and actions. An example of an advisory policy is one covering acceptable use of the Internet. This policy might state how employees can use the Internet during the course of business; if they violate the policy, it could lead to disciplinary action or dismissal.

- ▶ **Informative**—Designed not for enforcement, but for teaching. Their goal is to inform employees and/or customers. An example of an informative policy is a return policy on goods bought on the business's website.

Policies and Procedures

Policies are high-level documents developed by management to transmit its guiding strategy and philosophy to employees. Management and business process owners are responsible for the organization and design of policies to guide it toward success. Policies apply a strong emphasis to the words of management. They define, detail, and specify what is expected from employees and how management intends to meet the needs of customers, employees, and stakeholders. Policies can be developed internally, or can be based on international standards such as Common Criteria or ISO 17799:

▶ **Common Criteria**—A framework used to specify security requirements

▶ **ISO 17799**—Provides best practice recommendations for implementing good security management

One specific type of policy is the organization's *security policy*. Security policy dictates management's commitment to the use, operation, and security of information systems and assets. It specifies the role security plays within the organization. Security policy should be driven by business objectives and should meet all applicable laws and regulations. The security policy should also act as a basis to integrate security into all business functions. It serves as a high-level guide to develop lower-level documentation, such as procedures. The security policy must be balanced, in the sense that all organizations are looking for ways to implement adequate security without hindering productivity. The issue also arises that the cost of security cannot be greater than the value of the asset. Figure 2.4 highlights these concerns.

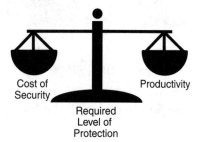

Cost of Security   Productivity

Required Level of Protection

FIGURE 2.4   Balancing security and productivity.

An auditor must look closely at all policies during the audit process and should review these to get a better idea of how specific processes function. As an example, the auditor should examine policies that have been developed for disaster recovery and business continuity. Some questions to consider are what kind of hardware and software backup is used; whether the software backup media is stored off site, and if so, what kind of security does the offsite location have, and what type of access is available? These are just a few of the items an auditor will be tasked with reviewing. The disaster recovery policy is an important part of *corrective control*.

Disaster recovery is discussed in detail in Chapter 9, "Disastor Recovery and Business Continuity."

During the audit, the auditor must verify how well policy actually maps to activity. You might discover that existing policy inhibits business or security practices. Operators might have developed better methods to meet specific goals. When faced with these situations, the auditor should identify the problem and look for ways to improve policy.

Policies don't last forever. Like most things in life, they need to be reviewed periodically to make sure they stay current. Technology becomes obsolete, new technology becomes affordable, and business processes change. Although it's sometimes easy to see that low-level procedures need to be updated, this also applies to high-level policies. Policies are just one level of procedural control. The next focus of discussion is on procedures.

Procedures

Procedures are somewhat like children—they are detailed documents built from the parent policy. Procedures provide step-by-step instruction. Like children, they are more dynamic than their parent policy. They require more frequent changes to stay relevant to business processes and the technological environment. Procedures are detailed documents tied to specific technologies and devices. Procedures change when equipment changes. The company might have a policy dictating what type of traffic can enter or leave the company's network, but a procedure would provide the step-by-step instruction on how the policy is to be carried out. As an example, if your company has a CheckPoint firewall, the procedure would provide step-by-step instruction on its configuration. If the company decided to migrate to a Cisco Adaptive Security Appliance (ASA), the policy would remain unchanged, but the procedure for configuration of the firewall would change.

During an audit, the auditor must review all relevant procedures and map them to employee behavior through direct observation or interview. Misalignment can mean that there are no existing procedures, that procedures don't map well to existing practices, or that employees have not had the proper or adequate training on the procedures they are tasked with following.

EXAM ALERT

System Demonstrations CISA exam candidates should be aware that direct observation is one way to identify problems between procedure and activity. As an example, if a policy specifies a lockout policy, yet, direct observation reveals that no lockout policy has been implemented, an auditor can then interview the employees to find out why. Is it a technical limitation, a failure to adhere to policy, or something else?

Standards, Baselines, and Guidelines

Standards are much more specific than policies. These tactical documents lay out specific steps or processes required to meet a certain requirement. Table 2.1 shows the relationship of these documents.

TABLE 2.1   Documentation/Level of Control

Level/Document	Policy	Standard	Procedure
Strategic	✓		
Tactical		✓	
Operational			✓

As an example, a standard might set mandatory requirements that all company email is to be encrypted. Although the standard does not specify how encryption is done, it does make clear that encryption is a required activity.

In the procedural sense, a *baseline* is a minimum level of security. This is the absolute minimum level that a system, network, or device must adhere to. As an example, an organization might set a baseline password length at seven characters; although passwords can be longer, they cannot be shorter than seven characters. Many times, baselines are usually mapped to regulatory or industry standards.

The final document left for discussion is the *guideline*. A guideline points to a statement in a policy or procedure to determine a course of action. As an example, the company might have a guideline stating that IS audits are to be performed at least once a year. Other procedures would detail how the audit should be carried out and what the audit should include. Guidelines are frequently referred to as best practices. Guidelines are not mandatory.

Reviewing Policies, Procedures, and Documentation

An audit of policies, procedures, and documentation can improve the quality of the control environment. Audits can verify that documents are being used in the way that management has authorized and intended them to be used. An audit can also help verify that policies are up-to-date and are adhered to. Per ISACA, the following items should be examined:

- ▶ Human resources documents
- ▶ Quality-assurance procedures
- ▶ Process and operation manuals
- ▶ Change-management documentation
- ▶ IT forecasts and budgets
- ▶ Security policies and procedures

- Organizational charts and functional diagrams

- Job details and descriptions

- Steering committee reports

Documents that deal with external entities should also be reviewed. A company might have contracts with vendors or suppliers for an array of products and services. How vendors are chosen, how the bidding process functions, what factors are used to determine the best bid, and what process is used to verify contract completion should all be reviewed. During the review process of policies, procedures, and documentation, any of the following might indicate potential problems:

- Excessive costs

- Budget overruns

- Late projects

- A high number of aborted projects

- Unsupported hardware changes or unauthorized purchases

- Lack of documentation

- Out-of-date documentation

- Employees unaware of or unknowledgeable about documentation

> **NOTE**
>
> **Policy and Compliance**   A policy review needs to take into consideration the testing of the policy for compliance.

Risk Identification and Management

Task

- Evaluate the risk management practices to ensure that the organization's IT related risks are properly managed.

Knowledge Statement

- Knowledge of risk management methodologies and tools

The first step in the risk-management process is to identify and classify the organization's assets. Information and systems must be assessed to determine their worth. When asset identification and valuation is completed, the organization can start the risk-identification process. Risk identification involves identifying potential risks and threats to the organization's assets. A risk-management team is tasked with identifying these threats. The team then can examine the impact of the identified threats. This process can be based on real dollar amounts or on gut feeling and intuition. When the impact is analyzed, the team can look at alternatives for handling the potential risks. Risks can be:

▶ **Accepted**—The risk is understood and has been evaluated. Management has decieded that the benefits outweigh the risk. As an example, the company might be considering setting up an e-commerce website. Although it is agreed that risks exist, the benefit of the added cash flow make these risks acceptable.

▶ **Reduced**—Installing a firewall is one method in which risk can be reduced.

▶ **Transferred**—The risk is transferred to a third party. As an example, insurance is obtained.

▶ **Rejected**—Depending on the situation, any one of the preceding methods might be an acceptable way to handle risk. Risk rejection is not acceptable, as it means that the risk will be ignored on the hope that it will go away or not occur.

The following sections look more closely at each step of the process.

The Risk-Management Team

The risk-management team is tasked with identifying and analyzing risks. Its members should be assembled from across the company and most likely will include managers, IT employees, auditors, programmers, and security professionals. Having a cross-section of employees from the company ensures that the team can address the many threats it must examine.

This team is not created in a void; it requires developing a risk-management program with a purpose. As an example, the program might be developed to look at ways to decrease insurance costs, reduce attacks against the company's website, or even verify compliance with privacy laws. After establishing the purpose of the team, the team can be assigned responsibility for developing and implementing a risk-management program. This is a huge responsibility because it requires not only identifying risks, but also implementing the team's recommendations.

Asset Identification

Asset identification is the task of identifying all the organization's assets. These can be both tangible and intangible. The assets commonly examined include:

- Hardware
- Software
- Employees
- Services
- Reputation
- Documentation

When looking at an asset, the team must first think about the replacement cost of the item before assigning its value. Actually, the value should be considered more than just the cost to create or purchase. These considerations are key:

- What did the asset cost to acquire or create?
- What is the liability if the asset is compromised?
- What is the production cost if the asset is made unavailable?
- What is the value of the asset to competitors and foreign governments?
- How critical is the asset, and how would its loss affect the company?

> **NOTE**
>
> **Placing a Value on Assets**—Asset valuation is an onerous task that requires a lot of expertise and work to do properly.

Threat Identification

The risk-management team can gather input from a range of sources to help identify threats. These individuals or sources should be consulted or considered to help identify current and emerging threats:

- Business owners and senior managers
- Legal counsel
- HR representatives

- IS auditors
- Network administrators
- Security administrators
- Operations
- Facility records
- Government records and watchdog groups, such as CERT and Bugtraq

A threat is any circumstance or event that has the potential to negatively impact an asset by means of unauthorized access, destruction, disclosure, or modification. Identifying all potential threats is a huge responsibility. A somewhat easier approach is to categorize the common types of threats:

- Physical threat/theft
- Human error
- Application error/buffer overflow
- Equipment malfunction
- Environmental hazards
- Malicious software/covert channels

A threat coupled with a *vulnerability* can lead to a loss. Vulnerabilities are flaws or weaknesses in security systems, software, or procedures. An example of a vulnerability is human error. This vulnerability might lead an improperly trained help-desk employee to unknowingly give a password to a potential hacker, resulting in a loss. Examples of losses or impacts include the following:

- Financial loss
- Loss of reputation
- Danger or injury to staff, clients, or customers
- Loss of business opportunity
- Breach of confidence or violation of law

Losses can be immediate or delayed. A delayed loss is not immediate; it has a negative effect on the organization after some period of time—in a few days, months, or years. As an example, an organization could have its website hacked and thus suffer an immediate loss. No e-commerce transactions would occur, technical support would have to be brought in to rebuild the web server, and normal processing would halt. All these are immediate losses. Later, when the local news channel reports that the company was hacked and that personal information was lost, the company would lose the goodwill of its customers. Some might remember this event for years to come and choose to use a competitor. This is a delayed loss.

Thus far, we have discussed building a risk-management team that has the support of senior management, identifying tangible and nontangible assets, and performing threat identification. Next, we analyze the potential risks that these threats pose.

Risk-Analysis Methods

After identifying the threats, the team can start to focus on the risk-analysis process. *Risk analysis* can be performed in one of two basic methods:

▶ **Quantitative risk assessment**—Deals with dollar amounts. It attempts to assign a cost (monetary value) to the elements of risk assessment and the assets and threats of a risk analysis.

▶ **Qualitative risk assessment**—Ranks threats by nondollar values and is based more on scenario, intuition, and experience.

Quantitative Risk Assessment

Performing a quantitative risk assessment involves quantifying all elements of the process, including asset value, impact, threat frequency, safeguard effectiveness, safeguard costs, uncertainty, and probability. This involves six basic steps, illustrated in Figure 2.5:

1. Determine the asset value (AV) for each information asset.

2. Identify threats to the asset.

3. Determine the exposure factor (EF) for each information asset in relation to each threat.

4. Calculate the single loss expectancy (SLE).

5. Calculate the annualized rate of occurrence (ARO).

6. Calculate the annualized loss expectancy (ALE).

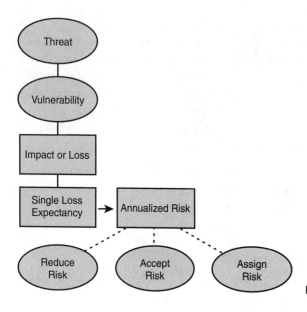

FIGURE 2.5   The risk-assessment process.

The advantage of a quantitative risk assessment is that it assigns dollar values, which is easy for management to work with and understand. However, a disadvantage of a quantitative risk assessment is that it is also based on dollar amounts. Consider that it's difficult, if not impossible, to assign dollar values to all elements. Therefore, some qualitative measures must be applied to quantitative elements. Even then, this is a huge responsibility; therefore, a quantitative assessment is usually performed with the help of automated software tools. Assuming that asset values have been determined as previously discussed and threats have been identified, the next steps in the process are as follows:

STEP BY STEP

2.1 Quantitative Risk Assessment

1. **Determine the exposure factor**—This is a subjective potential percentage of loss to a specific asset if a specific threat is realized. This is usually in the form of a percentage, similar to how weather reports predict the likelihood of weather conditions.

2. **Calculate the single loss expectancy (SLE)**—The SLE value is a dollar figure that represents the organization's loss from a single loss or the loss of this particular information asset. SLE is calculated as follows:

    Single Loss Expectancy = Asset Value × Exposure Factor

    Items to consider when calculating the SLE include the physical destruction or theft of assets, loss of data, theft of information, and threats that might delay processing.

3. **Assign a value for the annualized rate of occurrence (ARO)**—The ARO represents the estimated frequency at which a given threat is expected to occur. Simply stated, how many times is this expected to happen in one year?

4. **Assign a value for the annualized loss expectancy (ALE)**—The ALE is an annual expected financial loss to an organization's information asset because of a particular threat occurring within that same calendar year. ALE is calculated as follows:

   Annualized Loss Expectancy (ALE) =

   Single Loss Expectancy (SLE) × Annualized Rate of Occurrence (ARO)

   The ALE is typically the value that senior management needs to assess to prioritize resources and determine what threats should receive the most attention.

5. **Analyze the risk to the organization**—The final step is to evaluate the data and decide to accept, reduce, or transfer the risk.

Much of the process of quantitative risk assessment is built upon determining the exposure factor and the annualized loss expectancy. These rely heavily on probability and expectancy. When looking at events, such as storms or other natural phenomena, it can be difficult to predict their actual behavior. Yet over time, a trend can be established. These events can be considered *stochastic*. A stochastic event is based on random behavior because the occurrence of individual events cannot be predicted, yet measuring the distribution of all observations usually follows a predictable pattern. In the end, however, quantitative risk management faces challenges when estimating risk, and as such must rely on some elements of the qualitative approach.

Another item that is sometimes overlooked in quantitative risk assessment is the total cost of a loss. The team should review these items for such costs:

▶ Lost productivity

▶ Cost of repair

▶ Value of the damaged equipment or lost data

▶ Cost to replace the equipment or reload the data

When these costs are accumulated and specific threats are determined, the true picture of annualized loss expectancy can be assessed. Now the team can build a complete picture of the organization's risks. Table 2.2 shows sample results.

TABLE 2.2 Sample Assessment Results

Asset	Risk	Asset Value	EF	SLE	Annualized Frequency	ALE
Customer database	Loss of consumer data due to no backup	$118,000	78.06%	$92,121	.25	$23,030
E-commerce website	Hacked	$22,500	35.50%	$8,000	.45	$3,600
Domain controller	Power supply failure	$16,500	27.27%	$4,500	.25	$1,125

Although automated tools are available to minimize the effort of the manual process, these programs should not become a crutch to prevent businesses from using common sense or practicing due diligence. Care should also be taken when examining high-impact events, even for the probability. Many of us witnessed the 100-year storm that would supposedly never occur in our lifetime and that hit the Gulf Coast and severely damaged the city of New Orleans. Organizations must be realistic when examining such potential events and must openly discuss how the situation should be dealt with. Just because an event is rated as a one-in-a-hundred-year probability does not mean that it can't happen again next year.

Challenge

This challenge has you calculate a risk score. As part of your CISA duties, you have been asked to look over some risk score calculations. Your organization has installed a new email server valued at $2,500. The organization plans to use it to connect its 65 client computers to the Internet for email access. Currently, this server does not have software installed for spam, content filtering, or antivirus. Your research indicates that there is a 95% chance that the new email server will become infected. If such an infection were to occur, three-fourths of the data could be lost. Without antivirus, there's a good chance that a virus could bring down the network for up to four hours and divert the four-member support team from normal duties. An approved vendor has offered to sell a site license for the needed software for $175. Can you calculate the ALE? Where do you start?

1. The first step is to examine the exposure factor. This has been calculated at 75%. Remember that the exposure factor identifies the percentage of the asset value that will be affected by the succesful execution of the threat.

2. Next, calculate the single loss expectancy (SLE). The SLE value is a dollar figure that represents the organization's loss from a single loss or the loss of this particular IT asset. SLE is calculated as $1,875. The formula is as follows:

   Single Loss Expectancy = Asset Value × Exposure Factor

   Given an asset value of $2,500 and exposure factor of 75%, the resulting SLE will be $1,875.

3. Assign a value for the annualized rate of occurrence (ARO). The ARO is a value that represents the estimated frequency at which a given threat is expected to occur. Simply stated, how many times is this expected to happen in one year? Your research indicates that there is a 95% chance (.95) that an infection will occur in one year.

(continues)

(continued)

4. Assign a value for the annualized loss expectancy (ALE). The ALE is an annual expected financial loss to an organization's IT asset because of a particular threat occurring within that same calendar year. ALE is calculated as follows:

(ALE) = (SLE) × **(ARO)**

or

$1,875 (SLE) × .95 (ARO) = $1,781 (ALE)

5. The final step is to evaluate the data and decide to accept, reduce, or transfer the risk. Therefore, would the purchase of antivirus be a good deal for the company? The answer is "yes" because $1,781 (ALE) – $175 (antivirus) = $1,606 (savings).

EXAM ALERT

Qualitative Risk Assessment Process   For the exam, you must know the steps used to perform a qualitative risk assessment. You will also want to note that this is the preferred method for performing risk assessment.

Qualitative Risk Assessment

Maybe you're thinking that there has to be another way to perform the assessment. If so, you're right. Qualitative assessment is scenario driven and does not attempt to assign dollar values to components of the risk analysis. A qualitative assessment ranks the seriousness of threats and sensitivity of assets by grade or class, such as low, medium, or high. You can see an example of this in NIST 800-26, a document that uses confidentiality, integrity, and availability as categories for a loss. It then rates each loss according to a scale of low, medium, or high. Table 2.3 displays an example of how this process is performed. A rating of low, medium, or high is subjective. In this example, the following categories are defined:

▶ **Low**—Minor inconvenience; can be tolerated for a short period of time but will not result in financial loss.

▶ **Medium**—Can result in damage to the organization, cost a moderate amount of money to repair, and result in negative publicity.

▶ **High**—Will result in a loss of goodwill between the company, client, or employee; may result in a large legal action or fine, or cause the company to significantly lose revenue or earnings.

TABLE 2.3   Performing a Qualitative Assessment

Asset	Loss of Confidentiality	Loss of Integrity	Loss of Availability
Customer credit card and billing information	High	High	Medium
Production documentation	Medium	Medium	Low
Advertising and marketing literature	Low	Low	Low
HR (employee) records	High	High	Medium

The downside of performing a qualitative assessment is that you are not working with dollar values; therefore, this lacks the rigor that accounting teams and management typically prefer.

Other types of qualitative assessment techniques include these:

▶ **The Delphi Technique**—A group assessment process that allows individuals to contribute anonymous opinions.

▶ **Facilitated Risk Assessment Process (FRAP)**—A subjective process that obtains results by asking a series of questions. It places risks into one of 26 categories. FRAP is designed to be completed in a matter of hours, making it a quick process to perform.

NOTE

Blending Qualitative and Quantitative Methodologies   When it is not possible to calculate specific items quantitatively, qualitative methods can be used. This is known as *semiquantitative analysis*.

Management Practices and Controls

Task

▶ Evaluate the IT organizational structure and human resources (personnel) management to ensure that they support the organization's strategies and objectives.

Knowledge Statement

▶ Knowledge of the IT human resources (personnel) management

Management is tasked with the guidance and control of the organization; they are the individuals who are responsible for the organization. Although companies heavily depend on technology, a large part of management's duties still deals with people. People are key to what can make a company successful. Therefore, a large portion of management's duties depends on its people skills, including interaction with employees and with those outside the traditional organizational boundaries. *Outsourcing* is an example of this. This might not be a phrase that some people like, but it's a fact of life that companies depend upon an array of components and services from around the world. As an example, consider Dell Computer. Dell might be based in Round Rock, Texas, yet its distribution hub is in Memphis, Tennessee; Dell assembles PCs in Malaysia, yet has customer support in India. Many other parts come from the far corners of the globe. The controls that a company places on its employees and contracts, and its agreements with business partners and suppliers, must be examined and reviewed. The next several sections focus on good management practices. Let's start by reviewing employee management.

Employee Management

Employee management deals with the policies and procedures that detail how people are hired, promoted, retained, and terminated. Employees can have a huge impact on the security of the company. Consumeraffairs.com has attributed more than 54% of instances of lost data or security breaches to employees, and only 34% to outside hackers. This should serve as a sad but true reminder that people are the weakest link in security. Insiders have greater access and opportunity for misuse than outsiders typically do. Whether it's malicious, accidental, or intentional, insiders pose a real threat to security. Although there is no way to predict future events, employee risks can be reduced by implementing and following good basic HR practices. The first of these is good *hiring practices*.

Everyone Has Good HR Practices, Right?

On February 20, 2006, Dave Edmondson, CEO of Radio Shack, said, "For the last 11 years, it has been my privilege to be associated with Radio Shack. At this time, the board and I have agreed that it is in the best interest of the company for new leadership to step forward." What would cause the CEO of Radio Shack to step down?

Mr. Edmondson had come under increasing pressure to explain errors noted about his educational background. Although company records indicated that Edmondson had received a four-year bachelor degree, the listed college could report no record of the supposed degree. Radio Shack downplayed the incident by stating that, at the time Edmondson was hired in 1994, the company did not perform educational checks on employees even if they were hired into senior management positions.

Although it would be nice to think this is an isolated incident, in October 2006, a fake degree mill in Spokane, Washington, was shut down and the company's records revealed that more than 100 federal employees had purchased fake degrees from it. These individuals included a White House staff member, National Security Agency employees, and officials running the Iraq reconstruction program.

Everyone wants to get the right person for the job, but good HR practices require more than just matching a resume to an open position. Depending on the position to be filled, company officials need to perform due diligence in verifying that they have matched the right person to the right job. As an example, Kevin might be the best security expert around, but if it is discovered that he served a 10-year sentence for extortion and racketeering, his chances of being hired by an interested company will be slim. Some basic common controls should be used during the hiring practice:

▶ Background checks

▶ Educational checks

▶ Reference checks

▶ Confidentiality agreements

▶ Noncompete agreements

▶ Conflict-of-interest agreements

Hiring practices should be performed with due diligence. References can be checked, education verified, military records reviewed, and even drug tests performed, if necessary. When an employee is hired, he brings not only his skills, but also his background, history, attitude, and behavior. Many companies perform these searches in-house, and these can even be performed via the Internet. Figure 2.6 shows an example of one site offering such services.

FIGURE 2.6 ZABASearch, a background search site.

Once hired, employees should be provided with an employee handbook detailing employee code of conduct, acceptable use of company assets, and employee responsibilities to the company. Per ISACA, the handbook should address the following issues:

▶ Security practices, policies, and procedures

▶ Employee package of benefits

▶ Paid holiday and vacation policy

▶ Work schedule and overtime policy

▶ Moonlighting and outside employment

▶ Employee evaluations

▶ Disaster response and emergency procedures

▶ Disciplinary action process for noncompliance

Hiring is just the first step in good employee management. Auditors should verify that HR has a written, well-defined promotion policy. Employees should also know the process for promotion. These procedures should be defined and known by all employees so that this is seen as a fair, unbiased process. Closely related to promotion policy is performance evaluation. Assessments should occur on a predetermined schedule and should be based on known goals and results. A fair and objective process should be used. Pay raises and bonuses should be based strictly on performance.

Training is another area that falls under the responsibility of HR. Employees might not know proper policies and procedures if they are not informed and trained. Training increases effectiveness and efficiency. When a new process or technology is introduced in the organization, employees should be trained for proper operation. Training is also beneficial because it increases morale; it makes people feel better, so they strive to do a better job. Training categories include those for technical, personnel management, project management, and security needs.

NOTE

Security Awareness Programs Increase Awareness   Security awareness training must be developed differently for the various groups of employees that make up the organization. Successful employee awareness programs tailor the message to fit the audience.

Training can range from lunchtime programs to learning programs, multiday events, or degree programs. Common training methods include the following:

▶ In-house training

▶ Classroom training

▶ Vendor training

▶ On-the-job training

▶ Apprenticeship programs

▶ Degree programs

▶ Continuing education programs

If all this talk of work and training has made you tired, don't worry—many employees feel the same way. Therefore, our next topic is vacations—and not just any kind of vacation, but *required vacations*. A required vacation is not something that is done for the health or benefit of the employee. Required vacations are for the company to ensure that someone else does the regular employee's job tasks for at least a week. This control helps verify that improper or illegal acts have not been occurring. It also makes it harder for an employee to hide any misuse. Required vacations are just one of the employee controls that can be used. Another control is *rotation of assignment*, which allows more than one person to perform a specific task. This not only helps ensure a backup if an employee is unavailable, but it also can reduce fraud or misuse by preventing an individual from having too much control over an area. One other closely related control worth mentioning is *dual control*. Dual control requires two individuals to provide input or approval before a transaction or activity can take place.

The final topic for this section is termination. HR must have approved, effective *termination procedures* in place to address the termination of employees. These procedures should include procedures for voluntary and involuntary separation. Checklists should be included to verify that the employee has returned all equipment that has been in his possession, including remote access tokens, keys, ID cards, cell phones, pagers, credit cards, laptops, and software. Termination might not be a joyful or happy event, but there needs to be a defined process on how to address or handle the situation properly. The applicable policy must cover issues such as employee escort, exit interviews, review of NDAs, and suspension of network access.

Background Checks: It's a Brand-New Day!

Technology continues to change the way we do business. Imagine that your company has an employee who has had a little too much fun on a Friday night and gets arrested for a DWI. Luckily, the employee has enough cash to make bail and is back home before sunrise on Saturday morning. He believes that it's a brand-new day, time to start fresh again. It's all just a small misunderstanding that no one will ever find out about, right?

Wrong! Today companies such as Verified Person offer continuous employment checks to companies that subscribe to their service. Not only can the HR department use these services to check an individual's background before being hired, but they can continue to monitor employees throughout their employment. In other words, an employee's criminal and civil history can be monitored 24 hours a day, seven days a week.

So the guy who had too much to drink on Friday night has caused a report to be generated before he even reports to work on Monday morning. Employers can use this service to monitor employee misconduct, ranging from simple misdemeanors or bad checks to major felonies. State laws vary on how this technology can be used, but in some states, employers have the right to terminate an employee based on the information that has been reported. The belief that "it's a brand-new day" and "what happened last week is unknown" is no longer true. Today actions have consequences that can last a lifetime!

REVIEW BREAK

Employee controls help protect the organization and build good security. Notice how each of the controls in Table 2.4 is used and what the primary attributes are.

TABLE 2.4   Employee Controls

Item	Usage	Attributes
Background checks	Hiring practice	Helps match the right person to the right job
Required vacations	Uncovers misuse	Serves as a detective control to uncover employee malfeasance
Rotation of assignment	Prevents excessive control	Rotates employees to new areas
Dual control	Limits control	Aids in separation of duties
Nondisclosure agreement (NDA)	Aids in confidentiality	Helps prevent disclosure of sensitive information
Security training	Improves performance	Improves performance and gives employees information on how to handle certain situations

Sourcing

Task

▶ Evaluate IT contracting strategies and policies, and contract management practices to ensure that they support the organization's strategies and objectives.

Knowledge Statement

▶ Knowledge of the contracting strategies, processes, and contract management practices

Per ISACA, *sourcing* describes the means by which an organization obtains its information systems services. IS services can be provided in these ways:

- ▶ **Internally**—Insourced
- ▶ **Externally**—Outsourced
- ▶ **Combination**—Hybrid

Functions can also occur at a wide range of locations, such as inside and outside the company:

▶ **On-site**—Employees and contractors work at the company's facility.

▶ **Off-site**—Staff and contractors work at a remote location.

▶ **Off-shore**—Staff and contractors work at a separate geographic region.

Organizations should go through a source strategy to determine what information systems tasks must be done by employees. Third parties commonly provide these services:

▶ Data entry

▶ Application/web hosting

▶ Help desk

▶ Payroll processing

▶ Check processing

▶ Credit card processing

Key to this decision is determining whether a task is part of the organization's *core competency*, or proficiency that defines who the organization is. This is a fundamental set of skills or knowledge that gives the company a unique advantage. The company should analyze whether these tasks can be duplicated at another location and whether they can be performed for the same or less cost. Security should also play a role in the decision because some tasks take on a much greater risk if performed by others outside the organization. Any decision should pass a thorough business process review. As an example, does data entry report a large number of errors, is the help desk backlogged, or is application development more than three months behind schedule? Some of the most common outsourced tasks are data entry and processing. When a task is outsourced, a method for retaining accuracy should be done by implementing a *key verification* process. Key verification ensures that data entry was done correctly. For example, the company's data entry department might key in information just as the outsourcing partner does in India. After both data sets are entered, they are compared to verify that the information was entered correctly. Any keystroke that does not match flags an alert so that a data-entry supervisor can examine and verify it.

If the decision is made to outsource, management must be aware that it will lose some level of visibility when the process is no longer done in-house. Outsourcing partners face the same risks, threats, and vulnerabilities as the client; the only difference is they might not be as apparent. Because of this loss of control, every outsourcing agreement should contain a *right-to-audit*. Without a right-to-audit statement, the client would be forced to negotiate every type of audit or review of the outsourcing partner's operation. These negotiations can be time-consuming and very costly. Therefore, a right-to-audit clause is one of the most powerful mechanisms that a company can insist upon before an agreement is signed. Even if the outsourcing partner does not agree to a right-to-audit, it should at least provide the auditor with a copy of its statement of auditing standards 70 (*SAS-70*) report. An SAS-70 report verifies that the outsourcing partner has had its control objectives and activities examined by an independent accounting and auditing firm.

NOTE

SAS-70—One potential drawback of an SAS-70 report is that the audittee determines the scope of the audit. It's the auditor's responsibility when examining an SAS-70 report to validate that the scope and type of report present covers the needs of his review.

Another control that should be considered when outsourcing is a service level agreement (SLA). If the outsourcing provider will provide a time-sensitive process, an SLA is one way to obtain a guarantee of the level of service the outsourcing partner is agreeing to provide. The SLA should specify the uptime, response time, and maximum outage time to which they are agreeing. Choosing the right outsourcing partner is extremely important and should be done with the utmost care.

CAUTION

Measure Performance Before Signing Agreements   A right-to-audit will help verify future performance, but organizations should consider asking outsourcing providers to agree to a preagreement audit and measurement of uptime compliance before signing a contract.

Change Management and Quality Improvement Techniques

Knowledge Statements

▶ Knowledge of the use of maturity and process improvement models (e.g., CMM, CobiT)

▶ Knowledge of the use of control frameworks (e.g., CobiT, COSO, ISO 17799)

▶ Knowledge of quality management strategies and policies

As funny as it sounds, change is continuous today and occurs at a much faster rate than ever before. Processes, procedures, and technology all motivate the change process. As a CISA, you will be tasked with ensuring that all changes are documented, accounted for, and controlled.

Companies should have a well-structured process for change requests (CRs). The following steps are a generic overview of the change management process:

1. Request a change.

2. Approve the request.

3. Document the proposed change.

4. Test the proposed change.

5. Implement the change.

CRs are typically examined by a subject matter expert (SME) before being implemented. CRs must also be assessed to ensure that no change poses a risk for the organization. If an application or code is being examined for a potential change, other issues must be addressed, including how the new code will move from the coding to a production environment and how the code will be tested, as well as an examination of user training. Change management ensures that proper governance and control are maintained.

Quality Management

Quality management is an ongoing effort to provide IS services that meet or exceed customer expectations. It's a philosophy to improve quality and strive for continuous improvement. The auditor should be knowledgeable in these areas:

▶ Hardware and software requisitioning

▶ Software development

▶ Information systems operations

▶ Human resources management

▶ Security

Why are so many quality-management controls and change-management methods needed? Most companies move data among multiple business groups, divisions, and IT systems. Auditors must verify the controls and attest to their accuracy. ISO 9001 is one quality-management standard that is receiving widespread support and attention. ISO 9001 describes how production processes are to be managed and reviewed. This is not a standard of quality; it covers how well a system or process is documented. Companies that want to obtain 9001 certification must perform a gap analysis to determine what areas need improvement. The ISO 9001 is actually six documents that specify the following:

▶ Control of documents

▶ Control of records

- ▶ Control of nonconforming product

- ▶ Corrective action

- ▶ Preventive action

- ▶ Internal audits

TIP

Achieving ISO 9001:2000 Certification   ISO 9001 certification requires an organization to perform a gap analysis. This allows the company to identify shortcomings that must be addressed to obtain certification.

Being ISO certified means that the organization has the capability to provide products that meet specific requirements; this includes the process for continual improvement. Being ISO certified can also have a direct bearing on an IS audit because it places strong controls on documented procedures. Another ISO document that the auditor should be aware of is ISO 17799, which is considered a code of practice for information security. ISO 17799 is written for individuals who are responsible for initiating, implementing, or maintaining information security management systems. Its goal is to help protect confidentiality, integrity, and availability. ISO 17799 provides best-practice guidance on information security management and is divided into 12 main sections:

- ▶ Risk assessment and treatment

- ▶ Security policy

- ▶ Organization of information security

- ▶ Asset management

- ▶ Human resources security

- ▶ Physical and environmental security

- ▶ Communications and operations management

- ▶ Access control

- ▶ Information systems acquisition, development, and maintenance

- ▶ Information security incident management

- ▶ Business continuity management

- ▶ Compliance

Another means of quality management is the software *capability maturity model* (CMM), designed for software developers to improve the software-development process. The CMM enables software developers to progress from an anything-goes type of development to a highly structured, repeatable process. As software developers grow and mature, their productivity will increase and the quality of their software products will become more robust. The CMM has five maturity levels, described in Table 2.5.

TABLE 2.5 Capability Maturity Model

Maturity Level	Name	Description
1	Initial	This is an ad hoc process with no assurance of repeatability.
2	Repeatable	Change control and quality assurance are in place and controlled by management, although a formal process is not defined.
3	Defined	Defined processes and procedures are in place and used. Qualitative process improvement is in place.
4	Managed	Qualitative data is collected and analyzed. A process-improvement program is used.
5	Optimized	Continuous process improvement is in place and has been budgeted for.

Control Objectives for Information and Related Technology (*CobiT*) is a control framework that can be utilized to better control processes. It is considered a system of best practices. CobiT was created by the Information Systems Audit and Control Association (ISACA) and the IT Governance Institute (ITGI) in 1992. Although auditors can use CobiT, it is also useful for IT users and managers to help design controls and optimize processes. CobiT is designed around 34 key processes, which address the following:

▶ Performance concerns

▶ IT control profiling

▶ Awareness

▶ Benchmarking

Another process-improvement method includes enterprise resource planning (ERP). The goal of this method is to integrate all of an organization's processes into a single integrated system. There are many advantages of building a unified system that can service the needs of people in finance, human resources, manufacturing, and the warehouse. Traditionally, each of those departments would have its own computer system. These unique systems would be optimized for the specific ways in which each department operates. ERP combines them all into a single integrated software program that runs off a unified database. This allows each department to more easily share information and communicate with each other. Enterprise resource planning is seen as a replacement to business process reengineering, a management approach that attempted to improve the efficiency of the underlying processes. Business process reengineering was done in the following steps:

1. Envision

2. Initiate

3. Diagnose

4. Redesign

5. Reconstruct

6. Evaluate

Business process reengineering lost favor because it was closely associated with downsizing.

A final control worth mentioning is the Committee of Sponsoring Organizations of the Treadway Commission (COSO), which was designed to improve the quality of financial reporting. COSO was started in 1985 to review the causes of fraudulent financial reporting.

> **NOTE**
>
> **Who Pays for Change?** One change management practice is to charge the department and users of the services that have been updated. This is known as the "user pays" scheme. Basically, charges are forwarded to the users of the service.

Understanding Personnel Roles and Responsibilities

Knowledge Statement

▶ Knowledge of organizational structure, roles, and responsibilities related to the use and management of IT

Individuals can hold any number of roles or responsibilities within an organization. The responsibilities each employee has and to whom he or she reports should be noted. An auditor's first option for determining this information should be an organizational chart. After obtaining and reviewing the organizational chart, the auditor should spend some time reviewing each employee's area to see how the job description matches actual activities. The areas to focus attention on include these:

▶ Help desk

▶ End-user support manager

▶ Quality assurance manager

▶ Data manager

▶ Rank and file employees

▶ Systems-development manager

▶ Software-development manager

NOTE

Organizational Charts When performing audits, don't be surprised to find organizational charts that are missing, incomplete, or out-of-date. This is a common occurrence.

Employee Roles and Duties

Most organizations have clearly defined controls that specify what each job role is responsible for. An auditor should be concerned with these common roles within the IS structure:

▶ **Librarian**—Responsible for all types of media, including tapes, cartridges, CDs, DVDs, and so on. Librarians must track, store, and recall media as needed. They also must document when the data was stored and retrieved, and who accessed it. If data moves off-site, librarians track when it was sent and when it arrived. They may also be asked to assist in an audit to verify what type of media is still being held at a vendor's site.

▶ **Data-entry employee**—Although most data-entry activities are now outsourced, in the not-too-distant past, these activities were performed in-house at an information processing facility (IPF). During this time, a full-time data-entry person was assigned the task of entering all data. Bar codes, scanning, and web entry forms have also reduced the demand for these services. If this role is still used, key verification is one of the primary means of control.

▶ **Systems administrator**—This employee is responsible for the operation and maintenance of the LAN and associated components such as mid-range or mainframe systems. Although small organizations might have only one systems administrator, larger organizations have many.

▶ **Quality-assurance employee**—Employees in a quality-assurance role can fill one of two roles: quality assurance or quality control. Quality-assurance employees make sure programs and documentation adhere to standards; quality-control employees perform tests at various stages of product development to make sure they are free of defects.

▶ **Database administrator**—This employee is responsible for the organization's data and maintains the data structure. The database administrator has control over all the data; therefore, detective controls and supervision of duties must be observed closely. This is usually a role filled by a senior information systems employee because these employees have control over the physical data definition, implementing data definition controls and defining and initiating backup and recovery.

▶ **Systems analyst**—These employees are involved in the system development lifecycle (SDLC) process. They are responsible for determining the needs of users and developing requirements and specifications for the design of needed software programs.

▶ **Network administrators**—These employees are responsible for maintenance and configuration of network equipment, such as routers, switches, firewalls, wireless access points, and so on.

▶ **Security architect**—These employees examine the security infrastructure of the organization's network.

Segregation of Duties

Job titles can be confusing because different organizations sometimes use different titles for various positions. It helps when the title matches the actual job duties the employee performs. Some roles and functions are just not compatible. For an auditor, concern over such incompatibility centers on the risks these roles represent when combined. Segregation of duties usually falls into four areas of control:

▶ **Authorization**—Verifying cash, approving purchases, and approving changes

▶ **Custody**—Accessing cash, merchandise, or inventories

▶ **Record keeping**—Preparing receipts, maintaining records, and posting payments.

▶ **Reconciliation**—Comparing dollar amounts, counts, reports, and payroll summaries

---

NOTE

Segregation of Duties   In the United States, Sarbanes-Oxley legislation has served to increase concern about sensitivity around SOD. Auditors must now perform an in-depth review of this key control during their control audits.

Table 2.6 lists some of the duties that should not be combined because they can result in a control weakness.

TABLE 2.6   Separation of Duties

First Job Role	Combined (Yes/No)	Second Job Role
Systems analyst	No	Security administrator
Application programmer	Yes	Systems analyst
Help desk	No	Network administrator
Data entry	Yes	Quality assurance
Computer operator	No	Systems programmer
Database administrator	Yes	Systems analyst
System administrator	No	Database administrator
Security administrator	No	Application programmer
Systems programmer	No	Security administrator

EXAM ALERT

Separation of Duties   CISA exam candidates must understand which job duties should not be combined. Examples include security administrator/programmer and database administrator/network administrator.

Compensating Controls

Because of the problems that can occur when certain tasks are combined, separation of duties is required to provide accountability and control. When it cannot be used, compensating controls should be considered. In small organizations, it is usually very difficult to adequately separate job tasks. In these instances, one or more of the following compensating controls should be considered:

▶ **Job rotation**—The concept is to not have one person in one position for too long a period of time. This prevents a single employee from having too much control.

▶ **Audit trail**—Although audit trails are a popular item after a security breach, they should be examined more frequently. Audit trails enable an auditor to determine what actions specific individuals performed; they provide accountability.

▶ **Reconciliation**—This is a specific type of audit in which records are compared to make sure they balance. Although they're primarily used in financial audits, they are also useful for computer batch processing and other areas in which totals should be compared.

▶ **Exception report**—This type of report notes errors or exceptions. Exception reports should be made available to managers and supervisors so that they can track errors and other problems.

▶ **Transaction log**—This type of report tracks transactions and the time of occurrence. Managers should use transaction reports to track specific activities.

▶ **Supervisor review**—Supervisor reviews can be performed through observation or inquiry, or remotely using software tools and applications.

Chapter Summary

In this chapter, you learned about IT governance. Governance starts with senior management and extends down though the organization. Good governance requires that the goals of an organization's information systems (IS) department map to the goals of the company. Technology's role is to support the company and help it reach its goals. This requires strategy. Mapping the strategy of the company to the technology needs of the organization is the role of the steering committee.

Other requirements are policies, procedures, and standards. These documents not only provide a high-level view of the mission and direction of the company, but they also guide employees in their day-to-day activities. Auditors also play a role in governance. Auditors are tasked with reviewing the documents, standards, and policies that an organization has, to determine how closely they map to employee activities. Auditors might note missing documentation, obsolete documentation, or documentation that is not being followed. Auditors might also review job roles and responsibilities to understand the risks that an individual might pose to the company.

Key Terms

- ► Annualized loss expectancy
- ► Balanced score card
- ► Bottom-up policy development
- ► Capability maturity model
- ► CobiT
- ► Enterprise architecture
- ► Guideline
- ► Key verification
- ► Outsourcing
- ► Policy
- ► Procedure
- ► Qualitative risk assessment
- ► Quantitative risk assessment
- ► Required vacation

- ▶ Right-to-audit
- ▶ Risk analysis
- ▶ Rotation of assignment
- ▶ Security policy
- ▶ Standard
- ▶ Termination procedure
- ▶ Top-down policy development
- ▶ Vulnerability

Apply Your Knowledge

You have seen in this chapter the importance of risk assessment. Inventorying assets, determining the risk to those assets, and evaluating countermeasure options are all part of good IT governance.

Exercises

2.1 Determining the steps for quantitative risk assessment

In this exercise, you examine the proper order for quantitative risk assessment.

Estimated Time: 5 minutes

1. Place the following quantitative risk analysis steps and calculations in the proper sequential order (first step = 1, last step = 6):

_____ Determine the annual rate of occurrence (likelihood of occurrence).

_____ Identify threats to the asset.

_____ Determine the asset value (AV).

_____ Calculate the annualized loss expectancy for each asset.

_____ Calculate the single loss expectancy.

_____ Identify the exposure factor for each asset in relation to the threat.

2. Compare your results to the answers here:

    1. Determine the asset value (AV).

    2. Identify threats to the asset.

    3. Identify the exposure factor for each asset in relation to the threat.

    4. Calculate the single loss expectancy.

    5. Determine the annual rate of occurrence.

    6. Calculate the annualized loss expectancy for each asset.

2.2 Calculate single loss expectancy

In this exercise, you calculate single loss expectancy.

Estimated Time: 10 minutes

1. Examine Table 2.7 and fill in the ALE for each item shown.

TABLE 2.7   Annualized Loss Expectancy

IT Asset Name	SLE Value	Threat	ARO Value	ALE Value
Cisco PIX firewall	$4,795	DoS attack	.05	
WAN circuits (2 remote data centers)	$3,250	Power failure	.15	
Cisco 6500 switch/router	$5,400	Power failure	.15	
LAN connectivity	$18,500	Hardware failure	.12	
Gateway servers—Pentium 4s	$4,950	Power failure	.20	
Microsoft SQL Server	$6,000	Software vulnerability	.60	
Oracle SQL data (customer data)	$120,000	Hacker attack	.30	

2. Now compare your results to the values shown in Table 2.8:

TABLE 2.8   Annualized Loss Expectancy Values

IT Asset Name	SLE Value	Threat	ARO Value	ALE Value
Cisco PIX firewall	$4,795	DoS attack	.05	$239
WAN circuits (2 remote data centers)	$3,250	Power failure	.15	$487
Cisco 6500 switch/router	$5,400	Power failure	.15	$810
LAN connectivity	$18,500	Hardware failure	.12	$2,220
Gateway servers—Pentium 4s	$4,950	Power failure	.20	$990
Microsoft SQL Server	$6,000	Software vulnerability	.60	$3,600
Oracle SQL data (customer data)	$120,000	Hacker attack	.30	$36,000

3. Which item in Table 2.8 represents the greatest dollar risk when ranked per ALE?

4. What three methods can be used to deal with risk?

Exam Questions

1. Which of the following control documents describes a software-improvement process that is characterized by five levels, where each level describes a higher level of maturity?

   ○ **A.** ISO 17799

   ○ **B.** CMM

   ○ **C.** COSO

   ○ **D.** CobiT

2. A network administrator should not share the duties of which of the following roles?

   ○ **A.** Quality assurance

   ○ **B.** Systems administrator

   ○ **C.** Application programmer

   ○ **D.** Systems analyst

3. You are auditing a credit card payment system. Which of the following methods provides the best assurance that information is entered correctly?

   ○ **A.** Audit trails

   ○ **B.** Separation of data entry and computer operator duties

   ○ **C.** Key verification

   ○ **D.** Supervisory review

4. Which level of the CMM is characterized by its capability to measure results by qualitative measures?

   ○ **A.** Level 1

   ○ **B.** Level 2

   ○ **C.** Level 3

   ○ **D.** Level 4

5. Which of the following is most closely associated with bottom-up policy development?

   ○ **A.** Aligns policy with strategy

   ○ **B.** Is a very slow process

   ○ **C.** Does not address concerns of employees

   ○ **D.** Involves risk assessment

6. Which of the following offers the best explanation of a balanced score card?

   ○ **A.** Used for benchmarking a preferred level of service

   ○ **B.** Used to measure the effectiveness of IT services by customers and clients

   ○ **C.** Verifies that the organization's strategy and IT services match

   ○ **D.** Measures the evaluation of help-desk employees

7. Your organization is considering using a new ISP now that the current contract is complete. From an audit perspective, which of the following would be the most important item to review?

   ○ **A.** The service level agreement

   ○ **B.** The physical security of the ISP site

   ○ **C.** References from other clients of the ISP

   ○ **D.** Background checks of the ISP's employees

8. Separation of duties is one way to limit fraud and misuse. Of the four separation-of-duties controls, which most closely matches this explanation: "This control allows employees access to cash or valuables"?

   ○ **A.** Authorization

   ○ **B.** Custody

   ○ **C.** Recordkeeping

   ○ **D.** Reconciliation

9. Which of the following job roles can be combined to create the least amount of risk or opportunity for malicious acts?

   ○ **A.** Systems analyst and quality assurance

   ○ **B.** Computer operator and systems programmer

   ○ **C.** Security administrator and application programmer

   ○ **D.** Database administrator and systems analyst

10. You have been asked to perform a new audit assignment. Your first task is to review the organization's strategic plan. Which of the following should be the first item reviewed?

   ○ **A.** Documentation that details the existing infrastructure

   ○ **B.** Previous and planned budgets

   ○ **C.** Organizational charts

   ○ **D.** The business plan

Answers to Exam Questions

1. **B.** This capability maturity model specifies five levels of control for software maturity levels. Answer A is incorrect because ISO 17799 is a comprehensive set of controls designed to gauge best practices in information security. Answer C is incorrect because COSO was designed to help prevent and detect fraud in financial reports. Answer D is incorrect because CobiT was designed to aid in the development of good IT process and policies.

2. **C.** A network administrator should not have programming responsibilities. Answers A, B, and D are all duties that an administrator can hold, but the network administrator might have end-user responsibilities, aid in the system administration, and help in the early phases of design.

3. **C.** Key verification would provide the highest level of confidence. Answer A is incorrect because audit trails would provide details of the entered activities but would not improve accuracy. Answer B is incorrect because separating job roles would be an additional control but would not add any accuracy to the information that was entered incorrectly. Answer D is incorrect because supervisory review is a detective and compensating control, but is not the best answer.

4. **C.** Level 3 of the capability maturity model is considered the defined level. Level 3 is characterized by its capability to use qualitative measurements. Answers A, B, and D are incorrect because the levels do not feature qualitative measurement.

5. **D.** Bottom-up policy development addresses the concerns of operational employees because it starts with their input and concerns, and examines risk. Answers A, B, and C are incorrect because all these items are tied to top-down policy development. A top-down approach aligns with company policy, is a slow process, and might not fully address the concerns of employees.

6. **C.** A balanced score card is used to match the organization's information technology to the strategy of the organization. Answer A is incorrect because it is not used for benchmarking, answer B is incorrect because it is not used to measure effectiveness, and answer D is incorrect because it is not used to evaluate help-desk employees.

7. **A.** Anytime an outsourcing provider will provide a time-sensitive process, such as ISP services, an SLA is one way to obtain a guarantee of the level of service the outsourcing partner is agreeing to provide. The SLA should specify the uptime, response time, and maximum outage time they are agreeing to. Answer B is incorrect because physical security is important, but it is not the *most* important, in this case. Answers C and D are incorrect because neither would serve as an adequate measure for an independent evaluation of the ISP's service capability.

8. **B.** Custody is the access to cash, merchandise, or inventories. Answer A is incorrect because authorization describes verifying cash, approving purchases, and approving changes. Answer C is incorrect because recordkeeping deals with preparing receipts, maintaining records, and posting payments. Answer D is incorrect because reconciliation deals with comparing dollar amounts, counts, reports, and payroll summaries.

9. **D.** Database administrator and systems analyst are two roles that ISACA believes can be combined. Answers A, B, and C are incorrect because none of these positions should be combined. The auditor should understand how the combination of certain roles increases risk. As an example, a systems analyst should be discouraged from performing the duties of someone in a quality assurance role. If these roles are combined, quality-assurance levels could be compromised if strong compensating controls are not being used.

10. **D.** Before auditors can begin any technical duties, they must understand the environment in which they are working. The best way to do that is to review the business plan, which details the goals of the organization. Only after the business plan has been reviewed should the other items listed be reviewed. Therefore, answers A, B, and C are incorrect.

Need to Know More?

- COSO Guidelines: http://www.coso.org/

- CobiT Framework: http://www.isaca.org/cobit/

- IT Governance: http://en.wikipedia.org/wiki/Information_technology_governance

- Compensating Controls: http://www.cu.edu/security/ps/INTERNAL_CONTROLS. HTML

- Outsourcing to India: http://tinyurl.com/32kdu4

- Outsourcing to Follow the Sun: http://www.itbusinessedge.com/item/?ci=15816

- Who Should Pay for IS Services: http://tinyurl.com/3y9ljj

- Auditing Best Practices: http://internalaudit.wayne.edu/Internal/AuditBestPractices. htm

PART II

System and Infrastructure Lifecycle Management

CHAPTER THREE

Lifecycle Management

This chapter helps you prepare for the Certified Information Systems Auditor (CISA) exam by covering the following ISACA objectives, which include understanding the importance of lifecycle management and items such as the system development lifecycle. This chapter pairs with Chapter 4 to cover all of the tasks/knowledge statements and requirements you need to know that are included under the Systems and Infrastructure Lifecycle Management job practice area.

Tasks

Evaluate the business case for the proposed system development/acquisition to ensure that it meets the organization's business goals.

Evaluate the project management framework and project governance practices to ensure that business objectives are achieved in a cost-effective manner while managing risks to the organization.

Perform reviews to ensure that a project is progressing in accordance with project plans, is adequately supported by documentation, and status reporting is accurate.

Evaluate the process by which systems and/or infrastructure are maintained to ensure the continued support of the organization's objectives and are subject to effective internal control.

Evaluate the process by which systems and/or infrastructure are disposed of to ensure that they comply with the organization's policies and procedures.

Evaluate proposed control mechanisms for systems and/or infrastructure during specification, development/acquisition, and testing to ensure that they will provide safeguards and comply with the organization's policies and other requirements.

Evaluate the readiness of the system and/or infrastructure for implementation and migration into production.

Knowledge Statements

Knowledge of quality assurance methods

Knowledge of benefits management practices, (e.g., feasibility studies, business cases)

Knowledge of project governance mechanisms (e.g., steering committee, project oversight board)

Knowledge of project management practices, tools, and control frameworks

Knowledge of project success criteria and risks

Knowledge of configuration, change, and release management in relation to development and maintenance of systems and/or infrastructure

Knowledge of requirements analysis and management practices (e.g., requirements verification, traceability, gap analysis)

Knowledge of acquisition and contract management processes (e.g., evaluation of vendors, preparation of contracts, vendor management, escrow)

Knowledge of system development methodologies and tools, and an understanding of their strengths and weaknesses (e.g., agile development practices, prototyping, rapid application development [RAD], object-oriented design techniques)

Knowledge of the management of testing processes (e.g., test strategies, test plans, test environments, entry and exit criteria)

Knowledge of data conversion tools, techniques, and procedures

Knowledge of system and/or infrastructure disposal procedures

Knowledge of software and hardware certification and accreditation practices

Knowledge of post-implementation review objectives and methods (e.g., project closure, benefits realization, performance measurement)

Knowledge of system migration and infrastructure deployment practices

Outline

Study Strategies

This chapter addresses lifecycle management. Project management, business application development, and infrastructure and acquisition practices are the primary topics. A CISA candidate should review the following primary topics for the exam:

▶ Project-management structure

▶ The formalized steps of the project-management process: initiating, planning, executing, controlling, and closing

▶ Identification and definition of the steps of the system development lifecycle

▶ Alternative approaches to application development, such as prototyping and agile development

▶ Process-improvement practices

▶ Information systems maintenance practices

Introduction

Did you ever stop to think about how much of an auditor's work actually revolves around project management? After all, projects are temporary endeavors that have a defined beginning, middle, and end. Each audit you will be involved with will be unique. Each will have different requirements and specifications. This means that CISAs need to understand project management. This includes initiating, planning, executing, controlling, and closing projects.

Lifecycle management also requires that auditors understand the system development lifecycle (SDLC). Auditors can become deeply involved in the SDLC process. Auditors are responsible for helping to ensure that sufficient controls are designed during SDLC and that these controls work as expected. Controls must be tested and the overall design plan must be reviewed. Not all projects will use the same development method. Today many alternate development methods, such as prototyping, rapid application development, and agile development, are used. The auditor must understand each of these to fulfill his job duties. After the rollout of new applications, the auditor's job is not done. Systems require maintenance, review of changes, and review and redesign of processes. Throughout the lifecycle, auditors play a key role.

Project Management

Knowledge Statements

▶ Knowledge of project governance mechanisms (e.g., steering committee, project oversight board)

▶ Knowledge of project management practices, tools, and control frameworks

To be able to discuss project management, one must first define project management. Projects are temporary endeavors. The purpose of this one-time effort is to meet a defined goal of creating a specific product, service, or result. Projects are unique, in that when all the objectives are met, the project is terminated. Projects can be large or small, and can involve hardware, software, or networks. A project can even be used to create a product or service. Projects have unique attributes:

▶ A unique purpose

▶ A temporary nature

▶ A primary customer and/or sponsor

▶ Uncertainty

Projects are constrained by their scope, time, and cost; therefore, you must consider the following:

▶ **Scope**—How much work is defined? What do the sponsor and the customer expect from this project?

▶ **Time**—How long is this project scheduled to run? Does it have a defined schedule? When does the product need to be launched, or when does the service need to be operational? Answering these questions will help determine how long the project will run.

▶ **Cost**—How much money is this project expected to cost? Has the sponsor approved it?

Many approaches and standards exist to meet this triple constraint. The most well known of these approaches and standards are PMBOK (IEEE Standard 1490) Prince 2 (projects in a controlled environment) and Project Management Institute (PMI). Each of these standards is somewhat different, but they share common attributes. The following section looks at some of the common roles and responsibilities in project-management activities.

Roles, Responsibility, and Structure

The auditor should play an active part in the project-management process and know the various roles and responsibilities. Auditors should understand who is responsible and be able to identify key stakeholders, some of which include the following:

▶ **Senior management**—Provides necessary resources to complete project.

▶ **Stakeholders**—A person, group, or business unit that has a share or an interest in the project activities.

▶ **Project steering committee**—Ultimately responsible. Must ensure that the stakeholders' needs are met and oversee direction and scope of project. The committee acts as project-oversight board.

▶ **Project sponsor**—Works with the project manager to ensure success and is responsible for allocating funding for the project.

▶ **Project manager**—Responsible for day-to-day management of the project team.

▶ **Project team**—Responsible for performing operational tasks within the project.

▶ **Quality assurance**—Responsible for reviewing the activities of the project-management team and ensuring that output meets quality standards. This role/group does not necessarily act as part of the project team as a whole. QA activities can be carried out by external parties to the project team; including auditors.

Projects must take on an organizational form or framework, which can be either loosely structured or very rigid, in that the program manager has complete authority over the group and is assigned to the group for the duration of the project. Table 3.1 shows the primary types of project organizational forms.

TABLE 3.1   Project Organizational Forms

Name	Description
Pure project	Formal authority is held by the project manager.
	The team may also have a dedicated project work area.
Influence	The project manager has no real authority, and the functional manager remains in charge.
Weak matrix	The project manager has little or no authority and is part of the functional organization.
Balanced matrix	The project manager has some functional authority, and management duties are shared with functional managers.
Strong matrix	In this more expensive model, the project has members assigned for dedicated tasks. The advantage is this offers a greater level of authority.

Project Culture and Objectives

Teams take on a unique culture. Project managers can play a part in developing a healthy culture by holding a kick-off meeting that allows team members to get to know each other. The kick-off meeting also gives the project manager a forum in which to discuss the goals of the project and what tasks need to be completed to meet the desired goal. The program manager might also want to use this time to perform some team-building activities, such as having the group develop a team name, establish a mission statement, or even create a project logo.

As the team progresses, it typically goes through four stages:

▶ Forming

▶ Storming

▶ Norming

▶ Performing

Throughout these ups and downs, the team must stay clearly focused on the deliverables. Some deliverables are considered main objectives, and others are considered nonobjectives. The main objectives are directly linked to the success of the project; nonobjectives add value by clarifying and defining the main objectives. The project-management process usually starts with the team working on an *object breakdown structure* (OBS), which defines each component of the project and their relationship to each other. The OBS can help make sure the team doesn't leave anything out and that all requirements are clearly defined. Next, a *work break-down structure* (WBS) can be developed. A WBS is process oriented and shows what activities need to be completed in a hierarchical manner. It allows for easy identification of tasks that need to be completed. One advantage of the WBS is that tasks are defined as achievable work units. Figure 3.1 shows an example of a WBS.

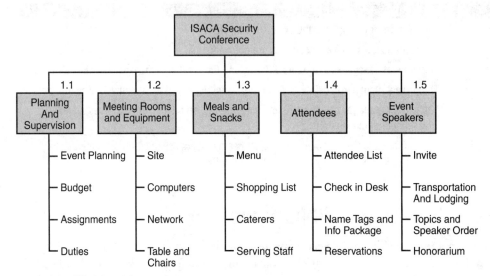

FIGURE 3.1 Work breakdown structure.

NOTE

Work Breakdown Structure Developing the work breakdown structure is an important task at the start of the project-management process because it identifies specific tasks and specifies what resources are needed for completion of the task.

Project-Management Practices

Tasks

▶ Evaluate the project management framework and project governance practices to ensure that business objectives are achieved in a cost-effective manner while managing risks to the organization.

▶ Perform reviews to ensure that a project is progressing in accordance with project plans, is adequately supported by documentation, and status reporting is accurate.

Knowledge Statement

▶ Knowledge of project success criteria and risks

Project-management practices are designed to increase the likelihood of overall success. Good project-management practices can help ensure that the goals of the project are met. The three constraints of project management include the following:

- ▶ **Scope**—The scope of the project can be better defined by understanding areas/activities/personnel needed to complete the project. For example, software projects must define how big the applications will be. Will the project involve a few thousand lines of code or millions of lines of code?

- ▶ **Time**—Time can be better established by building a project timeline that lists each task and specifies a timeframe for each.

- ▶ **Cost**—Cost can be determined by examining the lines of code, the number of people in the project team, and the time needed for each phase of the project.

The following sections discuss each of these constraints in more detail.

Project Initiation

Project initiation is the first stage. Sometimes attention and effort are focused on the endpoint and final deliverable. Projects must be managed carefully during the initiation stage. At this point, a project sponsor seeks to obtain funding and approval for a project through a project initiation document (PID). The PID is used to obtain authorization for the project to begin. It justifies the project to management, clearly defines the scope of the project, documents all roles and responsibilities, and sets up and runs a project office environment.

Project Planning

Project planning is the part of project management that relates to schedules and estimation. The project manager must develop a realistic estimate of how much time the project will take and determine what tasks must be accomplished. A big part of project planning involves not just time, but also the identification and quantification of all required resources. Task management is not just about handing out tasks to each member of the team; it is about determining who is most capable of accomplishing each task. Program Evaluation and Review Technique (PERT) charts and Gantt charts are two tools to help; each is discussed later in the chapter. Project planning requires that the sequence of tasks be determined. Some tasks can be performed in any order, whereas others must flow in a specific order. As an example, building a house requires the foundation to be laid before the walls can be built. Each of these tasks must have a time estimate performed; the project manager must determine how long each task will take. Needed resources will vary depending on the task. As in our previous example, a foundation requires concrete and rebar, while walls require wood and nails. The following sections look at some of the pieces of project planning. The first is estimating software cost and size.

Software Cost Estimation

Most of us put a lot of effort into cost estimation in our personal lives. When considering a new job offer, most of us look closely at the cost of living in a different area; likewise, when shopping for a new car, most people check with several dealerships to find the best deal. The business world is constrained by the same budget factors. These components drive up the cost of software:

▶ **The chosen source code language**—Using an obscure or unpopular language will most likely drive up costs.

▶ **The size of the application**—The size or complexity of the application has a bearing on cost. As an example, the *level of security needed* is something that will affect the complexity of a given application. This also has a direct correlation to the *scope* of the project.

▶ **The project time constraints**—If a project is projected to be completed in one month versus three months, this might mean that more overtime needs to be paid, along with fees for rushed services.

▶ **Computer and resource accessibility**—If resources are available only during certain times, the output of the project team will most likely be reduced.

▶ **Project team experience**—Every individual has a learning curve that adds cost to inexperienced team members.

▶ **The level of security needed**—A project that needs very high levels of security controls will take additional time and effort to develop.

One early cost model, developed by Barry Boehm, is known as the Constructive Cost Model (COCOMO). It was designed as a simple cost model for estimating the number of person-months required to develop software. It is now considered obsolete, replaced by COCOMO II in 1995. This model considers "what if" calculations to determine how changes to personnel, resources, or staffing affect project cost. Figure 3.2 shows what the COCOMO II model looks like. It can be run online at http://sunset.usc.edu/research/COCOMOII/index.html. COCOMO II can also be used with standard spreadsheet applications such as Microsoft Excel.

Model: Post-architecture
Calibration: COCOMOII.2000
Current rule base implementation

Size

	SLOC	% Design Modified	% Code Modified	% Integration Required	Assessment and Assimilation (0% - 8%)	Software Understanding (0% - 50%)	Unfamiliarity (0-1)
New							
Reused		0	0				
Modified							

Rate each cost driver below from Very Low (VL) to Extra High (EH). For **HELP** on each cost driver, select its name.

	Very Low (VL)	Low (L)	Nominal (N)	High (H)	Very High (VH)	Extra High (EH)

Scale Drivers

	VL	L	N	H	VH	XH
Precedentedness	○ VL	○ L	● N	○ H	○ VH	○ XH
Development Flexibility	○ VL	○ L	● N	○ H	○ VH	○ XH
Architecture/Risk Resolution	○ VL	○ L	● N	○ H	○ VH	○ XH
Team Cohesion	○ VL	○ L	● N	○ H	○ VH	○ XH
Process Maturity	○ VL	○ L	● N	○ H	○ VH	○ XH

FIGURE 3.2 COCOMO software estimation.

Now that you have a reasonable idea of the software cost estimates, the next step is to examine methods to determine software size, in terms of lines of code.

> **NOTE**
>
> **The Constructive Cost Model** COCOMO was developed in 1981 and has been replaced with COCOMO II.

Software Size Estimates

Traditional software sizing has been done by counting *source lines of code* (SLOC). This method of software sizing was developed because early programs were written in FORTRAN or other line-oriented languages. To give some idea of how big programs can be, Linux 2.6 had about 5.7 million lines of code. With programs of such size, counts are usually done in *kilo lines of code* (KLOC). This method does not work as well in modern development programs because additional factors affect the overall cost, such as the complexity of the application/ program being written. This method determines cost solely on one factor—length of code. Considering that development packages can generate hundreds of line of code from only a few mouse clicks demonstrates that this model is not as useful as in years past. One solution to this is *function point analysis* (FPA).

FPA is a method that the ISO has approved as a standard to estimate the complexity of software. FPA can be used to budget application-development costs, estimate productivity after project completion, and determine annual maintenance costs. FPA is based on the number of inputs, outputs, interfaces, files, and queries. Figure 3.3 shows an overview of function point analysis.

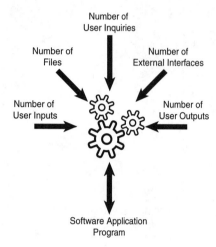

FIGURE 3.3 Function point analysis.

Per ISACA, function points are first computed by completing a table, as demonstrated in Table 3.2. The purpose of the table is to determine whether the task is simple, average, or very complex. One way to determine this subjective weighting factor is to apply the Halstead Complexity Measures (http://www.sei.cmu.edu/str/descriptions/halstead.html). The five functional point values are the number of user inputs, number of user outputs, number of user inquiries, number of files, and number of external interfaces. Take a moment to review Table 3.2.

TABLE 3.2 Computing Metrics of Function Point Analysis

Measurement Parameter	Count	Simple	Weighing Factor Average	Complex	Results
Number of user inputs		X3	4	6	=____
Number of user outputs		X4	5	7	=____
Number of user inquiries		X3	4	6	=____
Number of files		X7	10	15	=____
Number of external interfaces		X5	7	10	=____
Total count:					

> **CAUTION**
>
> **Function Point Metrics**   If an organization decides to use function point metrics, it must develop criteria for determining whether an entry is simple, average, or complex.

When the table is completed, the organization can use the computed totals to run through an algorithm that determines factors such as reliability, cost, and quality, such that:

- Productivity = FP/person-month

- Quality = defects/FP

- Cost= $/FP

With these calculations completed, the project team can identify resources needed for each specific task.

> **EXAM ALERT**
>
> **Function Point Analysis**   Exam candidates should know that when assessing the scope of an application-development project, function point analysis is one of the best techniques for estimating the scope and cost of the project.

Scheduling

With software size and cost determined, the project team can turn its attention to scheduling. Scheduling involves linking individual tasks. The relationship between these tasks is linked either by earliest start date or by latest expected finish date. The Gantt chart is one way to display these relationships.

The Gantt chart was developed in the early 1900s as a tool to schedule activities and monitor progress. Gantt charts show the start and finish dates of each element of a project, and also show the relationship between each activity in a calendar-like format. They are one of the primary tools used to communicate project schedule information. Gantt charts use a baseline to illustrate what will happen if a task is finished early or late.

Program Evaluation and Review Technique (PERT) is the preferred tool for estimating time when a degree of uncertainty exists. PERT uses a critical-path method that applies a weighed average duration estimate.

PERT uses probabilistic time estimates to estimate the best and worst time estimates. Basically, PERT uses a three-point time estimate to develop best, worst, and most likely time estimates. The PERT weighted average is calculated as follows:

PERT Weighted Average = Optimistic Time + 4 × Most Likely Time + Pessimistic Time ÷ 6

A PERT chart is used to depict this information. Each chart begins with the first task that branches out to a connecting line that contains three estimates:

▶ The most optimistic time in which the task will be completed

▶ The most likely time in which the task will be completed

▶ The worst-case scenario or longest the task will take

This line is then terminated by another node, which signifies the start of another task. Figure 3.4 shows an example of a PERT chart.

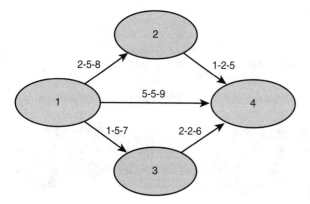

FIGURE 3.4 PERT chart.

As an example, suppose that the project team has been assigned to design an online user-registration system for the organization and that one task is to develop the Java input screen the user will use to enter personal data. It might be reasonable to estimate that this task will take five work days to complete. With PERT, the best and worst completion time would also be factored in. To get a better example of how an estimate would be performed with PERT, consider the following step-by-step example.

STEP BY STEP

3.1 Calculating Time Estimates with PERT

1. Determine the average amount of time to complete the task. In the previous example, this was estimated to be five work days.

2. Estimate the best possible completion time for the task. For this step by step, assume that it is three work days.

3. Estimate the worst possible completing time. For this step, assume 10 work days.

4. Plug these values into the PERT weighted average formula:

   $(3 + 10 +(4 \times 5) \div 6)= 5.5$ days

5. The value of 5.5 days would be recorded as the critical path time.

Critical Paths

Project management mirrors life, in that anything can go wrong. Things can happen to affect the time, cost, or success of a project. That is why all project-management techniques compute the critical path, or the sequence of tasks that must be completed on schedule for the project to be finished on time. We can expand on the house-building project we used in an earlier example. Having a foundation is a task on the critical path; it must be completed before the walls and roof can be built. Exterior painting is not on the critical path and can be done at any time once the foundation, walls, and roof are completed.

Critical path methodology (CPM) determines what activities are critical and what the dependencies are between the various tasks. CPM is accomplished by the following:

▶ Compiling a list of each task required to complete the project

▶ Determining the time that each task will take, from start to finish

▶ Examining the dependencies between each task

Critical tasks have little flexibility in completion time. The critical path can be determined by examining all possible tasks and identifying the longest path. Even if completed on time, this path indicates the shortest amount of time in which the project can be completed. CPM offers real advantages over Gantt, in that it identifies this minimum time. If the total project time needs to be reduced, one of the tasks on the CPM path must be finished earlier. This is called *crashing*, in that the project sponsor must be prepared to pay a premium for early completion as a bonus or in overtime charges. The disadvantage to CPM is that the relation of tasks is not as easily seen as it is with Gantt charts.

EXAM ALERT

Critical Path Methodology Exam candidates should understand that CPM is considered a project-management planning and control technique.

Timebox Management

Timebox management is used in projects when time is the most critical aspect and software projects need to be delivered quickly. It is used to lock in specifications and prevent creep. As an example, if given time, engineers might overengineer a system or decide to add more functionality or options. Although users might appreciate the added functionality, these items add time to the build phase and slow progress. Timeboxing counteracts this tendency by placing a very rigid time limit on the build of the system. When using timeboxing, the project time must never slip or be extended. If the project manager foresees time problems, he should consider corrective action, such as reducing the scope of the project or adding manpower or resources.

Project Control and Execution

Project control requires the collection, measurement, and dissemination of information and project performance. The bulk of the budget will be spent during the execution of the project. It is entirely possible that project changes might be needed. If so, the changes to the project must be recorded. Changes typically result in additional funds, manpower, or time. Auditors must be aware of any changes and must examine how this could affect any existing controls and the overall project. The auditor must also be concerned with end-user training. When new software products are released to users, the users must be trained on how the application works, what type of authentication is required, and how overrides or dual controls work.

Closing a Project

The last step in the project-management process is to close the project. Projects are, after all, temporary endeavors. At the conclusion of the project, the project manager must transfer control to the appropriate individuals. The project closing includes the following tasks:

▶ Administrative closure

▶ Release of final product or service

▶ Update of organizational assets

At the close of the project, surveys or post-project reviews might be performed. This is a chance to survey the project team and end users to gauge their satisfaction with the project and examine how things could have been done differently or what changes should be implemented next time. A postmortem review is similar but is usually held after the project has been in use for some time.

Challenge

As you must realize by this point in the chapter, understanding the project-management process is important. This challenge exercise has you complete the PERT calculations in Table 3.3. A new software update project has three items that have been determined to be in the critical path. You have been asked to compute critical path times.

▶ The build process has a minimum of 30 days, a maximum of 70 days, and an average of 45 days.

▶ The testing process has a minimum of 12 days, a maximum of 20 days, and an average of 14 days.

▶ The deployment process has a minimum of 5 days, a maximum of 15 days, and an average of 7 days.

TABLE 3.3 Challenge Question

Item	Description	Critical Path Time
1	Build	
2	Test	
3	Deploy	
Total time		

Verify your answers by using Table 3.4.

TABLE 3.4 Challenge Answer

Item	Description	Critical Path Time
1	Build	46 Days
2	Test	18 Days
3	Deploy	8 Days
Total time		72 Days

If you had difficulty completing this challenge, review the section titled "Project Planning." The text and examples should help you relearn this material and understand what just happened in this challenge exercise. After review, try this challenge again.

Business Application Development

Tasks

▶ Evaluate the business case for the proposed system development/acquisition to ensure that it meets the organization's business goals.

▶ Evaluate proposed control mechanisms for systems and/or infrastructure during specification, development/acquisition, and testing to ensure that they will provide safeguards and comply with the organization's policies and other requirements.

▶ Evaluate the readiness of the system and/or infrastructure for implementation and migration into production.

▶ Evaluate the process by which systems and/or infrastructure are disposed of to ensure that they comply with the organization's policies and procedures.

Knowledge Statements

▶ Knowledge of benefits management practices, (e.g., feasibility studies, business cases)

▶ Knowledge of quality assurance methods

▶ Knowledge of the management of testing processes (e.g., test strategies, test plans, test environments, entry and exit criteria)

▶ Knowledge of data conversion tools, techniques, and procedures

▶ Knowledge of system and/or infrastructure disposal procedures

▶ Knowledge of software and hardware certification and accreditation practices

▶ Knowledge of post-implementation review objectives and methods (e.g., project closure, benefits realization, performance measurement).

▶ Knowledge of system migration and infrastructure deployment practices

▶ Knowledge of requirements analysis and management practices (e.g., requirements verification, traceability, gap analysis)

▶ Knowledge of acquisition and contract management processes (e.g., evaluation of vendors, preparation of contracts, vendor management, escrow)

Business application development is largely a product of the systems development lifecycle (SDLC). New applications are typically created when new opportunities are discovered, when companies want to take advantage of new technology or use technology to solve an existing problem. Organizations use a structure approach for these reasons:

- ▶ To minimize risk

- ▶ To maximize return

- ▶ To establish controls so that the likelihood that the software meets user needs is high

As an auditor, you are not expected to be an expert programmer or understand the inner workings of a Java program. Instead, the auditor must know how to manage the development process so that adequate controls are developed and implemented. The auditor must be able to review information at each step of the process and provide input on the adequacy of controls being designed. Auditors are also responsible for reporting independently to management on the status of the project and the implementation of controls. Auditors might also become more deeply involved in the process, based on their individual skills and abilities. Now let's look more closely at how the SDLC process works.

Systems-Development Methodology

The SDLC is designed to produce high-quality software in a structured way that minimizes risk. The traditional approach to SDLC is the waterfall model, illustrated in Figure 3.5. The name of the waterfall model comes from the fact that progress flows from the top to the bottom progressing through each phase. W.W. Royce originally described the model as having seven phases. Some variations show it as having five or six phases. ISACA uses a modified model that has five primary phases and the post implementation phase.

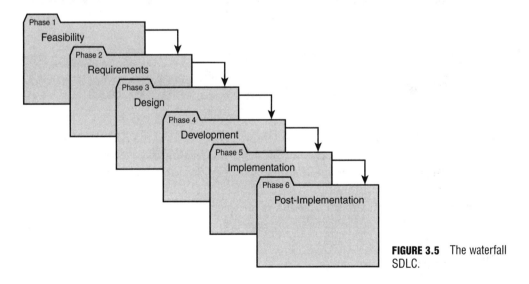

FIGURE 3.5 The waterfall SDLC.

As Figure 3.5 illustrates, the waterfall model starts with a feasibility study and progresses through implementation. The advantage of this model is that it is well known and extremely stable when requirements are not expected to change and the architecture is well known. Table 3.5 describes each phase of the SDLC.

TABLE 3.5 SDLC Overview

SDLC Phase	Description
Feasibility	Benefits are determined at this phase of the SDLC.
Requirements	At this phase, the purpose of the project must be defined. What needs of the user will this project meet?
Design	Based on the requirements and user input, a specification should be developed. At this point, the auditor must verify all required controls are in the design.
Development	At this phase, developers begin to write code, and verification and testing occur.
Implementation	At this phase, final user testing occurs and the application is placed into operation.
Post-Implementation	At the conclusion of the preceding five steps, a formal review should occur to evaluate the adequacy of the system. A cost-benefit analysis and review can be performed to determine the value of the project and to improve future projects.

EXAM ALERT

Design Phase   Exam candidates should understand that auditors must verify controls during the design phase of the SDLC.

EXAM ALERT

Waterfall Model   A primary characteristic of the classic waterfall model is that when each step ends, there is no turning back.

The National Institute of Standards and Technology (NIST) defines the SDLC in NIST SP 800-34 as "the scope of activities associated with a system, encompassing the system's initiation, development and acquisition, implementation, operation and maintenance, and ultimately its disposal that instigates another system initiation." Therefore, the goal of the SDLC is to control the development process and add security checks at each phase. The failure to adopt a structured development model will increase risk and the likelihood that the final product may not meet the customer's needs. The following sections describe each phase of the SDLC in more detail.

Phase 1: Feasibility

In this step, the feasibility of the project is considered. The cost of the project must be discussed, as well as the potential benefits that it will bring to the system's users. A payback analysis must be performed to determine how long the project will take to pay for itself. In other words, the payback analysis determines how much time will lapse before accrued benefits will overtake accrued and continuing costs. Figure 3.6 illustrates an example of this. If it is determined that the project will move forward, the team will want to develop a preliminary timeline. During the feasibility phase, everyone gets a chance to meet and understand the goals of the project.

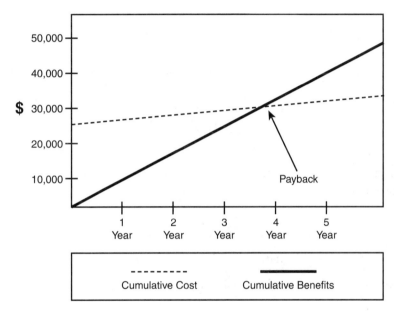

FIGURE 3.6 Charting the payback period.

Phase 2: Requirements Definition

This phase entails fully defining the need and then mapping how the proposed solution meets the need. This requires the participation of management as well as users. Users should also be involved because they should have input on how the applications are designed.

At this phase, an *entity relationship diagram* (ERD) is often used. An ERD helps map the requirements and define the relationship between elements. The basic components of an ERD are an entity and a relationship. An entity is very much like a database, in that it is a grouping of like data elements. An entity has specific attributes, which are called the entity's primary key. Entities are drawn as a rectangular box with an identifying name. Relationships describe how entities are related to each other and are defined as a diamond. ERDs can be used to help define a data dictionary. When a data dictionary is designed, the database schema can be developed. The database schema defines the database tables and fields, and the relationship between them. Figure 3.7 shows the basic design of an ERD. The completed ERD will be used in the design phase as the blueprint for the design.

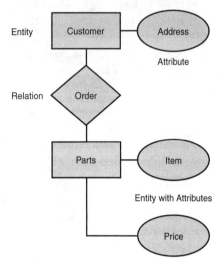

FIGURE 3.7 Entity relationships diagram.

During the requirements phase, auditors must verify the requirements and determine whether adequate security controls are being defined. These controls should include the following mechanisms:

- ▸ **Preventive**—Preventive controls can include user authentication and data encryption.

- ▸ **Detective**—Detective controls can include embedded audit modules and audit trails.

- ▸ **Corrective**—Corrective controls can include fault tolerance controls and data integrity mechanisms.

EXAM ALERT

SDLC Requirements Phase   You might be tested on the fact that user acceptance plans are usually developed during the requirements phase.

Build Versus Buy

Although this is not a step in the SDLC, an organization might decide to buy a product instead of building it. The decision typically comes down to time, cost, and availability of a pre-designed substitute. Figure 3.8 shows how this affects the SDLC process.

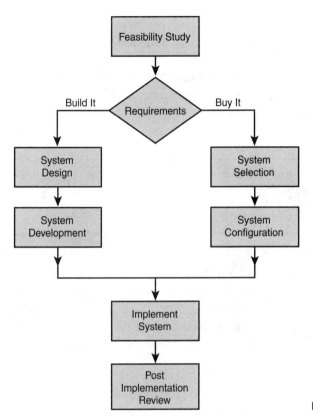

FIGURE 3.8 Build versus buy.

Before moving forward with the option to buy, the project team should develop a request for proposal (RFP) to solicit bids from vendors. Vendor responses should be closely examined to find the vendor that best meets the project team's requirements. Some of the questions that should be asked include these:

▶ Does the vendor have a software product that will work as is?

▶ Will the vendor have to modify the software product to meet our needs?

▶ Will the vendor have to create a new, nonexistent software product for us?

The reputation of the vendor is also important. Is the vendor reliable, and do references demonstrate past commitment to service? When a vendor is chosen, the last step is to negotiate and sign a contract. Auditors will want to make sure that a sufficient level of security will be designed into the product and that risks are minimized.

Phase 3: Design

During the design phase, users might not be involved, but the auditor will still be working in an advisory role. The auditor must again check that security controls are still in the design and test documents. Test plans should detail how security controls will be tested. Tests should be performed to validate specific program units, subsystems, interfaces, and backup/recovery. Change-control procedures should be developed to prevent uncontrolled changes.

> **CAUTION**
>
> **Scope Creep**   *Scope creep* is the addition of products, features, or items to the original design so that more and more items are added on. This is sometimes refered to as the "kitchen sink syndrome." Scope creep is most likely to occur in the design phase. Little changes might not appear to have a big cost impact on a project, but they will have a cumulative effect and increase the length and cost of the project.

There are ways to decrease design and development time. *Reverse engineering* is one such technique. Reverse engineering converts executable code into human-readable format and can be performed with tools such as IDA Pro. This is a somewhat controversial subject because, although reverse engineering has legitimate uses, a company could use it to disassemble another company's program. Most software licenses make this illegal. Reverse engineering is also sometimes used to bypass access-restriction mechanisms.

Phase 4: Development

During the development phase, programmers work to develop the application code. Programmers might use online programming facilities so that many programmers can access the code directly from their workstation. Although this typically increases productivity, it also increases risk because someone might gain unauthorized access to the program library. Programmers should strive to develop modules that have high cohesion and low coupling. Cohesion addresses the fact that a module is focused on a single task. Coupling is the measurement of the interconnection between modules. Low coupling means that a change to one module should not affect another. Figure 3.9 demonstrates this concept.

> **NOTE**
>
> **Cohesion and Coupling**   Programmers should strive to develop modules that have high cohesion and low coupling.

During development, auditors must verify that input and output controls, audit mechanisms, and file-protection schemes are used. Examples of input controls include dollar counts, transaction counts, error detection, and correction. Examples of output controls include validity checking and authorizing controls. Testing these controls and the functionality of the program is an important part of this phase. Testing can be done by using one of the following testing methods:

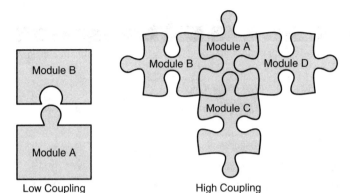

Low Coupling

High Coupling

FIGURE 3.9 High and low coupling.

▶ **Top down**—Top-down testing starts with a depth or breadth approach. Its advantage is that it gets programmers working with the program so that interface problems can be found sooner. It also allows for early testing of major functions.

▶ **Bottom up**—Bottom-up testing works up from the code to modules, programs, and all the way to systems. The advantage of bottom-up testing is that it can be started as soon as modules are complete; work does not have to wait until the entire system is finished. This approach also allows errors in modules to be discovered early. Most application testing follows the bottom-up approach.

Regardless of the chosen approach, test classifications are divided into the following categories:

▶ **Unit testing**—Examines an individual program or module

▶ **Interface testing**—Examines hardware or software to evaluate how well data can be passed from one entity to another

▶ **System testing**—A series of tests that can include recovery testing, security testing, stress testing, volume testing, and performance testing. Although unit and interface testing focus on individual objects, the objective of system testing is to assess how well the system functions as a whole.

▶ **Final acceptance testing**—When the project staff is satisfied with all other tests, *final acceptance testing*, or user acceptance testing, must be performed. This occurs before the application is implemented into a production environment.

Table 3.6 lists some other types of tests that are used for requirement verification.

TABLE 3.6 Testing Types

Test Type	Description
Alpha test	The first and earliest version of an application, followed by a beta version. Both are considered prereleases.
Pilot test	Used as an evaluation to verify functionality of the application.
White-box test	Verifies inner program logic. This is typically cost-prohibitive on a large application or system.
Black-box test	Integrity-based testing that looks at inputs and outputs.
Function test	Validates the program against a checklist of requirements.
Regression test	Verifies that changes in one part of the application did not affect any other parts in the same application or interfaces.
Parallel test	Parallel tests involve the use of two systems or applications at the same time. The purpose of this test is to verify a new or changed system or application by feeding data into both and comparing the results.
Sociability test	Verifies that the system can operate in its targeted environment.

Before coding can begin, programmers must decide what programming language they will use. To some measure, the organization will decide this. For example, if the company has used FORTRAN for engineering projects for the last 25 years, it might make sense to do so for the current project. Programming has evolved, and there are five generations of programming languages:

- ▶ **Generation Five (5GL)**—Natural language

- ▶ **Generation Four (4GL)**—Very high-level language

- ▶ **Generation Three (3GL)**—High-level language

- ▶ **Generation Two (2GL)**—Assembly language

- ▶ **Generation One (1GL)**—Machine language

Figure 3.10 shows the five generations of languages and an example of each with their syntax.

> **CAUTION**
>
> **Citizen Programmers** Organizations might have many individuals who have the ability to write code, but this does not mean they are *authorized* to write code. These citizen programmers can have a detrimental effect on security. No single user should ever have complete control over the development of an application program.

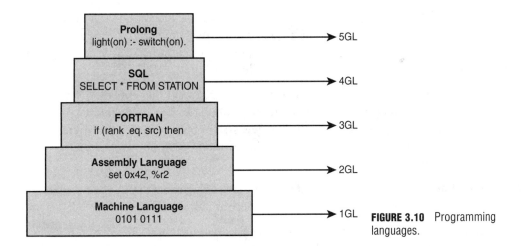

FIGURE 3.10 Programming languages.

Phase 5: Implementation

In the implementation phase, the application is prepared for release into its intended environment. Final user acceptance is performed, as are certification and accreditation. This is typically the final step in accepting the application and agreeing that it is ready for use. *Certification* is the technical review of the system or application. Certification testing might include an audit of security controls, a risk assessment, or a security evaluation. *Accreditation* is management's formal acceptance of a system or application. Typically, the results of the certification testing are compiled into a report, and management's acceptance of the report is used for accreditation. Management might request additional testing, ask questions about the certification report, or accept the results as is. Once accepted, a formal acceptance statement is usually issued.

EXAM ALERT

SDLC Implementation Phase   You might be tested on the fact that final user acceptance testing is performed during the implementation phase.

Now it is time to roll out the application to the users. Some support functions will need to be established. Items such as maintenance, support, and technical response must be addressed. Data conversion might also need to be considered. If an existing system is being replaced, data from the system might need to be migrated to the new one. Computer-aided software engineering (CASE) is used for program and data conversions.

Hopefully, some of the users have been involved throughout the process and can help in the training process. The training strategy can include classroom training, online training, practice sessions, and user manuals. The rollout of the application might be all at once or phased in over time. Changeover techniques include the following:

▶ **Parallel operation**—Both the old and new systems are run at the same time. Results between the two systems can be compared. Fine-tuning can also be performed on the new system as needed. As confidence in the new system improves, the old system can be shut down. The primary disadvantage of this method is that both systems must be maintained for a period of time.

▶ **Phased changeover**—If the system is large, a phased changeover might be possible. With this method, systems are upgraded one piece at a time.

▶ **Hard changeover**—This method establishes a date at which users are forced to change over. The advantage of the hard changeover is that it forces all users to change at once. However, this introduces a level of risk into the environment because things can go wrong.

Phase 6: Post-Implementation

In the post-implementation phase, some might be ready to schedule a party and declare success. What really needs to be done is to assess the overall success of the project. Actual costs versus projected costs should be reviewed to see how well cost-estimating was done at the feasibility phase. Return on investment (ROI) and payback analysis should be reviewed. A gap analysis can determine whether there is a gap between requirements that were or were not met. An independent group might conduct performance measurement, such as an audit. If this is the case, it should not be done by auditors who were involved in the SDLC process. Overall, post-implementation should answer the following questions:

▶ Is the system adequate?

▶ What is the true ROI?

▶ Were the chosen standards followed?

▶ Were good project-management techniques used?

Disposal

Applications and systems don't last forever. This means that, at some point, these systems must be decommissioned and disposed of. This step of the process is reached when the application or system is no longer needed. Those involved in the disposal process must consider the disposition of the application. Should it be destroyed or archived, or does the information need to be migrated into a new system? Disk sanitization and destruction are also important, to ensure confidentiality. This is an important step that is sometimes overlooked. Table 3.7 outlines a sample policy for data disposal.

> **NOTE**
>
> **Disposal**   Typically, disposal of an existing application might be required when the maintenance cost surpasses the benefits/returns from the application.

TABLE 3.7   Sample Media Destruction Policy

Media	Wipe Standard	Description
Rewriteable magnetic media (floppies, tape, hard drive, flash drives, and so on.)	Three-pass wiping or degaussing	DOD 5220.22-M 3 pass drive wipe or the use of electric degaussing
Optical media (CD-RW, DVD-RW, DVD+RW, CD-R, DVD-R, etc.)	Physical destruction	Physical destruction of the media by shredding or breaking

Data Disposal Is a Big Problem

Whereas hard-drive size and performance has continued to grow at a rapid pace, hard-drive standards have remained relatively unchanged. Without getting too deep into technical standards, this means that you can plug a 10-year-old hard drive into a modern computer, and it will probably work. Most of us use a shredder on a daily basis, but few have probably ever sanitized a hard drive. Whether your company is planning to sell old hard drives, give them to charity, or just throw them away, you need to make sure the data on the drives is impossible to recover.

If you are thinking that most companies already do this, consider the following: Two researchers from MIT bought 158 used hard drives from eBay. Out of the 158 hard drives, 129 had data that the researchers were able to copy. Some of the data on these drives included personal information, company HR records, medical information, a pharmacy's database, and another database with 3,700 credit card numbers. You can read more about their findings at http://tinyurl.com/2y8gcy

These statistics clearly indicate that most companies don't have a data-destruction policy, or the policy is flawed. If the company doesn't have a data-destruction policy, the first step is to develop one. You might want to consider physically destroying drives if they contain highly sensitive information. If a policy already exists, it should be reviewed. Activities such as formatting actually do not erase a drive. Drive wiping, which writes the drive with alternating patterns of ones and zeros, must be used to completely remove the contents of the drive. The higher the number of passes, the lower the probability that even the finest magnetic tracks can be detected. The Department of Defense (DOD 5220.22-M) recommends seven passes, for top security.

REVIEW BREAK

The CISA needs to understand business application development. Table 3.8 outlines each step in the SDLC and its defining attributes.

TABLE 3.8   SDLC Implementation Phases

Phase	Title	Attributes
Phase 1	Feasibility	A business case is required for justification.
Phase 2	Requirements	The problem definition requires user input.
Phase 3	Design	This covers the design of the program security controls and change management.
Phase 4	Development	Programmers become deeply involved in their work at this phase. Testing begins here.
Phase 5	Implementation	The system is deployed and new users are trained. Certification and accreditation are performed.
Phase 6	Post-Implementation	Project review is performed, along with ROI calculations to determine the cost-effectiveness of the project.
Disposal	Retirement	Systems must eventually be retired; at such time, data must be migrated, archived, or destroyed.

Alternative Application-Development Techniques

Knowledge Statement

▶ Knowledge of system development methodologies and tools and an understanding of their strengths and weaknesses (e.g., agile development practices, prototyping, rapid application development [RAD], object-oriented design techniques)

Globalization has increased the pace of change and reduced the amount of time that organizations have to respond to changes. The new system must be brought online quickly. The SDLC is not the only development methodology used today. As an auditor, you must be knowledgeable of other development methods and have a basic understanding of their operations. Some popular models include the following:

▶ **Incremental development**—Defines an approach that develops systems in stages so that development is performed one step at a time. A minimal working system might be deployed while subsequent releases build on functionality or scope.

▶ **Spiral development**—The spiral model was developed based on the experience of the waterfall model. The spiral model is based on the concept that software development is evolutionary. The spiral model begins by creating a series of prototypes to develop a solution. As the project continues, it spirals out, becoming more detailed. Each step passes through planning, requirements, risks, and development phases.

▶ **Prototyping**—The prototyping model reduces the time required to deploy applications. Prototyping uses high-level code to quickly turn design requirements into application screens and reports that the users can review. User feedback can fine-tune the application and improve it. Top-down testing works well with prototyping. Although prototyping clarifies user requirements, it can result in overly optimistic project timelines. Also, when change happens quickly, it might not be properly documented, which is a real concern for the auditor.

NOTE

Prototyping   The advantage of prototyping is that it can provide real savings in development time and costs.

▶ **Rapid application development (RAD)**—RAD uses an evolving prototype and requires heavy user involvement. Per ISACA, RAD requires well-trained development teams that use integrated power tools for modeling and prototyping. With the RAD model, strict limits are placed on development time. RAD has four unique stages, which include concept, functional design, development, and deployment.

EXAM ALERT

Rapid Application Development   The CISA exam might question you on the fact that RAD uses prototyping as its core development tool.

These models share a common element, in that they all have a predictive lifecycle. This means that when the project is laid out, costs are calculated and a schedule is defined.

A second category of application development can be defined as *agile software development*. With this development model, teams of programmers and business experts work closely together. Project requirements are developed using an *iterative* approach because the project is both mission driven and component based. The project manager becomes much more of a facilitator in these situations. Popular agile development models include the following:

▶ **Extreme programming (XP)**—The XP development model requires that teams include business managers, programmers, and end users. These teams are responsible for developing useable applications in short periods of time. Issues with XP are that teams are responsible not only for coding, but also for writing the tests used to verify the code. Lack of documentation is also a concern. XP does not scale well for large projects.

▶ **Scrum**—Scrum is an iterative development method in which repetitions are referred to as *sprints* and typically last 30 days. Scrum is typically used with object-oriented technology and requires strong leadership and a team meeting each day for a short time. The idea here is for more planning and directing tasks from the project manager to the team. The project manager's main task is to work on removing any obstacles from the team's path.

> **NOTE**
>
> **Reengineering** Reengineering converts an existing business process. Reengineering attempts to update software by reusing as many of the components as possible instead of designing an entirely new system.

Challenge

A variety of alternate application-development techniques exist. This challenge has you complete Table 3.9 and describe each one of these techniques.

TABLE 3.9 Application-Development Methods

Application Method	Description of Method
Incremental	
Waterfall	
Spiral	
Prototyping	
Rapid application development	
Extreme programming	
Scrum	

Use the preceding section on alternate application-development techniques if you need help filling out this table.

Application-Development Approaches

Applications are written in a programming language. Programming languages can be low level so that the system easily understands the language; they also can be high level, enabling humans to easily understand them but requiring translation for the system. The programs used to turn high-level programs into object- or machine-readable code are known as interpreters, compilers, or assemblers. Most applications are compiled. The information also can be grouped for the development process in various ways, including data-oriented system development, object-oriented systems development, component-based development, and web-based application development. Table 3.10 describes these methods in more detail.

TABLE 3.10   Application-Development Approaches

Name	Attribute	Description
Data-oriented system development (DOSD)	Uses a process of focusing on software requirements by focusing on data and its structure	DOSD eliminates problems with porting and conversion because the client uses the data in its predescribed format. Stock exchanges, airlines, and bus and transit companies use DOSD.
Object-oriented systems development (OOSD)	Uses a process of solution specifications and models, with items grouped as objects	OOSD works with classes and objects, and is used in computer-aided manufacturing and computer-aided software engineering. OOSD is valued because it can model complex relationships, work with many data types, and meet the demands of a changing environment.
Component-based development (CBD)	Uses a process of enabling objects to communicate with each other	The benefit of CBD is that it enables developers to buy predeveloped tested software from vendors that are ready to be used or integrated into an application. Microsoft's Component Object Model (COM), Common Object Request Broker Architecture (CORBA), and Enterprise JavaBeans (EJB) are examples of component models.
Web-based application development (WBAD)	Uses a process to standardize code modules to allow for cross-platform operation and program integration	WBAD offers standardized integration through the uses of application-development technologies such as Extensible Markup Language (XLM). Its components include Simple Object Access Protocol (SOAP), Web Services Description Language (WSDL), and Universal Description, Discovery, and Integration (UDDI). Buffer overflows are of particular concern to WBAD.

Information Systems Maintenance Practices

Task

▶ Evaluate the process by which systems and/or infrastructure are maintained to ensure the continued support of the organization's objectives and are subject to effective internal control.

Knowledge Statement

▶ Knowledge of configuration, change, and release management in relation to development and maintenance of systems and/or infrastructure

When a system moves into production, the thought might be that the work is done. This is not the case. Changes need to be made and must be done in a controlled manner. The integrity of the application and source code must be ensured. Most organizations use a change-control board that includes a senior manager as the chairperson and individuals from various organizational groups. The change-control board is responsible for developing a change-control process and also for approving changes.

Although the types of changes vary, change control follows a predictable process:

1. Request the change.

2. Approve the change request.

3. Document the change request.

4. Test the proposed change.

5. Present the results to the change-control board.

6. Implement the change, if approved.

7. Document the new configuration.

Documentation is the key to a good change-control process. All system documents should be updated to indicate any changes that have been made to the system or environment. The system maintenance staff or department responsible for requesting the change should keep a copy of the change approval.

The auditor should ensure that backup copies of critical documents are created. These documents should be kept off-site in case of a disaster or other situation. The auditor should also watch for the possibility of unauthorized changes because of poor oversight or the lack of proper security controls. Items to look for include the following:

- ▶ Changes are implemented directly by the software vendor, without internal control.

- ▶ Programmers place code in an application that has not been tested or validated.

- ▶ The changed source code has not been reviewed by the proper employee.

- ▶ No formal change process is in place.

- ▶ The change review board has not authorized the change.

- ▶ The programmer has access to both the object code and the production library.

Finally, this does not mean that a situation will never arise in which a change does not have to go through the change-control process. Emergency changes might have to be made. These typically occur because of situations that endanger production or halt a critical process. In these situations, it is important to maintain the integrity of the process. These changes should be followed up by procedures to ensure that standard controls are applied retroactively. If programmers are given special access or an increased level of control, the accounts and mechanisms they use should be closely monitored.

Chapter Summary

This chapter covered the systems development lifecycle and project management. These topics are important to the auditor from the standpoint of governance. Throughout these processes, the auditor has a leadership role. This chapter's goal was to introduce the auditor to the various steps, review the activity performed at each stage, and help the auditor become familiar with the terms and concepts used in software development.

Key Terms

- ▶ Accreditation
- ▶ Bottom-up testing
- ▶ Certification
- ▶ Critical path methodology (CPM)
- ▶ Entity relationship diagram (ERD)
- ▶ Function point analysis (FPA)
- ▶ Kilo lines of code (KLOC)
- ▶ Object breakdown structure (OBS)
- ▶ Reverse engineering
- ▶ Source lines of code (SLOC)
- ▶ Top-down testing
- ▶ Work breakdown structure (WBS)

Apply Your Knowledge

This chapter introduced you to the role an auditor plays in the development of new applications and systems. As such, it is important that you understand some common project-management techniques.

Exercises

3.1 Project Management

In this exercise, examine different project-management techniques.

Estimated Time: 30 Minutes

Part 1

1. Find someone who works as a project manager at your organization, and see if you can interview this person by phone, by email, or in person. Formulate several questions to ask about the project-management process. Ask what types of concerns he has when working on software projects. Ask what methods are used to calculate project time and whether PERT, CPM, RAD, prototyping, or other techniques are used.

2. Search the Web for *function point analysis* and *source lines of code*. Record the number of hits you get for each, and examine any interesting articles found.

Part 2

1. Examine Table 3.11 and calculate the totals with the values shown.

TABLE 3.11   Function Point Analysis

Measurement Parameter	Count	Weighing Factor			
		Simple	Average	Complex	Results
Number of user inputs	10		4		=____
Number of user outputs	2		5		=____
Number of user inquiries	3		4		=____
Number of files	6		10		=____
Number of external interfaces	3		7		=____
Total count:					

2. Next, go to http://www.effortestimator.com/ and download the demo version of FPApal.

3. Once downloaded, install the program, select **Open Project** from the File menu, and enter the same values, as shown in Table 3.11. Figure 3.11 shows the program.

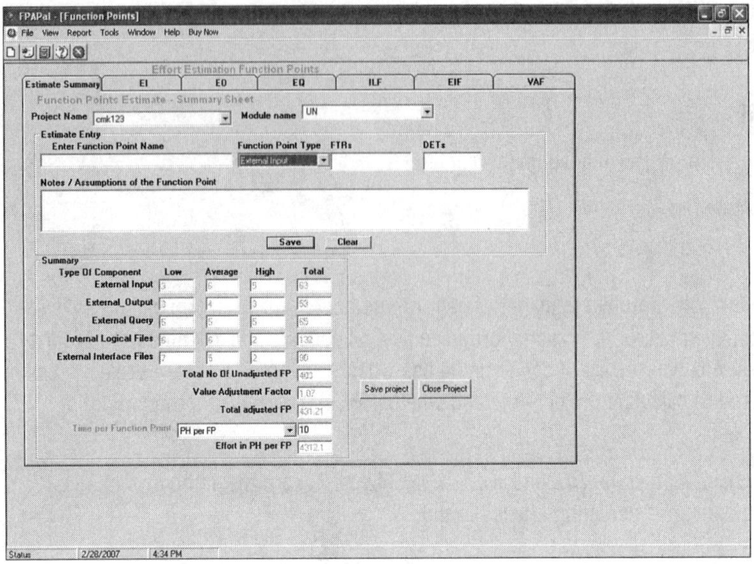

FIGURE 3.11 FPApal.

4. Compare the results between the manual and automated methods. Were they the same?

   Yes _____ No _____

Exam Questions

1. During which step of the SDLC is final user acceptance usually performed?

   O **A.** Design

   O **B.** Development

   O **C.** Implementation

   O **D.** Requirements

2. When planning to add time constraints to a project, which of the following should be examined most closely?

   O **A.** Budget

   O **B.** Critical path

   O **C.** Skills of the project team

   O **D.** Tasks that require the most time

3. During the post-implementation review, which of the following activities should be performed?

- ○ **A.** Perform an ROI
- ○ **B.** Design the audit trail
- ○ **C.** Complete an entity relationship diagram
- ○ **D.** Perform acceptance testing

4. Which of the following types of tests is used to verify that the proposed design will function in its intended environment?

- ○ **A.** Regression testing
- ○ **B.** Function testing
- ○ **C.** Pilot testing
- ○ **D.** Sociability testing

5. Which of the following development methods is known to not work well for large projects?

- ○ **A.** Spiral model
- ○ **B.** Rapid application development
- ○ **C.** Scrum
- ○ **D.** Extreme programming

6. Programming languages that most closely map to database management are found at what generational level?

- ○ **A.** 2GL
- ○ **B.** 3GL
- ○ **C.** 4GL
- ○ **D.** 5GL

7. Which of the following does the PERT weighted average consider?

- ○ **A.** High cost, low cost, best cost
- ○ **B.** Average cost plus 5%
- ○ **C.** Best time, worst time, average time
- ○ **D.** Average time plus 5%

8. This type of changeover process requires all users to get up to speed in advance so that a defined changeover can be set to a fixed date.

   ○ **A.** Fallback scenario

   ○ **B.** Abrupt changeover

   ○ **C.** Phased changeover

   ○ **D.** Parallel changeover

9. Entity relationship diagrams are built using two essential components. These include which of the following?

   ○ **A.** Processes and attributes

   ○ **B.** Processes and decision blocks

   ○ **C.** Entities and relationships

   ○ **D.** Nouns and adverbs

10. Which of the following development techniques uses short cycles, referred to as sprints, and is focused on object-oriented technology?

   ○ **A.** Spiral model

   ○ **B.** Rapid application development

   ○ **C.** Scrum

   ○ **D.** Extreme programming

Answers to Exam Questions

1. **C.** Implementation is the stage at which user acceptance is usually performed. Therefore, answers A, B, and D are incorrect.

2. **B.** The critical path is the sequence of activities that must be completed on time for the project to stay on schedule. Delays of any items on the critical path will slow the entire project. Answers A, C, and D are incorrect because, although the budget, team skills, and individual tasks are all items to consider, the critical path should be examined first because that will affect all other items.

3. **A.** Following implementation, a cost-benefit analysis or ROI should be performed. Answer B is incorrect because the audit trail should be designed during the design phase. Answer C is incorrect because an ERD should be performed during the requirements phase. Answer D is incorrect because final acceptance testing should be performed during the implementation phase.

4. **D.** Sociability testing is performed to confirm that a new or modified system will work in its intended environment. Answer A is incorrect because regression testing verifies that changes have not introduced errors. Answer B is incorrect because function testing verifies that systems meet specifications. Answer C is incorrect because pilot testing is used for limited evaluations.

5. **D.** Extreme programming does not work well for large project teams. Extreme programming requires that teams include business managers, programmers, and end users. These teams are responsible for developing useable applications in short periods of time. Answer A is incorrect because the spiral model is based on the concept that software development is evolutionary. The spiral model begins by creating a series of prototypes to develop a solution. As the project continues, it spirals out, becoming more detailed. Each step passes through planning, requirements, risks, and development phases. Answer B is incorrect because RAD requires well-trained development teams that use integrated power tools for modeling and prototyping. Answer C is incorrect because scrum uses short cycles referred to as sprints and is focused on object-oriented technology.

6. **C.** Fourth-generation languages (4GL) are most commonly used for databases. Examples of 4GLs include Focus, natural, and dBase. Answer A is incorrect because 2GL is assembly language. Answer B is incorrect because 3GL includes languages such as FORTRAN, Pascal, and C. Answer D is incorrect because 5GLs are very high-level languages such as LISP and PROLOG.

7. **C.** PERT is used to schedule, organize, and coordinate tasks. The PERT weighted average examines the shortest time, average time, and longest time a task is scheduled to be completed. Therefore answers A, B, and D are incorrect.

8. **B.** The abrupt changeover requires the establishment of a cut-off date so that all users must switch to the new system by then. Answer A is incorrect because a fallback scenario is used for data conversion and to ensure that the new application is ready for use. Answer C is incorrect because a phased changeover is gradual. Answer D is incorrect because a parallel changeover brings the new system online while the old is still in operation.

9. **C.** Entity relationship diagrams are built using two essential components that include entities and relationships. Therefore answers A, B, and D are incorrect.

10. **C.** Scrum uses short cycles referred to as sprints and is focused on object-oriented technology. Answer A is incorrect because the spiral model is based on the concept that software development is evolutionary. The spiral model begins by creating a series of prototypes to develop a solution. As the project continues, it spirals out, becoming more detailed. Each step passes through planning, requirements, risks, and development phases. Answer B is incorrect because RAD requires well-trained development teams that use integrated power tools for modeling and prototyping. Answer D is incorrect because extreme programming requires that teams include business managers, programmers, and end users. These teams are responsible for developing useable applications in short periods of time.

Need to Know More?

▶ Which Development Method Is Right for Your Company: http://tinyurl.com/2do5ws

▶ Prototyping: http://www.umsl.edu/~sauter/analysis/prototyping/proto.html

▶ On Overview of RAD: http://csweb.cs.bgsu.edu/maner/domains/RAD.htm

▶ Fundamentals of Function Point Analysis: http://www.ifpug.com/fpafund.htm

▶ PERT, CPM, and Gantt: http://studentweb.tulane.edu/~mtruill/dev-pert.html

▶ Building Security Controls into the SDLC: http://tinyurl.com/27hurl

▶ Auditing the SDLC: http://tinyurl.com/24x7ah

CHAPTER FOUR

System Infrastructure Control

This chapter helps you prepare for the Certified Information Systems Auditor (CISA) exam by covering the following ISACA objectives, which include understanding the importance of system infrastructure and control.

Tasks

Perform post-implementation review of systems and/or infrastructure to ensure that they meet the organization's objectives and are subject to effective internal control.

Evaluate the processes by which systems and/or infrastructure are developed/acquired and tested to ensure that the deliverables meet the organization's objectives.

Perform periodic reviews of systems and/or infrastructure to ensure that they continue to meet the organization's objectives and are subject to effective internal control.

Knowledge Statements

Knowledge of risk management practices applied to projects

Knowledge of control objectives and techniques that ensure the completeness, accuracy, validity, and authorization of transactions and data within IT systems applications

Knowledge of enterprise architecture related to data, applications, and technology (e.g., distributed applications, web-based applications, web services, *n*-tier applications)

Outline

Study Strategies

This chapter addresses system infrastructure control. As such, this chapter discusses application controls and how these controls can be audited to verify their functionality. This chapter also examines business application systems and looks at the risks with such items as electronic funds transfer and electronic banking. A CISA candidate should review the following primary topics for the exam:

▶ Application controls for input, output, and processing

▶ Data integrity auditing and verification of the accuracy of controls

▶ Electronic commerce and electronic data interchange

▶ Security issues surrounding email

▶ How decision support systems are used for efficiency and effectiveness

Introduction

Before an IS auditor can begin an audit of infrastructure or application systems, the auditor must understand the environment. Modern application processes can be highly complex. As an example, consider a few steps in a simple e-commerce transaction:

1. The customer must browse the merchant's online store.

2. The customer must complete an order form and store their personal information and credit card number.

3. The customer must review and approve the form.

4. The merchant must send a notice to the customer that the order was received and being processed. About the same time, the credit card information should be making its way through the bank's payment system.

5. The bank must verify the credit card and send payment to the merchant.

6. The order is shipped.

This is a high-level overview of the steps. This level of complexity means that an auditor must understand many controls in relation to the business. This process can be highly complex. Issues such as when the order was processed, where the customer's data is stored, where the product is shipped from, and how the financial transaction occurs are all relevant isssues. Without this knowledge, the auditor cannot verify that proper security measures have been implemented.

Programmed and Manual Application Controls

Knowledge Statement

▶ Knowledge of control objectives and techniques that ensure the completeness, accuracy, validity, and authorization of transactions and data within IT systems applications

This section discusses programmed and manual application controls as they relate to input, output, and processed information. These controls can be either manually or automatically programmed. Automated controls include validation and edit checks, programmed logic functions, and controls. Manual controls are those that auditors or staff manually verify, such as the review of reconciliation reports, and exception reports. The purpose of both automated and manual controls is to verify the following:

- ▶ The validity of data processed is ensured.

- ▶ The accuracy of data processed is ensured.

- ▶ The data is stored so that controls maintain the security of the data so that accuracy, validity, confidentiality, and integrity of the data is maintained.

- ▶ Processed data is valid and meets expectations.

Auditors can perform control checks by doing the following:

- ▶ Discovering and identifying application components so that transaction flow can be analyzed.

- ▶ Determining the appropriate audit procedures to perform tests to evaluate strengths and weaknesses of the application.

- ▶ Analyzing test results.

- ▶ Validating the results and reporting on the application's effectiveness and efficiency. The results should also be measured against good programming standards and compared against management's objectives for the application.

NOTE

Setting the Scope of the Review   The audit engagement letter should set out clearly the types of matters that will be reviewed during the audit and the scope of such review.

Business Process Controls

Before controls can be examined, an auditor must understand the business strategy and the business process. To understand business objectives and strategy, start with the company's business plan. Next, review the long- and short-term goals. Long-term goals are considered strategic and focus on activities planned for the next three to five years. Short-term goals are tactical and address immediate concerns that are no more than 18 months into the future. Finally, review the organization's goals. After reviewing this background information, examine process flow charts. Next, review application controls, data integrity controls, and controls for business systems. Table 4.1 provides an overview of input, processing, and output controls.

TABLE 4.1 Business Process Controls

Input Controls	Processing Controls	Output Controls
Input authorization	Processing	Logging
Batch controls	Validation	Security signatures
	Editing	Report distribution
		Balancing and reconciliation

The following sections look at each category of control in more detail, beginning with input controls, moving on to processing controls, and finally covering output controls.

Input Controls

When reviewing input controls, the auditor must ensure that all transactions have been entered correctly. Whatever controls are used, they should be capable of checking that input is valid. This becomes important because in many automated systems, the output of one system is the input of another. In such situations, data should be checked to verify the information from both the sending and receiving applications.

Controls can be either automated authorization or manual authorization. As an example, consider the last time you were at your local discount store and, at checkout, a sales item did not ring up at the advertised price. Most likely, you had to wait for the clerk to signal a supervisor to advise of the error in the sales price. The supervisor then had to enter a second-level password to authorize the price change. This is a *manual authorization control*. Other types of authorization controls include these:

▶ Signatures on forms or documents approving a change.

▶ Password controls that are required to process a change.

▶ Client identification controls that allow only certain clients to authorize the change. As an example, the clerk at the local market cannot authorize a price override, yet the manager can by using their access login.

A *batch control* is a second type of input control. Batch controls combine transactions into a group. This group then has a value assigned. The total of this transaction can be based on dollar amounts, total counts, total document numbers, or hash totals. Figure 4.1 illustrates an example of a batch control. Notice that the billing system has a count of 312. This number should match the count in the receivables system.

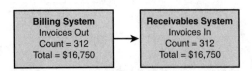

FIGURE 4.1 Batch control.

Total dollar amounts verify that each item totals up to the correct batched total amount. *Total item counts* verify the total counts match. As an example, if 312 items were ordered, 312 items should have been processed and shipped. *Total document numbers* verify that the total number of documents in the batch equals the total number of documents processed. Documents could be invoices generated, orders, or any document count that is used to track accuracy. *Hash totals* are generated by choosing a selected number of fields in a series of transactions. These values are computed again later to see if the numbers match. An incorrect value indicates that something has been lost, entered incorrectly, or corrupted somehow. As an example of hashing, consider that the totaling of part numbers on an order normally provides no usable value, but the total can be compared to the shipping order to verify accuracy, as illustrated in Figure 4.2. Notice how both the order and shipping entry are equal at 370373.

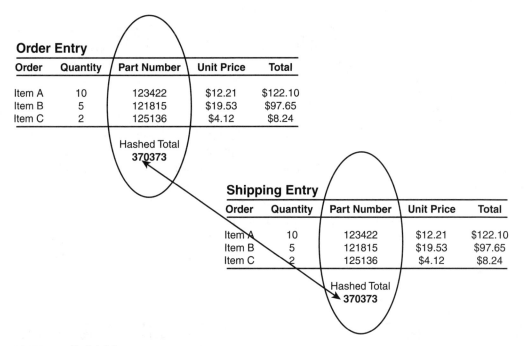

FIGURE 4.2 Hash totals.

> **NOTE**
>
> **Hash Totals** The use of hash totals is similar to how cryptographic hashing algrothims such as MD5 or SHA1 are used to verify integrity.

> **EXAM ALERT**
>
> **Batch Controls** Be aware that the CISA exam might ask questions about what is considered a valid batch control. Test candidates should understand each type and know that batch controls are used to detect loss, duplication, or corruption of data.

Batch controls must be combined with the proper follow-up procedures. For example, if rejected items are resubmitted, controls must be in place to detect this anomaly. Additionally, procedures must be in place to follow up on any discrepancies found when batch controls are performed. Batch balancing is used to verify that the batch was processed correctly. This can be accomplished by comparing computer-generated batch quantities to manual batch counts. Control accounts can also be used. Control accounts write an initial batch value to a data file. After processing, the processed value is compared to the initially stored value. An example of this can be seen in *batch registers*. Batch registers allow for the manual recording of batch totals. These are saved and then compared to totals that are generated by the system. If they do not agree, the batch can be rejected.

Processing Controls

Processing controls are used to ensure the accuracy, completeness, and timeliness of data during online or batch processing. Controls should be in place to verify that data is processed only through authorized routines. Processing controls should be designed to detect problems and initiate corrective action. If procedures are in place to override these controls, their use should be logged. Individuals who have the ability to override these controls should not be the same ones responsible for reviewing the log. Edit controls can be used after the data has been entered into the system but before it has been processed. Edit controls can be considered a type of preventive control. Table 4.2 describes edit controls, and Figure 4.3 shows an example of existence and completion checks.

TABLE 4.2   Processing Edit Controls

Validation Edit	Description
Sequence check	Sequence numbers ensure that all data falls within a given range. For example, checks are numbered sequentially. The day's first check that was issued had the number 120, and the day's last check was number 144. All checks issued that day should fall between those numbers, and none should be missing.
Limit check	Data to be processed should not exceed a predetermined limit. For example, the weekly sale item is limited to five per customer. Sales over that amount should trigger an alert.

TABLE 4.2 *Continued*

Validation Edit	Description
Range check	A range check ensures that a date is within a predetermined range. For example, a range check might verify that the data is after 01/01/2000 and before 01/01/2010.
Validity check	This type of check looks at the validity of data.
Reasonableness check	This check verifies the reasonableness of the data. For example, if an order is usually for no more than 20 items and the order is for 2,000 items, an alert should be generated.
Table look-ups	This check verifies that the data matches the data in a look-up table.
Existence check	An existence check verifies that all required data is entered. Figure 4.3 provides an example.
Key verification	Key verification requires a second employee to reenter the data. A match must occur before the data can be processed.
Check digit	A check digit verifies accuracy. A check digit is a sum of a value appended to the data.
Completeness check	This check ensures that all required data has been added and that no fields contain null values. Figure 4.3 provides an example.
Duplicate check	This check ensures that a data item is not a duplicate. For example, before payment is made, accounts payable verify that invoice number 833 for $1,612 has not already been paid.
Logical relationship check	This type of edit check verifies logic. If one condition is true, additional items must also be true. For example, in 2008 if the data shows that an applicant is old enough to vote, logic dictates that person must have been born before 1989.

EXAM ALERT

Validation Edit Controls CISA exam candidates must understand that validation edit controls are applied before processing and are therefore considered a type of preventive control.

Now that you understand edit controls, turn your attention to processing controls used to ensure that the data remains unchanged until processed by an authorized process. Table 4.3 outlines the control techniques used to protect the integrity of the data.

FIGURE 4.3 Existence and completeness check.

TABLE 4.3 Processing Control Techniques

Processing Control	Description
Manual recalculations	Some transactions might be recalculated to ensure that processing is operating correctly.
Editing	A program instruction controls input or processing of data to verify its validity.
Run-to-run totals	Various stages of processing ensure the validity of data.
Programming controls	Software-based controls flag problems and initiate corrective action.
Reasonableness verification	This control ensures the reasonableness of data. For example, if someone tries to process a negative amount through a payment system, a reasonableness control should flag the result as invalid.
Limit checks	This control sets bounds on what are reasonable amounts. For example, someone might attempt to order 565 flat-screen TVs.
Reconciliation of file totals	This refers to the act of balancing debits, credits, and totals between two systems. This control should be performed periodically to verify the accuracy and completeness of data.
Exception reports	This type of report should be generated when transactions appear to be incorrect.

EXAM ALERT

Run-to-Run Totals   The CISA exam might ask about specific process-control techniques. For example, run-to-run totals enable you to ensure the validity of data through various stages of processing.

Data File Controls

Data files or database tables can be one of four types:

- *System-control parameters* control values such as how much money can be transferred in a single transaction with approval.

- *Standing data* refers to information that is somewhat static. An example of standing data is a customer's name, address, and phone number. Because these values do not frequently change, an alteration should be controlled and should require authorization.

- *Balance data* refers to various values and totals that might be held temporarily during processing. These values should be strictly controlled; any manual alteration of these values should require authorization and be logged.

- *Transaction files* deal with the transmission of information between two systems or applications. Transaction files should be managed with exception reports or validation checks. Figure 4.4 shows an example of this in which the billing and receivables do not match. This, in turn, generates an exception report that notes the problem.

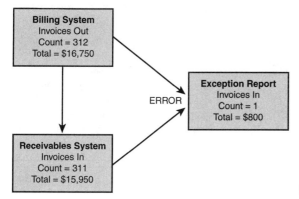

FIGURE 4.4 Exception report.

The four data file types can have various controls applied to them:

- **Before-and-after image reports**—By taking a snapshot of computer data before and after a transaction, you can determine what changes have been made to data.

- **Maintenance error reporting**—Procedures should be established to verify that any errors or exceptions are rectified and reconciled. The employee who generated the transaction should not have the authorization to clear the error.

- **Internal and external labeling**—Internal labeling ensures that proper data files are used and that all information is present. External labeling applies to removable media.

▸ **Data file security**—This control should ensure that individuals who process data cannot bypass validity checks, clear logs, or alter stored data.

▸ **One-to-one checking**—Documents entered for processing should match processed totals.

▸ **Transaction logs**—Transactional information such as date, time, terminal, user ID, and so on should be recorded to create a usable audit trail.

▸ **Parity checking**—Data integrity should be verified in the event of a transmission error.

Output Controls

Output controls are designed to provide assurance in data that has completed processing. Output data must be delivered accurately in a timely manner so that it is useful in the decision-making process. Output controls should be designed to ensure that the data is distributed and stored in a secure manner. Sensitive data should have sufficient controls to monitor usage and control who has access to it. These controls will vary, depending on whether the information is centrally stored or distributed to end-user workstations.

NOTE

Output Printer Controls   Auditors should be aware that one way to control distribution is to place controls on data that limit what information is to be printed and to whose printer it should be directed. For example, some reports might be configured so that they are printed only to the supervisor's printer. Software printing controls are another example of this. Products such as Adobe PDF and others can be used to limit printing or embed password controls for viewing or printing.

Per ISACA, output controls should address the following:

▸ Logging and storage of sensitive negotiable and critical forms

▸ Negotiable instruments, forms, and signatures that are computer generated

▸ Distribution control

▸ Balancing and reconciliation of control totals

▸ Output errors that should be logged and reviewed

▸ Retention records that specify how long output data should be stored or maintained

Challenge

This chapter covers the importance of application controls. In this challenge, you identify and describe some of these controls.

1. Fill in the descriptions and names of edit controls described in Table 4.4.

TABLE 4.4   Identifying Edit Controls

Validation Edit	Description
Sequence check	
Limit check	
Range check	
Validity check	
Reasonableness check	
Table look-ups	Verifies that all required data is entered
Key verification	
Check digit	Ensures that all required data has been added and that no fields contain null values
Duplicate check	
Logical relationship check	

2. Use the information from the preceding section to verify your answers.

Auditing Application Controls

Tasks

▶ Perform periodic reviews of systems and/or infrastructure to ensure that they continue to meet the organization's objectives and are subject to effective internal control.

▶ Evaluate the processes by which systems and/or infrastructure are developed/acquired and tested to ensure that the deliverables meet the organization's objectives.

Application software is the engine behind automated business transactions. These systems might process payroll, manage inventory, or even invoice and bill customers. Most users see only the application interface, but what does the application really do? The auditor should be most concerned about the limits, controls, and rules that define how the application interacts with the organization's data.

Understanding the Application

One of the first questions the auditor should ask is, what does the application do? How this question is answered will vary from organization to organization and from case to case. The auditor can start by asking for documentation. If the application was developed in-house, system-development methodology documents might be available. These documents will provide the auditor with insight into what the user requirements were and what cost-benefit analysis was done to justify development of the application. Functional design specifications should also be reviewed. These specifications are a great resource because they detail how the application is designed and what it was developed to achieve. If the application has been in use for a while, program-change documents that list any changes or updates also might exist. Checking outstanding bugs and issues in release note documentation and software build information also can provide good information. After reviewing these documents, the auditor can develop an application flowchart to accomplish the following:

▶ Validate every input to the system against the applicable criteria

▶ Review logical access controls and authorization controls

▶ Evaluate exception handling and logging

▶ Examine data flow to find control weaknesses

With an understanding of the application and knowledge of how transactions flow through the application, the auditor can move to the next step: observing and testing.

Observation and Testing

A big part of an auditor's job involves observation. Auditors are tasked with observing how users interact with the application. Auditors should also test the limits of the application. Buffer overflows are one concern. Buffer overflows can occur when attackers try to stuff more than the total number of characters allowed in a field. The design specification might state that the application does not accept negative numbers, but is that actually the case? If you enter a negative number or a negative quantity in a field, will the application actually accept it? It shouldn't. Figure 4.5 presents an example of a poorly constructed application entry form. Notice the grand total of –$2,450.99.

The Solution Firm - Demo Application Entry Form			
DESCRIPTION	QTY	Unit Price	Total Price
SNR142 1 Carat Diamond Ring Color: Gold Select Ring Size Review Item	1	($2450.99)	($2450.99)
Total			($2450.99)
Coupon [ ] View coupon status		0.00	($2450.99)
Shipping UPS Ground ▾ Calculate my shipping			
Gift Certificate [ ] View gift certificate status			
Grand Total			$-2450.99
To remove an item, change the Qty to Zero, then click "Recalculate"			
Continue Shopping Recalculate Clear Cart Check Out Now (Step 1 of 3)			

FIGURE 4.5 Sales entry form.

Even if the application was to accept an invalid entry as shown in Figure 4.5, activity reports should track the IP address or terminal number used to complete the entry. Logging should also track the date and time of activity. In addition, invalid entries should be logged so that violation reports can be created.

CAUTION

Tracking Violators Tracking violators can be a real challenge in the distributed world of the Internet. Proxy servers, anonomizers, and network address translation (NAT) make the prospect of identifying an individual user much harder.

When working with applications, auditors should observe and test the items listed in Table 4.5.

TABLE 4.5 Observation and Test

Observation/Test	Details
Separation of duties	Auditors should verify separation of duties because it provides control by limiting the ability of each employee. As an example, one department might have the capability to issue checks but must send the check to a second department for signature.
Input authorization	Auditors should review records to verify who is authorized to access applications. If supervisor override is used frequently, this might signal problems.
Balancing	Auditors should verify that run-to-run totals are reconciled on a timely basis.
Report distribution	Auditors should review report distribution logs to see who has access to view and print reports. Controls used to limit the distribution of reports should also be reviewed.
Error correction and control	Auditors should review past error corrections and verify that they are viewed and addressed in a timely manner.
Access control and authorization	Auditors should verify that access is limited to individuals who have a clearly demonstrated need. Testing can be performed to ensure that access controls are in place as specified.

Data Integrity Controls

Data integrity testing is performed to ensure the accuracy, completeness, consistency, and authorization of data. Integrity testing is considered a substitutive test. Data can be stored in files or in databases.

> **NOTE**
>
> **Data Integrity Testing** Data integrity testing is the best method of examining the accuracy, completeness, consistency, and authorization of data. Data integrity testing can be used to find failures in input and processing controls.

Data stored in databases has unique requirements because it differs from data stored or processed by an application. Database integrity testing can be performed through several methods. *Referential integrity* guarantees that all foreign keys reference existing primary keys, as demonstrated in Figure 4.6.

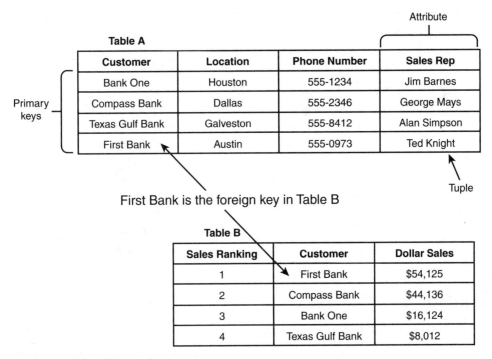

FIGURE 4.6 Referential integrity.

Controls in most databases should prevent the primary key from being deleted when it is linked to existing foreign keys. *Relational integrity* ensures that validation routines test data before it is entered into a database and that any modification can be detected. A third integrity control is *entity integrity*. As an example, in Figure 4.6, the primary keys are names of banks; *entity integrity* ensures that each tuple contains a primary key. Without the capability to associate each primary key with a bank, entity integrity cannot be maintained and the database is not intact.

Online data integrity has somewhat different concerns because online databases most likely are distributed or clustered for performance and fault tolerance. Online databases work in real time. This might mean that several databases must be updated simultaneously. These complexities mean that the *ACID test* should be applied:

► **A**tomicity, to divide work so that the results are either all or nothing

► **C**onsistency, to ensure that transactions are processed only if they meet system defined integrity constraints

► **I**solation, to ensure that each transaction is isolated from all others until complete

► **D**urability, to ensure that when a transaction is processed, the transaction cannot be rolled back and is accurate

Attacking Integrity and Access Controls

Attacks typically require means, motive, and opportunity. Most attackers prefer to keep their activities secret, but that is not always the case. Eric McCarty decided to set up a personal blog to broadcast the fact that he had hacked the University of Southern California (USC).

McCarty was denied admission to USC. After being notified that he was not accepted, McCarty hacked a student application system that included student data such as names, social security numbers, birthdates, and addresses. McCarty succeeded in breaking in undetected, but his failure to remain silent proved to be his demise.

McCarty contacted reporters and notified them that he had hacked USC. This information was turned over to law enforcement, McCarty's home was raided, and federal investigators found evidence of the crime. McCarty pleaded guilty to a plea bargain that sentenced him to three years of probation, six months of home detention, and almost $36,800 in damages. You can read more about the case at http://www.securityfocus.com/news/11411.

Application System Testing

Application testing is a critical part of the audit process. Testing enables the auditor to evaluate the program, review its controls, and monitor the transaction process. The primary methods used for application testing are as follows:

- ▶ **Snapshots**—These are used to monitor and record the flow of data through an application. Although snapshots require an in-depth knowledge about the application, they are useful in verifying logic.

- ▶ **Mapping**—Unlike snapshots, mapping verifies program logic that might not have been performed or tested. This is useful because it might detect undiscovered problems.

- ▶ **Tracing and tagging**—Tagging is used to mark selected transactions. Tracing enables these tagged transactions to be monitored.

- ▶ **Using test data**—This type of test uses test data to verify program operation. This technique requires little knowledge of the environment and does not require the review of the source code.

- ▶ **Base case system evaluation**—This compressive test uses test data that was developed to thoroughly test the environment. This method is useful because it requires great effort and close cooperation among various internal groups.

- ▶ **Parallel operation**—Both old and new systems process data so that the results can be compared.

▶ **Integrated test facility**—This test method creates a fictitious entity in a database to process sample test transactions at the same time live input is being processed.

▶ **Parallel simulation**—Another useful audit tool uses computer programs to simulate program logic.

▶ **Transaction selection**—This method of testing uses audit software to determine what transactions should be processed.

NOTE

Base case system evaluation   Using test data that was developed in a comprehensive manner is known as *base case system evaluation*.

Continuous Online Auditing

Testing a system once before rollout might provide a baseline of information, but it offers no ongoing feedback on the operation of the application. Continuous online auditing gives auditors the tools needed to perform ongoing monitoring. Continuous online auditing produces audit results either at real-time intervals or after a short period of time. This method actually can reduce costs because the need for conventional audits might be reduced or eliminated. In a conventional audit, the auditor has a limited amount of time to design tests and examine data. Continuous online auditing greatly increases the quantity and scope of data available to the auditor. With continuous auditing, the auditor can evaluate data on an ongoing schedule and alert management to problems as needed. Paperwork is reduced and the auditor can electronically examine application data and report problems directly as needed.

Continuous online auditing also increases security. Consider a bank that allows online access to customer accounts and funds. Although such systems are convenient for users, they present additional risk for the bank. Continuous online auditing allows the bank to monitor transactions as they occur. If some type of misuse occurs, the time between the misuse and discovery is greatly reduced. If additional controls are needed, they can be deployed in a shortened time frame. Overall, five continuous audit techniques exist, as described in Table 4.6.

TABLE 4.6   Continuous Audit Techniques

Name	Description	Level of Complexity	Issues and Concerns
Systems control audit review file and embedded audit modules (SCARF/EAM)	The application must contain embedded audit software to act as a monitoring agent.	◆◆◆◆◆	Cannot be used to interrupt regular processing

(continues)

TABLE 4.6 *Continued*

Name	Description	Level of Complexity	Issues and Concerns
Integrated test facilities	Live and dummy data is fed into the system. The results of the dummy data are compared with precalculated results.	◆◆◆◆	Should not be used with test data
Continuous and intermittent simulation (CIS)	CIS simulates the transaction run. If data meets certain criteria, the simulator logs the transaction; otherwise, processing continues.	◆◆◆	Requires examination of transactions that meet specific criteria
Snapshots	This technique tags transactions and then takes snapshots as the data is moved from input to output.	◆◆◆	Requires an audit trail
Audit hooks	This technique uses embedded hooks that act as red flags if certain conditions are met.	◆◆	Detects items that meet specific criteria

EXAM ALERT

Continuous Audit Techniques   The CISA exam might ask you to describe the unique attributes of each continuous audit technique. As an example, you should understand that snapshots require an audit trail.

REVIEW BREAK

Auditing application controls is a big piece of system infrastructure. Table 4.7 describes the four major steps and activities performed during each phase of application auditing.

TABLE 4.7 Review Break: Auditing Applications

Phase	Activity
Understanding the application	Validation of every input to the system against the applicable criteria
	Review of logical access control and authorization controls
	Evaluation of exception handling and logging
	Examination of data flow to find control weaknesses
Observation and testing	Separation of duties
	Input authorization
	Balancing
	Report distribution
	Error correction and control
	Access control and authorization
Data integrity controls	Referential integrity
	Relational integrity
	Entity integrity
Application system testing	Snapshots
	Mapping
	Tracing and tagging
	Use of test data
	Base case system evaluation
	Parallel operation
	Integrated test facility
	Parallel simulation
	Transaction selection
Continuous online auditing	Systems control audit review file and embedded audit modules (SCARF/EAM)
	Integrated test facilities
	Continuous and intermittent simulation (CIS)
	Snapshots
	Audit hooks

Auditing Systems Development, Acquisition, and Maintenance

Task

▶ Perform post-implementation review of systems and/or infrastructure to ensure that they meet the organization's objectives and are subject to effective internal control.

Knowledge Statement

▶ Knowledge of risk management practices applied to projects

In the past, software development consisted of one lone programmer writing code to meet the needs of a small group or department. Today's systems are much more complex, in that systems might be used by different branches located in different areas of the world or accessed by users through the Internet. Many more legal regulations and requirements, such as Safe Harbor or Sarbanes-Oxley, also must be satisfied. This means that coding must be performed by teams of programmers with the help of architects, analysts, testers, auditors, and end users that must all work together. To manage such a large endeavor, the system development lifecycle was created.

The auditor role in this process is to work with the development team to ensure that the final product meets user requirements while possessing adequate controls. Throughout the system development lifecycle, the auditor should work with the development team to minimize risks and exposures. The following list provides the general steps an auditor should follow during the development process.

STEP BY STEP

4.1 Auditing Systems Development

1. Determine the objectives and user requirements of the project.

2. Perform a risk assessment that identifies threats, risks, and exposures.

3. Assess existing controls to determine whether they will adequately reduce risk to acceptable levels. Discuss any needed changes with the development team.

4. Monitor the development process and evaluate controls as they are designed and created.

5. Evaluate the system during rollout, and review audit mechanisms to ensure that they function as designed.

6. Take part in any post-implementation reviews.

7. Verify system-maintenance procedures.

8. Review production library control to ensure the needed level of security.

Project Management

Implementing good application controls is just part of the task. Organizations must also use good project-management techniques. The auditor should be involved throughout the development process to minimize risk and ensure that adequate controls are in place. An auditor must evaluate the level of oversight that a project committee has over the process. Other issues, such as reporting, change control, and stakeholder involvement, are also important. Table 4.8 lists additional issues that the auditor should perform per ISACA recommendations. Although this is not a complete list, it should give you an overall idea of how important it is for the auditor to play a proactive role in the process.

TABLE 4.8   Audit Controls and Quality-Assurance Checks

Stage	Items to Review
Feasibility	Examine proposal and documentation
	Assess the criticality of the user's needs
	Evaluate how effectively the chosen solution meets the user's needs
	Investigate the possibility of an alternate or existing solution
Requirements definition	Assess total cost of the project and verify that the project sponsors have approved
	Examine the conceptual design and verify that it meets user demands
	Evaluate the possibility of embedded audit routines
	Examine the proposed user acceptance plans
Software-acquisition process	Examine the RFP to ensure that it is complete
	Examine vendor contracts
	Verify that the legal department has approved the vendor contract
Design and development	Study system flowcharts
	Evaluate input, process, and output controls
	Examine proposed audit trails and determine the usefulness
	Review how the system will handle erroneous input and data

(continues)

TABLE 4.8 *Continued*

Stage	Items to Review
Testing	Examine proposed test plans
	Verify audit trails, error processing, and error reports
	Evaluate user documentation and manuals
	Review test results
	Examine system security
Implementation	Examine system documentation
	Examine system parameters
	Examine any data-conversion activities to verify correctness
Post-implementation	Review requirements and user needs to verify that the systems meet user needs
	Examine user satisfaction and cost-benefit analysis
	Examine the change-request process
	Examine error logs
System change procedures	Determine whether emergency change procedures exist
	Evaluate the separation of production code from test code and access security controls
	Interview end users to determine their satisfaction with the turnaround of the change process

EXAM ALERT

Project Management Audit Activities The CISA exam expects candidates to understand what activities occur at each stage of the project-management process. As an example, user-acceptance test plans are reviewed at the requirements definition stage.

Business Application Systems

Knowledge Statement

▶ Knowledge of enterprise architecture related to data, applications, and technology e.g., distributed applications, web-based applications, web services, *n*-tier applications)

Audit programs require an understanding of the application being reviewed. One good place to start is reviewing application system flowcharts. Business applications can be categorized according to where they are used or by their functionality. Business application programs are used for accounting, payroll, inventory, sales, and so on. These systems can be used in e-commerce systems, for web-based applications, in electronic banking, and even for electronic payment systems. The following sections describe each of these systems in greater detail.

TIP

Flowcharts   Flowcharts are one of the first things an auditor should examine when evaluating business application systems.

E-Commerce

Electronic commerce, or e-commerce, is about the buying, selling, and servicing of goods via the Internet. The process usually begins with a company advertising its goods on a website. When a buyer finds the goods he or she is looking for, the buyer adds them to a shopping cart. Upon checkout, the buyer is redirected to a secure web page so that credit card and shipping information can be entered. E-commerce saw tremendous growth in the 1990s because it enabled businesses to offer better prices than in brick-and-mortar stores. E-commerce has none of the overhead of these traditional models. Although that model has somewhat held, many companies have moved to a bricks-and-clicks model that supports both online and offline presences. E-commerce models can be broken down into four basic categories (see Figure 4.7):

- **Business to business (B-to-B)**—Transactions between two or more businesses, such as a business and its suppliers.

- **Business to consumer (B-to-C)**—Transactions between businesses and consumers. This area is one of the greatest growth areas for e-commerce. For companies that don't sell products directly to their customer, there are brokers that can act as middlemen to sell products for them.

- **Business to government (B-to-G)**—Transactions between business and government, such as the online filling of legal documents and reports.

- **Business to employee (B-to-E)**—Transactions between business and employees. This model can be seen when organizations set up internal websites and portals for employee services such as health care, job benefits, and payroll.

E-commerce adds an additional level of challenge to the organization because data and applications must now protect availability, integrity, and confidentiality 24 hours a day, seven days a week. Companies must also be careful in handling customers' personal information and payment information such as credit cards. Authentication and nonrepudiation are important aspects of this because customers need to know that they are really dealing with the company, not an impostor.

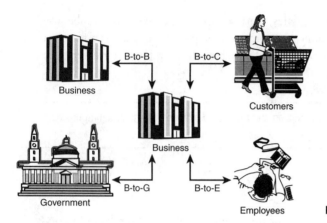

FIGURE 4.7   E-commerce models.

NOTE

B-to-C   Business-to-consumer e-commerce offers the greatest capability to reshape business models.

Electronic Data Interchange

Electronic data interchange (EDI) is a technology designed to facilitate the exchange of data between computer systems. It was designed to bridge the gap between dissimilar systems. EDI is used to exchange invoices, shipping notices, inventory updates, and so on in a format that both the sending and receiving systems can understand. *ANSI X12* is the most common of the formats used. EDI offers real benefits for organizations: It reduces paperwork and results in fewer errors because all information is transmitted electronically. Traditional EDI consists of the following components:

▶ **Communications handler**—The method used to transmit and receive electronic documents. Much of this activity occurs via the Internet.

▶ **EDI interface**—The EDI interface handles data as it is being passed between the two organizations' applications. Security controls are usually placed here. The EDI interface is comprised of the EDI translator and the application interface.

▶ **Application system**—The application system is the program responsible for processing documents that have been sent or received. Additional controls are usually not placed here.

NOTE

Value-added network (VAN)   Before the rise of the Internet, VANs, which are private networks, were the primary communications handlers. The Internet disrupted the VAN's business because many companies found it cheaper to move data via the Internet.

EDI adds a new level of concern to organizations because documents are processed electronically. One big concern with EDI is authorization. This means that EDI process should have an additional layer of application control. These controls can be used to address the issue of authorization, as well as lost or duplicate transactions and issues of confidentiality and invalid distribution. Some common controls include these:

- ▶ Transmission controls to validate sender and receiver

- ▶ Manipulation controls to prevent unauthorized changes to data

- ▶ Authorization controls to authenticate communication partners

- ▶ Encryption controls to protect the confidentiality of information

Auditors should seek to verify that these common controls have been implemented. Other controls include the deployment of *audit monitors*, which are devices used to capture EDI activity as it is sent or received. The auditor should also review systems that process inbound transactions to make sure that each transaction is properly logged, as well as use transaction totals to verify that totals agree with those collected by trading partners.

CAUTION

EDI and Internal Controls   The impact of EDI on internal controls means fewer opportunities for review and authorization.

Email

Email enables individuals to communicate electronically through the Internet or a data communications network. Although email is the most used Internet application, it raises some security concerns. Specifically, email is usually clear text, which means anyone can easily read it. Email can be spoofed to mask the true identity of the sender. Email also is a major conduit for spam, phishing, and viruses. Users need to be made aware of these problems. Email carries a number of legal and regulatory requirements which are expected to grow in the coming years. Email actually uses two underlying services—Simple Mail Transfer Protocol (SMTP) and Post Office Protocol (POP). The following steps describe basic email operation.

STEP BY STEP

4.2 Basic Email Operation

1. The user opens an email program such as Outlook to create an email message.

2. After the email is created and addressed to the recipient, the user sends the email.

3. The email is forwarded to an SMTP server, which provides a message transfer agent (MTA). Just as the postal service sorts mail using a zip code, email messages are sorted by domain. As an example, in an email addressed to training@thesolutionfirm.com, the domain is thesolutionfirm. This domain identifies where the message is to be forwarded.

4. The MTA forwards the email toward its final destination.

5. The email is delivered to the destination mail server, where it waits until the recipient user retrieves it.

6. The email is retrieved using Post Office Protocol version 3 (POP3) and is displayed via Outlook on the recipient's computer.

Users must be educated that sensitive information (such as social security numbers) should not be sent by clear-text email. If an organization has policies that allow email to be used for sensitive information, encryption should be used. This requires an evaluation of the business needs. If only some information is to be encrypted, Pretty Good Privacy (PGP) might be the best option. However, if full-time encryption is needed, the company might want to use link encryption or standards such as Secure Multipurpose Internet Mail Extensions (S/MIME) or Privacy Enhanced Mail (PEM).

Business Intelligence

The objective of business intelligence is to reduce decision-making time and increase the value of the decision. Business intelligence is much like having a crystal ball because the organization can make better decisions in a shorter period of time. Thus, the organization can compare itself to its competitors. Business intelligence is also useful in helping understand customer needs as well as the capabilities of the firm. In addition, business intelligence is useful in risk management; it can help the business spot unusual trends, odd transactions, and statistics on loss and exposure. To properly implement an infrastructure to support business intelligence, the business must design and develop a data architecture, such as the one shown in Figure 4.8.

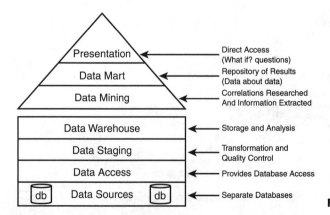

FIGURE 4.8 Data architecture.

These components encompass the data architecture:

- **Data sources**—The actual data sources reside here. As an example, a grocery store might have customer reward card scanners at each checkout, so that customers using the card have each item recorded on their account.

- **Data access**—This layer is responsible for connecting the data sources with the data staging layer. As an example, the grocery store might process sales to customers with reward cards to a local database.

- **Data staging**—This layer is responsible for copying and formatting data into a standard format for the data warehouse layer.

- **Data warehouse**—Data is captured by many databases and organized into subject-oriented usable groupings. As an example, the grocery store collects all the data from various stores across the country into this one centeralized database. This allows them to drill up or drill down and obtain information by region or by item.

- **Data mining**—Large volumes of data are searched for specific patterns. For example, if a grocery store examines paper plate sales, does it see that the same customers purchase plastic cutlery?

- **Data mart**—At this layer resides some type of relational database that enables the user to move the data around to extract specific components that they are looking for. At this point, the user can extract data about data.

- **Presentation layer**—This is the top of the model, the point at which users interact with the system. This layer can include such applications as Microsoft Access and Excel.

EXAM ALERT

Data warehouse   Exam candidates are expected to know that data warehouses are subject oriented.

Together these components provide the structure for a business intelligence system. Once developed, this system can be used in different ways, including scorecarding, customer relationship management, decision support systems, document warehouses, data mining, and supply chain management.

NOTE

Data warehouse accuracy   The quality of data in the data warehouse is dependent upon the accuracy of the source data.

Phone Number Please?

Many consumers have heard the phrase "phone number, please" while in the checkout line. You might have even been asked, "Do you have our customer rewards card?" What is all this tracking really about? It is the increasingly popular process of *data mining*. Companies ask for various pieces of information such as phone numbers or zip codes because most users don't mind providing such information. This information allows additional data mining through the process of enhancement.

Stores can pass this information to database companies such as Acxiom, ChoicePoint, and Experian to tie the information back to a unique identity. The enhanced information might include hobbies, demographic information, the number of people in the household, and even email addresses. All of this allows companies to evaluate the value of the customer. The compiled information can be fed into a decision system to make marketing decisions such as sending the consumer a specific offer, offering them a discount, or even targeting them for specific goods or services. Much of this process is hidden from consumers. Although companies find the information useful for data mining, customers should look closely at the company's privacy policy before revealing too much personal information.

Decision Support System

A decision support system (DSS) helps managers solve problems. DSS uses models and mathematical techniques, and usually is designed with fourth-generation programming (4GL) tools. This makes the systems flexible and adaptable, yet not always as efficient as lower-level programming tools might deliver. DSS models include the following:

- ▶ **Model-driven DSS**—Uses models based on statistics, finance, or simulation. These are designed to help users make a decision. An example of this can be seen in the dicodess project at http://dicodess.sourceforge.net/.

- ▶ **Communication-driven DSS**—Designed to facilitate sharing so that more than one person can work on a task. Lotus Notes is an example of a communication-driven DSS. Lotus Notes was used for just such a purpose after 9/11 when it served as a DSS to help rebuild an emergency operation center.

- ▶ **Data-driven DSS**—Can access a variety of internal and external data to analyze outcomes. Companies such as Oracle, IBM, and Microsoft are some of the leaders in this field as they build products that support data warehousing.

- ▶ **Document-driven DSS**—Manipulates and manages unstructured information. eRoom is an example of a document-driven DSS.

- ▶ **Knowledge-driven DSS**—Based on rules, facts, and knowledge. It is used for problem solving and to provide answers.

DSS models share these common characteristics:

- Used for decision making
- Used for goal seeking
- Perform simulation
- Linkable
- Perform "what if" modeling
- Provide time series analysis

In the end, the true test of a DSS is in its capability to help the user make a better decision.

> **NOTE**
>
> **Communication-driven DSS**   Microsoft Netmeeting is an example of a communication–driven DSS.

Artificial Intelligence and Expert Systems

Auditors should understand artificial intelligence and expert systems, and know that these systems are used to solve complex problems. An expert system is a computer program that contains the knowledge base and set of rules needed to extrapolate new facts from existing knowledge and inputted data. The Prolog and LISP programming languages, used most in developing such systems, are both considered 5GL languages. At the heart of these systems is the knowledge base.

As an example, imagine the knowledge that an auditor can obtain after 20 years on the job. Now consider the possibility of entering this knowledge into a knowledge base, enabling the expert to enter information into the program without a software engineer or programmer. Expert systems are typically designed for a specific purpose. For example, a hospital might have one designed with various types of medical information entered so that if a doctor enters the symptoms of headache, sore jaw, and trouble swallowing, the knowledge base can scan existing data to determine that the patient is suffering from tetanus. The challenge with these systems is in ensuring that accurate data is entered into the system, that access controls are in place, that the proper level of expertise was used in developing the system, and that the knowledge base is secure.

Customer Relationship Management

Customer relationship management (CRM) refers to the tools, techniques, and software companies use to manage their relationship with customers. CRM solutions are designed to track and record everything you need to know about your customers. This includes items such as buying history, budget, timeline, areas of interest, and future planned purchases. Products designed as CRM solutions range from simple off-the-shelf contact-management applications to high-end interactive systems that combine marketing, sales, and executive information. CRM typically involves three areas:

▶ **Sales automation**—Automation of sales force management tasks

▶ **Customer service**—Automation of customer service processes such as requests, comments, complaints, and returns

▶ **Enterprise marketing**—Automation of business enterprise information such as trends, forecasts, business environment, and competition

Supply Chain Management

Supply chain management (SCM) is the science of matching buyers to sellers to improve the way businesses can acquire the raw materials they need to make the products or services they sell to customers. SCM begins with raw materials and ends with finished goods that have been delivered to the customer. SCM involves five basic components:

▶ **Plan**—Definition of the strategy used for managing resources and monitoring the supply chain

▶ **Source**—The process of choosing suppliers

▶ **Make**—The manufacturing process

▶ **Deliver**—The logistics of moving goods and services to the customer

▶ **Return**—The systems developed to return non-compliant products back to the manufacturer

SCM has become more popular as companies move to a global economy with increased competition. The opportunities SCM offers focus on key items in the supply chain process. First is the focus on keeping transportation costs as low as possible while also keeping enough raw material on hand—but no more than needed. With these two items handled properly, production improves as parts and raw materials are available as needed. This helps ensure that products are available to meet customer demand, thereby preventing loss of sales due to product shortages. The key to the SCM process is cooperation between companies in the supply chain and the business. Applying these principles can reduce inventory, increase the transaction speed by exchanging data in real time, and produce higher revenue.

Chapter Summary

Audit applications, systems, and electronic processes are important considerations for the CISA and require an understanding of process. Looking at flowcharts to learn the application is a good place to start. Next, the CISA must examine input, process, and output controls. The CISA can test and validate these controls in a variety of ways, including snapshots, mapping, and tracing and tagging. After all, application testing is a critical part of the process. Testing enables the auditor to evaluate the program and see if it really operates as specified.

The CISA must also be concerned with e-commerce. Although e-commerce provides the capability to be connected to vendors, customers, and others 24×7, it presents a new level of risk: Individuals outside the company can access payment systems and purchase accounting systems. With so much more at risk today and so many more critical decisions to be made, many companies turn to expert systems, data mining, and decision support systems to help solve problems.

Key Terms

- ▶ ACID test
- ▶ ANSI X12
- ▶ Audit monitors
- ▶ Balance data
- ▶ Batch control
- ▶ Entity integrity
- ▶ Hash totals
- ▶ Manual authorization control
- ▶ Referential integrity
- ▶ Relational integrity
- ▶ Standing data
- ▶ System-control parameters
- ▶ Total document numbers
- ▶ Total dollar amounts
- ▶ Total item counts
- ▶ Transaction files

Apply Your Knowledge

This chapter demonstrated the importance of various application controls. Although the ISACA does not test knowledge on the use of any type of application, Exam Prep titles are designed to provide a deeper understanding of the material. Testing application systems, performing integrity testing, and examining application code are all important concerns for the auditor. For this exercise, you will perform some software-auditing activities.

Exercises

4.1 Software Application Audit

In this exercise, you perform a basic audit of a sample of source code.

Estimated Time: 60 minutes

1. Pick an open-source software application to perform a security audit on. You can use standard Linux utilities or download a simple C program from http://www.cis.temple.edu/~ingargio/cis71/code/. After you choose a program, download it and save the source code on your local computer.

2. Determine the lines of source code. You might remember from Chapter 3, "Lifecycle Management," that this is done in two common ways: though lines of source code or function point analysis. Count the lines of code manually and record your result here:

   _____

   _____

   _____

3. Next, use a tool that automatically counts the lines of code for you. For instance, you can use a tool called K-LOC, which is available for download from http://www.analogx.com/contents/download/program/kloc.htm. After downloading, install the program and enter the name and path of the source code you are auditing. Enter the lines of code that K-LOC calculates here:

   _____

   _____

   _____

   Do the numbers entered here agree with those calculated in step 2?

4. Spend some time looking at the source code you downloaded. Look for anything that might be a problem or that you do not understand. Document any findings here:

   _____

   _____

   _____

5. Although a manual audit of a small program is possible, the task becomes much more difficult on larger programs. To ease that task, some programs automatically look at the code. One such tool is Rough Auditing Tool for Security (RATS), which you can download from http://www.securesoftware.com/resources/download_rats.html. After you download the program, install it on your computer.

6. RATS is a source code–scanning tool that enables an auditor to search for program trouble spots and can suggest remedies. Although it might not find every problem, it can detect potential buffer overflows, race conditions, and other common problems. When you execute RATS, it inspects each segment of code and signals an alert for each problem it finds. Spend some time using RATS to look through the application code you previously loaded.

7. Did RATS find any security holes or potential vulnerabilities? If so, describe them here:

_____

_____

_____

This exercise demonstrated how manual methods of an audit, such as counting lines of code or examining code for potential errors, can be supplemented by automated tools that aid in the process.

Exam Questions

1. Which one of the following is not an application system testing methodology?
   - A. Snapshots
   - B. Entity integrity
   - C. Mapping
   - D. Base case system evaluation

2. Which continuous auditing technique detects items that meet specific criteria?
   - A. Audit hooks
   - B. Snapshots
   - C. Integrated test facilities
   - D. Continuous and intermittent simulation

3. Which of the following best defines how a decision support system should be used?
   - A. It uses structured models to solve complex problems.
   - B. It is designed to support nontraditional support activities.
   - C. It is designed to answer structured problems.
   - D. It is designed to answer less structured problems.

4. You have been asked to recommend a control that can detect the following: "An order is normally for no more than 20 items, yet this order is for 2,000." Which control works best to detect this?

   ○ **A.** Validity check

   ○ **B.** Range check

   ○ **C.** Reasonableness check

   ○ **D.** Limit check

5. Decision support systems are usually developed with which of the following types of programming languages?

   ○ **A.** 2GL

   ○ **B.** 3GL

   ○ **C.** 4GL

   ○ **D.** 5GL

6. Referential integrity is best defined as which of the following?

   ○ **A.** Referential integrity ensures that validation routines exist to test data before it is entered into a database and that any modification can be detected.

   ○ **B.** Referential integrity ensures that each tuple contains a primary key.

   ○ **C.** Referential integrity guarantees that all foreign keys reference existing primary keys.

   ○ **D.** Referential integrity is used to divide work so that the results are either all or nothing.

7. Which of the following is most correct about electronic data interchange (EDI)?

   ○ **A.** EDI has no impact on internal or external controls.

   ○ **B.** EDI reduces internal controls.

   ○ **C.** EDI increases internal controls.

   ○ **D.** EDI has no impact on internal controls.

8. Which of the following specifies a control that is used after data has been entered into a system but before it has been processed?

   ○ **A.** Editing

   ○ **B.** Sequence check

   ○ **C.** Balancing

   ○ **D.** Input authorization

9. You have been asked to recommend a continuous audit technique. Which of the following would be considered the least complex?

   ○ **A.** Audit hooks

   ○ **B.** Systems control audit review file and embedded audit modules

   ○ **C.** Snapshots

   ○ **D.** Continuous and intermittent simulation

10. During the project-management process at the design and development phase, which of the following is not a required activity?

    ○ **A.** Study system flowcharts

    ○ **B.** Examine proposed test plans

    ○ **C.** Evaluate output controls

    ○ **D.** Examine proposed audit trails

Answers to Exam Questions

1. **B.** Valid application-testing methodologies include snapshots, mapping, tracing and tagging, using test data, and base case system evaluation. Answer B is an example of a data integrity control.

2. **A.** Audit hooks detect items that meet specific criteria. Answer B is incorrect because snapshots require an audit trail. Answer C is incorrect because integrated test facilities should not be used with test data. Answer D is incorrect because continuous and intermittent simulation requires examination of transactions that meet specified criteria.

3. **D.** Decision support systems (DSS) are software-based applications that help analyze data to answer less structured problems. DSS typically uses knowledge databases, models, and analytical techniques to make decisions. Answer A is incorrect because DSS does not use structured models to solve complex problems. Answer B is incorrect because DSS is designed to support traditional decision-making activities. Answer C is incorrect because DSS is designed to support unstructured problems.

4. **C.** A reasonableness check verifies the reasonableness of the data. Answer A is incorrect because a validity check is usually used with dates. Answer B is incorrect because range checks are typically used to verify that data is within a specified range. Answer D is incorrect because a limit check is used to verify that sales do not exceed a specified limit—as an example, limit one per customer.

5. **C.** Decision support systems are typically developed with 4GL programming languages. Answers A, B, and D are incorrect.

6. **C.** Referential integrity guarantees that all foreign keys reference existing primary keys. Answer A is incorrect because it describes relational integrity; it ensures that validation routines exist to test data before it is entered into a database and that any modification can be detected. Answer B is incorrect because it describes entity integrity; it ensures that each tuple contains a primary key. Answer D is incorrect because it defines ACID: atomicity, consistency, isolation, and durability. Atomicity is used to divide work so that the results are either all or nothing.

7. **B.** The impact of EDI on internal controls is that there are fewer opportunities for review and authorization. Answers A, C, and D are, therefore, incorrect.

8. **B.** An edit control is used with data that has been entered but not yet processed. A sequence check is an example of an edit control. Answers A, C, and D are incorrect because they are all examples of processing controls, which ensure that data remains unchanged until processed by an authorized process.

9. **A.** Audit hooks are considered the least complex because they use embedded hooks that act as red flags if certain conditions are met. Answer B is incorrect because using systems control audit review file and embedded audit modules requires embedded audit software and is considered one of the most complex. Answer C is incorrect because snapshots are considered moderately complex. Answer D is incorrect because continuous and intermittent simulation is also considered moderately complex; it simulates the transaction run.

10. **B.** The examination of proposed test plans is part of the testing phase. Items to be addressed during the design and development phase include studying flowcharts; evaluating input, output, and process controls; examining proposed audit trails; and reviewing how the system will deal with erroneous input.

Need to Know More?

▶ The Need for Audit of the SDLC: http://www.asosai.org/journal2002/articles_1.htm

▶ Is Your Internal Audit Effective?: http://www.gebbusinesssolutions.co.uk/documents/IAEffectivenessArticle.pdf

▶ ACID Compliance: http://www.fredosaurus.com/notes-db/transactions/acid.html

▶ The Evolution of Continuous Online Auditing: http://raw.rutgers.edu/continuousauditing/continuousonlineauditing-p1.html

▶ What Is a Decision Support System?: http://dssresources.com/papers/whatisadss/

▶ Project Management Basics: http://www.managementhelp.org/plan_dec/project/project.htm

▶ Data Mining: http://www.anderson.ucla.edu/faculty/jason.frand/teacher/technologies/palace/datamining.htm

▶ Supply Chain Management: http://www.scmr.com/

PART III

IT Service Delivery and Support

CHAPTER FIVE

Information Systems Hardware and Architecture

This chapter helps you prepare for the Certified Information Systems Auditor (CISA) exam by covering the following ISACA objectives, which include understanding system hardware and the architecture of operating systems and databases. This includes items such as the following:

Tasks

Evaluate service level management practices to ensure that the level of service from internal and external service providers is defined and managed.

Evaluate operations management to ensure that IT support functions effectively meet business needs.

Evaluate data administration practices to ensure the integrity and optimization of databases.

Evaluate change, configuration, and release management practices to ensure that changes made to the organization's production environment are adequately controlled and documented.

Evaluate the functionality of the IT infrastructure (e.g., network components, hardware, system software) to ensure that it supports the organization's objectives.

Knowledge Statements

Knowledge of service-level management practices

Knowledge of operations management best practices (e.g., workload scheduling, network services management, preventive maintenance)

Knowledge of database administration practices

Knowledge of the functionality of system software, including operating systems, utilities, and database management systems

Knowledge of capacity planning and monitoring techniques

Knowledge of processes for managing scheduled and emergency changes to the production systems and/or infrastructure, including change, configuration, release, and patch management practices

Knowledge of incident/problem management practices (e.g., help desk, escalation procedures, tracking)

Knowledge of software licensing and inventory practices

Knowledge of system resiliency tools and techniques (e.g., fault tolerant hardware, elimination of single point of failure, clustering)

Outline

Study Strategies

This chapter addresses information you need to review about computer hardware, operating systems, and related issues. A CISA must understand the technical environment to successfully perform the job tasks. A CISA candidate should review the following primary topics for the exam:

▶ Understand service-level management best practices

▶ Know what lights-out processes are

▶ Understand databases, their structure, and database-management systems

▶ Know the differences between distributed and centralized architectures

▶ Understand operation-management best practices

▶ Describe the change-control and change-management best practices

Introduction

In this chapter, you review information systems operations. This topic involves issues dealing with resource use monitoring, the help desk, and the issues of security involving programming code. Programming code must be handled carefully, and controls must be used to protect the integrity of source code and production applications. This chapter also discusses information systems hardware. This chapter reviews different types of computers, as well as the roles that computers fulfill, such as clients or servers. It also reviews components such as memory, storage, and interfaces. Hardware represents just one part of computer operations; software is another big piece. Computers cannot run without operating systems and software. The design of the operation system plays a big part in how easily controls can be implemented. This also holds true for databases, which hold sensitive information; the auditor must understand the architecture, structure, and controls.

Information Systems Operation

Tasks

▶ Evaluate service level management practices to ensure that the level of service from internal and external service providers is defined and managed.

▶ Evaluate operations management to ensure that IT support functions effectively meet business needs.

▶ Evaluate change, configuration, and release management practices to ensure that changes made to the organization's production environment are adequately controlled and documented.

Knowledge Statements

▶ Knowledge of service level management practices

▶ Knowledge of operations management best practices (e.g., workload scheduling, network services management, preventive maintenance)

▶ Knowledge of capacity planning and monitoring techniques

▶ Knowledge of processes for managing scheduled and emergency changes to the production systems and/or infrastructure, including change, configuration, release, and patch management practices

▶ Knowledge of incident/problem management practices (e.g., help desk, escalation procedures, tracking)

Information systems (IS) management has responsibility for IS operations and must develop policies and procedures to ensure that operations comply with management's strategy. Management must also allocate resources to ensure that resources are available to meet the needs of the organization. This requires deploying systems to monitor IS processes. Monitoring enables management to detect problems, measure the effectiveness of existing systems, and plan for upgrades as needed. Table 5.1 lists and describes the control functions for which IS operations are responsible.

TABLE 5.1 Control Functions

Function	Description
Planning	Efficient and effective use of the resources
	Upgrades and modification to system's process to meet management's goals and objectives
Reviewing	Audit logs and user activities
	Changes to operation schedule
Detecting	Unauthorized access attempts
	Incidents and problems
Monitoring	System performance
	Environmental control to make sure variables such as temperature and humidity are set to maintain the proper conditions for equipment
	Vulnerabilities discovered and addressed
Limiting	Physical access to those who have a need
	Logical access to code and applications to those who have a need
Ensuring	Backup so that operations can be recovered in a timely fashion
	Detailed schedules for operations employees working on all shifts
	Job accountability and adequate audit records collected

In many ways, IS operations is a service organization because it provides services to its users. Many IS departments have mission statements in which they publicly identify the level of service they agree to provide to their customers. When IS services are outsourced, this becomes an even bigger concern. The issue of service is usually addressed by means of a *service level agreement* (SLA). SLAs define performance targets for hardware and software. Some common types of SLAs include the following:

▶ **Uptime agreements (UAs)**—UAs are one of the most well-known type of SLA. UAs detail the agreed-on amount of uptime. As an example, these can be used for network services, such as a WAN link or equipment-like servers.

▶ **Time service factor (TSF)**—The TSF is the percentage of help desk or response calls answered within a given time.

▶ **Abandon rate (AR)**—The AR is the number of callers that hang up while waiting for a service representative to answer.

▶ **First call resolution (FCR)**—The FCR is the number of resolutions that are made on the first call and that do not require the user to call back to the help desk to follow up or seek additional measures for resolution.

IS operations are responsible for monitoring resources, incident/problem handling, infrastructure operations, help desk and support, and change management. The following sections examine each of these functions in more detail.

NOTE

Lights-Out Operations   Lights-out operations can take place without human interaction. These include job scheduling, report generation, report balancing, and backup.

Monitoring Resource Usage

Computer resources are considered a limited commodity because the company provides them to help meet its overall goals. Although many employees would never dream of placing all their long-distance phone calls on a company phone, some of those same individuals have no problem using computer resources for their own personal use. Consider these statistics from http://www.connections-usa.com: One-third of time spent online at work is non–work related, 70% of porn is downloaded between 9 a.m. and 5 p.m., and more than 75% of streaming radio downloads occurs between 5 a.m. and 5 p.m. This means that the company must have an effective monitoring program. Accountability should be maintained for computer hardware, software, network access, and data access. Other resources such as VoIP and email must also be monitored and have sufficient controls in place to prevent its misuse. In a high-security environment, the level of accountability should be even higher and users should be held responsible by logging and auditing many types of activities.

If there is a downside to all this logging, it is that all the information must be recorded and reviewed. Reviewing it can be expedited by using *audit reduction tools*. These tools parse the data and eliminate unneeded information. Another useful tool for an auditor is a *variance detection tool*, which looks for trends that fall outside the realm of normal activity. As an example, if an employee normally enters the building around 8 a.m. and leaves about 5 p.m., but now is seen entering the building at 3 a.m., a variance detection tool can detect this abnormality.

NOTE

Keystroke Monitoring   Capturing a user's keystrokes for later review is an example of monitoring. Users need to be made aware of such activities through acceptable use policies and warning banners.

Challenge

This exercise has you review the application log in Event Viewer on a Windows computer.

1. Click Start, Settings, Control Panel, Administrative Tools, Event Viewer.

2. On the left side of the screen under Tree, select the System Log. Figure 5.1 illustrates where the logs can be seen on the right side of the dialog box.

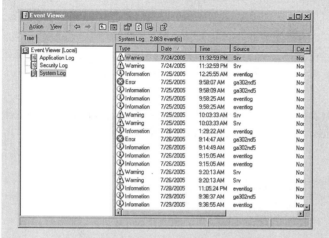

FIGURE 5.1 Event Viewer.

3. Choose an event to examine by double-clicking it.

4. After double-clicking the event, scroll down to the bottom of the Description box where you will find a URL that you can click on that takes you directly to the page on Microsoft's site (after you approve sending the information over the Internet, of course) that provides the explanation, possible causes, and recommended user action.

5. Repeat the process for another event ID and review the results.

Incident Handling

Things will go wrong, and technology does not always work as planned. Part of the process of monitoring is to verify that nothing out of the ordinary has occurred. If unusual activity is discovered, a method of handling the situation needs to be followed. This means that an incident-handling process must be established. Incident handling should follow a structured methodology that has smaller, manageable steps so that incidents can be dealt with in a logical fashion. This process starts with policies, procedures, and guidelines that should be developed before incidents occur. Although incident handling might seem to be a reactive process, it should be based on a proactive plan.

A big part of the plan should address priority. As an example, if the CEO calls about a printer problem and a production server crashes at the same time, parameters need to be established to determine what incidents are addressed first. The time between when an incident occurs and when it is addressed is called the *delay window*. Incident handling should look at ways to reduce the delay window to the smallest value possible. As an example, adding two extra people to the help desk might reduce the delay window from two minutes to under one minute of wait time. Incidents are typically caused by an underlying problem, which is the next topic for discussion.

Problem Management

A problem can be defined as an underlying cause of one or more incidents. Problem management is about more than mitigating an immediate incident; it's about preventing future problems and incidents.

When an incident is confirmed and the underlying problem is determined, the process moves into the known error state. Problem management follows a known process, as outlined in Figure 5.2.

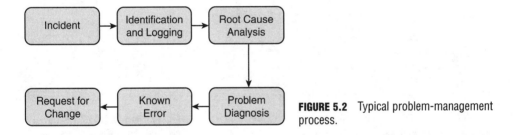

FIGURE 5.2 Typical problem-management process.

Note that the goal of the problem-management process is to find the root cause of problems and institute change management. Identifying problems and instituting change allows for the improvement of service and the reduction of problems. The department responsible for this process should track incidents, response time, and final resolution. These items are discussed in more detail next.

Tracking Abnormal Events

Audit logs help detect misuse, but a method of reporting and tracking abnormal events must be in place. IS operations are highly complex; when various types of hardware, software, and operating systems are combined, things are bound to occasionally go wrong and/or abnormal events are bound to occur. It's important to be able to track these events and document their occurrence. A manual log or an automated process can be used to perform this tracking activity. Recorded items should include errors caused by the following:

> ▶ Programs

> ▶ Systems

> ▶ Operators

> ▶ Networks

> ▶ Hardware

> ▶ Telecommunications systems

The contents of the log should be restricted. Only authorized individuals should be able to update items or post the final resolution. Separation of duties should be practiced so that the same person who can create log entries cannot close a log entry. Table 5.2 shows an example of what should be found in a log.

TABLE 5.2   Error Log Entry

Item	Description
Error Date	1/12/2007
Error Code	312
Error Description	Backup failed to initialize
Source of Error	Sales Backup Server
Error Reported by	Rueben James

The problem management's log should be reviewed periodically to ensure that problems are being addressed and that resolution is occurring in a timely manner. Problems that are not resolved within a reasonable period of time should be escalated. The mechanisms by which this happens should be detailed in policy and be thoroughly documented. Problem escalation should include the following information:

> ▶ Who can address the problem

> ▶ Lists of problems that require immediate response

> ▶ Types of problems that should be addressed only during normal working hours

EXAM ALERT

Auditing Problem Reports   The auditor should know to review the problem log to verify that problems are being resolved. Auditors must also check to see that the most appropriate department or individual is handling the problems.

Help Desk and Support

The help desk has the responsibility of providing technical support to the organization and its employees. The help desk is typically charged with identifying problems, performing root cause analysis, and tracking change management or problem resolution. Many companies provide help desk functionality by means of toll-free phone numbers, websites, or email. After a user contacts the help desk, he is issued a *trouble ticket*. Figure 5.3 shows an example of a web-based trouble ticket.

Submit New Trouble Ticket
ResTech > Trouble Ticket System > Submit New Trouble Ticket

Summary: Forgot Password

Description:
I have forgotten my password and tried several times to login to my domain. What do I need to do to reset the password?

Category: Network Security
Location:
Attached file: Browse...
Severity: High
Full Name: Jan Tankersly
E-mail: JanT@thesolutionfirm.com
Telephone: 555-1212

FIGURE 5.3 Example of a web-based trouble ticket.

Trouble tickets are assigned unique IDs, which are used to track the time of entry, response, and resolution. The trouble ticket is typically assigned a level of priority at the time it is created. As an example, most companies use a Level 1 help desk priority to answer common questions and easy-to-address problems. Level 1 help desk employees typically use a script or decision tree to step through possible problems and solutions. An example of a Level 1 connectivity script is shown here:

STEP BY STEP

5.1 Troubleshooting Connectivity Problems

1. Do you have connectivity to the web? Can you access the company webserver at
   `http://192.168.1.254`?

2. Can you ping 192.168.1.254? (Yes/No)

3. Can you verify that the network cable is attached to your computer and is connected to the wall jack? (Yes/No)

4. Open a command prompt and enter `ipconfig/all`. Can you please read off the settings? (Yes/No)

5. Click Start, Settings, Control Panel, Network Connections, Local Area Network Connection. Next select the Properties button. Now double-click on Internet Protocol. Please read off the values listed in each field. Are these correct? (Yes/No)

6. All obvious checks have been completed and the problem has not been resolved. Refer problem to Level 2 response.

Problems that cannot be resolved by Level 1 are escalated to Level 2 response. Level 2 help desk analysts handle the most difficult calls. Small organizations might have help desk analysts who answer all types of calls; however, many larger companies separate calls by the nature of the problem. Common teams include the following:

- **Deskside team**—Responsible for desktops and laptops

- **Network team**—Responsible for network issues

- **Application software team**—Responsible for application issues

- **Printer team**—Responsible for printers and printer-related problems

- **Telecom team**—Responsible for VoIP systems, PBX, voice mail, modems, and fax machines

NOTE

Crossover Responsibilities   In real life it can sometimes be a challenge to find out who is really responsible, as there can be some crossover within technologies and duties. For example, the Telecom team works the PBX, but the PBX has a VoIP firewall that the Network team administers.

Regardless of how the team is structured, it has several responsibilities:

- Document problems

- Prioritize issues

- Follow up on unresolved problems

- Close out problems

- Document results

The next section shifts the topic focus to change management and how it's related to help desk and problem management.

Change-Management Process

Change management is a formalized process whose purpose is to control modifications made to systems and programs. Without effective change-management procedures, situations can arise where unauthorized changes occur, potentially endangering the security of the organization or leading to operations being performed in an untested or unknown state. These questions must be asked during the change-management process:

- ▶ **Time scale**—How quickly is the change needed?

- ▶ **Scope**—How big of a change is needed?

- ▶ **Capability**—Does the company have the in-house skills and capability to implement change?

- ▶ **Cost**—What is the cost of the change?

- ▶ **Time completion**—What is the time frame to make the change?

- ▶ **Approval**—Who must approve the change and what is the approval process?

Companies typically customize the change-management process for their particular environment. The change-management process should be designed to ensure that the benefits of any potential change are properly analyzed and that changes to a system are made in a structured manner. On a higher level, change management consists of three stages, as illustrated in Figure 5.4.

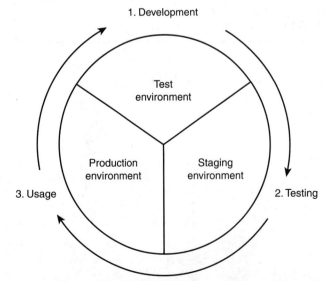

FIGURE 5.4 General change-management process.

Changes should be looked at closely to make sure that no proposed change affects the process negatively or reduces the quality of service. The change-management process should include steps for change development, testing, and usage. Change management should have an escape path so that changes can be backed out if the change is unsuccessful.

Program Library Systems

Change management is especially critical for program library systems, which typically control all applications, including accessing code and compiling it to an executable program. Program library systems should also contain an audit function so that the date, time, or name of a specific programmer that accessed the library can be identified. Accountability must be maintained so that the auditor can trace any changes to code or compiled programs. Specifically, these systems should prevent programmers from directly accessing production source code and object libraries. If a programmer needs the code, it should be released only through a third-party control group that has the capability to copy it to the programmer's library. If compiled code is to be placed back into production again, the programmer should not be able to do this directly. The programmer should again go through the control group and have it place the approved code back into the production library. Sufficient controls should be in place to prevent nonproduction code from inadvertently being executed in the production environment. Ensuring that these requirements are met is a complicated task that can be made easier by verifying that the program library system has certain capabilities:

▶ **Integrity**—Each piece of source code should be assigned a unique ID and version number. Security should be maintained through password-controlled directories, encryption, and regular backups.

▶ **Update**—Any changes or modification to source code should be tracked and an audit trail should be produced.

▶ **Reporting**—Controls should be in place to report changes to code or any modification.

▶ **Interface**—Library-management systems need to interface with the OS, access-control system, audit, and access-control mechanisms.

Auditors might be asked to verify existing source code at some point. If so, the auditor might want to use source code comparison software. This software compares a previously obtained copy of the source code to a current copy and can identify any changes. Although this is somewhat effective, it should be noted that after changes are entered into the code and then removed, they cannot be detected. As an example of this shortcoming, suppose that a programmer adds code to the accounting software to shave off a few cents from each transaction and then adds them to a secret account that he has set up. After compiling the code and placing it in production, the programmer removes the added lines of code from the source and returns it to its original state. The source code comparison software would not detect this.

EXAM ALERT

Source Code Comparison   A CISA candidate should be aware that source code comparison does have its limitations. As an example, it cannot detect a change in source code that has been changed and restored between checks. Compiled code must also be examined. The test might review these types of items.

These issues emphasize the fact that executable code must also be examined. Items such as time stamps and integrity checks can be examined on compiled code to make sure that nonvalidated programs are not in production. At no time should the programmer or developer have direct access to the production libraries. In some environments, users might create their own programs. This can be particularly challenging to the auditor because there are few controls in place. More than one user can use these programs, and, without the guidance of professional programmers, these programs might be flawed. Such programs can easily introduce flaws into data files.

Release Management

Release management is the discipline within software management of controlling the release of software to end users. Released software is software that has been approved for release to users. Releases can be divided into one of several categories:

▶ **Emergency fix**—These are updates that must be done quickly, sometimes referred to as a *patch*. An emergency fix is designed to fix a small number of known problems. These can be dangerous because they can introduce additional errors into the program.

▶ **Minor release**—Minor releases contain small enhancements or fixes that supersede an emergency fix. Minor releases are used to improve performance, reliability, or security.

▶ **Major release**—Major releases supersede minor releases and emergency fixes. They are designed to provide a significant improvement to the program. Major releases are usually scheduled to be released at predetermined times, such as quarterly, biannually, or yearly.

Updates to programs are also sometimes referred to as *patches*. A patch is an additional piece of code designed to remedy an existing bug or problem. As an example, Microsoft releases patches in three formats:

▶ **Hotfixes**—These updates address a single problem or bug encountered by a customer.

▶ **Roll-ups**—A roll-up fix combines the updates of several hotfixes into a single update file.

▶ **Service packs**—These are a collection of all hotfixes released since the application's release, including hotfixes released in previous service pack versions.

Each of these patch formats are distributed with release or patch notes which should be reviewed.

What is important about this process is that the organization has a schedule for deploying and updating applications. A rollout plan needs to be established and a system should be in place to test releases and phases of their use within the organization. An organization should also have a rollback plan so that it can back out of the process if something fails. The Quality Assurance group is responsible for overseeing much of this process. Quality Assurance personnel must verify that changes are authorized, tested, and implemented in a structured method. Most Quality Assurance groups follow a Plan-Do-Check-Act (PDCA) approach. This allows Quality Assurance to ensure quality and verify that changes to programs or applications are met and/or exceed customer needs.

Post-Deployment

Many might believe that in post-deployment, the job is complete; however, this is not the case. Programs and the data that programs use require ongoing protection. This means performing periodic vulnerability tests. After major changes, a business must perform an impact analysis, as well as secure certification and accreditation. Other post-deployment issues include these:

► Testing backup and recovery

► Ensuring proper controls for data and reports

► Verifying that security features cannot be bypassed or disabled

► Validating the security of system resources and data

Information Systems Hardware

Task

► Evaluate the functionality of the IT infrastructure (e.g., network components, hardware, system software) to ensure that it supports the organization's objectives.

Knowledge Statements

► Knowledge of capacity planning and monitoring techniques

► Knowledge of system resiliency tools and techniques (e.g., fault tolerant hardware, elimination of single point of failure, clustering)

This section reviews hardware used in organizations. It begins by reviewing the central processing unit (CPU) and then moves on to look at other components found in a computer.

The Central Processing Unit

At the heart of every computer is the CPU. The CPU is capable of executing a series of basic operations; it can fetch instructions and then process them. CPUs have four basic tasks: fetch, decode, execute, and write back. Because CPUs have very specific designs, the operating system must be developed to work with the CPU. CPUs have two primary components:

▶ **The arithmetic logic unit**—Computations are performed here, in the brain of the CPU.

▶ **The control unit**—This unit handles the sequence of operations for the CPU and is also responsible for the retrieval of instructions and data.

CPUs also have different types of registers to hold data and instructions. Together the components are responsible for the recall and execution of programs. CPUs have made great strides, as the timeline in Table 5.3 illustrates.

TABLE 5.3 CPU Advancements

CPU	Date	Transistors	Clock Speed
8080	1974	6,000	2MHz
80386	1986	275,000	12.5MHz
Pentium	1993	3,100,000	60MHz
Intel Core2	2006	291,000,000	2.66GHz

NOTE

The CPU   The CPU consists of the control unit, the arithmetic logic unit, and registers. The arithmetic unit performs computations and is the brain of the CPU.

CPUs can be classified according to several categories, based on their functionality:

▶ **Multiprogramming**—The CPU can interleave two or more programs for execution at any one time.

▶ **Multitasking**—The CPU can perform one or more tasks or subtasks at a time.

▶ **Multiprocessor**—The computer has the support for more than one CPU. As an example, Windows 95 does not support the multiprocessor, but Windows Longhorn does.

CPUs can operate in user mode or kernel mode. These modes specify what state the CPU is working in. Kernel mode is a privileged or supervisory state, which provides a greater level of protection. As an example, if the CPU is running the Windows operating system (OS) and needs to perform a trusted OS operation, it can do so in kernel mode; yet, if it needs to run an application of unknown origin, it can do so in user mode. This sets up rings of protection, as Figure 5.5 demonstrates. This model provides a level of access control and granularity. As you move toward the outer bounds of the user mode of the model, the ring numbers increase and the level of trust decreases. User mode is also sometimes called the general user state because this is the level in which most users operate.

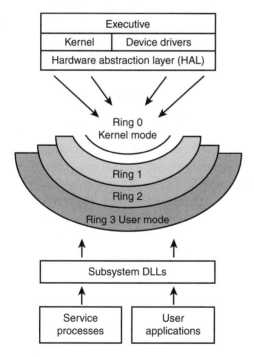

FIGURE 5.5 CPU operating modes.

NOTE

The CISA Exam Is Vendor Neutral No vendor-specific hardware or technology is included on the exam. If it is mentioned in this chapter, it is to better illustrate concepts or techniques.

One Man Who Changed the World

Modern computers would not be possible without the work of Jack Kilby. Although Jack applied to the Massachusetts Institute of Technology, he did not make the cut and failed to even achieve the minimum entrance score. He went on to get his electrical engineering degree from the University of Wisconsin. By the late 1950s, he was an employee of Texas Instruments.

In the summer of 1958, when most employees had left for summer vacation, Jack remained behind—not because he wanted to, but because he had not yet accrued enough days of vacation time. Jack used this time to put together a lab full of used, borrowed, and improvised equipment. Using this equipment, he designed the first semiconductor microchip. His efforts in the field paved the way for the CPUs we use today.

Whereas some might have been satisfied to coast on such a grand achievement, Jack went on to another first in 1966 by being part of the team that invented the handheld calculator. Jack died in 2005, but he lived long enough to see an industry grow from his first simple circuit to one that is worth hundreds of billions of dollars and that has changed the way we all live.

Memory

A computer is not just a CPU—memory is also an important component. When a CPU processes instructions, the results must be stored, most likely in *random access memory* (RAM). RAM is considered volatile memory because if power is lost, data is destroyed. RAM can be static because it uses circuit latches to represent binary data, or it can be dynamic. Dynamic RAM (DRAM) must be periodically refreshed every few milliseconds. RAM is not the only memory type; *read-only memory* (ROM) is a second type. ROM is used to permanently hold data so that even if the computer is turned off, the information remains; thus, it is considered nonvolatile. ROM is typically used to load and store firmware. Some common types of ROM include the following:

▶ Erasable Programmable Read-Only Memory (EPROM)

▶ Electrically Erasable Programmable Read-Only Memory (EEPROM)

▶ Flash memory

▶ Programmable logic devices (PLD)

A longer form of storage is secondary storage, also considered nonvolatile. *Hard disk drives* are an example of secondary storage. Hard drives have a series of platters, read/write heads, motors, and drive electronics contained within a case designed to prevent contamination. *Floppies*, or diskettes, are also considered secondary storage. The data on diskettes is organized in tracks and sectors. Tracks are narrow concentric circles on the disk. Sectors are pie-shaped slices of the disk. The disk is made of a thin plastic material coated with iron oxide. This is much like the material found in a backup tape or cassette tape. As the disk spins, the disk drive heads move in and out to locate the correct track and sector. It then reads or writes the requested track and sector.

Compact discs (CDs) are a type of optical media that use a laser/optoelectronic sensor combination to read or write data. A CD can be read-only, write once, or rewriteable. CDs can hold up to around 800 MB on a single disk. A CD is manufactured by applying a thin layer of aluminum to what is primarily hard, clear plastic. During manufacturing, or whenever a CD/R is burned, small bumps or, pits, are placed in the surface of the disk. These bumps, or pits, are converted into binary ones or zeros. Unlike the tracks and sectors of a floppy, a CD consists of one long spiral track that begins at the inside of the disk and continues toward the outer edge. *Digital video discs* (DVDs) are similar to a CD because both are a type of optical medium, but DVDs hold more data. The data capacity of DVDs ranges from 4.7 to 17.08 GB, depending on type—R, RW, RAM, 5, 9, 10, or 18. One contender for the next generation of optical storage is the *Blu-ray* Disc. These optical disks can hold 50 GB or more of data.

Memory cards and sticks are another form of storage. The explosion of PDAs, digital cameras, and other computerized devices has fueled their growth. One of the most well-known is the PC memory card that came out in the 1980s, originally called the Personal Computer Memory Card International Association (PCMCIA) card. Newer but smaller versions, such as a smart media card and multimedia cards, are not much bigger than a postage stamp. Since the late 1990s, USB memory drives have become increasingly popular. These floppy disk killers are nothing more than a Universal Serial Bus (USB) connector with a Flash memory chip. These devices can easily be found in 2 GB format and up. Many companies have become increasingly worried about such devices because they can hold such a large amount of information and can be easily moved in and out of the company's facility in someone's pocket or purse.

I/O Bus Standards

From a CPU point of view, the various adaptors plugged into the computer are external devices. These connectors and the bus architecture used to move data to the devices have changed over time. Some common bus architectures follow:

▸ **The ISA bus**—The Industry Standard Architecture (ISA) bus started as an 8-bit bus designed for IBM PCs. It is now obsolete.

▸ **The PCI bus**—The Peripheral Component Interface (PCI) bus was developed by Intel and served as a replacement for the ISA and other bus standards.

▸ **The SCSI bus**—The Small Computer Systems Interface (SCSI) bus allows a variety of devices to be daisy-chained off a single controller. Many servers use the SCSI bus for their preferred hard drive solution.

Two serial bus standards have also gained wide market share, USB and FireWire. USB overcame the limitations of traditional serial interfaces. USB devices can communicate at speeds up to 480 Mbps. Up to 127 devices can be chained together. USB is used for Flash memory, cameras, printers, and even iPods. One of the fundamental designs of the USB is that it has such broad product support, and many devices are immediately recognized when connected. The competing standard for USB is FireWire, or IEEE 1394. This design is found on many Apple computers and also on digital audio and video equipment. Because of licensing fees, FireWire has not gained the market share that USB has. Figure 5.6 shows USB and FireWire adaptors.

FIGURE 5.6 USB and FireWire adaptors.

CAUTION

Open USB and FireWire Ports   Open USB and FireWire ports can present a big security risk. Organizations should consider disabling ports or using a software package to maintain some type of granular control. New U3 memory sticks enable users to autoexecute programs, whether legitimate or malicious. This is an issue of growing concern.

Computer Types

Computers can be categorized by the role they play in the organization, their amount of processing power, and their architecture or design. Common types include servers, supercomputers, mainframes, client desktops, laptops, and PDAs, as described in Table 5.4.

TABLE 5.4   Computer Types

Computer Type	Description
Server	Computers that share resources such as applications, files, or web content with other computers and clients on a network. Servers are typically dedicated to one task, such as a web server, file server, or DHCP server.
Supercomputer	Large expensive computers that have great processing power. An example is the Cray supercomputer. Supercomputers can cost billions of dollars and have extremely vast capabilities.
Mainframe	Large general-purpose computers that once were the predominant type of computer. Mainframes are usually used in a centralized design and generally have their own proprietary operating systems.
Client	Desktops based on microprocessor technology, found throughout organizations. Client systems enable users to perform many activities, such as word processing and spreadsheet activities, locally. Client systems typically use either the Microsoft or Linux operating systems.
Laptop	Lightweight and easily transportable, laptops are similar to desktops but have built-in battery supplies and allow workers to make their computer mobile. One major problem is theft. Laptop computers should use encryption to protect confidential information from loss or exposure.
PDAs/Handhelds	Small computing devices, such as Blackberrys, Palm Pilots, and cell phones. These devices have some computing power along with the capability to check email, perform scheduling, and make and receive phone calls. Theft is also a problem for these devices.

Computer Configurations and Roles

Most companies today have their computers configured in one of two configurations: peer-to-peer or client/server. In a peer-to-peer network, each system is both a server and a client. Peer-to-peer systems split their time between these two duties. Peer-to-peer networks are usually found only in small networks because of the following concerns:

▶ Desktop systems are not optimized to be servers and usually cannot handle a large traffic load.

▶ A large number of requests will most likely degrade system performance.

▶ Peer-to-peer systems leave each user in charge of his own security, so many users are in charge, not one central body or department.

EXAM ALERT

Peer-to-Peer   Peer-to-peer networks do not scale well and are not efficient for large organizations. Peer-to-peer networks also suffer from security concerns that make them a poor choice for larger companies.

Client/server networks are configured in such a way that clients make requests and servers respond. Examples of client/server systems include Microsoft 2003 server and Novell NetWare. Client/server networks have the following characteristics:

- Servers are loaded with dedicated server software.

- Servers are designed for specific needs.

- User accounts and access privileges are configured on the server.

- Client software is loaded on the client's computer.

- Clients don't service other clients.

Within a client/server network, a server holds some basic defined roles. These are some of the most common configurations:

- **Print server**—Print servers are usually located close to printers and enable many users to access the printer and share its resources.

- **File server**—File servers give users a centralized site for storing files. This provides an easier way to back up a network because only one file server needs to be backed up, not all individual workstations.

- **Program server**—Program servers are also known as application servers. This service enables users to run applications that are not installed on the end user's system. This is a very popular concept in thin client environments. Licensing is an important consideration.

- **Web server**—Web servers provide web services to internal and external users via web pages. An example of a web address or uniform resource locator (URL) is www.theso-lutionfirm.com.

- **Database server**—Database servers store and access data. This includes information such as product inventory, price lists, customer lists, and employee data. Databases hold sensitive information and require well-designed security controls.

- **Proxy server**—Proxy servers stand in place of the client and provide indirect access. Proxy servers can provide caching services and improve security. Figure 5.7 shows an example of a proxy server.

Most networks have some common hardware elements. These are discussed in depth in Chapter 6, "Information Systems Used for IT Delivery and Support," but Table 5.5 introduces them.

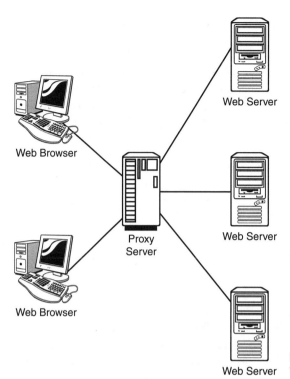

FIGURE 5.7   Proxy server for connection to website.

TABLE 5.5   Common Hardware Elements Used for IT Delivery

Name	Description
Firewall	A specialized device that inspects and either permits or denies traffic traveling into and out of the organization's network.
Intrusion-detection system (IDS)	A detective device that "sniffs" network or host traffic and inspects it for malicious content.
Intrusion-prevention system (IPS)	A preventive device that monitors network or host traffic and can block malicious content.
Router	A device used to link physically separate networks.
Switch	A data link device used to increase performance and reduce traffic collisions.
Load balancer	Distributes traffic among several different devices. Commonly used for distributing web traffic on large domains.
Hub	A physical-layer device used for connectivity.

Radio Frequency Identification

Radio frequency identification (RFID) tags are extremely small electronic devices that consist of a microchip and antenna. These devices send out small amounts of information when activated. Companies are excited about this technology because it means they can forget about barcode scanning and improve product management. As an example, employees can quickly scan an entire pallet of goods and record the information. An RFID tag can be designed in one of several different ways:

▶ **Active**—Active tags have a battery or power source that is used to power the microchip.

▶ **Passive**—These devices have no battery; the RFID reader powers them. The reader generates an electromagnetic wave that induces a current in the RFID tag.

▶ **Semipassive**—These hybrid devices use a battery to power the microchip, but they transmit by harnessing energy from the reader.

Passive RFID tags can hold about 2 KB of data, which is enough to hold more information than a bar code. Active RFID tags can hold even more information. Both types offer companies a wealth of information. If development of this technology proceeds as planned, RFID tags could someday allow retailers to add up the price of purchased goods as shoppers leave the store and deduct the charges directly from the customer's credit card. Another use for RFID tags is in the inventory and audit process. Current technology requires each item to be counted by hand. However, in the future, RFID readers strategically placed throughout the store would automatically determine the amount and type of a product sitting on the store's shelves.

Using RFID tags on animals and people has even been proposed. Some individuals have already implanted RFID tags. In response to a growing rabies problem, Portugal has passed a law that all dogs must be embedded with RFID devices. Government officials have advocated that these devices become a standard issue for individuals who work as firemen, policemen, or emergency rescue workers whose jobs place them in situations in which their identifications could become lost or destroyed.

Security concerns are based on the fact that some of these devices are less than half the size of a grain of rice, so their placement possibilities are endless. If these devices are used in retail services, some have expressed concern that such devices might not be disabled when the products are taken home. Some even fear that high-tech thieves might someday be able to park outside your home and scan to determine what valuables are worth stealing.

> **NOTE**
>
> **RFID Passports**   In 2006, the United States and many European countries began using RFID passports. Although some envision this technology as a way to hold biometric information and better guard the nation's borders, others fear potential vulnerabilities. One such vulnerability was realized in August 2006 when German hackers succeeded in cloning a Dutch RFID e-passport. Because of this event and other potential vulnerabilities, the United States has decided to place a metallic lining inside RFID passport covers in an attempt to prevent RFID passports from being scanned or snooped when closed.

Hardware Maintenance Program

Just as your car requires periodic oil changes and maintenance, hardware and equipment requires maintenance. It is usually much cheaper to maintain a piece of equipment than it is to repair it. Computers have a habit of trapping a large amount of dust that, over a period of time, coats all the inner components and acts as a thermal blanket. This layer of dust raises the operating temperature and reduces the lifespan of the equipment.

Internal employees might maintain some types of equipment, while vendors might service others. Regardless of who performs the maintenance, it should be documented and recorded. When performing an audit, the auditor should examine the existing procedures to make sure that a maintenance program has been developed, performed, and documented. If outside vendors are given access to sensitive areas, it should be verified that they are properly cleared before receiving access.

> **NOTE**
>
> **Tape-Management Systems**   Automated tape-management systems reduce errors and speed load time by automatically locating and loading tape volumes as needed.

Hardware Monitoring and Capacity Management

The best way to prevent problems is to monitor current activity. Monitoring should include the following:

- **Availability reports**—These reports indicate availability. The key to these reports is determining when and why resources are unavailable.

- **Hardware error reports**—These reports indicate hardware problems and can be used to look for recurring problems.

- **Utilization reports**—These reports look at overall usage and can be used to help plan needed upgrades to the infrastructure.

EXAM ALERT

Utilization CISA candidates should know that utilization rates above 95% require attention to determine needed upgrades and that short-term fixes might include countermeasures such as reducing unneeded activities or shifting schedules so that some activities take place at less demanding times, such as the late-night or second shift.

Capacity management provides the capability to monitor and measure usage in real time and forecast future needs before they are required. Capacity management requires analyzing current utilization, past performance, and capacity changes. Table 5.6 outlines the indicators for capacity-management issues.

TABLE 5.6   Capacity-Management Issues

Item	Indicator
CPU utilization	High usage indicates the need for a processor or computer upgrade.
Computer storage	Lack of space indicates the need for additional hard disk storage.
Network bandwidth	Low bandwidth might indicate the need for a network upgrade to gigabit.
Terminal utilization	High utilization might indicate the need for additional terminals.
Memory utilization	High memory usage indicates the need for additional memory.
Total number of users	Additional users usually indicate the need for more terminals or computers.
Application usage	High application usage requires inspection of licensing agreements.
Service level agreements	Growth requires a review of existing service level agreements.

REVIEW BREAK

Table 5.7 provides a comparison of various types of computer hardware and equipment. These are terms that the CISA should be familiar with. Each item in the table is followed by an attribute that offers an inherent quality or chacteristic that is worth noting.

TABLE 5.7   Comparison of Computer Hardware

Item	Attribute	Description
RAM	Volatile memory	RAM is used for short-term storage of information.
ROM	Static	ROM is used to hold information permanently.
EPROM	Erasable ROM	EPROM is ROM that can be erased and rewritten to, as needed.
CDs	Storage standard	In many ways, CDs have replaced floppies, up to about 800 MBs.
Thumb drives	Portable	The small size and massive storage of this new storage standard make it a potential security risk.

TABLE 5.7   Continued

Item	Attribute	Description
ISA bus	Old	The original design dates to the first IBM PCs.
SCSI bus	Commercial	Used by companies that need performance, the SCSI bus is slowly being replaced by the Serial ATA bus.
PCI	Widely used	This is found in almost all computers built today.
Firewall	Security	A firewall is used to control ingress or egress network traffic.
IDS	Detective device	An IDS can alert management to activity that could be a security risk.
Router	Logical device	A router connects networks logically and separates broadcast domains.
Switch	Performance	A switch increases performance by preventing collisions.
Hub	Connectivity	This physical-layer device forwards all traffic.

Information Systems Architecture and Software

Task

▶ Evaluate data administration practices to ensure the integrity and optimization of databases.

Knowledge Statements

▶ Knowledge of database administration practices

▶ Knowledge of the functionality of system software, including operating systems, utilities, and database management systems

▶ Knowledge of software licensing and inventory practices

Software differs from hardware: It is the code that runs on computer platforms. Software is loaded into RAM and executed by the CPU. Software can be used for an operating system, a database, access control, file transfer, a user application, and even network management. Before discussing operating systems and databases, you should review the different ways in which software can be developed and learn about some of its common attributes.

Software Development

At the core of systems architecture is computer hardware, which requires programs or code to operate. Programs can be hard-coded instruction or firmware, or can be executed by a higher-layer process. Regardless of the format, code must be translated into a language that the computer understands. The three most common methods of conversion are as follows:

▶ **Assembler**—An assembler is a program that translates assembly language into machine language.

▶ **Compiler**—A compiler translates a high-level language into machine language.

▶ **Interpreter**—An interpreter does not assemble or compile; it translates the program line by line. Interpreters fetch and execute.

One big hurdle that software developers face is that computers and humans speak very different languages. As an example, computers work well with assembly language, as demonstrated here:

```
mov al, 061h
ld length,%
mov bl, 10   ; hex=0ah or bin=00001010b
```

Humans work well with English and other high-level languages. To bridge this gap, many programming languages have been developed over the years—in fact, they date back to before the computer era. Programming languages are used to convert sets of instructions into a vocabulary, such as the assembly that a computer can understand. The goal is to convert instructions into a format that allows the computer to complete a specific task. Examples of common programming languages include the following:

▶ **COBOL**—Common Business-Oriented Language is a third-generation programming language used for business finance and administration.

▶ **C, C-Plus, C++**—The C programming language replaced B and was designed by Dennis Ritchie. C was originally designed for UNIX; it is popular and widely used, but vulnerable to buffer overflows.

▶ **FORTRAN**—This language features an optimized compiler that is widely used by scientists for writing numerically intensive programs.

▶ **Java**—A relatively new language developed in 1995 by Sun Microsystems, it uses a sandbox scheme for security.

NOTE

Sandbox Scheme   A sandbox scheme is a software security mechanism designed to limit the the ability of untrusted code. This allows programs from unknown or untrusted vendors to be executed on a system without the fear that the programs will access privileged commands.

▶ **Visual Basic**—This programming language was designed for anyone to use and makes it possible to develop practical programs quickly.

This list offers details on just some of the available programming languages. Others include .NET, Prolog, Python, Perl, and Ruby. Computer languages can be designed to be like machine language and can be made more natural so that humans can easily understand them. This is why languages are placed into generations. The generation of the programming language defines where it fits into this hierarchy. The five generations of computer languages are as follows:

- **Generation One**—Machine language

- **Generation Two**—Assembly language

- **Generation Three**—High-level language, such as FORTRAN

- **Generation Four**—Very high-level language, such as Structured Query Language (SQL)

- **Generation Five**—Natural language, such as Prolog or LISP

NOTE

Decompilers   When a programmer writes programs to be sold to the public, the source code normally is not provided. Decompilers can analyze the compiled code and rebuild the original source code. The software license might prohibit decompiling, but unscrupulous competitors or software hackers might still attempt it.

Operating Systems

An operating system (OS) is key to computer operation because it is the computer program that controls software resources and interacts with system hardware. The OS performs everything from low-level tasks to higher-level interaction with the user. The OS is responsible for managing resources such as the processor, memory, disk space, RAM, and so on. The OS also provides a stable, defined platform that applications can use. This allows the application to deal with the OS and not have to directly address the hardware. The OS is responsible for managing the following key resources (see Figure 5.8):

- **Input devices**—Keyboard, mouse, microphone, webcam, and so on

- **Output devices**—Monitor, printer, soundcard, and so on

- **Memory**—RAM, ROM, CMOS, virtual memory, and so on

- **CPU usage**—Available time, processing order

- **Network communication**—Modems, network interface card (NIC), Bluetooth, and so on

- **External storage**—DVD drive, CD-ROM drive, floppies, hard drive, USB drives, and so on

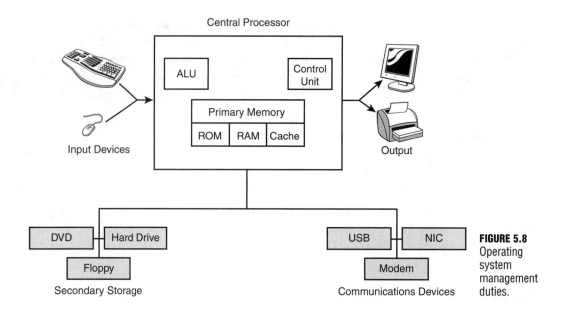

FIGURE 5.8
Operating
system
management
duties.

An OS has the capability to interact with the CPU in different ways so that there are different levels of control. In user mode, the operator has limited ability to perform privileged functions. In supervisory mode, the user has total access to the security kernel and has complete access to all memory, devices, and instructions. Some system utilities and other processes run in supervisory mode and, therefore, must be closely controlled because they could be used to bypass normal security mechanisms. Some types of malware, such as rootkits, have the capability to run in supervisory mode. This means that they can corrupt the kernel and do basically anything they want, including lie to the user about their presence, thereby avoiding detection.

EXAM ALERT

Supervisory Mode   CISA candidates should know that any user allowed to run programs in kernel mode can bypass any type of security mechanism and gain complete control of the system. Many system utilities run in supervisory mode and should be under strict control.

Secondary Storage

Other than using long-term storage of information and programs, the OS can use secondary storage. A modern OS can also use secondary storage for *virtual memory*, the combination of the computer's primary memory, RAM, and secondary storage, the hard drive. By combining these two technologies, the OS can make the CPU believe that it has much more memory than it actually does. If the OS is running short on RAM, it can instruct the CPU to use the hard drive as storage. Virtual memory uses the hard drive to save data in pages that can be swapped back and forth between the hard drive and RAM, as needed.

> **CAUTION**
>
> **Information Leakage** Security issues are possible with sensitive data written to swap that becomes accessible to non-supervisor users.

Although memory plays an important part in the world of storage, other long-term types of storage are also needed. One of these is sequential storage. Anyone who is old enough to remember the Commodore 64 knows about sequential storage: These earlier computers used a cassette tape recorder to store programs. Tape drives are a type of sequential storage that must be read sequentially from beginning to end. Indexed sequential storage is similar to sequential storage, except that it logically orders data according to a key and then accesses the data based on the key. Finally, the direct access method does not require a sequential read; the system can identify the location of the information and go directly to that location to read the data.

Data Communication Software

At a miminum level, data communications requires the following:

- ▶ A source (transmitter)
- ▶ A communication channel (voice, line, and so on)
- ▶ A receiver

In the world of electronic communications, the receiver is known as a *data sink*. The data sink is any electronic device that is capable of receiving a data signal. One-way communication is referred to as *simplex*. Two-way communication is known as *duplex*. Duplex communication systems allow both parties to send and receive date simultaneously. Data communication systems are designed to accurately transmit communication between two points. Without data communications, computer operations wouldn't be possible. One person who helped make that a reality was Bob Beaman. Bob helped lead the team that developed the American Standard Code for Information Interchange (ASCII) standard. ASCII was of great importance at the time it was developed in 1967 because it defined a 128-character set. This standard was used for years to come for computer communications. ASCII was not the first communication standard to be developed, however. The Extended Binary Coded Decimal Interchange Code (EBCDIC) was developed in early 1960 by IBM and designed for use with mainframe systems.

It debuted alongside the IBM 360. EBCDIC uses 8 bits and has a 256-character set. Unicode is an industry standard designed to replace previous standards. Unicode uses 16 bits, so it can support more than 65,000 unique characters. This makes it useful for languages other than English, including Chinese and Japanese characters.

Database-Management Systems

Databases provide a convenient method by which to catalog, index, and retrieve information. Databases consist of collections of related records, such as name, address, phone number, and date of birth. The structured description of the objects of these databases and their relationship is known as the schema. Databases are widely used. As an example, if you go online to search for flight times from Houston to Las Vegas, the information most likely is pulled from a database as well as the stored user's credit card number that was previously provided to the airline. If you are not familiar with databases, you need to know these terms:

▶ **Aggregation**—The process of combining several low-sensitivity items to produce a high-sensitivity data item.

▶ **Attribute**—An attribute of a component of a database, such as a table, field, or column.

▶ **Field**—The smallest unit of data within a database.

▶ **Foreign key**—An attribute in one table whose value matches the primary key in another table.

▶ **Granularity**—The control one has over someone's view of a database. Highly granular databases have the capability to restrict certain fields or rows from unauthorized individuals.

▶ **Relation**—Data that is represented by a collection of tables.

The data elements required to define a database are known as metadata. Metadata is best described as being data about data. As an example, the number 310 has no meaning, but when described with other data, it is understood as the information that represents the area code used for Beverly Hills and Malibu residents. Organizations treasure data and the relationships that can be deduced between the individual elements. That's data mining, the process of analyzing data to find and understand patterns and relationships between the data. The patterns discovered in this data can help companies understand their competitors and understand usage patterns of their customers to carry out targeted marketing. As an example, you might never have noticed that in most convenience stores the diapers are located near the refrigerated section of the store, where beer and sodas are kept. The store owners have placed these items close to each other as data mining has revealed that men are usually the ones that buy diapers in convenience stores, and they are also the primary demographic to purchase beer. By placing the diapers close by, both items increase in total sales. Although many of us might not naturally think of these types of relationships, data mining can uncover how seemingly unrelated items might actually be connected. Data mining operations require the collection of large amounts of data. All of this data can be stored in a data warehouse, a database that contains data from many different databases. These warehouses have been combined, integrated, and structured so that they can provide trend analysis and be used to make business decisions.

Many companies use knowledge-management systems to tie together all of an organization's information—databases, document management, business processes, and information systems—into one knowledge repository. This is referred to as customer relationship management (CRM). It's how businesses determine how to interact with their customers. Businesses use knowledge-management systems to further these goals. The knowledge-management system can interpret the data derived from these systems and automate the knowledge extraction. This knowledge-discovery process takes the form of data mining, in which patterns are discovered through artificial intelligence techniques.

Database Structure

Databases can be centralized or distributed depending on the database-management system (DBMS) that is implemented. The DBMS enables the database administrator to control all aspects of the database, including design, functionality, and security. Per ISACA, three primary types of database structures exist:

- Hierarchical database-management systems (HDMS)
- Network database-management systems (NDMS)
- Relational database-management systems (RDMS)

With the HDMS, the database takes the form of a parent-child structure. These are considered 1:N (one-to-many) mappings. Each record can have only one owner; because of this restriction, a hierarchical database often cannot be used to relate to structures in the real world. However, it is easy to implement, modify, and search. Figure 5.9 shows an example of an HDMS.

The NDMS was created in 1971 and is based on mathematical set theory. This type of database was developed to be more flexible than a hierarchical database. The network database model is considered a lattice structure because each record can have multiple parent and child records. Although this design can work well in stable environments, it can be extremely complex. Figure 5.10 shows an example of an NDMS.

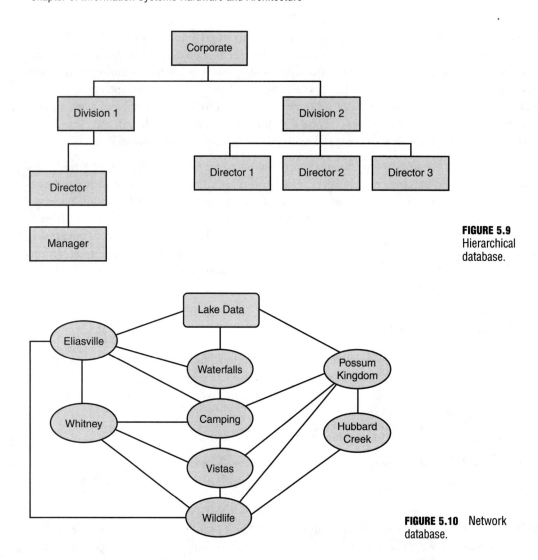

FIGURE 5.9
Hierarchical
database.

FIGURE 5.10 Network
database.

An RDMS database is considered a collection of tables that are linked by their primary keys. This type of database is based on set theory and relational calculations. Many organizations use software based on the relational database design, which uses a structure in which the data and the relationship between the data are organized in tables known as *tuples*. Most relational databases use SQL as their query language. Figure 5.11 shows an example of an RDMS.

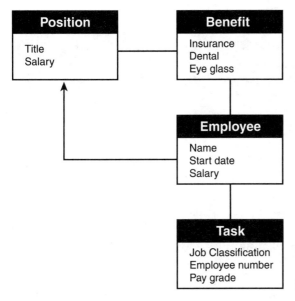

FIGURE 5.11 Relational database.

All databases need controls that protect the integrity of the data. Database transactions are protected through the use of controls. Integrity must be protected during storage and transactions. Controls to protect the integrity of the data during storage include the following:

▶ Enforcing security so that access to the database is restricted

▶ Defining levels of access for those who must have access to the database

▶ Establishing controls to verify the accuracy, completeness, and consistency of the data

Controls can be put into place during transactions. These are sometimes referred to as the ACID test, which is defined as follows:

▶ **Atomicity**—The results of a transaction are either all or nothing.

▶ **Consistency**—Transactions are processed only if they meet system-defined integrity constraints.

▶ **Isolation**—The results of a transaction are invisible to all other transactions until the original transaction is complete.

▶ **Durability**—After completion, the results of the transaction are permanent.

EXAM ALERT

ACID Test   You might be asked in the CISA exam about database management and how to tell if it is adequate for handling transactions. Adequate systems have atomicity, consistency, isolation, and durability.

Software Licensing Issues

Have you ever stopped to read an End-User License Agreement (EULA)? If you haven't, don't feel bad—many other users never have. The EULA is a type of contract between the software manufacturer and the end user. EULAs specify the terms of the conditions under which the end user can use the computer program or software. EULAs and software licensing are issues of concern for a CISA because companies have a legal and moral obligation to use software only in an approved manner. Companies caught using illegal software can be subjected to fines, legal fees, and bad press, being identified as a company that uses illegal software. The Business Software Alliance (http://www.bsa.org) pursues companies for illegal software. According to its website, in one case, the defendant received a jail term of more than seven years. IS auditors should review policies and procedures to verify that the company has rules in place that prohibit the use of illegal software. Some companies have employees sign an agreement stating that they will not install or copy software illegally. An IS should also perform random samples of users' computers to verify that they are loaded only with authorized, approved programs. The users' applications should be checked against a list of approved programs. Other controls include these:

▶ Disabling the local installation of software

▶ Installing application metering

▶ Using thin clients

▶ Performing regular compliance scans from the network

EXAM ALERT

Site Licensing   The CISA exam might ask you about ways to reduce illegal usage of software. One useful control to prevent unlawful duplication of software on multiple computers at a company's site is to purchase site licensing. This allows the software to be loaded on as many computers as needed at the organization.

Chapter Summary

This chapter examined information systems operations and discussed how controlling and monitoring are two big concerns. You can't roll out a new system overnight; this must be planned and budgeted for over time. Monitoring is so important because it enables the company to discover needs early on and gives the company more time to plan for change. Monitoring is also important because it enables the company to track response. If someone calls the help desk, does he get help in an hour, or must he wait two weeks? Monitoring also allows for the discovery of repetitive problems and catches errors early on before they become major problems.

This chapter also reviewed computer hardware, offering an in-depth look at hardware items such as the CPU, RAM, and ROM. It introduced the concept of integrity as it applies to the CPU and OS. Specifically, systems can run in different states. In the general user state, users are limited in their ability to access privileged functions. In the supervisor state, users can access the most privileged areas of the system. Supervisor state provides unrestricted access to all areas of the system.

Finally, this chapter discussed databases. As an auditor, your primary concerns are with database design, access, administration, interfaces, and portability. Databases can take on different designs, such as hierarchical, network, or relational. Access deals with the various ways in which a database can be accessed and what controls, such as indexes, are in place to minimize access time.

Key Terms

- ▶ Arithmetic logic unit
- ▶ Assembler
- ▶ Audit reduction tools
- ▶ Blu-ray Disc
- ▶ Compact disc (CD)
- ▶ Compiler
- ▶ Control unit
- ▶ Delay window
- ▶ Digital video disc (DVD)
- ▶ Emergency fix
- ▶ Floppy

- ▶ Hard disk drive

- ▶ Hierarchical database-management systems (HDMS)

- ▶ Interpreter

- ▶ Major release

- ▶ Minor release

- ▶ Network database-management system (NDMS)

- ▶ Radio frequency identification (RFID)

- ▶ Random access memory (RAM)

- ▶ Read-only memory (ROM)

- ▶ Relational database-management system (RDMS)

- ▶ Service level agreement (SLA)

- ▶ Trouble ticket

- ▶ Variance-detection tools

- ▶ Virtual memory

Apply Your Knowledge

This chapter covered IT delivery and support. The two exercises presented here show you how to check a computer to verify that it is running legal software and show you how to measure latency or delay.

Exercises

5.1 Product Validation

In this exercise, you learn how to verify that you are not running a counterfeit copy of the Windows operating system.

Estimated Time: 10 minutes

1. Go to http://www.microsoft.com/resources/howtotell/en/default.mspx. This site provides information on how to tell if the Microsoft operating system software you are running is a valid copy.

2. Click on the counterfeit link, http://www.microsoft.com/resources/howtotell/en/counterfeit.mspx. This page gives you information on how you can detect pirated software and illegal copies.

3. Launch the counterfeit gallery to see examples of what counterfeit software looks like.

4. Now return to the previous page, http://www.microsoft.com/resources/howtotell/en/default.mspx, and click on the Windows validation assistant.

5. Click on the Run Windows Validate Now button and follow the onscreen instructions.

6. You have now validated the copy of Windows you are running on your computer.

5.2 Measuring Latency

In this exercise, you learn how to use the `ping` command to measure latency.

Estimated Time: 10 minutes

1. Go to Start, Run and enter **cmd** to open a command prompt.

2. At the command prompt, enter **ping 127.0.0.1**. This is the local loopback address. You should see a time of less than 10ms.

3. Now ping your local gateway. If you do not know the address, you can discover it by typing **ipconfig/all** at the command line. After pinging your default gateway, you should still see a time of less than 10ms.

4. Now ping an Internet address, such as 64.233.161.99. In the following example, the time increases to 40ms:

```
C:\>ping 64.233.161.99
Reply from 64.233.161.99: bytes=32 time=40ms TTL=245
Reply from 64.233.161.99: bytes=32 time=40ms TTL=245
Reply from 64.233.161.99: bytes=32 time=40ms TTL=245
Reply from 64.233.161.99: bytes=32 time=30ms TTL=245
```

5. Now ping an even more distant site. I am in the United States, so I chose http://www.google.cn. My pings took even longer—about 51ms in this example:

```
C:\>ping www.google.cn
Reply from 72.14.203.161: bytes=32 time=50ms TTL=242
Reply from 72.14.203.161: bytes=32 time=51ms TTL=242
Reply from 72.14.203.161: bytes=32 time=51ms TTL=242
Reply from 72.14.203.161: bytes=32 time=52ms TTL=242
```

These results prove that `ping` can be used to measure latency and that generally the delay increases with congestion or as distance to the target increases.

Exam Questions

1. Which of the following is the most important concern for an auditor reviewing the contracts for delivery of IT services?

   ○ **A.** Service-level agreements

   ○ **B.** Help desk

   ○ **C.** Problem management

   ○ **D.** Nonessential backup

2. In web services, a proxy server is most often used for which of the following:

   ○ **A.** Reduce the load of the client system

   ○ **B.** Improve direct access

   ○ **C.** Interface to access the private domain

   ○ **D.** Provide high-level security services

3. You have been asked to audit a database to evaluate the referential integrity. Which of the following should you review?

   ○ **A.** Field

   ○ **B.** Aggregation

   ○ **C.** Composite key

   ○ **D.** Foreign key

4. Which of the following is the most important security concern when reviewing the use of USB memory sticks?

   ○ **A.** The memory sticks might not be compatible with all systems.

   ○ **B.** The memory sticks might lose information or become corrupted.

   ○ **C.** Memory sticks can copy a large amount of data.

   ○ **D.** Memory sticks' contents cannot be backed up.

5. You are an auditor for a financial organization and have been asked which of the following would be the best tool to detect abnormal spending patterns and flag them:

   ○ **A.** Relational database

   ○ **B.** Manual audit techniques

   ○ **C.** Neural network

   ○ **D.** Intrusion-prevention system

6. Which of the following is the most common failure with audit logs?

◯   **A.** Audit logs can be examined only by auditors.

◯   **B.** Audit logs use parsing tools that distort the true record of events.

◯   **C.** Audit logs are not backed up.

◯   **D.** Audit logs are collected but not analyzed.

7. The `ping` command can be used to measure which of the following?

◯   **A.** Latency

◯   **B.** Best path

◯   **C.** Computer configuration

◯   **D.** Firewall settings

8. Which of the following is the greatest concern with the use of utility software?

◯   **A.** It can be used to scan or defrag a hard drive.

◯   **B.** It runs with privileged access.

◯   **C.** It might not have controls that log who used it or when.

◯   **D.** It can be used to improve operational efficiency.

9. Which of the following are two primary components of the CPU?

◯   **A.** RAM, cache, and the logic processing unit

◯   **B.** The control unit and the scalar processor

◯   **C.** The control unit and the arithmetic logic unit

◯   **D.** The primary address unit and the arithmetic logic unit

10. Which of the following is the primary bus standard today?

◯   **A.** PCI

◯   **B.** ISA

◯   **C.** MCA

◯   **D.** VESA

Answers to Exam Questions

1. **A.** Service-level agreements are the most important concern for the auditor because they specify the agreed-upon level of service. Answer B is incorrect because although the help desk is important, it is not used to measure delivery of service; the same is true for answer C, problem management. Answer D is also incorrect because a nonessential backup would not be important here.

2. **C.** Proxies provide several services, including load balancing and caching. Most importantly, the proxy stands in place of the real client and acts as an interface to the private domain, thereby preventing direct access. Answer A is incorrect because the proxy is not used to reduce the load of a client. Answer B is incorrect because a proxy prevents direct access. Answer D is incorrect because although proxy servers provide some level of security, they do not allow high-level security such as an application or kernel firewall.

3. **D.** The foreign key refers to an attribute in one table whose value matches the primary key in another table. Answer A is incorrect because the field refers to the smallest unit of data within a database. Answer B is incorrect because aggregation refers to the process of combining several low-sensitivity items to produce a higher-sensitivity data item. Answer C is incorrect because the composite key refers to two or more columns that together are designated as the computer's primary key.

4. **C.** Memory sticks can copy and hold large amounts of information. This presents a security risk because someone can easily place one of these devices in his pocket and carry the information out of the company. Although answers A, B, and D are important, they are not the most important security concern.

5. **C.** Neural networks use predictive logic and can analyze data and learn patterns. Answer A is incorrect because a relational database would not be useful in detecting fraud or abnormal spending. Answer B is incorrect because manual audit techniques could be used but would not be the most efficient or cost-effective. Answer D is incorrect because intrusion-prevention systems typically examine traffic entering the organization from the Internet and attempt to alert and prevent malicious activity.

6. **D.** One of the most common problems with audit logs is that they are collected but not analyzed. Many times no one is interested in the audit logs until someone reports a problem. Answers A, B, and C are all important concerns but are not the most common failure.

7. **A.** The `ping` command can be used to measure latency. Answer B is incorrect because `ping` does not specify best path. Answer C is incorrect because `ping` is not used to verify the computer configuration; that is the `IP config` command. Answer D is incorrect because `ping` is not used to verify firewall settings.

8. **B.** Utility programs can operate outside the bounds of normal security controls and function in a supervisor state. Thus, these utilities must be controlled and restricted. Answer A is incorrect because it is not a concern, but an advantage. Answer C is incorrect because although not having an audit trail is a concern, of most concern is the fact that utility programs can be very powerful. Answer D is incorrect because, again, it is an advantage, not a disadvantage.

9. **C.** Two primary components of the CPU include the control unit and the arithmetic logic unit. Therefore, answers A, B, and D are incorrect.

10. **A.** The PCI, or Peripheral Component Interface, bus was developed by Intel and served as a replacement for the ISA, MCA, and VESA bus standards. Therefore, answers B, C, and D are incorrect.

Need to Know More?

▶ How CPUs Work: http://computer.howstuffworks.com/microprocessor.htm

▶ Problem Management Techniques: http://www.daveeaton.com/scm/PMTools.html

▶ USB Description: http://www.interfacebus.com/Design_Connector_USB.html

▶ Understanding Databases: http://msdn2.microsoft.com/en-us/library/ms189638.aspx

▶ Auditing Databases: http://en.wikipedia.org/wiki/Database_audit

▶ Database Security: http://www.governmentsecurity.org/articles/DatabaseSecurityCommon-sensePrinciples.php

▶ Capacity Management: http://www.smthacker.co.uk/capacity_management.htm

CHAPTER SIX

Information Systems Used for IT Delivery and Support

This chapter helps you prepare for the Certified Information Systems Auditor (CISA) exam by covering the following ISACA objectives, which include understanding the importance of system infrastructure and control. This includes items such as the following:

Tasks

Evaluate the use of capacity and performance monitoring tools and techniques to ensure that IT services meet the organization's objectives.

Evaluate problem and incident management practices to ensure that incidents, problems or errors are recorded, analyzed, and resolved in a timely manner.

Evaluate the functionality of the IT infrastructure (e.g., network components, hardware, system software) to ensure it supports the organization's objectives.

Knowledge Statements

Knowledge of systems performance monitoring processes, tools, and techniques (e.g., network analyzers, system utilization reports, load balancing)

Knowledge of the functionality of hardware and network components (e.g., routers, switches, firewalls, peripherals)

Outline

Study Strategies

This chapter addresses information you need to know about service delivery. An array of equipment, transmission protocols, and devices operate as the heartbeat of modern organizations. Although this array is transparent to most employees, these systems deliver email, provide connectivity to the Internet, allow file sharing, and support print services and a range of other services. Auditors must understand these complex systems. Listed here are some of the primary topics a CISA candidate should review for the exam:

▶ Understand how to analyze network capacity

▶ Know the ways in which performance is measured

▶ Know how to analyze a network and verify that it meets the needs of the organization

▶ Describe basic network equipment such as hubs, switches, routers, and firewalls

▶ Describe LAN, WAN, and networking protocols including TCP/IP, Frame Relay, X.25, wireless, and so on

Introduction

This chapter introduces networking technology. Not all networks are created equal. Different protocols are used on local area networks (LANs), metropolitan area networks (MANs), and wide area networks (WANs). Some of these protocols, such as Transmission Control Protocol/Internet Protocol (TCP/IP), might be familiar to you; however, others, such as Frame Relay, X.25, or Asynchronous Transfer Mode (ATM), might not. The CISA must understand these protocols and the equipment that interconnects the network. These components include hubs, bridges, switches, routers, and firewalls. The design of the network and the type of equipment used can have a big impact on the level of security provided. An IS auditor must be aware of these issues and also be able to examine the level of services provided by the network. In addition, auditors must be able to determine the capacity constraints of the network. Just as every modern freeway has a maximum level of capacity, so does the network. It is important to know the current demand and expected future demand requirements. This knowledge provides for the proper planning and budgeting of current and future control requirements. This chapter begins by examining network architectures and the types of networks.

Network Infrastructure

Knowledge Statement

▶ Knowledge of the functionality of hardware and network components (e.g., routers, switches, firewalls, peripherals)

The network infrastructure encompasses all the protocols, hardware, and systems used to provide network services. Networks can be local or distant. Local networks must use an agreed-upon set of protocols and a standardized cabling method. This might be coaxial cable, twisted-pair cable, or even a wireless system. Distant networks must also have an agreed-upon way to communicate with other distant systems. They, too, need cabling and protocols to operate. Without agreed-upon standards, the Internet would not be possible. TCP/IP is one of these common protocols. The equipment to connect all these systems must also be capable of interacting with the various protocols and communication schemes. Routers are one such piece of equipment. Routers form the backbone of the Internet. The following section begins to examine the concepts behind network infrastructure more deeply by first defining the different network types.

Network Types

Throughout time, there has always been a need to share information. Years ago, that might have been by paper, fax, or phone. Today the computer network has taken over that task. The development of the desktop computer in the 1980s caused a paradigm shift. Much of this change would not have been possible without the capability to link these desktop PCs together. Some of this work had been done decades earlier. Back in 1975, the Digital, Intel, and Xerox (DIX) group released the first official Ethernet product. Ethernet is the standard for *local area networks* (LANs). The computers and other devices in a LAN communicate over a small geographical area, such as the following:

▶ A section of a one-story building

▶ The whole floor of a small building

▶ Several buildings on a small campus

▶ A work office or home network of computers

> **NOTE**
>
> **The Father of the Ethernet** Robert Metcalfe is commonly referred to as the Father of the Ethernet. The first designs for the protocol were created in 1975 at a National Computer Conference. Metcalfe went on to form 3Com, a successful networking equipment company.

Although it is nice to have computers and other networked devices communicate locally, many times the need exists to communicate on a larger scale. For devices that need to communicate on a citywide level, the *metropolitan area network* (MAN) was created. The MAN is a network that interconnects a region larger than what's covered by a LAN. A MAN can include a city, geographic region, or large area. If you work for a company that owns several buildings located in different states or countries, that network is part of a *wide area network* (WAN). A WAN spans geographic distances that are too large for LANs and MANs. WANs are connected by routers. When two LANs are connected over a distance, they form a WAN. You might think this covers just about all the possible different network types, but a few more are worth mentioning. One such type is the *personal area network* (PAN), which allows a variety of personal and handheld electronic devices to communicate over a short range. A subset of the PAN is known as a *wireless PAN* (WPAN). Bluetooth is one technology that makes use of WPANs. The three classifications of Bluetooth include the following:

▶ **Bluetooth Class 1**—Up to 100m of range and 100mW of power

▶ **Bluetooth Class 2**—Up to 20m of range and 2.5mW of power

▶ **Bluetooth Class 3**—Up to 10m of range and 1mW of power

Finally, there are *storage area networks* (SANs). A SAN is a network of storage disks and devices. SANs are used to connect multiple servers to a centralized pool of disk storage. SANs improve system administration by allowing centralizing storage instead of having to manage hundreds of servers, each with its own disks.

Network Standards and Protocols

Task

▶ Evaluate the use of capacity and performance monitoring tools and techniques to ensure that IT services meet the organization's objectives.

Communication systems need some type of model for devices to communicate and understand what the other devices need. Over the years, various standards have been developed to make this possible. These standards and protocols set up rules of operation. Protocols describe how requests, messages, and other signals are formatted and transmitted over the network. The network will function as long as all computers are consistent in following the same set of rules for communication. Protocols, such as TCP/IP, and standards, such as the Open Systems Interconnect (OSI), are two examples of network rules. These rules have helped build the Internet and the worldwide data networks we have today. The goal of any set of network standards is to provide the following:

▶ Interoperability

▶ Availability

▶ Flexibility

▶ Maintainability

Many groups have been working toward meeting this challenge, including the following:

▶ International Organization for Standardization (ISO)

▶ American Institute of Electrical and Electronics Engineers (IEEE)

▶ Internet Engineering Task Force (IETF)

▶ International Telecommunications Union–Telecommunications Sector (ITU-T)

The next section discusses one of these organizations, the ISO, in greater detail.

The OSI Model

The ISO is recognized for its development of the Open Systems Interconnect (OSI) reference model. The ISO set the worldwide standards for its work in developing a common approach to networking. Its goal was for all vendors to adopt its standard networking architecture for all hardware and software products, thereby enabling all network users to communicate with each other regardless of the computer products owned or used. The OSI model was developed in 1984 and defines networking as a seven-layer process. Within the OSI model, the data is passed down from layer to layer. It begins at the application layer and ends at the physical layer, as shown in Figure 6.1. The data is then transmitted over the medium toward the target device, back up the stack to the application layer of the target machine. The seven layers of the OSI model are: application, presentation, session, transport, network, data link, and physical.

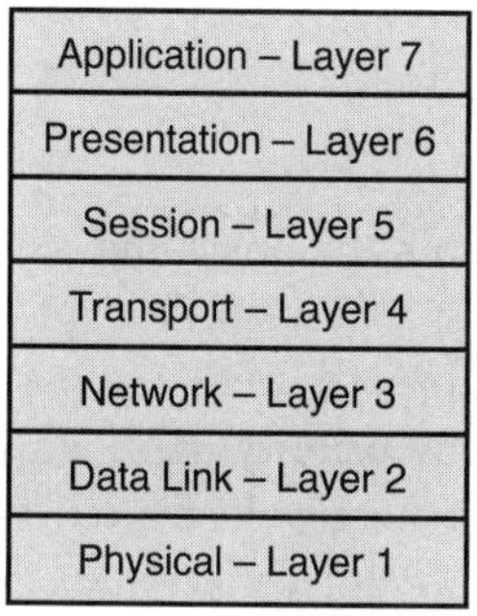

| Application – Layer 7 |
| Presentation – Layer 6 |
| Session – Layer 5 |
| Transport – Layer 4 |
| Network – Layer 3 |
| Data Link – Layer 2 |
| Physical – Layer 1 |

Figure 6.1   The OSI model.

Most people remember the OSI model by one of the many acronyms that have been thought of over the years. One way to remember it is to use the following mnemonic device:

All (application—Layer 7)

People (presentation—Layer 6)

Seem (session—Layer 5)

To (transport—Layer 4)

Need (network—Layer 3)

Data (data link—Layer 2)

Processing (physical—Layer 1)

Today the OSI model is widely used as a guide in describing the operation of a networking environment and serves as a teaching model for all other protocols. The following sections describe and examine how each layer of the OSI model is designed to operate. Let's get started by reviewing the application layer and then working our way down the stack.

EXAM ALERT

The OSI Model   CISA candidates need to know the seven layers of the OSI model (from Layer 1 to Layer 7): physical, data link, network, transport, session, presentation, and application layer.

The Application Layer

Layer 7 is known as the application layer. Recognized as the top layer of the OSI model, this layer serves as the window for application services. This is the layer that users are most knowledgeable of. The application layer serves as the interface for applications, such as email and web browsers. Without the application layer, email and the Web would not exist and our computers would be unable to interpret and sort the data transmitted by other computers. Layer 7 is not the application itself, but rather the channel through which applications communicate. Think of this in terms of preparing to send a present to a friend—the application layer would be equivalent to buying the gift.

The Presentation Layer

Layer 6 is known as the presentation layer. Consider the gift analogy from the preceding section. At Layer 6, this is when you are now ready to take the gift to the post office. It will require packaging. Although some might be content in placing the gift in a paper package, the post office will require a specific type of box if you want to send the gift by priority mail. This means that the presentation layer is concerned about presentation. Data must be formatted so the application layer can understand and interpret the data. The presentation layer is skilled in translation; its duties include encrypting data, changing or converting the character set, and performing protocol conversion. Data compression is also performed at the presentation layer.

The Session Layer

Layer 5 is known as the session layer. Its purpose is to allow two applications on different computers to establish and coordinate a session. A session is simply a name for a connection between two computers. Ports are defined at the session layer. Ports are used to identify the application being used. For example, port 21 is used for File Transfer Protocol (FTP), and port 80 is used for Hypertext Transfer Protocol (HTTP). When a data transfer is completed, the session layer is responsible for tearing down the session.

The Transport Layer

Layer 4 is known as the transport layer. While the network layer routes your information to its destination, the transport layer ensures completeness by handling end-to-end error recovery and flow control. Without the transport layer, the network would be unreliable. Transport-layer protocols include (1) *Transmission Control Protocol* (TCP), a connection-oriented protocol that provides reliable communication through the use of handshaking, acknowledgments, handling error detection, and session teardown; and (2) *User Datagram Protocol* (UDP), a protocol without a connection that offers speed and low overhead as its primary advantage. As an example, when I take my package to the post office, I must now decide how to ship it. Should I send it return receipt with delivery confirmation (TCP), or shall I just pay for parcel post (UDP) and hope it gets there?

The Network Layer

Layer 3 is known as the network layer. The network layer is tied to routers and routing. The network layer is responsible for the movement of data from network A to network B. The network layer is the home of the *Internet Protocol* (IP). IP acts as a postman determining the best route from the source to the target network. Like a postman, IP does not examine the contents of the packet (letter or package); it simply makes a best effort at delivery. Network-layer components include the following:

▶ Routers

▶ Routing protocols

▶ Packet filters

The Data Link Layer

Layer 2 is known as the data link layer. The data link layer is responsible for formatting and organizing the data before sending it to the physical layer. It is also responsible for error handling. The data link layer must frame up packets and deal with the local delivery of traffic within a single LAN. A frame is a logical structure in which data can be placed. When a frame reaches the target device, the data link layer is responsible for stripping off the data frame and passing the data packet up to the network layer. Data link–layer components include the following:

▶ Bridges

▶ Switches

▶ Network interface cards (NICs)

▶ Media Access Control (MAC) addresses

The Physical Layer

Layer 1 is known as the physical layer. Bit-level communication occurs here. The bits have no defined meaning on the wire, but the physical layer defines how long each bit lasts and how it is transmitted and received. All the electrical, mechanical, and functional requirements of the network are specified at this level. The physical layer even establishes parameters to define whether a data bit is a one or zero. Returning to our previous example, this is where your package and many others are all loaded on the mail carrier's truck and bound for delivery. Physical-layer components include the following:

▶ Copper cabling

▶ Fiber cabling

▶ Wireless system components

▶ Wall jacks and connectors

▶ Ethernet hubs

At the bottom of the OSI model or stack, the data is broken into electrical signals and transmitted on the fiber, wire, or wireless system used. When the targeted system receives it, the information is pushed back up the stack until it arrives at the application layer and is passed to the appropriate service. Figure 6.2 illustrates this process.

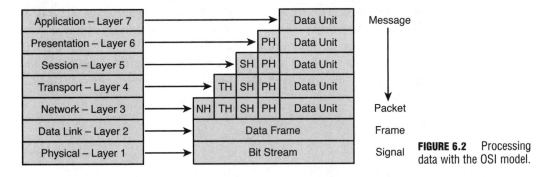

FIGURE 6.2 Processing data with the OSI model.

Network Services and Applications

Networks can provide a wide array of applications and enable users to share common services such as file sharing. Networks give users the capability to share files and folders with other users. Users can have read, write, or full control. A common means of sharing files remotely is *File Transfer Protocol* (FTP), an application used to move files from one computer to another. FTP operates on ports 20 and 21. Email service is another common network service and one of the most widely used network services. Email uses two protocols. *Simple Mail Transfer Protocol* (SMTP) is the first. SMTP is designed for the exchange of electronic mail between network systems. All types of computers can exchange messages with SMTP. It operates on port 25. The second protocol used by email is *Post Office Protocol* version 3 (POP3), which provides a simple, standardized way for users to access mail and download messages from a mail server to their own computer. POP3 operates on port 110.

Print services are another well-used network service. Print services enable users to use network printers to manage and print documents to remote network printers. *Terminal-emulation software* (TES) is a category of network service that enables users to access remote hosts. These hosts then appear as local devices. An example of TES is *Telnet*, which allows a client at one site to establish a session with a host at another site. The program passes the information typed at the client's keyboard to the host computer system. Telnet sends passwords and other information in clear text. Telnet operates on port 23.

The network-management service is used to control and maintain the network. IT does so by monitoring the status of devices and reporting this information back to a management console. Network-management services allow the effective use of the network and help alert staff of problems before they become critical. *Simple Network Management Protocol* (SNMP) is the protocol commonly used for network management. SNMP was designed to be an efficient and inexpensive way to monitor networks. The SNMP protocol allows agents to gather information. The agent gathers network statistics and reports it back to its management station. Most corporations use some type of SNMP management. SNMP operates on port 161.

Directory services are the means by which network services are identified and mapped. Directory services perform services similar to that of a phone book as it correlates addresses to names. An example of directory services can be seen in the *Domain Name Service* (DNS), which performs address translation. DNS converts *fully qualified domain names* (FQDNs) into a numeric IP address. An example of a FQDN is www.thesolutionfirm.com. DNS can take this name and resolve its proper IP address, 112.10.8.5. DNS operates on port 53.

No discussion on network services would be complete without mentioning the Internet and the *Hypertext Transfer Protocol* (HTTP). HTTP has helped make the Web the popular tool it is today. The HTTP connection model is known as a *stateless connection*. HTTP uses a request/response protocol in which a client sends a request and a server sends a response. HTTP operates on port 80.

Comparing the OSI Model to the TCP/IP Model

Although the OSI model was great in theory, it was never fully implemented. Instead, TCP/IP was implemented in its place. TCP/IP is the foundation of computer communications. Its development can be traced back to the U.S. Department of Defense (DoD). TCP/IP is similar to the OSI model but consists of only four layers instead of seven, as illustrated in Figure 6.3.

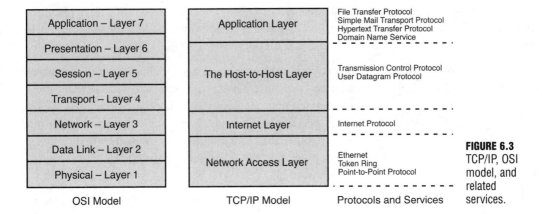

FIGURE 6.3
TCP/IP, OSI model, and related services.

The Network Access Layer

The network access layer corresponds to Layers 1 and 2 of the OSI model. The network access layer is responsible for physical delivery of IP packets via frames. The most common frame type is *Ethernet*. Ethernet is a CSMA/CD *(Carrier Sense Multiple Access/Collision Detection)* technology that places data into frames. Frames contain the source and destination addresses and are referred to as *Media Access Control* (MAC) addresses. MAC addresses are 6 bytes long. Most tools such as analyzers display MAC addresses in hexadecimal, which look something like this: 00 00 0C 12 34 67. The information found in the Ethernet header and trailer is 18 bytes total. Ethernet frames can carry between 46 and 1,500 bytes of data.

Token Ring is the second most used LAN protocol after Ethernet. Whereas Ethernet is a collision-detection protocol, Token Ring is a collision-avoidance protocol. As an example, consider going to a noisy party with your friends. Everyone's talking and the only way to be heard is by waiting for a brief period of slience and then jumping into the conversation. That's how Ethernet works—it's contention-based. Ethernet is quite different from Token Ring. A collision-avoidance protocol such as Token Ring is like going to a very reserved dinner party with your CEO and senior management. Everone is very reserved and as long as one person is talking, everyone else stays silent and waits for their turn to speak. This type of protocol is deterministic as the only one that can speak is the one with the token. The *Point-to-Point Tunneling Protocol* (PPTP) is also found at the network access layer. PPTP is used to tunnel private information over the public Internet and is widely used in *virtual private network* (VPN) products.

The Internet Layer

The internet layer maps to OSI Layer 3. This layer contains the information needed to make sure the data can be routed through an IP network. Whereas MAC addresses are considered a physical address, an IP address is considered a logical address. IP divides networks into logical groups known as *subnetworks* (subnets). IPv4, the current version of IP, uses 32-bit addresses. These addresses are laid out in a dotted-decimal notation. The IPv4 address format is four decimal numbers separated by decimal points. Each of these decimal numbers is 1 byte in length, to allow numbers to range from 0 to 255. Three primary ranges of logical addresses are used:

▶ **Class A networks**—Class A networks consist of up to 16,777,214 client devices; their address range can extend from 1 to 126.

▶ **Class B networks**—Class B networks host up to 65,534 client devices; their address range can extend from 128 to 191.

▶ **Class C networks**—Class C networks can have a total of 245 devices; their address range can extend from 192 to 223.

NOTE

IPv6   The next version of IP is IPv6. Although it might not be seen in many places in the U.S. yet, it is much more common in Europe. Besides offering better security, IPv6 also features 128-bit addressing, which allows for the growing need for IP addresses for many years.

If the internet layer deals with logical addresses and the network access layer deals with physical addresses, how do the two layers communicate? These two layers overcome these problems by using the *Address Resolution Protocol* (ARP). The purpose of ARP is to map known IP addresses to unknown MAC addresses. This two-step process is performed by first sending a message to all devices on the LAN requesting the receiver's physical address. If a device recognizes the address as its own, it issues an ARP reply to the sender of the ARP request. A good way to correlate the difference between physical and logical addresses is to think of the postal service. As an example, if I were to send a postcard to my mom, I would need to place her physical address on the postcard, such as 1313 Mockingbird Lane. I also need a logical address to place on the postcard—in this case, Betty Gregg. Together the logical address and the physical address allow delivery to the end address. Networks provide the capability to send information to more than one device at a time. Actually, there are three different ways to send data packets:

▶ **Unicast**—A packet transmitted from the sender to one receiver

▶ **Multicast**—A packet transmitted from the sender to a group of receivers

▶ **Broadcast**—A packet transmitted from the sender to all other devices on the network

The internet layer is also where some *routing protocols* reside. Routing protocols direct packets toward their intended destination. Routing protocols are based on distance or link state. *Distance-vector protocols* make a decision on the best route to the destination by determining the shortest path, calculated by counting hops. Each router counts as one hop. *Routing Information Protocol* (RIP) is one of the most well-known distance-vector protocols. A major shortcoming of a distance-vector protocol is that the path with the lowest number of hops might not be the optimum route; the path with the lower hop count might have considerably less bandwidth than the one with the higher hop count. *Link-state routing protocols* are the second type of routing. Link-state protocols determine the best path by metrics, such as delay or bandwidth. Link-state routing is considered more robust than distance-vector routing. *Open Shortest Path First* (OSPF) is probably the most common link-state routing protocol and many times is used as a replacement to RIP.

EXAM ALERT

The Internet Layer   Test candidates should be aware that the internet layer is primarily responsible for routing and logical addressing. Protocols such as IP and OSPF can be found at the internet layer.

The Host-to-Host Layer

The host-to-host layer corresponds to OSI Layers 4, 5, and 6. The host-to-host layer provides end-to-end delivery. This is accomplished by either the *Transmission Control Protocol* (TCP) or *User Datagram Protocol* (UDP).

TCP is a reliable protocol that provides for confirmed delivery of data. TCP gets its reliability by performing a three-step handshake before data is sent, using acknowledgments, and performing a four-step shutdown at the conclusion of communication, as illustrated in Figure 6.4.

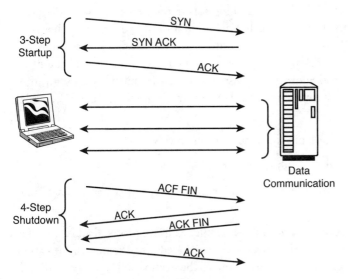

FIGURE 6.4   TCP setup, data flow, and shutdown.

UDP provides unconfirmed delivery and offers none of the handshaking process that is performed with TCP. Although this lowers reliability, it increases speed. UDP offers no guarantee of delivery and is used for applications and services that require speed. An example of a UDP application is *voice over IP* (VoIP), illustrated in Figure 6.5.

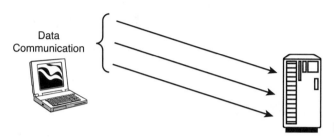

Data
Communication

FIGURE 6.5 UDP communication flow.

The Application Layer

The application layer maps to OSI Layers 6 and 7. The application layer is responsible for application support. Applications are typically mapped not by name, but by their corresponding port. Ports are placed into TCP and UDP packets so the correct application can be passed to the required protocols below.

Although a particular service might have an assigned port, nothing specifies that services cannot listen on another port. An example of this is HTTP, whose assigned port is 80. Your company might decide to run this on another port, such as 8080. As long as your web browser knows on what port to find the application, this will not present a problem. Standard ports are used primarily to make sure that services can be easily found. Table 6.1 lists some common ports.

TABLE 6.1   Common Port Numbers

Port	Service	Protocol
20/21	FTP	TCP
22	SSH	TCP
23	Telnet	TCP
25	SMTP	TCP
53	DNS	TCP/UDP
67/68	DHCP	UDP
80	HTTP	TCP
110	POP3	TCP
161	SNMP	UDP

Two common network services found at the application layer are the *Domain Name Server* (DNS) and *Dynamic Host Configuration Protocol* (DHCP). DNS performs address translation by resolving known *fully qualified domain names* (FQDNs) to IP addresses. DNS uses UDP for DNS queries (resolutions) and TCP for zone transfers. DHCP is used to provide IP addresses automatically. DHCP also provides the DNS server, gateway IP address, and subnet mask to a local system upon startup if it is configured to use DHCP. This four-step process is described in more detail here:

STEP BY STEP

6.1 Dynamic Host Configuration Protocol Operation

1. You can remember the DHCP process with the mnemonic DORA: discovery, offer, request, and acceptance. The first step is discovery. At this step, the host initially sends a broadcast in an attempt to discover a DHCP server on the network.

2. The second step is the offer. At this step, the DHCP server detects the computer that is looking for the DHCP service and responds with an offer of an IP address.

3. The third step is the request. At this step, the client receives the offer on an address and, in most cases, accepts it. To accept, the client must send an official request for the same IP address offered previously by the DHCP server.

4. The fourth step is the acceptance. At this step, the DHCP server completes the transaction by sending an acceptance message and marking the particular IP address "in use" for the specific host.

Network Design

Networks can use a variety of topologies. The topology is the physical design of the network. Topologies include bus, star, ring, and mesh. Table 6-2 provides an overview of each topology.

TABLE 6.2 Description and Features of Various Topologies

Topology	Feature	Advantage	Disadvantage
Bus	A single length of cable is used.	The design is simple.	The design is hard to expand.
			One break can disable the entire segment.
Star	Devices all connect to a central wiring point.	Expansion does not disrupt other systems.	More cable is required.
		A cable failure affects only one device.	A hub or switch is required.
Ring	Devices are connected in a loop.	The design is easy to troubleshoot and fault tolerant if dual rings are used.	Network expansion creates a disruption.

TABLE 6.2   *Continued*

Topology	Feature	Advantage	Disadvantage
Mesh	All points have redundant connections.	Multiple links provide greater fault tolerance.	The design is expensive to implement.
		Expansion requires little or no disruption.	

A *bus topology* consists of a single cable in which all computers are linked. The cable is terminated on each end. Older LAN technologies, such as 10BASE-5 and 10BASE-2, used a bus topology. Bus designs suffer problems ranging from low speeds to network outages because a single break can bring down the entire network. A *star topology* links each device via a hub or switch. Wires radiate outward from the switch in a starlike pattern. Although this design uses the most cable, a single break in a cable affects only one device. This is one of the most widely used LAN topologies. The *ring topology* is characterized by the fact that no endpoints or terminators exist. The layout of a ring network is that of a continuous loop of cable in which all networked computers are attached. Ring networks can span great distances and offer high performance. Token Ring and FDDI networks are two examples of protocols that use a ring topology. The *mesh topology* connects all devices with many redundant connections. This type of design offers the greatest amount of redundancy. The Internet is an example of a mesh network. Figure 6.6 illustrates each of these designs.

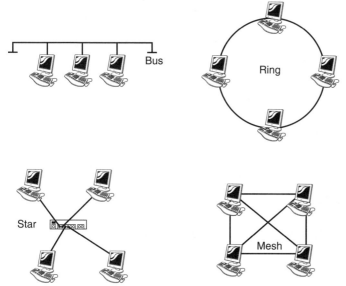

FIGURE 6.6   Common network designs.

> **NOTE**
>
> **Network Redundancy** Full-mesh networks provide the most protection against network failure. If each device has a separate link to each other, the network will provide the greatest amount of fault tolerance.

Network Cabling

Network topology and network cabling are closely associated, and both are part of network architecture. Cabling choices can include wire, fiber, and wireless systems. Although each approach has specific advantages, they all share some common disadvantages. One such disadvantage is *attenuation*, which is the reduction of signal. As the signal travels farther away from the transmitting device, the signal becomes weaker in intensity and strength. Therefore, all signals need periodic reamplification and regeneration.

Signals can be transmitted between devices in one of two basic methods:

▶ **Baseband** transmissions use a single channel to communicate. As an example, Ethernet uses a baseband transmission scheme. Baseband allows only one signal to be transmitted at any one time.

▶ **Broadband** uses many channels or frequencies. As an example, cable television is a broadband technology, as is a *digital subscriber line* (DSL). DSL broadband enables the user to make a phone call and surf the Internet at the same time.

Baseband and broadband systems need a transmission medium. If the choice is copper cable, the choices include *coaxial* and *twisted-pair cables*. Coaxial cable, widely used in the early days of networking, consists of a single solid copper wire core that uses a braided shield for the second conductor. Both conductors are covered with a plastic or insulative coating. Coaxial cable standards include 10BASE-5 (500 meters) and 10BASE-2 (185 meters). Twisted-pair cable (100 meters) is the more popular cabling choice. You can look in almost every wiring closet in any organization and find this type of cabling. Twisted-pair cable comes in many different speeds and is rated in categories. Category (Cat) 3 is 10Mbps, Cat 5 is 100Mbps, and Cat 6 is rated for 1Gbps. The primary difference between these cables is the number of twists per foot. The higher the twist counts, the greater the speed. The most common connector used is the RJ-45. Twisted-pair cable can be purchased in a shielded or unshielded version. Unshielded, which is known as UTP, is cheaper, but shielded cable, known as STP, does a better job at preventing interference.

> **EXAM ALERT**
>
> **What's Burning?** Guarding the health and safety of employees is always a concern. Therefore, plenum-grade cable is designed for use in the crawl spaces of a building. Plenum-grade cable is coated with a fire-retardant coating and is designed to not give off toxic gasses and smoke as it burns.

Our next cabling option is *fiber-optic* cable. Whereas twisted-pair and coaxial cabling use copper wire, fiber uses strands of glass that carry light waves representing the data being transmitted. Fiber-optic cabling can be multimode or single mode. Multimode fiber-optic cabling usually is found in LANs and is powered by LEDs. Single-mode fiber-optic cable is powered by laser light and is used in WANs. Common fiber-optic standards include 10BASE-F, which is rated for 10Mbps, and 100BASE-FX, which is rated for 100Mbps.

EXAM ALERT

Fiber Is a Good Choice Fiber offers advantages over copper cable because it does not radiate signals and is harder to tap.

The final transmission method for discussion is wireless communication. Wireless systems can include wireless LAN protocols, such as 802.11b, 802.11g, and 802.11n. Each of these is designed for LANs and can transmit at speeds from 11Mbps to greater than 1Gbps. Advantages of these systems are that they can be set up easily and do not require a cable plant. Long-range wireless systems include radio systems, microwave radio systems, and satellite systems. Satellite systems have the capability to allow communications to span the globe, but they can introduce a delay because it takes about 300ms to transmit up to the satellite and back down to earth. Table 6.3 discusses each cabling option in more detail.

TABLE 6.3 Cabling Standards

Type	Use	Topology	Length	Access Standard
Copper Cable	10BASE-T, 10Mbps 100BASE-TX, 100Mbps 1000BASE-TX, 1Gbps	Star	100m 100m 100m	Ethernet CSMA/CD
Coaxial Cable	10BASE5, 10Mbps 10BASE2, 10Mbps	Bus	500m 185m	802.3
Fiber Cable	10BASE-F, 10Mbps 100BASE-FX, 100Mbps 1000BASE-LX, 1000Mbps	Bus, star, or mesh	Long distances. For example, 10BASE-F can range up to 2,000 meters.	802.3, 802.3ae, and 802.5
Wireless LAN Protocol	In the 2.4GHz bandwidth	Wireless	Depends. As an example, 802.11b can range from 100 to 500 feet.	802.11

Choosing the right topology is important. Services such as VoIP and *streaming video* can place high demands on the network. To make sure the right infrastructure is deployed, the following questions should be asked:

▶ **What applications will be used on the network?**—Demanding applications require high performance. *Ten Gigabit Ethernet*, *Gigabit Ethernet* and *Asynchronous Transfer Mode* (ATM) are three possible choices.

▶ **What amount of bandwidth is needed?**—Modern LANs demand increasing amounts of bandwidth. Virtual machines and increased Internet traffic raise the demand for bandwidth. Whereas 10Mbps connectivity with hubs was once sufficient, 100Mbps switched connectivity is now seen as the minimum.

▶ **How much money does the company have to spend?**—The price of network equipment has been declining for several years. However, the cost to recable a facility is high. This has led many companies to consider wireless as a real alternative.

> **NOTE**
>
> **Wireless**   Wireless can be considered problematic when it comes to security. Issues such as social engineering, MITM attacks, free Wi-Fi, and so on must be considered before making the move to wireless networking.

▶ **Is remote management required?**—Depending on the equipment purchased, it might or might not have the capability for remote management. The need for remote management must be balanced against the budget.

Cable Review

Imagine that you have been asked to review your company's cabling upgrade options. As an auditor, how would you describe the advantages and disadvantages of each of the potential solutions?

1. Complete this challenge by completing the following chart.

Topology	Feature	Advantage	Disadvantage
Star			
Bus			
Ring			
Mesh			

2. Use the information from the preceding sections to verify your answers.

Network Equipment

Before beginning any discussion on network equipment, we present some basic terms to ensure that you understand common issues related to network equipment. As discussed previously the most widely used LAN protocol is Ethernet. As a baseband technology, only one device can transmit at a time. *Collisions* occur when more than one device in the same collision domain attempts to transmit at the same time. Therefore, a collision occurs when two devices attempt to transmit at the same time. *Collision domains* are defined by the devices that share the same physical medium. As an example, Figure 6.6 displays a bus network with three computers. These three computers all share the same collision domain. Another term you should be aware of is *broadcast domain*. A broadcast domain is a group of devices that can receive other devices' broadcast messages. Routers usually serve as the demarcation line for broadcast domains.

Now let's work up the stack and discuss some of the various types of networking equipment. First up for review is the *repeater*, which is nothing more than an amplifier that can be used to extend the range of the physical network. A repeater receives the signal, regenerates the signal, and forwards it. Not far up the food chain above repeaters are *hubs*. Hubs are simply multiport repeaters that provide physical connectivity by allowing all the connected devices to communicate with one another. A hub is basically a common wire to which all computers have shared access. Hubs are on the decline because of their low maximum throughput and their security vulnerabilities. Collisions are a big problem with hubs—any time utilization approaches 20% or more, the number of collisions skyrockets and the overall average throughput decreases. Switches have replaced hubs.

One other older technology worth mentioning is the Layer 2 *bridge*. Bridges predate Layer 2 switches; they are software based and much slower than hardware-based switches. Bridges separate collision domains and act as a store-and-forward device. Another big problem with bridges is that they pass broadcast traffic. Much like hubs, bridges have mostly disappeared from the corporate network.

Layer 2 switches perform in much the same way as a hub, with the exception that switches segment traffic. They operate at the data link layer of the OSI model. Because of this design, each port on a switch is a separate collision domain. On an Ethernet, LAN switches segment traffic by observing the source and destination MAC address of each data frame. These MAC addresses are stored in a *random access memory* (RAM) lookup table, which can then be used to determine which port traffic should be forwarded to. The frame is forwarded to only that switch port; therefore, other ports never see the traffic. Switches provide higher throughput than a hub and can function in full duplex. Not all switches are made the same. Switch manufacturers have developed various ways to handle incoming frames, such as store-and-forward and cut-through. Store-and-forward waits for the frame to be completely inputted into the switch before forwarding. A cut-through design is faster because the frame is quickly forwarded to the targeted device.

> **NOTE**
>
> **Layer 3 Switching**   Although traditionally switches are seen as Layer 2 devices, switches can be found at Layer 4 and work up to Layer 7. Higher-layer switches are known as content switches, content services switches, or application switches.

Routers reside at Layer 3 of the OSI model and are used to bridge dissimilar networks, join distant networks, and separate broadcast domains. Routers forward packets from one network to another based on network-layer information. For most networks, this information is an IP address. The IP address identifies the targeted host device. The router uses routing protocols to identify the best path from the source router to the destination device.

Closely related to routers are *gateways*. A gateway is a network device that is equipped for interfacing with another network that uses different protocols. In other words, gateways provide protocol conversion and, according to ISACA, can be found at Layer 4 and higher.

Modems are also a common piece of networking equipment. The word *modem* is short for *modulate/demodulate*. Modems convert a digital signal to an analog signal for transmission over the phone line. Modems are considered data communications equipment because they enable users to use phone lines to connect to distant computer networks. Modems are tasked with separating data into bits, synchronizing the signal with the distant computer, and then transmitting the sequence of bits sequentially.

The final piece of network equipment for review is the *wireless access point* (wireless AP). Wireless APs are used for LAN communication and started becoming popular in 2000. Wireless APs enable users to connect wireless devices to form a wireless network. Wireless APs are usually connected to a wired network and can relay data between wired and wireless devices. Table 6.4 provides an overview of the primary types of network equipment.

TABLE 6.4   Network Equipment

Equipment	OSI Layer	Description
Gateway	OSI Layer 4 or higher	Gateways operate at the transport layer and above. Gateways translate each source-layer protocol into the appropriate destination-layer protocol. As an example, an application-layer gateway is found at Layer 7.
Router	OSI Layer 3	Routers are used to connect distant sites connected by a WAN, improve performance by limiting physical broadcast domains, and ease network management by segmenting devices into smaller subnets, rather than one large network.

TABLE 6.4 *Continued*

Equipment	OSI Layer	Description
Switch	OSI Layer 2	Switches are hardware based and provide logical segmentation by observing the source and destination physical address of each data frame. Networking virtual LANs (VLANs) is one function that many switches can provide. VLANs separate various ports on a switch, therefore segmenting traffic much like a Layer 3 router function would.
Bridge	OSI Layer 2	Bridges connect two separate collision domains and provide physical segmentation. Bridges are software based and do not block broadcast traffic.
802.11 Wireless Access Devices	OSI Layer 2	Wireless access points can be found on OSI Layer 2, while those devices with routing capabilities can be found on OSI Layer 3.
Hub	OSI Layer 1	Hubs connect individual devices and provide physical connectivity so that devices can share data. Hubs amplify and regenerate the electrical signals. They are similar to repeaters, except that hubs have multiple ports.
Repeater	OSI Layer 1	Repeaters are designed only to boost signal strength and remove noise. Repeaters were designed to overcome cable distance limitations.

EXAM ALERT

Know Networking Equipment   Exam candidates should understand what each piece of networking equipment does and where it fits into the OSI model. Know where devices operate.

OSI Model Challenge

Most likely, you are familiar with what this chapter has covered with the OSI model. In this challenge exercise, you fill in the layers of the OSI model and place the scrambled items in their proper position.

1. Review the items shown in Table 6.5.

TABLE 6.5   OSI Equipment and Protocols

Layer	Layer Name	Equipment	Protocol or Service
	Network	Hubs	IP
	Physical	Routers	UDP
	Application	Switches	TCP

(continues)

(continued)

TABLE 6.5   Continued

Layer	Layer Name	Equipment	Protocol or Service
	Data link	Gateways	Telnet
	Transport	Copper cable	HTTP
	Presentation	Repeaters	Ethernet
	Session	Bridges	Token Ring

2. Place the items shown in Table 6.5 in their proper order in Table 6.6.

TABLE 6.6   Blank OSI Challenge Table

Layer	Layer Name	Equipment	Protocol or Service

3. Compare your answers as created in Table 6.6 to the completed Table 6.7.

TABLE 6.7   Completed OSI Challenge Table

Layer	Layer Name	Equipment	Protocol or Service
1	Physical	Copper cable	
		Hubs	
		Repeaters	
2	Data link	Switches	Ethernet Token Ring
		Bridges	
3	Network	Routers	IP
4	Transport	Gateways	TCP UDP
5	Session	Gateways	
6	Presentation	Gateways	
7	Application	Gateways	HTTP Telnet

Firewalls

The term *firewall* has been used since the 1990s and describes a device that guards the entrance to a private network. Firewalls were developed to keep out unauthorized traffic. Firewalls have undergone generations of improvements so that today several different types of firewall exist. These include the packet filter, application proxy, circuit proxy, and stateful inspection.

Packet filter firewalls operate at Layer 3 of the OSI model. Packet filters look at the packet header to determine whether to block or pass traffic. Packet filters can be thought of as the first generation of firewalls. They inspect the TCP/IP headers and make a decision based on a set of predefined rules. Packet filters simply drop packets that do not conform to the predefined rule set. These rules can include the following:

- ▶ Source IP address

- ▶ Destination IP address

- ▶ TCP/UDP source port

- ▶ TCP/UDP destination port

- ▶ TCP flags (SYN, FIN, ACK, and so on)

Packet filters are considered stateless. This means that they store no information about the state of the session, which, in turn, means that packet filters are simple and fast but are vulnerable to attack. Spoofing is an example of a packet filter vulnerability.

One advancement in the firewall was the development of the proxy. By definition, the word *proxy* means "to stand in place of." Therefore, a proxy is a hardware or software device that can perform address translation and communicates with the Internet on behalf of the network. The real IP address of the user remains hidden behind the proxy server. The host running the proxy service is known as an *application gateway*. Application proxies provide a higher level of security.

As you can see in the Step-by-Step 6.2, application proxies offer increased security because they don't allow untrusted systems to have a direct connection to internal computers. Application proxies accept packets from the external network, copy the packets, inspect them for irregularities, change the addresses to the correct internal device, and then put them back on the wire to the destination device. An application proxy operates at Layer 7 of the OSI model. For the application proxy to work correctly, it must understand the protocols and applications with which it is working.

STEP BY STEP

6.2 Application Proxy Process

1. The internal user generates a web request for www.yahoo.com.

2. The application proxy receives the request and alters the source address from the internal user to the address of the application proxy. The application proxy then forwards the request to the web server.

3. The web server www.yahoo .com receives the request and replies to the application proxy.

4. The application proxy checks its state table and uses this information to convert the destination address from the address of the application proxy to the address of the internal user. The data is inspected and then is forwarded to the internal user.

5. The internal user receives the data from www.yahoo.com from the application proxy.

Somewhere below an application proxy is a circuit-level proxy, which operates at Layer 5 of the OSI model. A circuit-level proxy closely resembles a packet-filtering device because it makes decisions on addresses, ports, and protocols. It does not provide the depth of security that an application-level proxy does because it does not inspect higher-layer applications. Its advantage is that it works with a wider range of protocols. Application proxies and circuit-level proxies do have something in common because both have the capability to maintain state. Stateful-inspection firewalls have the capability to keep track of every communication channel, with a state table. Because of this, they are considered an intelligent firewall. Packet filters do not have this capability.

EXAM ALERT

Application Proxy It is important to note that the application proxy provides the greatest level of protection because it inspects at all levels of the OSI model.

Firewall Configuration

Firewall configurations include *packet filtering, dual-homed gateway, screened host, and screened subnet*. A single-tier packet filter design has one packet-filtering router installed between the trusted and untrusted network, usually the Internet and the corporation's network. The problems with this design become amplified as the network grows larger and because the *packet filter* has limited capabilities. Figure 6.7 illustrates this design.

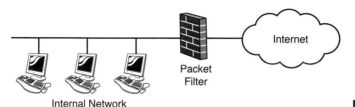

FIGURE 6.7   Packet filtering.

A *dual-homed gateway* is an improvement over the basic packet-filtering router. Dual-homed gateways consist of a bastion host that has two network interfaces. One important item is that IP forwarding is disabled on the host. Additional protection can be provided by adding a packet-filtering router in front of the dual-homed host. Figure 6.8 illustrates this design.

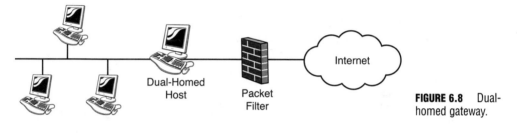

FIGURE 6.8   Dual-homed gateway.

NOTE

Bastion Hosts   The term *bastion host* has come to define the servers located in a DMZ or an untrusted area. These servers are designed much differently than those found in the internal network. Bastion hosts are typically hardened so that nonessential services are removed. Bastion hosts commonly perform tasks such as Web, email, DNS, and FTP.

The *screened host firewall* adds a router and screened host. The router is typically configured to see only one host computer on the intranet network. Users on the intranet have to connect to the Internet through this host computer, and external users cannot directly access other computers on the intranet. Figure 6.9 illustrates this design.

The *screened subnet* sets up a type of *DMZ*, a term that comes from the no man's (demilitarized) zone that was set up between North and South Korea following the Korean War in the 1950s. DMZs are typically set up to give external users access to services within the DMZ. Basically, shared services such as the Internet, email, and DNS can be placed within a DMZ; the DMZ would provide no other access to services located within the internal network. Screened subnet and DMZs are the basis for most modern network designs. Figure 6.10 illustrates this firewall design.

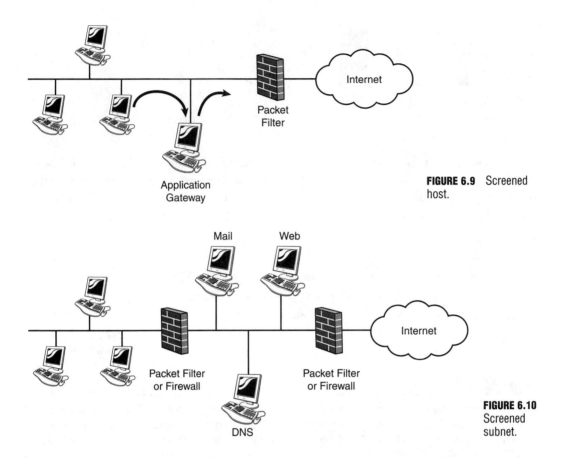

FIGURE 6.9 Screened host.

Application Gateway

FIGURE 6.10 Screened subnet.

All this talk of DMZs and screened subnets brings up one final issue—Network Address Translation (NAT). NAT allows a single device, such as a router or firewall, to act as an agent between the Internet and a local network. NAT was originally designed to deal with the shortage of IPv4 addresses. NAT is addressed in RFC 1631. Besides conserving public IP addresses, NAT provides security by providing address translation. This means that only a single, unique IP address is all that is needed to support an entire group of computers.

Wide Area Networks

Wide area networks (WANs) are much different than LANs. Whereas almost all companies own their LAN infrastructure, very few own their WAN infrastructure. Running a cable along the side of the interstate from Los Angeles to New York is usually not feasible. WANs and LANs also use very different protocols. WAN protocols are designed for the long-haul transmission of data. CISAs must understand WAN protocols and should focus on issues such as redundancy and fault tolerance. WAN protocols can be placed into two broad categories: *packet switching* and *circuit switching*.

Packet Switching

Packet-switched networks share bandwidth with other devices. They are considered more resilient and work well for on-demand connections with bursty traffic. Packet-switched protocols packetize data in much the same manner as the Ethernet or a Token Ring would. The data is placed into a frame structure. Let's look at some different types of packet-switching protocols and services:

- ▶ **X.25**—Although it might sound like a government secret spy plane, X.25 is actually one of the original packet-switching technologies. It was developed in 1976 and operates at the physical, data link, and network layers of the OSI model. Once used extensively, X.25 is no longer widely used. X.25 has speeds of up to 56Kbps and is considered reliable.

- ▶ **Frame Relay**—Think of this technology as the son of X.25. Frame Relay improved upon X.25 and relies more on the upper layers of the OSI model for error handling. Frame Relay controls bandwidth usage by use of a *committed information rate* (CIR). The CIR specifies the maximum guaranteed bandwidth that the customer is guaranteed. Although higher rates might be possible, the CIR represents the level the service provider is committed to providing. If additional bandwidth is available, the data will pass; if no additional bandwidth is available, the data is marked with discard eligibility and discarded.

- ▶ **Asynchronous Transfer Mode (ATM)**—This cell-switching technology operates at the data link layer of the OSI model. ATM is an asynchronous protocol that supports classes of service. ATM provides high bandwidth for bursty traffic and works well for time-sensitive applications. Because the switching process occurs in hardware, delays are minimized. ATM can be used on LANs or WANs.

- ▶ **Multiprotocol Label Switching (MPLS)**—MPLS is a framework that provides for the efficient switching of traffic flows through IP, ATM, and Frame Relay networks. Addresses are read just once as the packet enters the cloud, thereby providing more efficient routing. MPLS features class-of-service so that packets can be prioritized.

> **NOTE**
>
> **Voice over IP (VoIP)**   Although it is not a packet-switching protocol, VoIP is carried on packet-switched networks in IP packets. Networks that have been configured to carry VoIP treat voice communications as just another form of data. Auditors should be aware of VoIP because of its security issues such as eavesdropping, the potential for denial of service, and also because loss of the data network can disable VoIP.

Circuit Switching

Circuit switching is the second type of WAN technology up for discussion. Telecommunication providers have used circuit switching since 1891, when a Kansas City undertaker patented the first one. The most common form of circuit switching is the *plain old telephone service* (POTS).

▶ **POTS**—This humble voice-grade analog telephone service is used for voice calls and for connecting to the Internet and other locations via modem. Modem speeds can vary from 9,600bps to 56Kbps. Although the POTS service is relatively inexpensive, very reliable, and widely available, it offers only low data speeds.

▶ **Integrated Services Digital Network (ISDN)**—This circuit-switched technology has worldwide usage and is similar to POTS, except that the signal is 100% digital. ISDN uses separate frequencies called channels on a special digital connection. It consists of B channels used for voice, data, video, and fax services, and a D channel used for signaling by the service provider and user equipment. The D channel operates at a low 16Kbps, and the B channels operate at a speed up to 64Kbps. By binding the B channels together, ISDN can achieve higher speeds. ISDN is available in two levels, *basic rate interface* (BRI) and *primary rate interface* (PRI). ISDN BRI features two 64 B channels and one 16Kbps D channel; ISDN PRI features 23 64 B channels and one 16Kbps D channel.

▶ **T-carriers**—This service is used for leased lines. A leased line is assigned to specific locations. Users pay a fixed fee for this service. An example of the T-carrier is T1, which uses time-division multiplexing and has a composite data rate of 1.544Mbps. T3s are the next available choice, with a composite data rate of 45Mbps.

▶ **Digital subscriber line (DSL)**—This circuit-switched technology provides high bandwidth and works over existing telephone lines. Most DSL services are asymmetric, which means that the download speed is much faster than the upload speed. DSL is considered an "always on" circuit-switched technology.

REVIEW BREAK

This chapter covers a lot of technology. This review break has been designed to help you review some of the key terms that deal with LAN and WAN protocols.

Item	Usage	Attributes
Ethernet	LAN protocol	Contention-based protocol, CSMA/CD
Token Ring	LAN protocol	Collision-avoidance protocol CSMA/CA
ATM	WAN protocol	Packet-switching technology
X.25	WAN protocol	Packet-switching technology
Frame Relay	WAN protocol	Packet-switching technology, features a CIR
DSL	WAN protocol	Circuit-switching technology
POTS	WAN protocol	Circuit-switching technology
ISDN	WAN protocol	Circuit-switching technology, two types include BRI and PRI

Wireless Networks

Today more wireless devices are available than ever before, from Bluetooth to HiperLAN, HomeRF, and Wireless LAN (WLAN). One of the most popular wireless standard families of specifications is the *802.11* standards, which the IEEE developed. Wireless system components include the following:

▶ **Service Set IDs (SSID)**—For a computer to communicate or use the WLAN, it must be configured to use the same Service Set ID (SSID). The SSID distinguishes one wireless network from another.

▶ **Wireless access points**—A wireless access point is a centralized wireless device that controls the traffic in the wireless medium and can be used to connect wireless devices to a wired network.

▶ **Wireless networking cards**—These are used much like wired networking cards: They connect devices to the wireless network.

▶ **Encryption**—802.11 encryption standards include the aging *Wired Equivalent Privacy* (WEP) protocol, which was designed to provide the same privacy a user would have on a wired network. WEP is based on the RC4 symmetric encryption standard. Newer encryption standards include *WiFi Protected Access* (WPA) and WPA2.

Implementations of 802.11 include 802.11b, 802.11a, 802.11i, 802.11g, and 802.11n. Table 6.8 provides details for each.

TABLE 6.8   WLAN Standards and Details

IEEE WLAN Standard	Rated Speeds	Frequencies
802.11b	11Mbps	2.4000–2.2835GHz
802.11a	54Mbps	5.725–5.825GHz
802.11i	54Mbps	2.4000–2.2835GHz
802.11g	54Mbps	2.4000–2.2835GHz
802.11n	540Mbps	2.4000–2.2835GHz

Wireless devices can use a range of techniques to broadcast, the three most common of which are as follows:

▶ **Orthogonal frequency-division multiplexing (OFDM)**—OFDM splits the signal into smaller subsignals that use a frequency-division multiplexing technique to send different pieces of the data to the receiver on different frequencies simultaneously.

▶ **Direct-sequence spread spectrum (DSSS)**—DSSS is a spread-spectrum technology that uses a wide range of radio frequencies. Small pieces of data are then mapped to a pattern of ratios called a *spreading code*. The higher the spreading code, the more resistant the signal is to interference, but with less available bandwidth. As an example, the Federal Communication Commission (FCC) requires at least 75 frequencies per transmission channel. The transmitter and the receiver must be synchronized to the same spreading code.

▶ **Frequency-hopping spread spectrum (FHSS)**—FHSS works somewhat differently, by dividing a broad slice of the bandwidth spectrum into smaller subchannels of about 1MHz. The transmitter then hops between subchannels. Each subchannel is used to send out short bursts of data for a short period of time. This period of time is known as the *dwell time*. For devices to communicate, each must know the proper dwell time and must be synchronized to the proper hopping pattern.

Table 6.9 summarizes the primary wireless standards.

TABLE 6.9   WLAN Standards and Details

Service	Frequency	Max Speed	Transmission Scheme	Security Feature
802.11a	5GHz	54Mbps	OFDM	WEP
802.11b	2.4GHz	11Mbps	DSSS	WEP
802.11g	2.4GHz	54Mbps	OFDM/DSSS	WPA
802.11i	2.4GHz	11Mbps	DSSS	WPA, TKIP, WPA2 AES, RADIUS
Bluetooth	2.45GHz	2Mbps	FHSS	PPTP, SSL, or VPN
HomeRF	2.4GHz	10Mbps	FHSS	SWAP

Auditors must examine wireless systems closely and verify that these systems being used are configured per security policy. Some general concerns arise with these systems. One big concern is that wireless networks don't end at the organization's outer walls; the signal can extend far beyond. This raises the issue of confidentiality because unauthorized individuals can intercept the signal. Another concern is that most wireless systems can have security disabled by default, even if security is being used; weak security mechanisms such as WEPs are insecure. WEPs can be broken in less than five minutes. Even if stronger encryption mechanisms are being used, it's important that the encryption key be periodically changed. Long-term use of static keys is a big security concern.

Portable Wireless Devices

Smaller wireless devices can also be a concern. Camera phones enable users to take photos in otherwise secure areas. PDAs and Blackberrys can be easily lost or stolen. It's unfortunate, but these devices usually lack the level of security of desktop systems and servers. Organizations need to implement policies and procedures to address the following issues with these devices:

▶ **Identification and authentication**—Handheld devices should use passwords or have some other type of authentication controls. After a preset number of password attempts, the device should lock or disable itself.

▶ **Applications and programs**—Controls should be used to limit what types of programs can be loaded on handheld devices. The organization's security policy should define what users can install or what is allowed.

▶ **Storage cards and memory**—Most handheld devices have memory slots for additional storage. Storage cards are an easy way to expand memory, but they can also be removed, lost, or stolen. Because of these concerns, organizations should consider a security policy requiring that all such cards use encryption.

▶ **Data transfer**—Handheld devices offer the capability to store, copy, or send large amounts of information via email. Company policy should specify who is allowed to use these devices and what usage is acceptable.

▶ **Backup and restore**—Handheld devices can be lost, stolen, or transferred to other employees. Company policies should specify how information is to be backed up, restored, or wiped.

▶ **Lost or stolen device**—Easily one of the most pressing security issues of handheld devices. Depending on how the previous items are addressed, a lost device can be anything from a nuisance to a high-level security threat.

Internet

Before you can access the Internet, you need an *Internet service provider* (ISP). ISPs are the companies that provide communication services and the capability to connect to the Internet. ISPs connect to *national service providers* (NSPs). NSPs are the big brothers of ISPs and consist of major telecommunications companies, such as MCI, AT&T, and so on. The NSPs provide a mesh of telecommunication lines that crisscross the United States and span the world. The points at which traffic from an ISP hits the backbone of the Internet are known as *national access points*. These are much like a series of tubes used to route traffic through different parts of the country.

Although many believe that the Internet and the World Wide Web are the same, this is not correct. The term *Internet* was first used in a paper in 1974 when Vinton Cerf from Stanford was writing about TCP/IP. The Internet is a network of networks that is publicly accessible. The Internet provides support for many protocols and applications, such as email and the World Wide Web. Tim Berners-Lee invented the World Wide Web in 1989. The World Wide Web is an array of documents, papers, and resources linked by hyperlinks and URLs. The *Hypertext Markup Language* (HTML) and *Hypertext Transfer Protocol* (HTTP) standards originally defined the Web architecture. HTTP is a relatively simple, stateless, ASCII-based protocol. Unlike other applications, an HTTP TCP session does not stay open waiting for multiple requests and their responses. HTTP is based on TCP and typically runs on port 80. HTTP has only four stages:

1. Open the TCP request to the IP address and port number in the URL.

2. Request a service by sending request headers to define a method such as GET.

3. Complete the transaction by responding with response headers that contain data.

4. Close the TCP connection and do not save any information about the transaction.

There's more to the Web than HTTP. The standard web application is the web browser. Well-known web browsers include Internet Explorer, Netscape Navigator, and Mozilla Firefox. The transport protocol might be HTTP, but it can also be used with *Secure Sockets Layer* (SSL) or other protocols to provide encryption. When a user enters an address into the web browser, it is done in the form of a *uniform resource locator* (URL). Basically, the URL just identifies the address on the World Wide Web that the user is requesting. For example, if the user is looking for http://www.thesolutionfirm.com/CISA_training, the URL is broken down as follows:

▸ http:// identifies the protocol being used.

▸ www.thesolutionfirm.com identifies the web resource "www" and the server "thesolutionfirm" being contacted.

▸ CISA_training identifies the directory being requested.

Cookies are another component of the Internet and web browsers. Basically, they make the stateless HTTP protocol stateful—normally, as a user moves from one web page to another, HTTP has no way of keeping up with where the user has been or what he or she is doing. Cookies allow activity to be tracked. For example, if you visit http://www.yahoo.com and set up a personalized home page, that information is stored in a cookie so that each time you visit the Yahoo! website, the cookie can be retrieved and your preferences loaded. Cookies make possible the capability to store shopping lists or add items to an online shopping cart that can be processed later. The dark side of cookies is that they are sometimes used to hold passwords or other sensitive information and may have a long expiration time. Anyone can retrieve this information, which can endanger the security of the user.

Web pages don't always have to be static; many have active content. Java applets operate within a controlled environment. Java operates within a sandbox environment to provide some security. This functionality can be attacked and, therefore, is susceptible to risk.

NOTE

Consider these points about Java:

▶ Java is a compiled high-level language.

▶ It can be used on any type of computer.

▶ It uses a sandbox security scheme.

Common Gateway Interface (CGI) is another web-based machine-independent software program. CGI is used to extend the functionality of a web application but has some security risk. Its purpose is to allow web servers to call external routines and programs. CGI code must be closely examined because any bug can allow an attacker to gain unauthorized access to the web server. Other web security issues include cross-site scripting and malicious JavaScript.

The final issue of the Internet is one of privacy because the Internet knows no boundaries. Data, personal information, credit card numbers, and even medical records can be easily moved from one country to another. The systems used to store such sensitive information could be of high or low security. Auditors must look at such issues closely and ensure that the level of control provided meets internal, government, and industry standards. Privacy is addressed in laws such as the European Union Safe Harbor Privacy Principles.

Network Administration and Control

Tasks

▶ Evaluate problem and incident management practices to ensure that incidents, problems, or errors are recorded, analyzed, and resolved in a timely manner.

▶ Evaluate the functionality of the IT infrastructure (for example, network components, hardware, system software) to ensure it supports the organization's objectives.

Knowledge Statement

▶ Knowledge of system's performance monitoring processes, tools, and techniques (e.g., network analyzers, system utilization reports, load balancing)

Networks are highly complex technical systems. The purpose of the network is to support the strategy and needs of the company. This requires ongoing monitoring and planning for future growth and changes. It takes time to make upgrades, so planned changes must be worked out months, if not years, in advance.

Help-desk personnel should prepare help-desk reports to track help-desk requests and detail the types of requests received. These can range from password resets to server errors or application availability issues. Help-desk reports can spot trends and identify problems before they become critical. One problem users might complain of is the lack of availability or latency of the network. *Latency* is the delay that information will experience from the source to the destination. Latency can be caused because data must travel great distances or because of high volumes of network traffic and inadequate bandwidth. Latency can be measured with the ping command:

```
C:\>ping www.yahoo.com
Reply from 209.191.93.52: bytes=32 time=20ms TTL=57
Reply from 209.191.93.52: bytes=32 time=20ms TTL=57
Reply from 209.191.93.52: bytes=32 time=20ms TTL=57
Reply from 209.191.93.52: bytes=32 time=20ms TTL=57
Ping statistics for 209.191.93.52:
    Packets: Sent = 4, Received = 4, Lost = 0 (0% loss),
Approximate round trip times in milli-seconds:
    Minimum = 20ms, Maximum =  20ms, Average =  20ms
```

In this example, you can see that the average time to reach www.yahoo.com was 20ms. Although this is a simple way to measure latency, a group of tools can provide much more information on the status of the network. Some of these tools include the following:

▶ Online monitors that analyze network traffic for accuracy or errors

▶ Downtime report tools that watch WAN lines to track interruptions or any loss of service

Some tools can be used to analyze an individual packet on the network and review their structure. Such tools are referred to as protocol analyzers. Protocol analyzers are software tools that are loaded onto a host system. These programs place the host's network card in promiscuous mode so that all data packets on that segment of the network can be captured and observed. Sniffers operate at the data link layer of the OSI model and enable the user to see all the data contained in the packet, even information that might be better off unseen.

Other tools, such as Simple Network Management Protocol (SNMP), can monitor network equipment and track their level of performance. SNMP uses a network console that queries network devices on a regular basis and displays their status. SNMP agents are required on each device that the network administrator seeks to manage. The agents pull this information from the *management information base* (MIB) and then respond to the request. SNMP version 1 lacks security. Version 3 of SNMP offers security and encryption. Big Brother Software, illustrated in Figure 6.11, is an example of network-monitoring software.

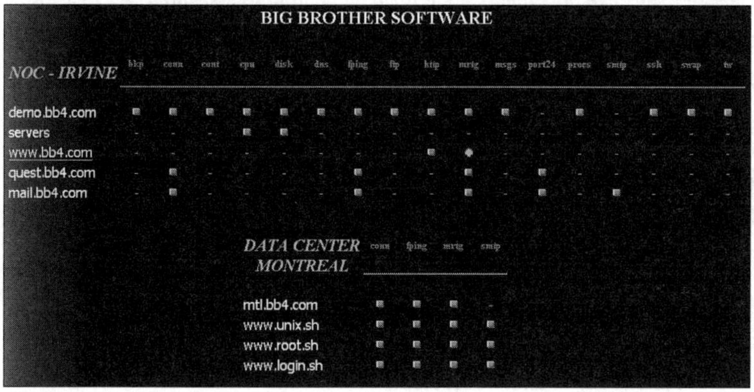

FIGURE 6.11 Big Brother, a network-monitoring tool.

Remote Monitoring (RMON) is a network-monitoring tool supported by a series of probes. RMON enables network administrators to monitor and analyze devices such as routers and switches on a LAN. The type of information RMON probes return includes items such as errors, packet statistics, bandwidth data, and device statistics.

The Dark Side of Network Management

Network-management tools are good for tracking the status of the network and monitoring its overall health. Just remember that a balance must always exist between usability and security. Consider an example of why that's so important. SNMP runs on ports 160 and 161, which should be blocked at the firewall and key network points. Although the administrator might want to leave these open for remote management, the danger is that an attacker might also find out that these ports are open. If that holds true, the attacker can simply use the same type of tools to get an in-depth look at the network. The capability to manage must always be balanced against the need for security.

Risks to Network Infrastructure and Controls

One key task for the auditor is to assess the network infrastructure for potential threats. The auditor should assess existing controls to evaluate their effectiveness at minimizing risks. Table 6.10 lists some of the physical controls that should be verified. Table 6.11 lists some of the logical controls that should be verified.

TABLE 6.10   Auditing Physical Network Controls

Item	Present
Verify that the wiring closet is physically secure.	Yes/No
Perform site survey to verify that no unauthorized wireless devices are being used.	Yes/No
Verify that the server facility is at the proper temperature and humidity.	Yes/No
Ensure that servers are secured and not kept in an area from which they can easily be removed.	Yes/No
Make sure that network manuals and sensitive documents are not left lying around unsecured.	Yes/No
Observe the storage of backup media and make sure it is stored in the proper location.	Yes/No
Visually search for passwords in the general area of networked computers.	Yes/No

TABLE 6.11   Auditing Logical Network Controls

Item	Present
Verify network session logoff.	Yes/No
Verify password-protected screensaver.	Yes/No
Review organizational charts and the described duties of network administrators and operators.	Yes/No
Interview users to verify the awareness of policies and procedures.	Yes/No
Review network documentation to verify that it is current and up-to-date.	Yes/No
Review LAN user profiles and make sure they are set to the appropriate level and are based on the employee's need to know.	Yes/No

Chapter Summary

This chapter reviewed the systems used for IT delivery and support. To better understand these systems, we reviewed concepts such as the OSI model, a seven-layer model that defines networking in a layered fashion. Although the OSI model is widely used for teaching, the system most associated with networking today is TCP/IP, a four-layer model that combines some of the layers found in the OSI model. The TCP/IP model is based on protocols such as IP, a routable protocol used to carry high-layer headers and data. IP commonly carries TCP or UDP. TCP is a connection-oriented protocol used for reliability. UDP is a connectionless protocol used for speed. TCP carries applications such as HTTP and FTP. UDP carries applications such as DHCP, TFTP, and DNS queries.

An IS auditor is expected to understand this technology and know how the various pieces of networking equipment work. The CISA should look closely at the technology the organization uses and examine its controls and potential vulnerabilities. Technology is a great benefit, but without proper controls, it can present many dangers.

Key Terms

- Address Resolution Protocol (ARP)
- Asynchronous Transfer Mode (ATM)
- Attenuation
- Baseband
- Broadband
- Broadcast
- Bus topology
- Carrier Sense Multiple Access/Collision Detection (CSMA/CD)
- Circuit switching
- Coaxial cable
- Collision domain
- Collisions
- Committed information rate (CIR)
- Common Gateway Interface (CGI)
- Cookies

- ▶ Digital subscriber line (DSL)
- ▶ Direct-sequence spread spectrum (DSS)
- ▶ Discovery, offer, request, acceptance (DORA)
- ▶ DMZ
- ▶ Domain name server (DNS)
- ▶ Domain Name Service (DNS)
- ▶ Dual-homed gateway
- ▶ Dwell time
- ▶ Dynamic Host Configuration Protocol (DHCP)
- ▶ Ethernet
- ▶ Fiber-optic cable
- ▶ File Transfer Protocol (FTP)
- ▶ Frequency-hopping spread spectrum (FHSS)
- ▶ Fully qualified domain names (FQDN)
- ▶ Gateway
- ▶ Gigabit Ethernet
- ▶ Hub
- ▶ Hypertext Markup Language (HTML)
- ▶ Hypertext Transfer Protocol (HTTP)
- ▶ Integrated Services Digital Network (ISDN)
- ▶ Internet Protocol (IP)
- ▶ Internet service provider (ISP)
- ▶ Latency
- ▶ Layer 2 bridge
- ▶ Layer 2 switch
- ▶ Management information base (MIB)
- ▶ Media Access Control (MAC)
- ▶ Mesh topology

▶ Metropolitan area network (MAN)

▶ Modem

▶ Multicast

▶ Multiprotocol Label Switching (MPLS)

▶ National access point

▶ National service providers (NSP)

▶ Open Shortest Path First (OSPF)

▶ Orthogonal frequency-division multiplexing (OFDM)

▶ Packet filtering

▶ Packet switching

▶ Personal area network (PAN)

▶ Plain old telephone service (POTS)

▶ Point-to-Point Tunneling Protocol (PPTP)

▶ Repeater

▶ Ring topology

▶ Router

▶ Routing Information Protocol (RIP)

▶ Routing protocol

▶ Screen host firewall

▶ Screened host

▶ Screened subnet

▶ Service Set ID (SSID)

▶ Simple Mail Transfer Protocol (SMTP)

▶ Simple Network Management Protocol (SNMP)

▶ Spreading code

▶ Star topology

▶ Subnet

▶ Terminal-emulation software (TES)

- ▶ Token Ring
- ▶ Transmission Control Protocol (TCP)
- ▶ Twisted-pair cable
- ▶ Unicast
- ▶ Uniform resource locator (URL)
- ▶ User Datagram Protocol (UDP)
- ▶ Virtual LAN (VLAN)
- ▶ Virtual private network (VPN)
- ▶ Voice over IP (VoIP)
- ▶ Wide area network (WAN)
- ▶ WiFi Protected Access (WPA)
- ▶ Wired Equivalent Privacy (WEP)
- ▶ Wireless access point (wireless AP)
- ▶ Wireless PAN (WPAN)

Apply Your Knowledge

This chapter has reviewed many aspects of logical security and discussed how computer networks operate.

In this exercise, you examine the TCP/IP model, identify OSI model components, and describe common firewall characteristics.

Exercises

6.1 Identifying TCP/IP Components

Estimated Time: 10 minutes

1. Using Figure 6.12 and your knowledge of TCP/IP, determine what LAN protocol is being used.

   _____

```
⊞ Frame 34 (912 bytes on wire, 912 bytes captured)
⊞ Ethernet II, Src: Netgear_1f:26:58 (00:09:5b:1f:26:58), Dst: 192.168.123.254 (00:00:94:c6:0c:4f)
⊞ Internet Protocol, Src: 192.168.123.101 (192.168.123.101), Dst: www.isaca.org (65.245.209.55)
⊞ Transmission Control Protocol, Src Port: 1628 (1628), Dst Port: http (80), Seq: 814, Ack: 392, Len: 858
⊟ Hypertext Transfer Protocol
  ⊞ GET /template.cfm?template=/ContentManagement/ContentDisplay.cfm&ContentID=2905 HTTP/1.1\r\n
    Host: www.isaca.org\r\n
    User-Agent: Mozilla/5.0 (Windows; U; Windows NT 5.0; en-US; rv:1.7.12) Gecko/20050915 Firefox/1.0.7\r\n
    Accept: text/xml,application/xml,application/xhtml+xml,text/html;q=0.9,text/plain;q=0.8,image/png,*/*;q=0.5\r\n
    Accept-Language: en-us,en;q=0.5\r\n
    Accept-Encoding: gzip,deflate\r\n
    Accept-Charset: ISO-8859-1,utf-8;q=0.7,*;q=0.7\r\n
    Keep-Alive: 300\r\n
    Connection: keep-alive\r\n
    Referer: http://www.google.com/search?client=firefox-a&rls=org.mozilla%3Aen-US%3Aofficial_s&hl=en&q=CISA+EXAM&btnG=Google+S
    Cookie: __utma=92022786.186025636.1161183212.1162669681.1162679061.8; __utmz=92022786.1162679061.8.8.utmccn=(organic)|utmcs
    \r\n
```

FIGURE 6.12 Network analyzer capture.

2. Refer to Figure 6.12 and identify the proper transport protocol.

3. Referring to Figure 6.12, what application-layer protocol is in use?

You should have answered 1-Ethernet, 2-TCP, and 3-HTTP.

4. Place the following items into the proper layers of the OSI model: MAC addresses, ASCII, TCP, IP, and HTTP.

_____ Application

_____ Presentation

_____ Session

_____ Transport

_____ Network

_____ Data link

_____ Physical

5. Place the following pieces of equipment into the proper layer of the OSI model: fiber, routers, hubs, switches, bridges, packet filters, application proxy firewall.

_____ Application

_____ Presentation

_____ Session

_____ Transport

_____ Network

_____ Data link

_____ Physical

Answers to questions 4 and 5 are as follows:

Application—HTTP, application proxy firewall

Presentation—ASCII

Session

Transport—TCP

Network—IP, routers, packet filters

Data link—MAC addresses, switches, bridges

Physical—Fiber, hubs

Exam Questions

1. Which of the following is the best example of a method to measure latency?

   ○ **A.** SNMP management tool

   ○ **B.** `ping` command

   ○ **C.** traceroute

   ○ **D.** RMON

2. Which of the following is the proper order for the OSI model from the bottom up?

   ○ **A.** Data link, media access, network, transport, session, presentation, application

   ○ **B.** Physical, data link, network, transport, session, presentation, application

   ○ **C.** Physical, data link, network, transport, presentation, session, application

   ○ **D.** Data link, physical link, network, transport, presentation, session, application

3. Which type of data transmission is to a group of devices on a LAN?

   ○ **A.** Unicast

   ○ **B.** Multicast

   ○ **C.** Anycast

   ○ **D.** Broadcast

4. Which of the following is the best explanation of ARP?

   ○ **A.** ARP resolves known domain names to unknown IP addresses.

   ○ **B.** ARP resolves known IP addresses to unknown MAC addresses.

   ○ **C.** ARP resolves known IP addresses to unknown domain names.

   ○ **D.** ARP resolves known MAC addresses to unknown IP addresses.

5. Which of the following best matches the description of a packet-switching technology with a committed information rate?

   ○ **A.** T1

   ○ **B.** ATM

   ○ **C.** X.25

   ○ **D.** Frame Relay

6. Which of the following is a fiber-optic cable standard?

   ○ **A.** 1000BASE-TX

   ○ **B.** 1000BASE-LX

   ○ **C.** 10BASE-T

   ○ **D.** 100BASE-TX

7. An auditor has been asked to perform a network audit. Which of the following is the best place for the auditor to start?

   ○ **A.** Review help-desk report

   ○ **B.** Review database architecture

   ○ **C.** Interview users

   ○ **D.** Review network diagrams

8. Which of the following network designs offers the highest level of redundancy?

   ○ **A.** Bus

   ○ **B.** Star

   ○ **C.** Ring

   ○ **D.** Mesh

9. Which of the following devices would best be suited for reducing the number of collisions on a LAN?

   ○ **A.** Switch

   ○ **B.** Hub

   ○ **C.** Bridge

   ○ **D.** Router

10. Which of the following statements best describes packet switching?

   ○ **A.** Packet switching allows the customer to determine the best path.

   ○ **B.** Packet switching takes a dedicated path established by the vendor.

   ○ **C.** Packet switching allows the vendor to determine the best path.

   ○ **D.** Packet switching takes a dedicated path established by the client.

Answers to Exam Questions

1. **B.** Latency can be caused because data must travel great distances or because of high volumes of network traffic and inadequate bandwidth. Latency can be measured with the `ping` command. Answer A is incorrect because SNMP is used for network management. Answer C is incorrect because traceroute is used to determine the path that traffic takes from one network to another. Answer D is incorrect because RMON is another example of a network-management tool.

2. **B.** The proper order for the OSI model from the bottom up is physical, data link, network, transport, session, presentation, application. Therefore, answers A, C, and D are incorrect.

3. **B.** Network traffic on a LAN can be addressed to one device, many devices, or all devices on the network. Sending information to a group is known as a multicast. Answer A describes one device; answer C describes a technique used in IPv6, which is a directed broadcast; and answer D describes the transmission to everyone.

4. **B.** ARP resolves known IP addresses to unknown MAC addresses. This two-step process is performed by first sending a message to all devices on the LAN requesting the receiver's physical address. If a device recognizes the address as its own, it issues an ARP reply to the sender of the ARP request. Answers A, C, and D are incorrect because they do not properly describe the ARP process.

5. **D.** Frame Relay controls bandwidth usage with a *committed information rate* (CIR) that specifies the maximum guaranteed bandwidth that the customer is guaranteed. Although higher rates might be possible, the CIR represents the level the service provider is committed to providing. Answer A, T1, does not use a CIR and is not packet switching. Answer B, ATM, does not use a CIR. Answer C, X.25, does not use a CIR.

6. **B.** Some of the standards for optical fiber cabling include 10BASE-F, 100BASE-FX, and 1000BASE-LX. Answers A, C, and D are all copper cabling standards.

7. **D.** Reviewing network diagrams is usually the best place for the auditor to start. This gives the auditor a foundational understanding of the network. Although answers A, B, and C are all items that can be performed, they should not be the starting point of the audit.

8. **D.** A mesh offers the highest level of redundancy. Answers A, B, and C are incorrect.

9. **A.** A switch is best suited for reducing the number of collisions on a LAN. Switches segment physical networks. Answer B is incorrect because a hub provides only physical connectivity. Answer C is incorrect because a bridge is inferior to a switch. Bridges are software based and are much slower. Answer D is incorrect because a router is an OSI Layer 3 device.

10. **C.** Packet switching allows the telecommunication's vendor to determine the best path. The vendor is free to route the packetized traffic through the network as it sees fit. Answer A is incorrect because the customer does not determine the path. Answer B is incorrect because packet switching does not use a dedicated path. Answer D is incorrect because the client does not set a dedicated path for packet-switched traffic.

Need to Know More?

▶ A Beginner's Guide to Wireless Security: http://www.pcstats.com/articleview.cfm?articleID=1489

▶ A Guide to Understanding Firewalls: http://www.hslanj.org/Ambrose.pps

▶ An Introduction to Internet Firewalls: http://csrc.nist.gov/publications/nistpubs/

▶ The OSI Model: http://en.wikipedia.org/wiki/OSI_model

▶ Understanding TCP/IP: http://www.cisco.com/univercd/cc/td/doc/product/iaabu/centri4/user/scf4ap1.htm

▶ Network Cabling Basics: http://www.datacottage.com/nch/basics.htm

▶ A Quick Guide to Common Attacks: http://www.windowsecurity.com/articles/Common_Attacks.html

▶ The History of the Internet: http://www.elsop.com/wrc/h_web.htm

▶ Cookies, the Hidden Truth: http://www.cookiecentral.com/

PART IV

Protection of Information Assets

7

CHAPTER SEVEN

Protection of Logical Assets

This chapter, along with Chapter 8, "Physical Security," covers the Protection of Information Assets job practice area of the Certified Information Systems Auditor (CISA) exam. This portion of the exam makes up 31% of the material. Although Chapter 8 looks at many of the physical aspects of this job practice area, Chapter 7 helps you prepare for the CISA exam by covering the following ISACA tasks and knowledge statements, which focus on understanding the importance of the protection of logical assets:

Tasks

Evaluate the design, implementation, and monitoring of logical access controls to ensure the confidentiality, integrity, availability, and authorized use of information assets.

Evaluate network infrastructure security to ensure confidentiality, integrity, availability, and authorized use of the network and the information transmitted.

Evaluate the processes and procedures used to store, retrieve, transport, and dispose of confidential information assets.

Knowledge Statements

Knowledge of the techniques used for design, implementation, and monitoring of security (e.g., threat and risk assessment, sensitivity analysis, privacy impact assessment)

Knowledge of logical access controls for the identification, authentication, and restriction of users to authorized functions and data (e.g., dynamic passwords, challenge/response, menus, profiles)

Knowledge of logical access security architectures (e.g., single sign-on, user identification strategies, identity management)

Knowledge of physical security systems and practices (e.g., biometrics, access cards, cipher locks, tokens)

Knowledge of attack methods and techniques (e.g., hacking, spoofing, Trojan horses, denial of service, spamming)

Knowledge of processes related to monitoring and responding to security incidents (e.g., escalation procedures, emergency incident response team)

Knowledge of network and Internet security devices, protocols, and techniques (e.g., SSL, SET, VPN, NAT)

Knowledge of intrusion detection systems and firewall configuration, implementation, operation, and maintenance

Knowledge of encryption algorithm techniques (e.g., AES, RSA)

Knowledge of public key infrastructure (PKI) components (e.g., certification authorities, registration authorities) and digital signature techniques

Knowledge of virus detection tools and control techniques

Knowledge of security testing and assessment tools (e.g., penetration testing, vulnerability scanning)

Knowledge of voice communications security (e.g., voice over IP)

Knowledge of the processes and procedures used to store, retrieve, transport, and dispose of confidential information assets

Knowledge of controls and risks associated with the use of portable and wireless devices (e.g., PDAs, USB devices, Bluetooth devices)

Outline

Study Strategies

This chapter addresses the information you need to know for the protection of logical assets. An organization might have the best physical controls in the world, but they are of little use if no logical security is present. A large portion of the CISA exam deals with logical access and controls, such as encryption, firewalls, antivirus software, and intrusion detection. A CISA candidate should review the following primary topics for the exam:

▶ The importance of information security

▶ Logical access exposures

▶ Basic network infrastructure controls

▶ The role of encryption

▶ The steps to audit information security mechanisms

▶ The steps to audit network security controls

Introduction

We live in a changing world. At one time, the greatest threat an organization faced was physical in nature. This is no longer the case; computers and networks have flattened the world and changed the playing field. Organizations are no longer accessible only through their doors and windows. The invention of the Internet and the rise of e-commerce means that companies are connected on a global scale 24×7. Although this has been a time of good growth for e-commerce, it also presents new challenges, such as the protection of personal information and intellectual property, protection against intrusions, and prevention of denial-of-service attacks.

This chapter discusses the ways in which logical security can be attacked, how it can be strengthened, and how you, as an IS auditor, can verify that the organization's logical security controls are sufficient to protect vital assets. As an IS auditor, these are all issues that concern you. Anyone who has watched the news knows that there has been no shortage of high-profile breaches of security over the last several years. Privacy Rights International reports that, just in the month of June 2006, more than one million names and social security numbers were stolen through either loss of physical assets or breach of logical security. Industry groups, trade groups, state governments, and federal governments have responded to these problems by implementing stronger guidelines for controls. These address issues such as control of personal information, copyrights, intellectual property, sensitive data, and access control. Many of these laws, policies, and procedures require certain levels of security controls.

The Goals of Logical Security

Task

▶ Evaluate network infrastructure security to ensure confidentiality, integrity, availability, and authorized use of the network and information transmitted.

Security controls implemented within an organization should be layered so that if any one security mechanism fails, another can take its place. That is the concept of *defense-in-depth*, building security in layers. If one layer is breached, you have multiple layers beneath it to continue protecting your organization's assets. Defense-in-depth is about finding a balance between the protection, cost, and value of the informational asset. For example, if you have an information-classification system but also have encrypted data, you have two security controls in place. In this example, strong controls have been placed on who has access to the information and the physical devices where the information is located has been secured, and, when in transit, that information is transmitted only in encrypted form. This does not mean that the information cannot be attacked or disclosed, but it does mean that you have placed several effective overlapping layers that will deter its release.

Information Security Protection Mechanisms

Knowledge Statement

▶ Knowledge of the techniques for design, implementation, and monitoring of security (e.g., threat and risk assessment, sensitivity analysis, privacy impact assessment)

What is the single most important thing to know about protection mechanisms and controls? The controls work best when layered one after another or on top of each other. This provides defense-in-depth and makes it difficult for an attacker or wrongdoer to bypass all the layers of control successfully or without being detected. Building defense in depth provides for better security. This is one of the primary goals of a CISA. The auditor must understand these controls and ensure that they provide a level of assurance.

Of course, the IS auditor cannot accomplish the overall job of security alone. This requires a structure of control:

▶ **The organization**—The organization is bound by legal and ethical concerns to provide a certain level of protection for critical assets.

▶ **Senior management**—The top tier of the company must provide guidance and support to drive an effective security-management program. These individuals are ultimately responsible.

▶ **Policies and procedures**—These documents provide the framework that will be used to motivate the security-management program. They must take into account the mission and objectives of the organization, but also must maintain compliance with all state, federal, and local laws. Policies are important because they serve as a declaration of management's concern with protecting privacy.

▶ **Security awareness and education**—This critical component is sometimes overlooked. Without training, how will employees know what policies are important? Most employees want to do the right thing, but training is required to map that desire to the knowledge of what needs to be done. Many types of security training and awareness can be performed, and each has a specific task. As an example, nondisclosure agreements (NDAs) remind employees of what information they are forbidden to disseminate. Likewise, email-awareness programs alert employees to the danger of clicking on links of unsolicited emails.

▶ **Monitoring and compliance**—Even the best security program in the world has little value if it is not monitored and lacks a mechanism to establish accountability. Many organizations must maintain accountability not only to their organizations, but also to state and federal laws. HIPAA and SOX are two good examples.

▶ **Incident handling and response**—An incident that affects logical security must be investigated and examined to determine what went wrong. This requires incident response policies and procedures. Part of an effective response is education. Learning what went wrong and educating users about the reason can prevent future incidents.

The Role of Confidentiality, Integrity, and Availability

Proper assurance means that the logical controls to protect the confidentiality, integrity, and availability of the organization's information assets have been examined. Confidentiality addresses the fact that sensitive information in storage or in transit is protected from prying eyes that should not have access. Integrity seeks to maintain the correctness of the information, which helps establish trust in the information's correctness. Availability addresses the fact that information and systems should be available to authorized users when needed. The CISA typically reviews the information and systems in part by examining the policies, procedures, and logical controls that have been implemented. The following sections look at some of the key players responsible for the security of the organization.

Roles and Responsibilities

Information security requires responsibility and a host of individuals in many different roles. Together these individuals help build a structure that creates, controls, maintains, and verifies the security of information and systems. Some key players and their responsibilities are as follows:

▶ **IS security steering committee**—These are individuals from various levels of management who represent the different departments of the organization. They meet to discuss and make recommendations for security issues.

▶ **Executive management**—These individuals are ultimately responsible for the security practices of the organization. Executive management might delegate day-to-day responsibility to another party, but they cannot delegate overall responsibility for the security of the organization.

▶ **Security advisory group**—These individuals are responsible for reviewing security issues with the chief security officer, as well as reviewing security plans and procedures.

▶ **Chief privacy officer**—This individual is responsible for maintaining compliance with local, state, and federal privacy laws. This includes the privacy of employees and customers.

▶ **Chief security officer**—This individual is responsible for the day-to-day security of the organization and its critical assets.

▶ **Process owner**—This individual is responsible for specific processes and for verifying that appropriate security controls are in place and functioning. Responsibilities include the day-to-day management of the assets. The process owner's work focuses on policies and procedures that dictate how an asset is used or maintained. Controlling access, adding and removing privileges for individual users, and ensuring that the proper controls have been implemented are part of the process owner's daily tasks.

▶ **Developers**—These individuals develop code and applications for the organization. They are responsible for implementing the proper security controls within the programs they develop.

▶ **Information security auditor**—This individual is responsible for examining the organization's security procedures and mechanisms. Their job is to provide an independent view on the effectiveness of the organization's security controls. How often this process is performed depends on the industry and its related regulations. As an example, the healthcare industry is governed by HIPAA regulations and requires yearly reviews. Regardless of the industry, senior management should document and approve the audit process.

Information Assets

Before any security controls can be developed, the organization must know what assets it has. One of the most important steps for securing the organization's assets is to identify and inventory all known assets. As an example, a bank that is in charge of protecting a customer database with names, social security numbers, and addresses would want to place a much higher level of control on these assets than it would another database that contained the locations, manager names, and phone numbers of all the bank's local branches. Without a complete and accurate inventory of all components and assets, an asset valuation, criticality, or importance evaluation cannot be performed. When recording information about the organization's assets, you should record the following information:

▶ **Asset identification**—An alphanumeric, barcode, or other means of tagging and identification

▶ **Asset location**—The location of the asset

▶ **Asset risk**—The risk of the asset

▶ **Asset protection**—What type of protection mechanisms are used

▶ **Asset group**—The group or department to which the asset belongs

▶ **Asset owner**—The owner of the asset

Information Classification

Not all of the assets you identify will have the same value. As in the preceding bank example, customer social security numbers have a much greater value than a list that contains branch locations and phone numbers. The best way to classify information is to place it into categories based on the value of the information. When the value is known, it becomes much easier to decide on the level of resources that should be used to protect the data. It wouldn't make sense to spend more on protecting something of lesser value or worth.

Each level of classification that's established should have specific requirements. Luckily for us, others have done much of this work; two widely used schemes already exist to manage and control information: military and commercial (see Table 7.1).

TABLE 7.1 Data Classification Types

Commercial Business Classifications	Military Classifications
Confidential	Top secret
Private	Secret
Sensitive	Confidential
Public	Sensitive
	Unclassified

EXAM ALERT

Know the Two Types of Data-Classification Systems   For the exam, you need to know that information can be classified by a military (confidentiality-based) system or a commercial (integrity-based) system. You should also know the labels used for both.

Regardless of which model is used, the following questions help determine the proper placement of the information:

▶ Who owns the asset?

▶ Who controls access rights and privileges?

▶ Who approves access rights and privileges?

▶ What level of access is granted to the asset?

▶ Who currently has access to the asset?

Other questions the organization must address to determine the proper placement of the information include these:

▶ How old is the information?

▶ What laws govern the protection of the information?

▶ What regulations pertain to the information's disclosure?

▶ What regulations or laws govern data retention?

▶ What is the replacement cost if the information is lost or corrupted?

Privacy Issues

Information classification is only one piece of good security. Control should be placed on sensitive information to prevent it from ending up in the hands of the wrong individual. Privacy of personal information is a very important issue. Companies need to address this concern early by developing a company-wide policy based on a *privacy impact analysis* (PIA). A PIA should determine the risks and effects of collecting, maintaining, and distributing personal information in electronic-based systems. The PIA should be used to evaluate privacy risks and ensure that appropriate privacy controls exist. Existing controls should be examined to verify that accountability is present and that compliance is built in every time new projects or processes are planned to come online. The IS auditor can use the PIA to review how information is handled or to help build a case for stronger controls.

The PIA is tied to three items:

▶ **Technology**—Any time new systems are added or modifications made, reviews are needed.

▶ **Processes**—Business processes change, and, even though a company might have a good change policy, the change-management system might be overlooking personal information privacy.

▶ **People**—Companies change employees and others with whom they do business. Anytime business partners, vendors, or service providers change, the impact of the change on privacy needs to be reexamined.

Privacy controls tend to be overlooked for the same reason many security controls are. Management might have a preconceived idea that security controls will reduce the efficiency or speed of business processes. To overcome these types of barriers, senior management must make a strong commitment to security and demonstrate their support. A key component of the process is security awareness and training. Most managers and users do not instinctively know about good security practices; they require education. Part of the educational process involves increasing the awareness level of the costs involved if sensitive information is lost. Risk-assessment activities aid in the process by informing employees of the actual costs for the loss of security. This helps justify the controls needed to protect sensitive information. One of the controls is system access, our next topic of discussion.

Privacy and Trust

Organizations must guard privacy and trust to protect their employees, customers, and image. This was a difficult lesson that the Guidance Corporation learned in late December 2005. The Guidance Corporation is one of the leading companies that develops a variety of products for incident response, misuse discovery, and digital forensics.

(continues)

(continued)

Because of the company's line of business, it most likely found it difficult to send out notices in December 2005 advising of a breach of security that exposed the details of approximately 3,800 credit cards. The credit card numbers were held in an unencrypted database along with the name, address, and phone number of each customer. The breach was first noticed by a customer who complained about having his credit card cancelled.

The company has now stated that it will no longer store this information in such an insecure manner, but it leaves room to speculate on whether the company performed a privacy impact analysis at the very beginning. Although Guidance is not the only company that has experienced such a dilemma in the last few years, this makes clear that if it can happen to a company known for its ability to find and track intrusions, it most certainly can happen to other less technical and adept companies.

System Access

System access involves who has access to what. It is much better to practice the principle of *deny all*, blocking all access. Afterward, allow only the minimum level of access needed. The alternative is to *allow all* and give full open access, and then decide to take away specific types of access from employees. People don't like to lose access, even if it is to a resource they do not use. Logical access is about the controls that allow individuals to read, write, change, or delete information or programs. This is a technical privilege; as such, system-access controls can be placed into four broad categories or layers, as illustrated in Figure 7.1: networks, platforms, databases, and applications.

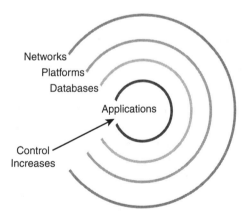

FIGURE 7.1 Four layers of security controls.

The network and platform layers provide the broadest level of control. These generalized controls usually mandate how users log onto systems, what type of access control is used, what type of traffic is allowed, and who has access. Database and application controls are more granular. These controls are much more specific: They might specify how the user can use the data, whether it can be modified, and who can erase it. Table 7.2 highlights some examples of access controls.

TABLE 7.2   Access Control Types

Access Privilege	Access Right
No access	No access permitted
Read	Can read but cannot make changes
Write	Can write to file and make changes
Execute	Can execute a program
Delete	Can delete a file
Change	Can read, write, execute, or delete
Full control	Has all abilities to execute, change, create, or delete

These layers of control help support basic security concepts such as the following:

▶ **Need to know**—Means that even if someone has the required access, that person may obtain information only if he or she has approval for the information.

▶ **Least privilege**—Addresses the fact that individuals are given only the minimum level of information needed to perform their job.

▶ **Separation of duties**—Used to prevent too much power or control in the hands of one person. Separation of duties forces malicious users to collude if they want to launch a successful attack.

It is not uncommon for employees to be resistant to these types of controls. Auditors must make sure these principles are in use when security controls are being designed or reviewed.

Problems with system access usually begin when employees are hired and can continue through the employee's lifecycle. First, it's a known fact that many companies still use a manual provisioning process. When an employee is entered into the system, he or she is manually added to an HR database to establish an employee record. The information usually is then forwarded to the IT department. The IT group creates a profile and grants access based on information from HR or the hiring manager. This allows system access to be granted. The user now has been provisioned, and his or her approval is recorded. In many organizations, this process can take up to two weeks. In addition to the time involved, this process can induce the following problems:

▶ Manual requests for system access rights are slow and reduce user productivity.

▶ Manual processes can cause access errors.

▶ Manual request forms might not be fully completed.

▶ Precise audit reports are time-consuming and, therefore, require sampling.

▶ Many access profiles might not even be valid.

One final important item that the IS auditor must be aware of is *access creep*. Simply stated, access creep occurs as employees move from one job to another within the organization. Each time they transfer or get promoted, they pick up greater system access with increased privileges. This means that organizations must periodically look at individual access rights and ensure that they correspond to a level of least privilege for the tasks to which they have been assigned. Any level of access that exceeds this need should be removed. This concern is restricted not just to current employees, but also to former ones and contractors. When individuals leave the organization, their access rights should be terminated. One way to address this is to automate the system access process with the existing HR system. Then when an employee transfers, gets promoted, demoted, or leaves the organization, access rights should be immediately adjusted. This raises security and increases the effectiveness of access controls. Reports from Gartner Inc. indicate that access creep is one of the biggest problems that organizations face. This is a big problem in systems that are not automated.

System Access-Control Models

System access is about more than how users access resources. It's also about what they can access. Access-control models dictate how users access data and objects. These controls establish specific rules that govern how subjects access data, whether they can access data, and what they can do with the data after it is accessed. Three broad categories of access-control models exist:

▶ Discretionary access control (DAC)

▶ Mandatory access control (MAC)

▶ Role-based access control (RBAC)

Discretionary Access Control

The discretionary access control (DAC) model is titled because access control is left to the owner's discretion. DAC enables owners to activate security controls as they see fit. Consider an analogy of DAC in a peer-to-peer network. In such a configuration, each user is responsible for his or her own security and has the ability to allow or deny other users access to the system or resources. In a DAC environment, the owner is left to determine whether other users have access. The DAC concept includes two key components:

▶ **File and data ownership**—This concept states that all objects within a system must have a designated owner. If objects do not have an owner, they are left unprotected.

▶ **Access rights and permissions**—This concept determines the owner's control of access rights. Access rights include read, write, modify, and execute privileges. These controls are typically configured through some type of access control list (ACL). The ACL identifies users who have authorization to specific information.

Table 7.3 diagrams a sample ACL.

TABLE 7.3   Access Control Rights

Subject	Object 1	Object 2	Object 3	Object 4
Larry	No access	No access	Read	Read/write
Moe	Read	Read	Read/write	Full control
Curly	Full control	Full control	Full control	Full control

Mandatory Access Control

A mandatory access control (MAC) model is static and based on a predetermined list of access privileges; therefore, in a MAC-based system, access is determined by the system rather than the user. The MAC model is typically used by organizations that handle highly sensitive data, such as the U.S. Department of Defense (DoD), National Security Administration (NSA), Central Intelligence Agency (CIA), and Federal Bureau of Investigation (FBI). Systems based on the MAC model use sensitivity labels and are prohibitive in nature; anything that is not explicitly allowed is also denied. Labels such as top secret, secret, and sensitive are assigned to objects. When a user attempts to access an object, the label is examined for a match to the subject's level of clearance. If a match is not found, access is denied. Important items to know about the MAC model include these:

▶ It's considered a requirement of a need-to-know system.

▶ It has more overhead and is nondiscretionary.

▶ All users and resources are assigned a security label.

EXAM ALERT

Know the Differences Between DAC and MAC   For the exam, you need to know that DAC allows the user to control access, whereas MAC uses sensitivity labels and offers the user no control.

Role-Based Access Control

Role-based access control (RBAC), the third type of access control, gives a user certain preestablished rights to objects. These rights are assigned to users based on their roles in the organization. Banks, casinos, and other organizations that have very defined roles use RBAC models. Assigning access rights and privileges to a group instead of an individual reduces the burden on administration.

> **NOTE**
>
> Although DAC, MAC, and RBAC are the three types of access-control models you will need to know for the CISA exam, you should be aware that other models do exist, such as content-dependent access control, lattice-based access control, and rule-based access control.

Logical Access Controls

Knowledge Statements

▶ Knowledge of logical access controls for the identification, authentication, and restriction of users to authorized functions and data (e.g., dynamic passwords, challenge/response, menus, profiles)

▶ Knowledge of logical access security architectures (e.g., single sign-on, user identification strategies, identity management)

▶ Knowledge of physical security systems and practices (e.g., biometrics, access cards, cipher locks, tokens)

Logical access controls address one of the most important topics of this chapter—the controls are put into place to protect against unauthorized access by insiders or outsiders to networks and logical resources.

User identification and authentication (verifying that users are who they say they are) are considered the first steps of the process.

The next step is to decide where the user's identity will be verified. This can be done in one centralized location, or it can be decentralized so that the process occurs closest to the user. The problem of remote access must also be considered. In most organizations, a number of users can log on remotely. Controlling this process and reducing the risk of unauthorized users from gaining remote access is a major concern.

Finally, all users, remote and local, must be held accountable for their actions. This requires the implementation of detective systems to monitor compliance and detect misuse. More than just systems are needed to detect misues, one also needs processes and people. The failure to correctly implement any of the controls can lead to many different types of security risks and vulnerabilities as addressed in the following sections.

Identification and Authentication (I&A)

The first step of granting access to the user is the process of identification. Identification asserts the user's identity and is considered a *one-to-many search process* because the system must match the user to a unique identity. Identity is needed as it provides accountability and holds users responsible for their actions. The most common way for users to identify themselves is by presenting user identification (user ID) such as a username, account number, or personal identification number (PIN). Authentication is the second step in the I&A process. It is commonly referred to as a *one-to-one process* because it is a comparative process; no search is involved. Three authentication methods exist:

▶ **Authentication by knowledge**—What a user knows

▶ **Authentication by ownership**—What a user has

▶ **Authentication by characteristic**—What a person is and does

Authentication by Knowledge

Of the three types, what a user knows is the most widely used method of authentication. This type of authentication is about *passwords*. Good passwords should be easy to remember but difficult for an attacker to guess. Passwords should initially be set by network administrators or generated by the system. Upon initial logon by the user, the password should be changed. Passwords should have a lockout threshold established. For example, if the user enters the wrong password three times in a row, the account should be disabled or locked for a predetermined length of time. If passwords need to be reset, the process should ensure that the user's identity is verified and that passwords are not passed in any insecure or open format. User identity can be verified by having the user answer several cognitive questions, such as high school attended, first pet's name, or first best friend; or by making the user retrieve the new password in person or by transmitting the password securely to the employee's supervisor.

Passwords are perishable; they grow stale and need to be changed on a regular basis. Most of us lack the cognitive ability to create several complex, unique, and unrelated passwords on a daily or weekly basis. Imagine the following situation: You have just started a new job, and your boss has asked that you create several login passwords. Do you invent hard-to-remember, complex passwords, something that you can easily remember when you return the next day, or do you write down the password? Most individuals will choose an easy password or write it down rather than risk forgetting the password and creating a bad impression. A Gartner study performed in 2000 reported the following facts about passwords:

▶ About 90% of respondents reported having passwords that were dictionary words or names.

▶ Another 47% used their name, the name of a spouse, or a pet's name.

▶ Only 9% used cryptographically strong passwords that are upper- and lowercase, alphanumeric, and at least fourteen charcters.

One of the responsibilities of an IS auditor is to verify password policies and make sure they are strong enough to protect the organization's assets. The preceding statistics offer a clear indication that many organizations still do not have good password policies. Good password policies should offer the following guidelines regarding password characteristics:

- ▶ Do not use personal information
- ▶ Are not comprised of common words or names
- ▶ Are complex and use upper- and lowercase letters, numbers, and characters (such as ! @#$%^&)
- ▶ Are changed regularly
- ▶ Have session timeouts
- ▶ Limit logon attempts to a small number of times, such as three successive attempts

Authentication by Ownership

This type of authentication—what a user has—can include various types of *tokens*, such as badge systems, smart cards, USB keys, and SecurID devices. Tokens are widely used in *two-factor authentication* schemes because they require something you have (the token) and something you know (a personal identification number). The system works in this general process:

STEP BY STEP

7.1 Asynchronous Challenge-Response

1. The server sends the user a value.
2. The value is entered into the token device.
3. The token performs a hashing process on the entered value.
4. The new, computed value is displayed on the LCD screen of the token device.
5. The user enters the displayed value into the computer for authentication.

NOTE

Know the Value of Two-Factor Authentication   Two-factor authentication requires two of the three following methods: something you know, something you have, or something you are. A bank card and PIN is an example of two-factor authentication; a password and a PIN is not.

Authentication by Characteristic

Authentication by characteristic—what a person is or does—is probably more familiar to you as *biometrics*. Biometric systems verify identity by either a physiological trait, such as a fingerprint or retina scan, or behavioral characteristic, such as a keystroke or signature pattern. Some common biometric types include the following:

▶ Fingerprint

▶ Hand geometry

▶ Palm scan

▶ Voice pattern

▶ Retina pattern/scan

▶ Iris pattern/recognition

▶ Signature dynamics

▶ Facial recognition

▶ Keystroke dynamics

Important concerns for the IS auditor when examining biometric systems include the following:

▶ **Accuracy**—Accuracy demonstrates how well the system can separate authentic users from imposters.

▶ **User acceptance**—Will users accept the system? The chosen biometric system must fit the environment.

▶ **Misuse**—Some users may even look for ways to bypass or cheat the system. With the right tools (some kind of putty or gel imprint), ingenuity, and a morally ambivalent coworker, an employee can "clock in" without even being there.

▶ **Processing speed**—Tied closely to user acceptance, processing speed indicates how fast the decision to accept or deny is determined. Slow systems tend to frustrate users and, thus, result in lower acceptance.

▶ **False reject rate (FRR)**—The FRR is the percentage of legitimate users who are denied access. This is also known as a Type I error.

▶ **False accept rate (FAR)**—This measurement is the percentage of users who are allowed access but who are not authorized users. It is also known as a Type II error.

▶ **Equal error rate (EER)**—This measurement indicates the point at which FRR equals FAR. Low numbers indicate that the system has greater accuracy.

EXAM ALERT

Know the Importance of Biometric Data-Protection Mechanisms CISA candidates must understand the value of biometric data and must verify that the information has an adequate mechanism in place to protect it from attack or disclosure.

More information on biometrics can be found in Chapter 8. No matter which of the three types of authentication methods is used, the user most likely will have to log on many times onto many different systems throughout the work day. One method to reduce the number of logins is single sign-on, the next topic of discussion.

Challenge

As you have been reading, authentication is an important control. For this challenge, review your own organization and measure how effective you believe its access control policy is. Create a solution by answering the following questions:

1. Does your organization use biometrics or tokens? Yes/No

2. If passwords are being used, does the user protect the password? Yes/No

3. Is a lockout policy enforced if the wrong password is entered? Yes/No

4. Are logon attempts of entering three wrong passwords consecutively established as the account lockout policy? Yes/No

5. Is password reuse prohibited? Yes/No

6. Are strong passwords required? Yes/No

7. Is the minimum length of password eight characters or more? Yes/No

If your organization is practicing good access control policy, you should have answered the majority of these questions with a "Yes."

Single Sign-On

Many users grow weary of having to log on to many different systems throughout the day to complete their required tasks. Single sign-on is an attempt to address the problem. If the organization is using passwords and single sign-on is not being used, each separate system requires the user to remember a potentially different username and password combination. Employees tend to bypass mental strain by writing down passwords and usernames. Single sign-on addresses this problem by permitting users to authenticate once to a single authentication authority, thereby being allowed access to all other protected resources without reauthenticating. Single sign-on can be seen as a process of consolidation that places the entire organization's functions of authentication and authorization in a single centralized location. This can include the following:

- Distributed systems

- Mainframe systems

- Local users

- Remote users

- Network security mechanisms

Implementing single sign-on is a challenge because most logical networks are heterogeneous. Networks, operating systems, mainframes, distributed systems, and databases must all be integrated to work together. Advantages to single sign-on include the following:

- Efficient logon process

- Stronger passwords created by users

- No need for multiple passwords

- Enforcement of timeout and attempt thresholds across the entire platform

- Centralized administration

Before you decide to run out and implement single sign-on within your organization, you should be aware that it is expensive, and if attackers gain entry, they now have access to everything. Including unique platforms also can be challenging. Examples of single sign-on systems include Kerberos, SESAME, KryptoKnight (by IBM), and NetSP (a KryptoKnight derivative). Kerberos is one of the most popular.

The Massachusetts Institute of Technology (MIT) created Kerberos. It provides four key services:

- **Security**—Kerberos protects authentication traffic so that a network eavesdropper cannot easily impersonate a user.

- **Reliability**—The service is available to users when needed.

- **Transparency**—For the end user, the process is transparent.

- **Scalability**—Kerberos supports everything from a small number of users to a large number of clients and servers. Kerberos consists of three parts: the client, the server, and a trusted third party (KDC) who mediates between them. The KDC is comprised of two systems:

> ▸ **Authentication service**—The authentication service issues ticket-granting tickets (TGTs) that are good for admission to the ticket-granting service (TGS). Before network clients can obtain tickets for services, they must obtain a TGT from the authentication service.

> ▸ **Ticket-granting service**—Clients receive tickets to specific target services through this service.

STEP BY STEP

7.2 Kerberos' Basic Operation

1. The client asks the KDC for a ticket, making use of the authentication service (AS).

2. The client receives the encrypted ticket and the session key.

3. The client sends the encrypted TGT to the TGS and requests a ticket for access to the application server.

4. The TGS decrypts the TGT by using its own private key and returns the ticket to the client, which allows it to access the application server.

5. The client sends this ticket along with an authenticator to the application server.

6. The application server sends confirmation of its identity to the client.

Remote Access Security

Technology has changed the workplace. Email, cell phones, and the Internet have changed when and how employees can work or connect to the organization's assets. Many employees don't even go into the workplace now. The International Telework Association and Council report that approximately 32 million people work at home at least part-time for an employer. These telecommuters pose a special challenge to security. Clients, consultants, vendors, customer representatives, and business partners might also require remote access to the organization. All of these users will expect the same level of access they would have if they were to connect locally. A well-designed architecture is required to provide this level of service. The CISA candidate must understand these issues and common connectivity methods.

EXAM ALERT

Know the Network's Points of Access When reviewing network access, the IS auditor should always find all points of access. This is a critical step and is required for a complete and thorough examination.

Connectivity methods can include dial-up. Although it's slow, it is usually low in cost, and most users are familiar with it. Concerns over dial-up include performance and low bandwidth, which means that time-sensitive, media-rich, and data-intensive applications don't perform well. Because of these constraints, an organization might choose a more dedicated connection. Dedicated connections provide greater security because they provide a private or dedicated link for the organization, but not at a much greater cost. This is a common approach for connecting remote business units. Two common methods for remote connectivity include Remote Access Dial-In User Service (RADIUS) and Terminal Access Control Access Control System (TACACS).

RADIUS uses a modem pool for connecting users to the organization's network. The RADIUS server contains usernames, passwords, and other information used to validate the user. Many systems use a callback system for added security control. When used, the callback system calls the user back at a predefined phone number. RADIUS is a client/server protocol used to authenticate dial-in users and authorize access. TACACS is a less popular approach and another remote access protocol that provides authentication, authorization, and accountability. TACACS is very similar to RADIUS. TACACS+, an upgrade to TACACS, was introduced in 1990 and offers extended two-factor authentication.

The Internet's popularity has made it an option for remote connectivity. That idea has matured into the concept of virtual private networks (VPNs). The Internet Engineering Task Force (IETF) defines a VPN as "an emulation of a private Wide Area Network (WAN) using shared or public IP facilities, such as the Internet or private IP backbones." The advantage of a VPN is that it is cheaper than a dedicated line. VPNs provide the same capabilities as a private network, but at a much lower cost. The biggest concern when using a VPN is privacy; after all, you're sending your company's traffic over the public Internet. Therefore, the traffic must be encrypted before being sent. All remote-access methods have a certain degree of risk:

▶ Denial of service

▶ Loss of physical control of the client's system

▶ Possibility that the client system will be hacked to gain remote access capability

▶ Possibility that the remote-access system will be hacked to gain access

These risks can best be addressed by good policies and procedures that specify using strong controls. Strong authentication should also be used to ensure that intruders cannot easily guess passwords or compromise remote-access systems. Encryption should also be a key component of any remote-access system; encryption is the best control that can be used to prevent the interception of information.

Know the Value of Encryption Encryption is the number-one control that can be used to protect information while being transmitted to and from a remote network to the organization's network.

Auditing and Logging

All access points to the network should have a means of logging to establish accountability. Access to network resources or attempts to access logical resources should be audited. Auditing enables the IS auditor to verify that access controls are working. The audit process can also be used to verify that each individual's responsibility is clearly defined. Employees should know they will be held accountable. Auditing is a good way to determine whether repetitive mistakes are being made or if someone is trying to gain unauthorized access. As a detective control, auditing provides a means of uncovering suspicious activity.

Auditing should be addressed in a policy so that employees know what to log, how to log, and when the logs should be audited. End users also need to be informed of the logging and auditing process, perhaps by acceptable use policies (AUPs). The end user also should be made aware of keystroke logging, email scanning, and Internet AUPs.

From a control standpoint, the IS auditor needs to examine log-retention policies to make sure they comply with local, state, or federal laws. If possible, audit records should be transferred to a centralized location. This makes audit and analysis easier for the appropriate administrator, and it makes log tampering harder for the malicious user because logs are not kept on the local system. Strong access controls to the logs, encryption, and integrity checks should also be considered. The idea behind integrity checks is to have a means of detecting log tampering. One good approach is for the auditor to periodically check the logs to make sure no one has attempted to exceed access privileges or gain access during unusual hours. Any control or procedure that bypasses normal security measures should be examined closely. As an example, *bypass label processing* can be used to bypass the normal process of reading a file security label. Because most access controls are based on security labels, this means normal security control could be bypassed.

Manual analysis of logs is time-consuming and tedious. It's best to use automated tools to log analysis. Although the CISA exam will not expect you to know the names of specific tools, you do need to know the types of tools that can be used when working with log files. *Attack-detection tools* are one type of audit tool that look for known attack signatures. For example, Betsy normally is able to log in on the first attempt, but now she has attempted to log in 5,000 times. This type of activity should be flagged for analysis.

Trend-/variance-detect tools are similar to *attack-detecting tools*, except that they scan for deviations to normal trends. As an example, there could be a problem if Betsy normally logs in at 9 a.m. but now is attempting to log in at 4 a.m.

Finally, *audit-reduction tools* reduce the volume of information to be examined to ease manual analysis.

The bottom line on auditing logs is that it requires a balance. That's because a system that produces auditing information takes a hit in performance as the number of auditable events increases. Reducing auditable events raises performance but reduces the amount of usable information. Even if performance was not a factor and we could audit every conceivable event, there would still be a huge burden on the analysis side. With so much information, it would be impossible to review it all. This means that collecting the information in the first place would be of little or no value. The art of auditing is best accomplished by balancing a required number of metrics to log and measuring that against the time and effort required to periodically review the logged data. This entire process should be documented and policy-driven.

Handling Confidential Information

Task

▶ Evaluate the processes and procedures used to store, retrieve, transport, and dispose of confidential information assets.

Knowledge Statement

▶ Knowledge of the processes and procedures used to store, retrieve, transport, and dispose of confidential information assets

Confidential information requires protection from the point of creation to the time of destruction or transfer to another entity. In far too many cases, information has been lost or exposed when having controls would have prevented the incident. Anyone looking for a good example of how not to handle sensitive media need look no further than the June 2000 incident at Los Alamos in which hard drives containing nuclear secrets were discovered missing. Later they were discovered behind a copier, but no one knew how they got there or where they had been. Your organization might not be storing nuclear secrets, but you most likely have sensitive information, such as backup files. Backup files need to be encrypted, and physically secured to minimize the risks of being lost or exposed. Databases are another area of concern; they contain sensitive information or items that might be personal in nature.

Off-site repair and storage is also sometimes overlooked. If a system is sent out for repair, is the information on that system removed before being shipped? Even if you have a *service level agreement* (SLA) that requires a repair person to come on-site for repair work on a defective hard drive or storage system, the repair person most likely will take the damaged drive when he or she leaves. Companies should consider what, if any, sensitive information might remain on the drive. Confidential information extends to more than hard drives and tapes; it also includes paper documents, floppy disks, CDs, DVDs, and USB thumb drives. Media can be disposed of in many acceptable ways. CDs can be destroyed, and magnetic media can be degaussed. Hard drives can be wiped. Wiping is the process of overwriting all addressable locations on the disk. The Department of Defense (DoD) drive-wiping standard #5220-22M states, "All addressable locations must be overwritten with a character, its complement, then a random character and verify." By making several passes over the media, an organization can further decrease the possibility of data recovery. Many methods can be used as long as they protect the sensitivity of the information and prevent information from ending up in the hands of the wrong person.

Common Attack Patterns

Knowledge Statement

▶ Knowledge of attack methods and techniques (e.g., hacking, spoofing, Trojan horses, denial of service, spamming)

Logical access control is one of the most targeted security mechanisms. Malicious individuals can use a variety of techniques to try to bypass logical access control or exploit its weaknesses. CISA exam candidates are expected to know about the different ways access control is attacked. The candidate also is expected to understand the various threats to the logical infrastructure. These attacks can be categorized as passive and active, as described in the following sections.

Passive Attacks

Passive attacks do not inject traffic into the network or attempt other types of activities that are active in nature. Sniffing is a good example of a passive attack. Sniffing is usually done with a network sniffer or analyzer. These utilities allow the user to examine traffic on the LAN. Sniffers have the capability to decode various types of protocols. They can place the network interface card into promiscuous mode so that all traffic on that segment of the network can be examined. This becomes a real problem when clear-text protocols, such as Password Authentication Protocol (PAP) and File Transfer Protocol (FTP), or others without encryption or weak encryption are being used. Attackers might try to intercept the authentication process between user and server to steal the user's credentials and launch an attack. Even sophisticated man-in-the-middle attacks can be attempted with toolkits such as DSNIFF (http://monkey.org/~dugsong/dsniff/).

An organization's electronic equipment (wireless keyboards, mouse devices, CRTs, Bluetooth devices, and so on) transmits a wide range of electronic signals. Although passive attacks would require equipment that typically only three-letter government agencies would possess, these attacks are possible. This might sound like science fiction, but the U.S. government was so concerned about the possibility of this type of attack that it created a program to study it. The program eventually became a standard and is known as TEMPEST. TEMPEST was designed to increase emanation security. It required copper shielding and faraday cages to block stray electronic signals. TEMPEST technologies have been replaced by technologies such as white noise and control zones. White noise uses special devices that send out a stream of frequencies that make it impossible for an attacker to distinguish the real information. A control zone is created by designing facilities, walls, floors, and ceilings to block electrical signals from leaving the area or room.

Network analysis is another type of passive attack. Many networks use Simple Network Management Protocol (SNMP) to monitor network equipment and devices. Tools such as HP OpenView and Solar Winds are used for these types of activities. Attackers can use the same tools to query devices and systems for range information, to map the network or gain information about its configuration or weaknesses.

Traffic analysis is another passive attack that can be useful even if two recipients are using encryption. Attackers can simply look at the flow of traffic to try to determine whether a major event will occur. This is called *inference*. As an example, the news media commonly watch people enter and leave the White House grounds. Most reporters go home at 5 p.m. but if they see Domino's Pizza drive up at 5 p.m., they might elect to stay later because there has been a change in normal traffic and they can infer that a major event is pending. Now let's turn our attention to active attacks.

Active Attacks

Active attacks inject traffic, modify systems, and seek to change settings to gain access or escalate privilege of the network or system. The least technical active attack is *social engineering*.

Social engineering predates the computer era. It's much like an old-fashioned con game that uses the art of manipulation to trick a victim into providing private information or improper access. Social-engineering attacks work because they attack the weakest link—people. Social-engineering attacks can be launched in person, on the phone, or via a computer. Attacks carried out in person can be as easy as an attacker using a disguise of a repair person or vending machine employee. Attacks on the phone can be carried out when an attacker calls the help desk and asks to have a password reset or seeks to gain privileged information. The low-ranking help desk employee might be bullied, feel scared, or feel coerced into giving out a password or other important information.

Email attacks are also common. These typically occur by means of the attacker spoofing a trusted party, such as eBay, Hotmail, PayPal, and Citibank. The attacker sends an official-sounding email asking the user to verify the Internet password via return mail. When doing so, the user's password is sent to the attacker, who can then access the victim's account at will. Training can go a long way toward educating employees on how to spot and prevent these attacks.

> **CAUTION**
>
> **Social-Engineering Attacks Are Very Effective** In 2003, the Infosecurity Europe conference performed a social-engineering attack in which they asked office personnel outside of their building if they would give away their passwords for a cheap pen. Almost 90% agreed.

Phishing is a newer form of social-engineering attack. It works by sending the victim an email from what appears to be an official site, such as a bank or credit card company. The email usually contains a link that promises to take the user to the real website to update, change, or modify their account. The real purpose of the email and link is to steal the victim's username, PIN, account number, or password.

Phishing, a Common Attack Vector

Phishing has become one of the most widely used types of social-engineering attack. Its goal is to lure the victim into revealing information of a sensitive or personal nature, including passwords and credit card details. These attacks lead victims to believe they are being approached by email from someone of a banking or credit institution.

A good example of a phishing attack can be seen in the story of Zachary Hill. According to his federal indictment, Hill was sentenced to four years in prison after he was caught in an extended phishing scheme. Hill was able to use his email scheme to access 473 credit card numbers, 152 sets of bank account numbers and routing numbers, and 566 sets of usernames and passwords for Internet service accounts.

Hill was enjoying the fruits of his scam by fixing up his Honda Accord. The indictment charged that Hill had used the fraudulently obtained credit card numbers to obtain goods and services for his car costing more than $47,000. His final mistake was being forgetful and using the same stolen credit card numbers to order parts from the same supplier more than once. This led FBI officers to make a personal delivery that eventually led to his arrest.

Pretexting is the practice of obtaining personal information about an individual under false pretenses. Pretexting is usually done when an individual wants more information about a certain individual to investigate their activities, such as to sue that person, to steal his or her assets, or to obtain credit in his or her name. One of the most well-known pretexting cases involves HP. Pretexters use a variety of techniques, but these are all simple variations of social-engineering techniques. The pretexter might call your cell phone provider and ask for a reprint of a bill. They also might call the bank and say they lost the checkbook, or even contact your credit card provider. In most cases, pretexting is illegal, and there are laws against pretending to be someone else to gain personal information.

Dumpster diving is another attack that requires no technical skill. Dumpster divers simply dig through the trash looking for key pieces of information. Sensitive information should be shredded, but this is not always the case. Post-it notes and other small pieces of trash can provide critical pieces of information to those seeking to gain sensitive information. As long as no trespassing takes place, dumpster diving is usually not illegal.

Now let's look at some of the more technologically involved attacks. First is *war dialing*. This is an older type of attack but occurs when an attacker uses a dialer program to dial through a range of numbers looking for one that has a modem attached to it. Some organizations still use modems for routers and other types of equipment that need out-of-band configuration capabilities. War dialing might also be performed to look for PBX systems to find dial-in to dial-out numbers for long distance call fraud.

Some threats to logical security do not involve a targeted attack such as those already described; some are much more random. *Viruses* are an example of this type of random attack. Fred Cohen was the first person to use the word *computer virus* in the 1980s. Since then, computer viruses have continued to grow, evolve, and change. Viruses can be boot sector, macro, or even file infectors.

Another destructive program is the *worm*. Worms require no interaction and can self-replicate. The first worm to be released on the Internet, in 1988, was named the Robert T. Morris worm, after its developer. Morris meant it to be only a proof of concept. Its release brought home the fact that worms can do massive damage to the Internet. The cost of the damage from the RTM worm is estimated to be between $10 million and $100 million.

One way to get a user to open a malicious program is by using a *Trojan horse*. Trojan horse programs enable a hacker to send what looks like a legitimate program to a user, such as games, animated greeting cards, or other small programs that are easily sent by email and are commonly used. When users run the program, they believe they are simply running a program, such as whack-a-mole or elf bowling. In reality, they may have installed malicious code.

Imagine that a company's programmer is able to access and change applications at will. What if this person could change the company's payroll application? The programmer might not destroy the code, but he might add a few lines into the code to have it checked for his employee number each week before printing checks. If his employee ID is verified, the program prints checks like normal. If his employee ID is not found, each check is printed but is made out to a random dollar amount. This is a *logic bomb*, designed to detonate sometime after the perpetrator leaves. A logic bomb can cause a great deal of damage: Because it is buried so deeply into the code, it is difficult to discover or detect before it becomes active.

Similar to the logic bomb is a *trap door*, a shortcut created by programmers during development. It acts as a hidden access point in the software or application and can aid in the testing process. When testing is completed, the trap door should be removed. If not, it can act as a hidden shortcut for attackers.

An *asynchronous attack* is a complex attack that targets timing. These are also known as a Time of Check (TOC) Time of Use (TOU) attacks, or a race condition because the attacker is racing to make a change to the object after it has been changed and just before it's used by the system. As an example, if a program creates a date file to hold the amount a customer owes, and the attacker can replace the value before the program reads it, the attacker can successfully manipulate the program. In reality, an IS auditor needs the help of a programmer or IT specialist to evaluate this complex attack.

Some attacks are launched for financial reasons. One example is a *rounding-down attack*. Rounding down skims off small amounts of money by rounding down the last few digits. For example, the amount $5,239,812.33 might be rounded down to $5,239,812.30. Similar to this attack is the *salami technique*, which slices off small amounts of money so that the last few digits are truncated. As an example, $5,239,812.33 might become $5,239,812.00. Both the rounding-down technique and the salami technique work under the concept that small amounts will not be missed; over a period of time, this can add up to big profits for the attacker. This type of attack can actually be seen in movies such as *Superman III* and *Office Space*.

A fragmentation attack might sound similar to a salami attack, but it's much different. Fragmentation is a normal process of the IP protocol. Attackers can fragment IP traffic to bypass firewalls and intrusion-detection systems (IDS). Some of these devices inspect only the first fragment and, if it's okay, pass all other fragments without inspection. These attacks use this flaw and later pass malicious code in fragments to allow them to pass without inspection. *Fuzzing* is another attack method. Fuzzing works by providing applications with random data. Many times the application does not have the capability to handle such data and simply crashes or allows an attacker unauthorized access. As an example, a simple program can be designed to distort (fuzz) the code found in a web page to examine how a web browser will respond. This technique was demonstrated at the 2006 CanSecWest Security Conference to examine cascading style sheets—about a dozen vulnerabilities were discovered.

In these next attacks, attackers break encryption schemes or crack passwords. Many passwords are based on weak dictionary words. Attackers are well aware of this and use such information to launch common password attacks. Attackers typically use one of three methods to crack passwords. First is the *dictionary attack*.

A dictionary attack uses a predefined dictionary to look for a match between the encrypted password and the encrypted dictionary word. Many dictionary files are available, ranging from sports, hobbies, and even the Klingon language. Many times, these attacks can be performed in just a few minutes if the user has used a well-known dictionary word. Although passwords are commonly stored in an encrypted format, password-cracking programs use a technique called *comparative analysis*. Each potential password found in a dictionary list is encrypted and compared to the encrypted password. If a match is obtained, the password has been discovered. If it's not obtained, the program continues on to the next word, computes its hashed value, and compares it to the hashed password.

The second type of password-cracking method is the *hybrid attack*, used to target individuals who use variations of a common word. As an example, focus on the word *password*. Hybrid password cracking would process the word as *Password, password, PASSWORD, PassWord, PaSSword,* and so on. Hybrid password cracking even attempts to add common prefixes, suffixes, and extended characters to try to crack the password. As another example, the word *password* would also be tried as *123password*, *abcpassword*, *drowssap*, *p@ssword*, *pa55w0rd*, and so on. These various attempts increase the odds of successfully cracking an ordinary word.

The third type of password attack is a *brute-force attack*, which attempts to use every combination of letters, numbers, and characters. Depending on the length and complexity of the original password, this attack can take hours, days, months, or years. To reduce the length of time this attack requires, rainbow tables are used to precompute password hashes.

> **NOTE**
>
> **Rainbow Tables** An advancement in cryptographic password attacks is the rainbow table. Instead of computing each hash one at a time and then comparing, a rainbow table is filled with precomputed hashed passwords. This form of time-memory tradeoff requires that a rainbow table be generated for all possibilities within a given range, such as 1- to 14-character alphanumeric passwords. If any password is a match, it is found in just a few seconds. The technique was first pioneered by Philippe Oechslin and is now incorporated into many password cracking programs.

Access can be gained in other ways, even if the attacker unsuccessfully recovers useful passwords. One technique is *masquerading*, in which the attacker pretends to be a trusted party. One common way masquerading attacks can occur is for the attacker to launch a session hijack. This attack allows a legitimate user to log on and for the attacker to immediately hijack the session and terminate the victim's connection. The attacker is left with an authenticated connection and the ability to masquerade as the victim.

Packet replay is another active technique that an attacker can use to gain access. As an example, the attacker might sniff an authentication session on the network and replay it later to try to gain unauthorized access. Using one-time passwords is a good defense against this type of attack.

If attackers simply want to harass users, they can simply target them for *spam* or *email bomb* them. An email bomb is nothing more than a program that sends a repeated series of messages to a victim's email account for the purpose of flooding the account or filling it with junk.

What if none of these techniques works for the attacker? In that situation, an attacker might decide to launch a *denial-of-service* (DoS) attack. Although this attack does not give the attacker access, it blocks legitimate users from using resources they have access to. Denial-of-service attacks consume resources to the point that legitimate access is not possible. Distributed DoS (DDoS) attacks work in much the same manner, except that they are launched from many more devices and add a layer between the attacker and the victim. Some older well-known DoS attacks include the following:

▶ **Ping of death**—A DoS that employs an oversized IP packet.

▶ **Smurf**—A DoS that sends a message to the broadcast of a subnet or network so that every node on the network produces one or more response packets.

- **Syn flood**—A DoS that manipulates the standard three-way handshake used by TCP.

- **Trinoo**—A DDoS that is capable of launching UDP flood attacks from various channels on a network.

Crash restarts and computer shutdowns are variations on the DoS. The attacker loads code that will shut down the system or cause it to crash. Before loading such code, the attacker alters a configuration so that when the system is restarted, a change occurs that gives the attacker operational control of the computer. The attacker now can take control of the system after it restarts with the new configuration.

After so much talk of attacks and the ways in which individuals can subvert security, let's turn our attention to more general items of network security. Network infrastructure and its security is the next topic.

> **NOTE**
>
> **Rename Default Accounts**   To increase the security of the network, a special system logon account should be renamed. Many operating systems and applications ship with default account names. As an example, Microsoft Windows ships with the default administrator account. Renaming these accounts makes it difficult for an attacker to identify common attack vectors.

Network Infrastructure

Knowledge Statements

- Knowledge of intrusion detection systems and firewall configuration, implementation, operation, and maintenance

- Knowledge of controls and risks associated with the use of portable and wireless devices (e.g., PDAs, USB devices, Bluetooth devices)

The network infrastructure includes the wide area network (WAN) and the local area network (LAN) and any devices connected to it, as well as programs and files that support the network operations. Per ISACA, the following are some of the basic controls that the network infrastructure should include:

- Network operations should be separated so that no one person has overall control.

- Operational duties should be rotated on a regular basis, if possible, to reduce the opportunity for misuse.

- Network controls should be maintained to verify accountability so that audit trials are available and periodically reviewed.

▶ Periodic audits and reviews should be performed to verify that employees are performing operations per written standards and that compliance is maintained.

▶ System efficiency should be periodically reviewed to verify adequate response time and verify that the network operates per required standards.

▶ Encryption should be used when possible to protect information in storage and in transit.

▶ Whenever possible, audit logs should be combined into one common location, to improve security management.

These controls can help facilitate the practice of good IT governance. Whenever possible, controls should be implemented so that users can be identified during every step of their activity and problems can be detected quickly. Let's now turn our attention to LAN security, client/server issues, the Internet, and the unique challenges that wireless systems pose.

Network and Internet Security

The ability of networked users to connect to the Internet and conduct business on a global scale has brought many benefits to business. Along with these opportunities come threats, which can originate from internal users misusing the Internet connection or from malicious outsiders. The Internet is the primary portal of attack. The opportunities and threats facilitated by the Internet present special challenges to the organization and require the development of controls that establish how the Internet can be used and what type of traffic is allowed to enter or leave the local network. The primary control is policy and procedure. As an example, these documents should specify what employees are allowed to use the Internet for. Policy might dictate that Internet usage is only for business-related activities. If you don't think that this is something that should be specified, consider the fact that http://www.the-tidings.com reports that 70% of all Internet porn activity occurs during working hours. Even if there is a good preventive control, such as policy, in place, there is still a need for a detective control. If employees don't adhere to policy, a way to detect such activity must be in place. Systems that detect misuse can help meet this challenge.

From outside the organization, hackers are the biggest risk. These individuals might be on the other side of the world; however, if they have an Internet connection to the organization, they have a potential access point. Hackers could theoretically break in and cause damage in many different ways, including damaging the network, defacing a website, stealing information, altering information, or even launching a denial-of-service attack. These potential risks mandate strong controls. Firewalls and intrusion-detection/-prevention systems are two of the primary systems used for perimeter security.

Firewalls

Firewalls are used to restrict access. This is usually from the Internet to the company's internal network. Firewalls are used to enforce company policy regarding what type of traffic is allowed to pass in and out of the company's network. Firewalls are chokepoints, just like gates in the physical world. Firewalls funnel all traffic through a controlled access point. A firewall can be hardware, such as a Cisco ASA, or software, such as a Checkpoint Firewall-1. One critical issue with firewalls is their configuration. Initial firewall configurations are as follows:

▶ **Allow all**—The firewall is left in an open state, and only items that are determined to be bad are prohibited. This is not the proper configuration.

▶ **Deny all**—This should be the default setting. In a deny-all configuration, everything is turned off and disallowed. Then only approved services are allowed after a business case has been made to justify their existence.

Firewalls have gone through what are considered generational improvements. The five generations of firewalls include the following:

▶ **Packet filtering**—Considered the first generation of firewalls. Packet filtering can be performed by routers and is the lowest form of packet inspection. Packet filters cannot keep track of status and make a pass or drop decision on items such as port, protocol, or IP address.

▶ **Stateful inspection**—Stateful inspection firewalls provide the same functionality as packet filters, but they can track the status of the session. Therefore, if a type of reply is presented to the firewall, it can actually look to see if this reply is in response to a valid request.

▶ **Proxy**—A proxy is referred to as a *circuit-level firewall* because it resides between a client and the Internet. A proxy stands in place of each party; it increases security by presenting a single IP address to the Internet and prevents direct access to an internal client.

▶ **Dynamic packet filtering**—This generation of firewall addressed the challenges of dynamic ports. As an example, when an FTP client communicates to an FTP server, a dynamically assigned port is used to transfer files and data. Historically, a firewall administrator might have left a wide range of high-order ports open for this activity. Dynamic packet filtering allows an open port to be generated as needed and then closed when the communication is completed.

▶ **Kernel proxy**—This is the fifth and most advanced type of firewall. A kernel proxy builds a virtual stack to examine each packet at each layer to ensure integrity. Not only is it fast, but it also can perform address translation.

Most modern firewalls have a mix of capabilities. As an example, the firewall may support both proxy and stateful inspection. You can read more about the generational improvement of firewalls at Cisco.com (http://tinyurl.com/2kgcbr). Although address translation is not specifically a firewall technology, it does help. *Network Address Translation* (NAT) was originally developed to address the growing need for IP addresses. NAT can be used to translate between private and public addresses. *Private IP addresses* are those that are considered unroutable, meaning that public Internet routers will not route traffic to and from addresses in these ranges. This concept is defined in RFC 1918. Three ranges of private addresses exist:

192.168.0.0–192.168.255.255
172.16.0.0–172.31.255.255
10.0.0.0–10.255.255.255

After the choice has been made to use a firewall, the next step is to determine how it will be implemented into the environment. Table 7.4 lists some common firewall configurations.

TABLE 7.4 Firewall Implementations

Configuration	Details
Screened host	This firewall is stateless, provides only minimal protection, is usually installed as a single point of protection, and is the most basic form of security.
Dual-homed host	This firewall depends on the computer that hosts it. It is implemented by installing two network cards in one computer.
DMZ	Devices in the demilitarized zone (DMZ) are more at risk than the protected inner network. The level of vulnerability depends on how well the host in the DMZ has been hardened.

NOTE

Firewall Terminology Stateless firewalls do not have the capability to track state. This type of firewall uses an access control list (ACL), which acts much like a set of rules. Depending on where the ACL is applied, traffic is matched to the list. Each packet is inspected to see if it matches any rules defined in the list. These rules can examine such items as information in the IP, TCP, or UDP header.

NOTE

DMZ A DMZ is a demilitarized zone, which is the portion of the network that lies between the trusted internal network and the untrusted external network. Common services that insiders or outsiders need to access are placed in the DMZ. Common services found in the DMZ include HTTP, DNS, and SMTP.

Even with a firewall configured and installed, there is a potential risk. When a firewall is in place, many individuals might have a false sense of security. Firewalls are not perfect: They cannot block insider attacks. They can be bypassed by means of modems and wireless access points. Finally, they can be misconfigured and maintenance can be neglected. Therefore, the firewall is not the "end all, be all" security product. Firewalls are just part of the layered approach to security; intrusion detection, our next topic, is another.

Intrusion-Detection Systems

Intrusion-detection systems (IDS) play a critical role in the protection of the IT infrastructure. *Intrusion detection* involves monitoring network traffic, detecting attempts to gain unauthorized access to a system or resource, and notifying the appropriate individuals so that counteractions can be taken.

IDS systems can be divided into two broad categories:

▶ **Network-based intrusion-detection systems (NIDs)**—NIDs are usually placed between the firewall and the corporate network. This allows the organization to detect intruders and plan the appropriate response.

▶ **Host-based intrusion-detection systems (HIDs)**—HIDs are used to monitor internal resources. HIDs can be used to monitor specific servers and systems for misuse or detection of an attempt to perform a privileged command.

IDS detection methods include the following:

▶ **Statistical**—Requires the administrator to use profiles of authorized activities or place them into the IDS so that it understands normal activity. A considerable amount of time is needed to make sure the IDS produce few false negatives. These systems trigger when individuals deviate from specified behavior.

▶ **Signature**—Requires the administrator to load a database of known attacks. As soon as the signatures are loaded into the IDS, it can begin to guard the network. These systems cannot guard against new attacks that have not yet been loaded into the IDS.

▶ **Neural**—Requires the administrator to place the IDS in learning mode so that it understands normal patterns of activity. It functions much like a statistical IDS. These systems can be fooled because the attack makes very small incremental changes.

Whatever type of IDS the organization uses, the real challenge is monitoring and maintenance. An IDS requires constant attention. A mistuned IDS is of little value because either it will produce alerts when an attack has not occurred, which is a false positive, or it will not trigger an alert when an attack really occurs, which is a false negative.

Figure 7.2 shows the four states in which an IDS can reside.

EXAM ALERT

Know the Valid State of an IDS   A CISA exam candidate should be aware that the most dangerous response is a false negative. A false negative means that an event did occur but an alert was not triggered.

	True	False
Positive	*True-Positive* An alarm was generated and is valid	*False-Positive* An alarm was generated, but no real event occurred to generate it
Negative	*True-Negative* An alarm was not generated and no event occurred	*False-Negative* An alarm was not generated and an event occurred that should have created an alert

FIGURE 7.2   IDS true/false matrix.

Another advancement in this type of technology is Intrusion Prevention Systems (IPS). An IPS is a preventive device. This technology was developed in the late 1990s to overcome the short-comings of intrusion detection. IPSs were designed to detect both known and unknown attacks and prevent them. Some vendors offer both IDS and IPS in a single device to create an effective self-defending network. What if an attacker bypasses the IDS or IPS? In these situations, or when an organization might need to set up a decoy to jail or hold an attacker, a *honey pot* might be the proper solution.

A honey pot consists of a single computer that appears to be part of a network but is actually isolated and protected from the production network. The honey pot is a type of sacrificial lamb. Honey pots are configured to appear to hold information that would be of value to an attacker but, in reality, hold nothing useful. Honey pots can be more than one computer. When an entire network is designed around these principles, it's called a *honey net*. A honey net is designed for the sole purpose of luring an attacker; they give security personnel advance notice of the intruder before they are able to target a real network segment.

Client/Server Security

Today most organizations don't use centralized systems such as mainframes. Mainframes made security a much easier task. Everything was centrally located which made it easier to secure. In the 1990s, mainframe systems started to lose more ground to client/server networks. Client/server networks are distributed; they help organizations respond more quickly to the challenges of business because they lack the controls of centralized systems. Because they are distributed, many more access points exist—and with them comes a greater level of risk. Good security requires examining each potential access point and discovering all potential exposures. The auditor will want to look closely at reducing the risk of these exposures. Many controls can be used to reduce client/server risks—for example:

▸ Disabling floppy drives

▸ Replacing CD/RW drives with read-only units

▸ Disabling the CD autorun feature

▸ Administratively locking USB drives

▸ Preventing unauthorized users from installing drivers or applications

▸ Activating password-protected screensavers

▸ Configuring autologoffs

▸ Requiring clients to store information on shared drives, not locally

▸ Using network-monitoring devices to watch for suspicious activity

▸ Ensuring that good password-change policies are in place

▸ Using strong authentication, such as biometrics or two-factor authentication

LAN Security

Most users spend little time thinking about LAN security and instead focus on performance and availability concerns. Because LANs are a distributed environment, security is more of a challenge. LANs typically use a mixture of cables and topologies, so many opportunities arise for misuse:

▸ Users can move laptops in and out of meeting rooms. This means many uncontrolled access points exist throughout the organization.

▸ Vendors and suppliers can ask for access to check email or to have web access. These systems can spread viruses on the internal network.

▸ Malicious users can run sniffing programs to look for sensitive information.

▸ Users can load programs and applications without concern for license agreements.

▸ Insiders can copy, modify, or disclose information that is of a sensitive nature.

▸ Uncontrolled changes to data and information might violate change management.

These concerns mean that it is very important for the IS auditor to understand the LAN and study its topology and configuration. The auditor will want to talk with the LAN administrator and review rights and responsibilities. It's important to remember that a network administrator is responsible for keeping services running and maintaining access, which is far different than the duties of a security officer. The auditor should examine the computer applications used on the LAN and review users' rights and roles. The auditor must also examine procedures and policies to see how they control security, design, naming conventions, and protocols.

Wireless LAN Security

Wireless LANs are data-communication systems that were developed to transmit data over electromagnetic waves. The most popular standard for wireless LAN services is the *802.11* family of specifications, developed by the IEEE for wireless LAN technology in 1997. Wireless LAN technology has grown at an astounding pace due to its cost and convenience. Users are no longer tied to LAN cabling and can take their laptops to meetings or move around the organization as necessary, while still having connectivity. Also, none of the cable plant issues associated with wired networks arise with wireless LANs. No longer must an organization spend the funds to string cabling to every corner of the facility. Wireless LAN technology allows a business to move into a new or existing facility without cabling and incur none of the usual costs of running a LAN drop to each end user. With so many advantages, it is easy to see why the IT industry has so quickly adopted this technology. However, proper placement of an access point to limit signal strength outside the facility is crucial to properly deploying a wireless LAN.

Wireless was not designed with security as a forethought. The original wireless security standard was the *Wired Equivalent Privacy* (WEP) protocol. WEP was designed only to provide the same privacy afforded to a user on a wired network. Although this offered some level of protection, wireless networks do not end at the organization's exterior walls. Wireless signals can extend to the parking lot, the street, or even a neighboring business. The IS auditor should look closely at wireless systems.

ISACA specifies six threats that are of the most concern to individuals who examine the security of wireless systems:

- ▶ Device theft
- ▶ Hackers/wackers
- ▶ Theft of service
- ▶ Malicious code
- ▶ Spying by competitors and foreign governments
- ▶ Denial of service

Wireless makes it easier to move about the organization while staying connected, so more employees most likely will be using PDAs, laptops, and other small, portable devices. This can result in high instances of theft. Whereas wired LANs had few outside threats, wireless systems have many. A large subculture consists of individuals who look for wireless networks;

those who deal specifically with wireless insecurities are known as wireless hackers or wackers. These individuals perform *war driving*, the act of canvassing an area to see how many wireless networks can be detected. The problem is that most wireless devices ship in an insecure state. Wireless manufacturers favor convenience over security in an effort to improve plug-and-play, out-of-box use for the end user. Implementing the security component is left to the discretion of the user. This increases risk because many users never turn on the wireless system's security features, which permit casual attackers to easily launch a drive-by attack. War driving has expanded to war walking, war boating, and even war flying. Others have taken to marking a network presence with chalk on the sidewalk or wall of a building. This is known as *war chalking*.

When an insecure network has been discovered, the wacker can use the company's network to upload or download spam, pornography, or illicit programs, or install malicious code on the company's network. Even worse, competitors or foreign nations can use the wireless network to remove trade secrets, new designs, or critical information on another business. These are all very real risks. Even if attackers cannot gain access, they can launch a denial-of-service attack. Unlike wired networks, some wireless networks are sensitive to interference and jamming. Jamming devices can be found quickly just by doing a Google search. You can find one example at the following site: http://www.spymodex.com/video.htm.

Wireless LANs are not the only wireless devices gaining ground in the workplace. *Bluetooth* is another. Bluetooth is a short-range communication technology that was designed for the development of personal area networks (PANs). These devices are relatively low power and are characterized by three classes:

▶ **Class 1**—Has the longest range (up to 100m) and has 100mW of power

▶ **Class 2**—Although not the most popular, allows transmission of up to 20m and has 2.5mW of power

▶ **Class 3**—The most widely implemented, with a transmission distance of 10m and 1mW of power

Although it is short range, this technology is still vulnerable to attack. Specialized antennas can be constructed to intercept Bluetooth signals from up to a mile away. Attacks against Bluetooth include Bluejacking and Bluesnarfing. Bluejacking allows an individual to send unsolicited messages over Bluetooth to other Bluetooth devices. Bluesnarfing is the theft of information from a wireless device. Tools such as RedFang and BlueBug exploit these vulnerabilities. Bluetooth is intergrated into many devices such as phones, PDAs, and computers—even many new cars now come equipped with Bluetooth. These vehicles can be targeted for whisper attacks that allow malicious individuals to listen in on the occupants (http://trifinite.org/trifinite_stuff_carwhisperer.html). If history provides us with a glimpse of the future, expect the exploits against Bluetooth to become more advanced and move in the direction of wireless

LAN exploits. With any wireless technology, the goal should be to ensure confidentiality, integrity, authenticity, and availability. The risks to wireless technologies are much greater than to wired networks.

Voice Communications

Knowledge Statement

▶ Knowledge of voice communications security (e.g., voice over IP)

Securing voice communication is a critical component of good security practice. When I was a child, my family lived in a rural area. Our phone was on what was called a party line. We shared a common phone line with three other families; each had a unique ring to let us know which party should answer the phone. Simply by picking up the phone, you could hear any of the other families having a conversation. Although modern voice communications have improved, there are still plenty of opportunities for those who want to eavesdrop on phone calls or play other types of malicious tricks. Actually, this activity has been going on for a long time.

Phreakers

Long before modern-day hacking, *phreakers* were practicing their trade. Phreaking is the art of hacking phone systems. This might sound like a rather complicated affair, but back in the early 1970s, John Draper discovered how to make free phone calls by using a Captain Crunch Whistle. The 2600Hz tone it produced is the same as what is required for bypassing the normal billing process.

Today phreakers still pose a threat to operational security by hacking into private branch exchange (PBX) systems and selling time on the victim's PBX phone network. These attacks might not be discovered for 30 days or more. By that time, the phreaker might have run up thousands of dollars in phone charges. PBX systems might not be their only target; voice over IP (VoIP) is another potential target.

PBX

A private branch exchange (PBX) is really nothing more than a telephone network that is located at the organization and operated by the company. A PBX can interface with many different types of equipment. Some companies even have modems connected to the PBX so that vendors can update or configure services. This can be a dangerous situation if the password and account information for the connection are not secured. Phreakers can use these connections to place free long-distance calls or even change the boring message of a CEO with one filled with obscenities.

Auditors must plan for enough time and resources to examine PBX systems and their features. Common features such as direct inward dial (DID) can be a real problem because an external party can use this to request a dial tone and then call anywhere in the world for free. Most PBX systems also have the capability to do call logging and auditing, which should be enabled to better track telecommunication activity. Finally, all fax machines and modems connected to the PBX should be identified and recorded with the proper documentation.

VoIP

In the not-too-distant past, IT professionals were tasked with running data services over voice networks. Today IT professionals face the new challenge of running voice services over data networks. The voice service that everyone is so eager to have is voice over IP (VoIP). After all, it's a great idea to use existing data networks to transmit voice services. VoIP offers organizations a low-cost alternative to traditional long-distance services. When the equipment and infrastructure is in place, there are very few additional charges.

VoIP functions by placing the voice data into packets and sending them over a packet-switched network. With so much going for it, you might wonder what the disadvantage is. Well, there are actually several. As VoIP is being transmitted over the data network, any break can cripple both the data network and the voice network. If the organization is using the Internet to route calls, none of the protection mechanisms of the publicly switched telephone network (PSTN) exist. Five hops, six hops, or even more intermediate systems might stand between the sender and the receiver. Any one of these could be used to intercept the call, listen to the call, or forward the call to a malicious third party. Although countermeasures are available, VoIP communication is vulnerable to many attacks, including spoofing, eavesdropping, and denial of service. For VoIP best practices, security tools, and in-depth information, check out the VOIP-SA group at http://voipsa.org.

Virus Protection

Knowledge Statement

▶ Knowledge of virus detection tools and control techniques

If the names Melissa, Code Red, Nimda, SQL Slammer, or I Love You are familiar to you, I am sure you can guess what the next topic is—malware. Whereas viruses require the interaction of a user, a worm has the capability to self-propagate. Poorly written viruses that bring down networks have lost traction in favor of more targeted attacks. Although this represents a change in tactics, the ongoing war against malware is not something that will most likely go away.

Viruses and worms cause a wide range of damage, from displaying messages to making programs work erratically, or even destroying data or hard drives. Generally, viruses attack four areas of the computer:

▶ **Executable applications**—Viruses that attach themselves to executable files.

▶ **The file allocation table (FAT)**—This area of the hard drive tracks the location of the system's files and data.

▶ **Boot sectors**—This area is required for startup of the operating system.

▶ **Data**—This includes any information stored in the computer, including word documents, graphics, text files, spreadsheets, and more.

To reduce the ongoing threat of computer viruses and worms, an organization must have a comprehensive and well-designed antivirus program. Effective antivirus requires administrative control in the form of policy that address program downloads and email attachments. Technical control is also required, including an up-to-date antivirus program. Antivirus programs can use one or more techniques to check files and applications for viruses, such as signature scanning, heuristic scanning, integrity checking, or activity blocking. Each method is effective and offers unique attributes. Many organizations use one type of antivirus on the company's servers and another type on the workstations, to build defense in diversity. This helps, as an individual antivirus program cannot be expected to catch 100% of all viruses.

Containing Threats to Information Security

Knowledge Statement

▶ Knowledge of processes related to monitoring and responding to security incidents (e.g., escalation procedures, emergency incident response team)

Although computer systems have brought great advances to the business world, criminals also can use them to their advantage. Computer crime can be a result of the following:

▶ **Computers used in a crime**—These crimes use computers as a tool much like criminals would use a crowbar or gun. As an example, whereas in the past a criminal might have used the post office for extortion or fraud, he might now use a computer and email to achieve the same goal.

▶ **Computers targeted as a crime**—These crimes are directed at computers. As an example, Mafia Boy targeted Yahoo! and eBay in 2000 for an extended distributed denial-of-service attack.

▶ **Computers are incidental in a crime**—Here the computer somehow aids the criminal. As an example, the criminal might keep a list of earnings from illegal gambling in an Excel spreadsheet instead of a little black book.

It's commonly thought that only one tenth of all the crimes that are committed against and that use computer systems are detected. These numbers might seem exceedingly low, but it is difficult to develop accurate numbers regarding the detection and reporting of computer crime. Although many crimes go undetected, others that are detected go unreported. After all, this is not something most companies want to talk about. Admitting to computer crime can have a negative impact on an organization's image, can make the company appear vulnerable, or can even motivate additional attacks. Computer crime can lead to many kinds of losses, including financial loss, legal costs, loss of credibility, disclosure of sensitive information, and even loss of competitive advantage. All this talk of computer crime might make you wonder who is committing such crimes. These individuals include the following:

▶ **Hackers**—These are expert software programmers capable of programming scripts, solving complex programming problems, and performing reverse-engineering on software. Hackers typically try to overcome the technical and physical barriers that restrict their access to information and systems.

▶ **Script kiddies**—A script kiddie is a young or inexperienced attacker who uses only well-known vulnerabilities and scripts to launch attacks. Script kiddies do not have any serious programming skills or an in-depth understanding of networks or operating systems. Most script kiddie attacks can be defended against by implementing good security controls and risk-mitigation strategies.

▶ **Black hats or crackers**—These hackers seek only to do damage or perform malicious activities. They are considered technically proficient and are usually able to exploit seemingly insignificant flaws or vulnerabilities.

▶ **Phreakers**—These individuals are considered the original hackers. Phreakers are interested in breaking into telecommunication and PBX systems. Their motive might be to exploit the system for free phone calls, for illegal use, or to provide telecommunication access to others for a profit. Phreakers can access telecommunication equipment, reprogram it, or even compromise user IDs and passwords to gain unauthorized use of facilities, such as voice mail.

▶ **Disgruntled employees**—These might be current or former employees who have lost respect and integrity in the organization. These feelings usually arise when individuals believe they were fired or terminated without cause, were slighted of a deserved promotion, were not given an increase in compensation, or were wrongly blamed for an incident. A disgruntled employee is an even greater threat if access rights and privileges were not properly terminated.

▶ **Cyberterrorists and cybercriminals**—These individuals might be funded by other countries, covert organizations, or industries. Their goal is to conduct clandestine or espionage activities on corporations illegally. Their activities include website defacement, a DoS attack, identity theft, financial theft, or potentially even compromise of critical infrastructures, such as nuclear power plants, electric plants, water plants, and so on.

▶ **Employees and end users**—These individuals can be dangerous because they have access to systems and might have broad knowledge about systems and their operations. Whereas outsiders might possess a motive for attack, insiders have the means and opportunity, making them a much bigger risk. These individuals might have poor moral judgement or simply be driven by the need for money or financial gain. They might sell inside secrets to competitors, or sell confidential info such as social security numbers or credit card numbers.

Emergency Response

To reduce the amount of damage that these individuals can cause, organizations need to have incident-response and -handling policies in place. These policies should dictate how the organization handles various types of incidents. Most companies set up a Computer Emergency Response Team (CERT) or a Computer Security Incident Response Team (CSIRT). The first CERT team got its start in 1988 as a result of the Morris worm, which knocked out more than 10% of the systems connected to the Internet Defense Advanced Research Projects Agency. Having a CERT team in place along with policies needed to function can give the organization an effective and efficient means of reducing the potential impact of these situations. These procedures should also give management sufficient information to decide on an appropriate course of action. By having these procedures in place, the organization can maintain or restore business continuity, defend against future attacks, and deter attacks by prosecuting violators. The goals of incident response are many; the steps to reduce damage from security incidents are well known and follow the format shown here:

STEP BY STEP

7.3 The Incident Process

1. **Planning and preparation**—The organization must establish policies and procedures to address potential security incidents.

2. **Identification and evaluation**—Automated systems should be used to determine whether an event occurred. Was the event real, not a false positive? The tools used for identification include IDS, IPS firewalls, audits, logging, and observation.

3. **Containment and mitigation**—Preplanning, training, and the use of predeveloped procedures are key to this step. The incident-response plan should dictate what action is required. The incident-response team must have had the required level of training to properly handle the response. This team also must know how to contain the damage and determine how to proceed.

4. **Eradication and recovery**—Containing the problem is not enough; it must be removed and steps must be taken to return to normal business processes.

5. **Investigate and closure**—What happened? When the investigation is complete, a report, either formal or informal, must be prepared. This is needed to evaluate any needed changes to the IR policies.

6. **Lessons learned**—At this final step, all those involved must review what happened and why. Most important, necessary changes must be put in place to prevent future problems. Learning from what happened is the only way to prevent it from happening again.

Incident-response team members need diverse skill sets. Members should come from various departments throughout the organization, such as the following:

▶ Information security

▶ Legal

▶ Human resources

▶ Public relations

▶ Physical security

▶ Network and system administrators

▶ IS auditors

Having a diverse group better prepares the team to deal with the many types of incidents that can occur. Per ISACA, auditors should review incident-response plans to make sure they have documented plans in place to deal with these common types of security incidents:

▶ Virus and worm attacks

▶ Malicious software

▶ Website attacks

▶ Unauthorized access

▶ Hardware theft and physical intrusion

▶ Unauthorized software

▶ Denial of service

▶ Slander and media misinformation

▶ Proper forensic response and investigation practices

Documentation to address each of these potential incidents is critical because investigating computer crime is so complex and involved. Missteps can render evidence useless and unusable in a court of law. This means that team members must be knowledgeable of the proper procedures and have training on how to secure and isolate the scene to prevent contamination. That is the role of computer forensics.

Computer Forensics

Computer forensics is the systematic step-by-step examination and analysis of data that is stored, retrieved, or processed on computer systems in a legal, approved way so that the evidence can be used in court if needed. Forensic specialists must know how to record evidence at the scene by taking photographs, documenting their activities in an investigator's notebook, interviewing suspects and witnesses, and knowing the proper procedures for collecting or seizing suspected systems or media. Doing all of this correctly protects the chain of custody and legality of the evidence.

Although law enforcement has been practicing forensics for a long time, the computer forensics field is relatively new to the corporate sector. This means that many IS auditors might not be highly skilled in auditing this important field. An IS auditor must look carefully at the policies and procedures that detail forensic activities during an audit. Such policies might address computers, but other devices could be subject to forensic analysis, including cell phones, PDAs, pagers, digital cameras, and USB thumb drives. Any existing policy must specify how evidence is to be handled. Mishandling can cost companies millions. The chain of custody helps protect the integrity and reliability of the evidence by providing an evidence log that shows every access to evidence, from collection to appearance in court. Because electronic information can be changed so easily, a rigid methodology should be followed:

1. **Identify and acquire**—The information must be identified and retrieved. Once in the custody of the investigator, a copy is usually created. Standard practice dictates making a bit-level copy, an exact duplicate of the original data. This enables the investigator to examine the copy while leaving the original copy intact.

2. **Preserve and authenticate**—Preservation is the act of maintaining the evidence in an unchanged state. This process requires that an investigator show that the data is unchanged and has not been tampered with. Authentication can be accomplished through the use of integrity checks and hashes such as MD5 and SHA.

3. **Analyze, record, and present**—The investigator must be careful to examine the data and ensure that any activity is documented. The investigator usually extracts evidence by examining drive slack space, file slack space, hidden files, swap data, Internet cache, and other locations such as the recycle bin. Specialized tools are available for this activity. All the activities of the investigator must be recorded to ensure that the information will be useable in court, if needed.

Because the collection of electronic information is such an important concern, the International Organization on Computer Evidence (IOCE) was appointed to develop international principles for the procedures relating to digital evidence. The goal was to develop standards and practices that many countries and states would recognize as legal that would allow digital evidence collected by one state to be used in the courts of another state. These principles can be found at the IOCE website (http://www.ioce.org) and are summarized as follows:

> ▶ When dealing with digital evidence, all of the generally accepted forensic and procedural principles must be applied.

> ▶ Upon seizing digital evidence, actions taken should not change that evidence.

> ▶ When it is necessary for a person to access original digital evidence, that person should be trained for the purpose.

> ▶ All activity relating to the seizure, access, storage, or transfer of digital evidence must be fully documented, preserved, and available for review.

> ▶ An individual is responsible for all actions taken with respect to digital evidence while the digital evidence is in his or her possession.

> ▶ Any agency responsible for seizing, accessing, storing, or transferring digital evidence is responsible for compliance with these principles.

Auditing Information Security

When auditing information security, the IS auditor is generally concerned with reviewing policies and procedures that have been implemented to protect confidentiality, integrity, and availability of data. The policies and procedures should set the tone for good security practices and should assign responsibility for a secure infrastructure. Policies on logical access control should be designed so that least privilege is established and users are granted access to only the minimum level of access needed to perform their assigned tasks.

Policies cannot be developed in a void. Effective security requires that employees are trained and aware of proper procedure. Users need to know why logging off before leaving for the day is a requirement, how social engineers con employees out of information or access, and how to practice safe computing.

Data Ownership

Data ownership refers to the classification of the organization's information and assignment of responsibility. Without assignment of responsibility, there is no way to ensure that the information is protected. Assigning an individual responsibility establishes accountability. Roles and responsibilities are as follows:

▶ **Data owners**—Typically, these are managers and directors who maintain responsibility for controlling the organization. Data owners are responsible for authorizing access, maintaining accurate records, and changing access rules, as necessary.

▶ **Data custodians**—Custodians are responsible for storing and safeguarding information.

▶ **Security administrators**—Administrators are responsible for designing, installing, and maintaining physical and logical security to protect data, programs, and equipment.

▶ **Data users**—Users are responsible for requesting access to resources and data needed to perform their required duties.

▶ **New users**—Users must complete security awareness training and sign acceptable use policies.

▶ **Auditor**—The auditor is responsible for reviewing data classification and user accountability, and verifying that activities match information security policy.

Data ownership does not extend indefinitely. When employees move to new jobs or are terminated, data access should be withdrawn. Common practice is to schedule the termination of data access while HR is meeting with or informing the employee of the end of their employment. The exit interview is also a good time to remind the individual of any NDAs or other agreements that might have been signed. These individuals should also be encouraged to seek outside employment opportunities. If unfriendly termination is known in advance, access should be restricted at the appropriate time to reduce the threat of potential damage.

Security Baselines

A security baseline should be implemented as a best practice. This is a starting point for security that the organization can adopt for its own well-being and to establish a record of due diligence. Table 7.5 outlines a basic security baseline.

TABLE 7.5   Security Baseline

Topics	Objectives
Antivirus	Automated antivirus with automatic updates at least weekly.
Backups	Involves regular intervals, encryption, and on-site storage in a secured area. Off-site storage should have the same or greater security as on-site storage.
Inventory	Established inventory system that logs new equipment and software before it is put into use. Item location and owner should also be recorded.
Minimizing of services	Risk reduction by practicing a principle of least privilege, or turning on and activating only the minimum services needed.
Patching	An automated process that minimizes work disruption.
Passwords	A strong password policy that enforces complex password requirements.
Reduction of vulnerabilities	Proactive security administration that addresses issues before they become problems. Best accomplished by a structured risk-management program.

Auditing Network Infrastructure Security

Task

▶ Evaluate the design, implementation, and monitoring of logical access controls to ensure the confidentiality, integrity, availability and authorized use of information assets.

Knowledge Statement

▶ Knowledge of security testing and assessment tools (e.g., penetration testing, vulnerability scanning)

A key piece of auditing infrastructure security is reviewing access control—keeping unauthorized individuals out. Access control is one of the most targeted security mechanisms. Auditors should test access-control mechanisms to make sure that access is allowed only after proper authentication. Remote access is another tempting target for attackers. Auditors should examine all remote access points and seek to promote centralized remote access controls when possible. Any traffic that originates outside the network should be untrusted. When reviewing planned access systems, the auditor should first make sure the level of access control is sufficiently strong for the value of asset it is protecting. The proposed solution should be cost-efficient while meeting business requirements.

Ethical Hacking and Penetration Testing

Penetration testing is the process of evaluating the organization's security measures using the same tools and techniques as a hacker. This type of security evaluation is also known as *ethical hacking* or as a *red team activity*. The idea is to look at the network of the organization from the perspective of an opponent. During a penetration (pen) test, operational control of computers might be the target, or the goal might simply be to plant a flag or download usernames and passwords to prove that vulnerabilities exist. The organization's security team might or might not be made aware of the pending test: In a blind test, the pen test team has no knowledge of the internal network. A double-blind test is similar, but with the added requirement that the internal security employees have no knowledge of the test. The pen test can also be internal, examining the security of the internal or external network; these attacks seek to gain control from outside the organization's security perimeter. After the test methodology is determined, the pen test team is responsible for determining the weaknesses, technical flaws, and vulnerabilities. Recommendations for addressing security shortcomings should be included. Test results should be delivered in a comprehensive report to management.

Several good documents detail ways to conduct penetration testing. One is NIST-800-42. Table 7.6 lists the different phases of penetration testing, according to NIST.

TABLE 7.6   The NIST Four-Step Pen Test Methodology

Stage	Description
Planning	At this step, a signed letter of authorization is obtained. The rules of engagement are established here. The team must have goals, know the time frame, and know the limits and boundaries.
Discovery	This stage is divided into two distinct phases:
	Passive—This step is concerned with information gathered in a very covert manner. Examples of passive information gathering include surfing the organization's website to mine valuable information and reviewing job openings to gain a better understanding of the technologies and equipment used by the organization.
	Active—This step of the test is split between network scanning and host scanning. As individual networks are enumerated, they are further probed to discover all hosts, determine their open ports, and attempt to pinpoint the OS. Nmap is a popular scanning program.
Attack	At this step, the pen testers attempt to gain access, escalate their privilege, browse the system, and finally expand their influence.
Reporting	In this final step, documentation is used to compile the final report. This report serves as the basis for corrective action, which can range from nothing more than enforcing existing policies to closing unneeded ports and adding patches and service packs.

NOTE

Ethical Hacking   Individuals interested in learning more about ethical hacking and pen testing should consider reading *Certified Ethical Hacker Exam Prep* (ISBN 978-0789735317) by the author of this book, Michael Gregg.

NOTE

OSSTMM   The Open Source Security Test Metholodogy Manual (OSSTMM) is a peer-reviewed methodology for performing security tests, which you can find at www.osstmm.org.

Throughout this pen test process, the security team should be in close contact with management to keep them abreast of any findings. The team should never exceed its level of authorization or attempt any type of test that has not been previously approved in writing. There shouldn't be any big surprises at the conclusion of these pen tests. Leading a pen test team is a huge undertaking that requires managerial, technical, and project-management skills. Although these activities can help uncover previously unknown vulnerabilities, other types of network security tests are also effective. Vulnerability scanning is probably the most effective of these techniques.

> **NOTE**
>
> **Implementing Compensating Controls**   During a pen test, team members try to exploit potential vulnera-bilities. If vulnerabilities are discovered that cannot be removed, the team should look for ways to imple-ment compensating controls.

Network Assessments

Vulnerability scanning tools scan the network for vulnerabilities. Some of these tools are com-mercial and require an annual subscription; others are open source and don't cost anything to initially acquire. These tools can be run against a single computer or a range of network addresses. Nessus is an example of a well-known vulnerability scanning tool. Nessus is now both an open source and a commercial tool. These tools can be used to run regularly sched-uled scans or can be used if a target system or network has been patched or changed due to upgrades. Periodic network assessments should also review a list of best practices to make sure security best practices are being followed. Table 7.7 presents a basic checklist of items.

TABLE 7.7   Network Assessment Checklist

Item	Finding
Strong authentication used?	Yes/No
Intrusion detection in place and tuned?	Yes/No
Firewalls deployed and properly configured?	Yes/No
Encryption used?	Yes/No
Antivirus present and updated?	Yes/No
Patch management used?	Yes/No
Application controls in place?	Yes/No

Tracking Change

Change management is a formalized process whose purpose is to control modifications made to systems and programs. Without effective change-management procedures, unauthorized changes to software could endanger the security of the organization. During an audit, controls to prevent unauthorized changes should be verified. Some common change controls include the following:

- **Separation of duties**—Development, administration, and operation duties should be performed by different individuals.

▶ **Controlling the development environment**—Software developers should have access restricted to a controlled area used only for code development.

▶ **Restricting access**—Access to source code should be restricted to only individuals who have a valid need.

Encryption

Knowledge Statements

▶ Knowledge of encryption algorithm techniques (e.g., AES, RSA)

▶ Knowledge of public key infrastructure (PKI) components (e.g., certification authorities, registration authorities) and digital signature techniques

▶ Knowledge of network and Internet security devices, protocols, and techniques (e.g., SSL, SET, VPN, NAT)

Encryption involves obscuring information and rendering it unreadable to those without special knowledge. Encryption has been used for many centuries by many cultures. Caesar had an encryption standard known as Caesar's Cipher, and the ancient Hebrews had one called ATBASH. Almost as long as there has been encryption, others have been trying to break encrypted messages. Breaking encrypted messages is known as cryptanalysis. In the ninth century, Abu al-Kindi published what is considered to be the first paper to discuss how to break cryptographic systems, titled "A Manuscript on Deciphering Cryptographic Messages." The importance of this information is that people have long been trying to protect sensitive information, while others have been trying to reveal it.

Although encryption cannot prevent the loss of data or protect against denial of service, it is a valuable tool to protect the assets of the organization. Encryption can be used to provide confidentiality, integrity, authenticity, and nonrepudiation. Before covering the nut and bolts of encryption, you need to know a few basic terms to better understand encryption and its components:

▶ **Algorithm**—The rules or mathematical formula used to encrypt and decrypt data.

▶ **Cryptography**—The study of secret messages, derived from the Greek terms *kryptos*, which means "hidden," and *grafein*, which means "to write."

▶ **Cipher text**—Data that is scrambled and unreadable.

▶ **Cryptographic key**—The value used to control a cryptographic process.

▶ **Plaintext**—Clear text that is readable.

- ▶ **Encryption**—The process of transforming data into an unreadable format.

- ▶ **Symmetric encryption**—Encryption method that uses the same key to encode and decode data.

- ▶ **Asymmetric encryption**—Encryption method that uses one key for encryption and a different key for decryption. Each participant is assigned a pair of keys, consisting of an encryption key and a corresponding decryption key.

Encryption Methods

Encryption systems must be strong, to serve their required purpose. The strength of the encryption system is based on several factors:

- ▶ **Algorithm**—Remember that this is the set of instructions used with the cryptographic key to encrypt plaintext data. Not all algorithms are of the same strength. For example, Caesar might have thought his system of encryption was quite strong, but it is seen as relativity insecure today.

- ▶ **Cryptographic key**—A user needs the correct key to encrypt or decrypt the information. As an example, when my brother was a teenager, my parents took the key to his car for violating curfew. Without the key, he had no way to use the car. Had he made a copy, access would have still been possible.

- ▶ **Key length**—Weak keys are easily subverted, whereas stronger keys are hard to break. How strong the key needs to be depends on the value of the data. High-value data requires more protection than data that has little value. More valuable information needs longer key lengths and more frequent key exchange to protect against attacks.

Modern encryption systems use either symmetric or asymmetric encryption. Each method has unique abilities and specific disadvantages. Symmetric encryption uses a single shared key to encrypt and decrypt data. Asymmetric encryption uses two different keys for encryption and decryption. Each user must maintain a pair of keys. The following sections discuss each of these methods in much more detail; however, first take a quick look at the advantages and disadvantages of each method, as shown in Table 7.8.

TABLE 7.8   Attributes of Symmetric and Asymmetric Encryption

Type of Encryption	Advantage	Disadvantage
Symmetric	Faster than asymmetric	Key distribution
		Provides only confidentiality
Asymmetric	Easy key exchange	Slower than symmetric encryption
	Can provide confidentiality and authentication	

Private Key Encryption

Symmetric encryption uses a single shared secret key for encryption and decryption. Symmetric algorithms include the following:

▶ **DES**—Data Encryption Standard, the most common symmetric algorithm

▶ **Blowfish**—A general-purpose symmetric algorithm intended as a replacement for the DES, replaced by Advanced Encryption Standard (AES) and Twofish

▶ **Rijndael**—A block cipher that the U.S. government adopted as the AES to replace DES

▶ **RC4**—Rivest Cipher 4, a stream-based cipher

▶ **RC5**—Rivest Cipher 5, a block-based cipher

▶ **SAFER**—Secure and Fast Encryption Routine, a block-based cipher

All symmetric algorithms are based on the single shared key concept, illustrated in Figure 7.3.

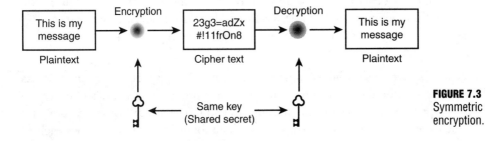

FIGURE 7.3 Symmetric encryption.

The strength of symmetric encryption depends on how well the private key is protected. One key is used to both encrypt and decrypt. The dual use of keys makes this system so simple and also causes its weakness. Symmetric encryption is fast and can encrypt and decrypt very quickly; it also is considered strong. Symmetric encryption is very hard to break if a large key is used. Even though symmetric encryption has its strengths, it also has disadvantages.

One disadvantage is key distribution. For symmetric encryption to be effective, there must be a secure method in which to transfer keys, and this must be done by some type of out-of-band method. As an example, if Bob wants to send Alice a secret message but is afraid that a third party can monitor their communication, how can he send the message? If the key is sent in clear text, the third party can intercept it. Bob could deliver the key in person, mail it, or even send a courier. None of these methods is practical in the world of electronic communication.

Another disadvantage of symmetric encryption is key management. For example, a user who needs to communicate with 10 people would need 45 unique keys. To calculate the numbers of keys needed in symmetric encryption, use this formula: $N (N - 1)/2$ or [10 (10 – 1)/2 = 45 keys]. As the number of users increases, so does the problem of key management.

One other problem with symmetric encryption is that it provides only confidentiality. If other services are needed, such as integrity or nonrepudation, asymmetric encryption must be considered.

Data Encryption Standard (DES)

The U.S. Bureau of Standards (NBS) published DES as a standard in 1977. NBS is now known as the National Institute of Standards and Technology (NIST). DES wasn't developed in a void; IBM had already developed it and named it Lucifer. To become a national standard, the algorithm was modified to use a 56-bit key and was officially adopted as a national standard in 1976. DES is considered a *block cipher* algorithm. The other type of symmetric algorithm is a *stream cipher*. Block and stream ciphers are defined as follows:

▶ **Block ciphers**—Divide the message into blocks for processing

▶ **Stream ciphers**—Divide the message into bits for processing

Because DES is a block cipher, it divides the input data into nice even blocks. If one block is short, padding is added to make sure all the blocks are the same size. DES processes 64-bit blocks of plain text and outputs 64-bit blocks of cipher text. DES uses a 56-bit key; therefore, the remaining 8 bits are used for parity. DES works by means of a permutation. This is a method of scrambling the input. This action is called a *round*, and DES performs this 16 times on every 64-bit block. DES has different modes of operation, such as Electronic Codebook (ECB) and Cipher Block Chaining (CBC).

Although DES has given years of useful service, nothing lasts forever; the same is true of DES, which became the victim of increased computing power. Just as Moore's law predicted, processing power has doubled about every 18–24 months. As a result, an encryption standard that might have taken years to brute-force in 1977 takes much less time to crack in 2007. The final demise of DES came in 1998, when the Electronic Frontier Foundation (EFF) was able to crack DES in about 23 hours. Although this sounds easy, the actual attack used distributed computing and required more than 100,000 computers. This demonstrated the need for stronger algorithms. The short-term fix for the problem was to implement 3DES, which can use two or three keys to encrypt data and performs what is referred to as *multiple encryption*.

3DES has a 168-bit key length. Even this was seen as just a stop-gap measure. Therefore, NIST began looking for a new system to replace DES. This new standard was to be referred to as the Advanced Encryption Standard (AES).

Advanced Encryption Standard (AES)

NIST provided the guidelines for AES so that vendors could submit their algorithm for review. At the conclusion of this process, NIST chose Rijndael (pronounced *rain doll*) as the choice for the AES standard. Rijndael is a block cipher that supports variable key and block lengths of 128, 192, or 256 bits. It is considered a fast, simple, robust encryption mechanism. Rijndael is also known to be very secure. Even if attackers used distributed computing and invested millions of dollars in computing power, Rijndael should be resistant to attacks for many years to come. Therefore, it is the symmetric algorithm of choice when high security is needed.

Public Key Encryption

Public key encryption is the second type of encryption method. It was designed to overcome the weaknesses of symmetric encryption and facilitate e-commerce. It's a rather new discovery: Dr. W. Diffie and Dr. M. E. Hellman developed the first public key exchange protocol in 1976. Public key encryption differs from symmetric encryption, in that it requires two keys: one to encrypt data and the second key to decrypt data. These keys are referred to as public and private keys. The public key can be published and given to anyone, whereas the user keeps the private key secret.

Public key cryptography is made possible by factoring large prime numbers or using discrete logarithms. Both make it possible to set up one-way functions. This is also called a trap-door function. For example, given the prime numbers of 387 and 283, it is easy to multiply them and get 109,521. However, if you are given the number 109,521, it's quite difficult to extract the two prime numbers of 387 and 283. The CISA exam will not expect you to calculate these numbers or perform advanced math. However, you will need to know that anyone who has the trap-door values can encrypt and decrypt, but anyone who lacks them can perform the function only in one direction. This functionality enables anyone with the public key to perform encryption and signature verification, while anyone with the private key can perform decryption and signature generation. Diffie-Hellman, RSA, and ECC are all popular asymmetric algorithms. Figure 7.4 illustrates public key encryption.

> **EXAM ALERT**
>
> **Know How Asymmetric Encryption Works**   With asymmetric encryption, the sender encrypts the information with the receiver's public key. The receiver decrypts the information with his or her own private key.

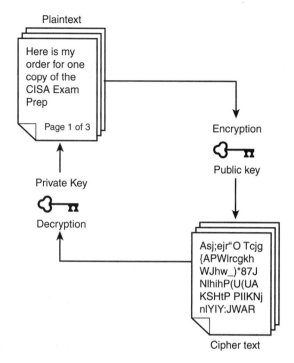

Plaintext

Here is my order for one copy of the CISA Exam Prep

Page 1 of 3

Encryption

Public key

Private Key

Decryption

Asj;ejr"O Tcjg {APWIrcgkh WJhw_)*87J NIhihP(U(UA KSHtP PIIKNj nIYIY:JWAR

Cipher text

FIGURE 7.4 Asymmetric (public key) encryption.

RSA Encryption

Ron Rivest, Adi Shamir, and Len Adleman developed RSA, which is strong even though it is not as fast as symmetric encryption. The RSA cryptosystem is found in many products, including Microsoft Internet Explorer and Mozilla Firefox. RSA supports a key size up to 2,048 bits. RSA is used for both encryption and digital signatures. Because asymmetric encryption is not as fast as symmetric encryption, many times the two are used together, thereby coupling the strengths of both systems. The asymmetric protocol is used to exchange the private key, and the actual communication is performed with symmetric encryption.

Elliptic Curve Cryptosystem (ECC)

ECC is another asymmetric algrothim. It requires less processing power than some of the previous algorithms discussed; it's useful in hardware devices such as cell phones and PDAs.

Quantum Cryptography

Quantum cryptography is seen as the next big step in encryption. Unlike traditional encryption, which is based on mathematics, quantum cryptography is based on the random polarization of photon light pulses. Any third-party attempt to intercept the photons will disturb the photons' quantum state and raise an alarm. This technology holds much promise. The first implementation of quantum cryptography was set up in 2004 in Cambridge, Massachusetts.

Hashing and Digital Signatures

Hashing is used to produce a message digest. Hashing verifies the integrity of data and messages. A well-designed message digest such as MD4, MD5, or SHA1 reduces a large amount of data to a small hash, as illustrated in Figure 7.5. Even a small change to the data produces a large change in the message hash.

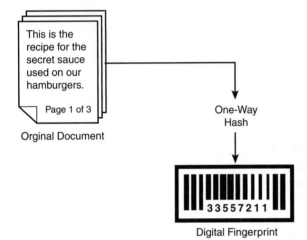

Digital Fingerprint   **FIGURE 7.5**   The digital signature process.

Now let's turn our attention to how hashing and asymmetric algorithms are used for authentication. The application of asymmetric encryption for authentication is known as a *digital signature*. Digital signatures are much like signatures in real life because they validate the integrity of the document and the sender. Algorithms used for digital signatures include MD4, MD5, SHA1, and HAVAL. Let's look at an example of how the digital signature process works:

STEP BY STEP

7.4 The Message Digest Process

1. Bob produces a message digest by passing a message through a hashing algorithm.

2. The message digest is encrypted using Bob's private key.

3. The message is forwarded to the recipient, Alice.

4. Alice creates a message digest from the message with the same hashing algorithm that Bob used. Alice then decrypts Bob's signature digest by using Bob's public key.

5. Alice compares the two message digests, the one originally created by Bob and the other that she created. If the two values match, Alice can be confident that the message is unaltered.

Public Key Infrastructure (PKI)

Per ISACA requirements, CISA candidates should have a basic understanding of *public key infrastructure* (PKI). PKI is a framework that consists of hardware, software, and policies to manage, create, store, and distribute keys and digital certificates. In face-to-face transactions, it's easy to know who you are dealing with. When dealing with companies over the Internet, it's hard to establish the same level of trust. The primary goal of PKI is to provide trust. It works much like a state driver's license bureau. As an example, to enter most airports, you must show proof of identification. In most cases, this is done with a driver's license. Airport employees trust driver's licenses because they have confidence in the state that issued them. Companies such as Verisign fill a very similar role in providing a level of trust between two unknown parties. PKI is built upon public key encryption. The components of the PKI framework include the following:

- ▶ **Certificate authority (CA)**—A person or group that issues certificates to authorized users. The CA creates and signs the certificate. The CA is the one that guarantees the authenticity of the certificate.

- ▶ **Certificate Revocation List (CRL)**—The CA maintains the CRL list. The list is signed to verify its accuracy and is used to report problems with certificates. When requesting a digital certificate, anyone can check the CRL to verify the certificate's integrity.

- ▶ **Registration authority (RA)**—The RA reduces the load on the CA. The RA cannot generate a certificate, but it can accept requests, verify an owner's identity, and pass along the information to the CA for certificate generation.

- ▶ **Certificate server**—The certificate server maintains the database of stored certificates.

- ▶ **X.509 standard**—This is the accepted standard for digital certificates.

When a user goes to a website that uses PKI, the certificate is presented to the user when they initiate a transaction. The user's system then checks the certificate by querying the certificate authority's database. If the certificate is valid, the transaction continues. Figure 7.6 shows a valid digital certificate. If there is a problem with the certificate, the user is notified, as shown in Figure 7.7.

FIGURE 7.6 A digital certificate.

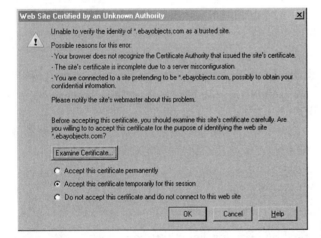

FIGURE 7.7 Certificate error.

NOTE

Digital Certificate Required Components   Digital certificates must always contain the owner's public key, the expiration date, and the owner's information.

Cryptographic Real-World Solutions

Although you need to know how encryption mechanisms work for the CISA exam, what is even more important to know is how the systems are used to provide real-world solutions. To better understand that concept, let us start by quickly reviewing the Open Systems Interconnect (OSI) reference model. The OSI reference model defines seven layers in which services, applications, and protocols are divided. Real-world cryptographic solutions can be found at many of these layers. It is generally agreed that cryptographic solutions exist at all except the physical layer. With so many choices of where to place a cryptographic solution, how do you know which is the right layer for implementation? That depends. Cryptographic solutions at the application layer are somewhat intrusive but offer the most flexibility because they can be designed to blend into the application and build a more seamless solution. Further down the stack, at the transport or network layers, encryption is more transparent yet more costly and can be complex because different systems and applications might need to communicate. Toward the bottom of the stack is the data link layer. Encryption added here is primarily for the LAN because different frame formats are designed according to different standards.

Now let's quickly review some of the better-known cryptographic systems that can be applied for confidentiality, integrity, and/or nonrepudiation:

▶ **Secure Shell (SSH)**—An application-layer program that provides secure remote access. It is considered a replacement for Telnet.

▶ **Secure Hypertext Transfer Protocol (S-HTTP)**—A superset of HTTP that was developed to provide secure communication with a web server. It has a low market share.

▶ **Secure Electronic Transaction (SET)**—An application-layer program developed by Visa and MasterCard to secure credit card transactions. SET uses a combination of digital certificates and digital signatures among the buyer, merchant, and the bank so that privacy and confidentiality are ensured.

▶ **Secure Multipurpose Internet Mail Extensions (S/MIME)**—A program that adds two valuable components to standard email, digital signatures, and public key encryption. Support also is provided for X.509 digital certificates.

▶ **Pretty Good Privacy (PGP)**—An application-layer secure mail solution that adds encryption and builds a web of trust. PGP requires users to sign and issue their own keys.

▶ **Secure Sockets Layer (SSL)**—Developed by Netscape Communications Corp. to provide security and privacy between clients and servers over the Internet. It's application independent and can be used with Hypertext Transfer Protocol (HTTP), Simple

Mail Transfer Protocol (SMTP), and File Transfer Protocol (FTP). SSL uses RSA public key cryptography and can provide confidentiality, integrity, authenticity, and nonrepudiation.

▶ **IP Security (IPsec)**—Widely used for VPNs. IPsec can provide encapsulated secure payload (ESP) and/or an authentication header (AH). ESP provides confidentiality by encrypting the data packet. AH provides integrity and authentication.

Table 7.9 provides an overview of some of these cryptographic solutions in relation to the OSI model.

TABLE 7.9 Attributes of Symmetric and Asymmetric Encryption and the OSI Reference Model

OSI Layer (ISO 7498-1)	Security Control	Security Model (ISO 7498-2)
Application	SSH, PGP, SET	Authentication
Presentation	SSL and TLS	Access control
Session		Nonrepudiation
Transport		Data integrity
Network	IPsec	Confidentiality
Data link	PPTP, L2TP, WEP	Assurance
Physical		Notarization

An organization could decide to use encryption that simply encrypts the data payload, known as *end-to-end encryption*. Or an organization might determine that everything needs to be encrypted, including the data and the header. That is known as *link-state encryption*. End-to-end encryption encrypts the message and the data packet, but the header, IP addresses, and routing information are left in clear text. The advantage of this type of encryption is speed. The disadvantage is that some information, such as addresses, are left in the clear. Link encryption encrypts everything, including the header, addresses, and routing information. Its advantage is that no one can determine the original source or the final destination. The disadvantage is that all intermediate devices, such as routers, must have the necessary keys, software, and algorithms to encrypt and decrypt the encrypted packets. This adds time and complexity.

With so many ways to encrypt data, you might think that these solutions could be used to build perfect security—unfortunately, that's not true. Attacks also can be launched against encryption systems, as discussed next.

Encryption Risks and Attacks

Attacks on cryptographic systems are nothing new. If malicious individuals believe that information has enough value, they will try to obtain it. Cryptographic attacks can use many methods to attempt to bypass the encryption someone is using. The attack might focus on a weakness in the code, cipher, or protocol, or might even attack key management. Even if they cannot decrypt the data, attackers might be able to gain valuable information just from monitoring the flow of traffic. E-commerce has increased the potential bounty for malicious users. Attackers typically target transactional databases in an attempt to steal names, social security numbers, credit card numbers, and so on. Common types of cryptographic attacks include the following:

▶ **Known plain-text attack**—This attack requires the hacker to have both the plain text and the cipher text of one or more messages. For example, if a WinZip file is encrypted and the hacker can find one of the files in its unencrypted state, the two then provide the attacker with both plaintext and ciphertext. Together these two items can extract the cryptographic key and recover the remaining encrypted, zipped files.

▶ **Cipher text–only attack**—This attack requires a hacker to obtain encrypted messages that have been encrypted using the same encryption algorithm. The attacker then looks for repetitions or patterns.

▶ **Man-in-the-middle attack**—This form of attack is based on hackers' ability to place themselves in the middle of the communications flow. Once there, they exchange bogus certificates and spoof each user.

Key size plays such a large role in the strength of an algorithm. Although 56-bit DES was cracked in about three days, it took many computers and cost more than $125,000. Larger key sizes equate to greater security. Increasing the key size by one doubles the work factor. Although (2^5) is just 16, (2^6) jumps to 32, and by incrementing only up to (2^{25}), you increase to a number large enough to approximate the number of seconds in a year. More often than not, encryption is cracked because users use weak keys or allow keys to become disclosed or compromised in some other way.

REVIEW BREAK

Encryption plays an important role in protecting sensitive information. Notice how each type of encryption service provides a specific control mechanism:

Item	Feature	Provides
DES	Symmetric encryption	Confidentiality
AES	Symmetric encryption	Confidentiality
RSA	Asymmetric encryption	Confidentiality, authentication
MD5	Hashing	Integrity
SHA	Hashing	Integrity
PKI	Key infrastructure	Confidentiality, integrity, authenticity and nonrepudiation
PGP	Email and file security	Confidentiality, integrity, authenticity, and nonrepudiation
SSL	Application independence	Confidentiality, integrity, authenticity, and nonrepudiation

Chapter Summary

In this chapter, you learned about mechanisms to protect information assets. This is an area of extreme importance to the IS auditor. These controls, including information classification, mandatory and discretionary controls, authentication, authorization, and accountability, can help protect the company's vital assets. The IS auditor needs to know how these controls are implemented and how they are monitored. You could have the best firewall or intrusion-detection system in the world, but if they are not properly set up, configured, and monitored, their value is almost insignificant. All this clearly points to the value of monitoring and control. The auditor plays an important role in this process.

Encryption is another one of these key defenses. Encryption can provide confidentiality, integrity, authentication, and nonrepudation. It's an amazing thing that one item has the potential to make such a huge difference. Just consider the lost laptop or exposed hard drive: If encryption is being used, there is now an effective barrier that must be compromised before information can be disclosed. Also, consider the value that cryptographic solutions that use PKI offer. With PKI, it is possible to perform commercial transactions with users all around the world with a high level of confidence. We can rest assured that the X.509 certificate we are presented with when we go to our bank's web page does, in fact, validate that we are truly dealing with our bank.

Without sufficient controls and the lack of a defense in-depth design, the many threats that endanger the organization could be realized. These threats include the many items discussed in the chapter, including passive sniffing attacks, password-cracking attacks, wireless security threats, denial-of-service attacks, and even malicious code, such as viruses and worms. Each of these threats present a real danger to the organization.

Key Terms

- ▶ Access control list
- ▶ Access rights and permissions
- ▶ Allow all or deny all
- ▶ Asymmetric encryption
- ▶ Asynchronous attack
- ▶ Attack-detecting tools
- ▶ Audit-reduction tools
- ▶ Biometrics
- ▶ Block cipher

- Bluetooth
- Brute force
- Bypass label processing
- Crash restarts
- Defense-in-depth
- Denial of service
- Dictionary attack
- Digital signature
- Dumpster diving
- Email bomb
- File and data ownership
- Hashing
- Hybrid attack least privilege
- Intrusion detection
- Logic bomb
- Masquerading
- Need to know
- Network Address Translation
- Packet replay
- Password
- Phishing
- Pretexting
- Principle of allow all
- Principle of deny all
- Privacy impact analysis

- ► Private Branch Exchange (PBX)
- ► Private IP addresses
- ► Public key infrastructure
- ► RADIUS
- ► Separation of duties
- ► Social engineering
- ► Stream cipher
- ► Symmetric encryption
- ► Token
- ► Trap door
- ► Trend-/variance-detect tools
- ► Trojan horse
- ► Two-factor authentication
- ► Virus
- ► Voice over IP (VoIP)
- ► War dialing
- ► War driving
- ► Wired Equivalent Privacy
- ► Worm

Apply Your Knowledge

You have seen in this chapter that the organization should have formalized security functions developed to protect the company's information assets. One proven method of protecting information is encryption. This exercise has you download and install a digital certificate. You will need an Internet connection and Microsoft Outlook to complete this exercise.

Exercises

7.1 Obtaining Digital Certificates

This exercise will step you through the process of obtaining a free digital certificate. These can be used with email, signing, or other noncommercial encryption processes.

Estimated Time: 10 Minutes

1. The first step in this task is to obtain a digital certificate. Many different vendors provide these; in this exercise, you will be downloading the certificate from Comodo, which provides free certificates for noncommercial use.

2. Go to http://www.comodogroup.com/products/certificate_services/index.html to get your free digital certificate. You will need to fill out a short form, and then download details will be emailed to you.

3. Open your email from Comodo and follow the link to the certificate download. This installs the certificate in your computer.

4. To use the certificate, open Outlook and Select **Tools** from the menu.

5. Select **Options** from the Tools menu.

6. On the Options menu, choose the **Security** tab.

7. Enter a name for your security setting into the **Security Settings Name** box.

8. Check **Default Security Setting for This Secure Message Format**.

9. Select your **Secure Email Certificate** from the **Select Certificate** dialog box.

10. Now view your certificate by selecting the **View Certificate** button. The Certificate menu displays four tabs that provide more detail about your certificate. Click on each one to learn more about the certificate. After examining it, click the **OK** button to return to the **Select Certificate** menu and click **OK** again to select the certificate.

11. While at the **Change Security Setting** menu, make sure **Send These Certificates with Signed Messages** is selected.

12. Click **OK** to return to the **Options** dialog box, and then click **OK** to return to Outlook. Your certificate is now installed.

13. To send a message with your new digital certificate, create a new message to send to a coworker or friend.

14. After creating the message, choose the **Options** button.

15. From the **Options** menu, select the **Security Settings** button. Now choose **Add Digital Signature to This Message** and select **OK**.

16. You have added the strength of nonrepudiation. You can now send your first signed email.

Exam Questions

1. Which of the following cryptosystems provides the best method to verify integrity?

   ○ **A.** DES

   ○ **B.** AES

   ○ **C.** MD5

   ○ **D.** RSA

2. Which of the following is the most effective control for viruses and worms?

   ○ **A.** A good backup policy

   ○ **B.** Scanning incoming email for viruses and worms

   ○ **C.** Policies that prohibit the use of media brought from home or downloaded from a non-work computer

   ○ **D.** Antivirus that is updated no less than weekly, that is online and active

3. A B-to-C e-commerce website is worried about security and has had talks about encryption. Specifically, they would like to set up a system that can monitor, detect, and alert on hacking activity. Which of the following would best meet the required needs?

   ○ **A.** Packet filtering

   ○ **B.** Intrusion detection

   ○ **C.** Stateful inspection

   ○ **D.** Asymmetric cryptography

4. Your company is considering a penetration test to review external security. They would like you, the company's lead IS auditor, to direct the project. Which of the following would be considered the first and most important for you to accomplish before you begin?

   ○ **A.** Establish a time frame for the test

   ○ **B.** Determine the team members

   ○ **C.** Get the support of the IT security group

   ○ **D.** Obtain written authorization

5. Which of the following best describes the type of IDS that works by learning users' activities so that it understands normal patterns of behaviors?

- ○ **A.** Statistical
- ○ **B.** Signature
- ○ **C.** Neural
- ○ **D.** Protocol

6. Which of the following is the highest priority for an IS auditor?

- ○ **A.** Designing and implementing security controls
- ○ **B.** Reviewing new policies and procedures
- ○ **C.** Controlling and monitoring data security and policies
- ○ **D.** Controlling and monitoring IDS and firewall activity

7. A team of auditors has just completed an audit of the organization. Which of the following findings should be considered the most critical?

- ○ **A.** Servers are not backed up on a regular basis.
- ○ **B.** Workstations are not backed up on a regular basis.
- ○ **C.** The business continuity plan is current but includes critical and noncritical items.
- ○ **D.** The password change policy is not being actively enforced

8. You have been asked to review your organization's computer forensics policy. Which of the following elements should be of the most concern to you while reviewing the documentation?

- ○ **A.** Incident response
- ○ **B.** Chain of custody
- ○ **C.** In-house forensic investigators
- ○ **D.** Commercial forensic software

9. When discussing data ownership, which of the following individuals has the responsibility of day-to-day management of the asset?

- ○ **A.** Security advisory group
- ○ **B.** Process owner
- ○ **C.** Chief privacy officer
- ○ **D.** Chief security officer

10. Several coworkers are installing an IDS, and you have been asked to make an initial review. One of the installers has asked which of the following is the worst condition for an IDS. Which is correct?

   ○ **A.** Positive

   ○ **B.** Negative

   ○ **C.** False positive

   ○ **D.** False negative

Answers to Exam Questions

1. **C**. MD5 is a hashing algorithm. Hashing algorithms are used to verify integrity. Answer A is incorrect because DES is a symmetric algorithm and offers confidentiality, answer B is incorrect because AES is also a symmetric algorithm that offers confidentiality, and answer D is incorrect because RSA is an asymmetric algorithm that generally offers confidentiality, authentication, and nonrepudiation.

2. **D**. An up-to-date antivirus system is the most effective means of preventing and controlling malicious software. Regular updates are required to ensure that the antivirus software has the capability to scan for the most current malicious code. Answer A is incorrect because backups will not prevent a virus infection and offer no control of malicious code. Answer B is incorrect because scanning email will prevent some malicious code, but there are other modes of entry. Answer C is incorrect because although policies are a good baselining control, they do not prevent employees from carrying out specific actions.

3. **B**. Intrusion detection is the best method of monitoring and detecting break-ins or attempts to attack via the Internet. Answer A is incorrect because packet filtering is a type of stateless inspection and can make a decision on only a set of static rules. Answer C is incorrect because stateful inspection is not specifically designed to detect and report hacking activities. Answer D is incorrect because encryption does not meet any of the company's stated goals.

4. **D**. The most important step of the pen test process is to obtain written authorization and approval. No testing should occur until this step is completed. Answer A is incorrect because timing is not the most important item; approval is. Answer B is incorrect because choosing team members is not the most important item; approval is. Answer C is incorrect because internal security might or might not be informed. Many times they are being tested to see if they detect any unusual activity or notice that pen testing is actually occurring.

5. **C**. A neural IDS works by first being placed in a learning mode so that it understands normal patterns of activity. Answer A is incorrect because this IDS detection method requires the administrator to use profiles of authorized activities or place them into the IDS so that it understands normal activity. Answer B is incorrect because signature IDS detection requires the administrator to load a database of known attacks. Answer D is incorrect because a protocol-decoding IDS is similar to a statistical IDS, yet it can keep track of the state of a session so that it can reassemble packets and look at higher-layer activity.

6. **C**. Data security is one of the primary duties of an auditor. This task is achieved by controlling and monitoring data security policies. Answer A is incorrect because auditors are usually not the individuals responsible for implementing security controls. Answer B is incorrect because an auditor is concerned not just with new policies, but also will all policies. Answer D is incorrect because the IT security group usually handles day-to-day activities of the IDS and the firewall.

7. **A**. Not backing up the servers on a regular basis is the most serious threat to the integrity and availability of informational assets. Answer B is incorrect because good control policies should dictate that users save critical information on network share drives. Answer C is incorrect because having a business continuity plan that goes into too much detail is not a problem. Answer D is incorrect because although poor password enforcement is a finding, it is not the most critical finding.

8. **B**. Chain of custody is the critical item that must be maintained during any forensic activity. Chain of custody concerns who collected the information and how it was documented, processed, stored, and handled. Answers A, C, and D are incorrect because incident response should be addressed in a separate set of policies. The organization might not use in-house investigators. Consultants might perform forensic activities. Forensic investigations might use Linux or other open source tools, but they do not have to be commercial.

9. **B**. The process owner has the responsibility of the day-to-day management of the asset. Answers A, C, and D are incorrect because the security advisory group is responsible for reviewing security issues, security plans, and procedures. The chief privacy officer is responsible for maintaining compliance with local, state, and federal privacy laws. The chief security officer is responsible for the day-to-day security of the organization.

10. **D**. The worst state for an IDS is a false negative, which means an event occurred yet no alarm was triggered. Therefore, answers A, B, and C are incorrect.

Need to Know More?

- Auditing Best Practices: http://tinyurl.com/ecx3o

- Firewall Evolution: http://tinyurl.com/yqqdb

- The History of IDS: http://www.securityfocus.com/infocus/1514

- Remote Access Best Practice: http://tinyurl.com/2gspo9

- Change Management: http://home.att.net/~nickols/change.htm

- Pen Testing Techniques: http://tinyurl.com/24g9ds

- Creating an Incident-Response Team: http://www.cert.org/csirts/Creating-A-CSIRT.html

- Social Engineering: http://tinyurl.com/yrzyxp

CHAPTER EIGHT

Physical Security

This chapter helps you prepare for the Certified Information Systems Auditor (CISA) exam by covering the following ISACA objectives, which include understanding the role and importance of physical security. This includes items such as the following.

Tasks

Evaluate the design, implementation, and monitoring of environmental controls to prevent or minimize loss.

Evaluate the design, implementation, and monitoring of physical access controls to ensure that information assets are adequately safeguarded.

Evaluate the processes and procedures used to store, retrieve, transport, and dispose of confidential information assets.

Knowledge Statements

Knowledge of environmental protection practices and devices (e.g., fire suppression, cooling systems, water sensors)

Knowledge of physical security systems and practices (e.g., biometrics, access cards, cipher locks, tokens)

Knowledge of data classification schemes (e.g., public, confidential, private, and sensitive data)

Knowledge of the processes and procedures used to store, retrieve, transport, and dispose of confidential information assets

Outline

Study Strategies

This chapter addresses information you need to know about physical security. An organization can have the best logical controls in the world; however, they are of little use if no physical security is present. Most of the information you need to pass the CISA exam deals with logical access and controls such as encryption, firewalls, antivirus software, and intrusion detection. Yet physical security is also required and is one of the items that must be examined during an audit. The following are the primary topics a CISA candidate should review for the exam:

▶ Understand the threats to physical security

▶ Know the ways in which a layered defense can be designed to provide defense-in-depth

▶ Know what controls, procedures, and mechanisms are needed to protect the safety of employees

▶ Describe the various types of physical access controls including gates, locks, and guards

▶ Know personal safety controls, including fire prevention and fire detection

Introduction

Physical security might not be a topic you automatically think of when you hear the words "IT audit," but it is a key component. You could have the best firewall, IDS, and wireless encryption in the world, yet it would do little good if someone can walk into your server room and simply walk out with a hard drive or computer. Physical security is not just about the protection of assets; it is also about people. This means having the right controls in place for the protection of life. This includes fire detection, alarm, and suppression systems; protection against blackout, humidity, and temperature controls; and plans and procedures in case of emergencies.

Physical Security

Tasks

▶ Evaluate the design, implementation, and monitoring of physical access controls to ensure that information assets are adequately safeguarded.

▶ Evaluate the design, implementation, and monitoring of environmental controls to prevent or minimize loss.

▶ Evaluate the processes and procedures used to store, retrieve, transport, and dispose of confidential information assets.

The most important aspect of physical security is control. If you can gain physical control of a device, it almost always means that this can be leveraged to control the behavior of the device. This is what makes physical security such an important piece of overall security. Physical security can be attacked from many different angles, from stealing data, to hardware modification, to the bypass of security controls. Each angle offers the potential to gain access or understanding of how a security control works.

It might be argued that physical security is more important now than at any time in the past. This bold statement holds true because businesses do have better logical controls—better firewalls, antivirus, IDS, and encryption—than ever. For the attacker or malicious individual, this can mean that physical access offers the most attractive means to target an organization. In the past, the few computers that an organization had were probably well-secured mainframes that were locked in a server room. Today there is a computer on every desk, a fax machine in every office, and employees with camera phones, PDAs, and iPods that can quickly move pictures or gigabytes of data out of the organization almost instantly. Many employees also have USB thumb drives that can hold a gigabyte of data or more. How many sensitive documents would one of these devices hold?

This section begins by looking at physical security exposures and then looks at some of the various types of physical security controls that can be used to protect the organization. These include equipment controls, area controls, facility controls, and personal safety controls. Next, you will learn about environmental protection practices and authentication and authorization.

Physical Security Exposures

Whereas logical security exposures are centered on disclosure, denial of service, and alteration, physical security exposures deal with *theft*, *vandalism*, and *destruction*. These threats can be caused by natural, man-made, or technical events. Companies might have to deal with several of these at the same time. We start by reviewing the types of natural events that organizations can be exposed to:

> ▶ **Floods**—Floods result from too much rain, when the soil has poor retention properties or when creeks and rivers overflow their banks. There's also the risk of internal building flooding from broken pipes, or a water main pipe breaking near or in the server/document storage room.

NOTE

Population Growth Is Booming in Storm-Prone Areas   Information from http://www.noaa.gov shows that Americans are moving disproportionately into storm-prone areas. From 1930 to 2000, the population of the United States rose only 230%, yet the population of storm-prone areas rose exponentially. For example, the population of Miami-Dade County rose 1,800%. Broward County, Florida, grew at a whopping 8,000% during the same time.

> ▶ **Fire**—Many controls such as smoke alarms and sprinklers can be put in place to minimize damage from this common natural disaster and reduce the threat to physical security.

> ▶ **Hurricanes and tropical storms**—Hurricanes are the most destructive force known to man. These natural events have the power to cause monumental damage. A good example of this was Hurricane Katrina, the power of which was enough to destroy New Orleans.

> ▶ **Tidal waves**—Tidal waves are also known as tsunamis. The word *tsunami* is based on a Japanese word that means "harbor wave." This natural phenomenon consists of a series of widely dispersed waves that cause massive damage when they come ashore. The December 2004 Indian Ocean tsunami is believed to have killed more than 230,000 people.

> ▶ **Earthquakes**—Earthquakes are caused from movement of the earth along fault lines. Many areas of the earth are vulnerable to earthquakes if they are on or near a fault line.

Although other chapters will focus more on disaster recovery and business continuity, it's possible that companies might have to deal with more than one physical threat at any particular time. For example, consider New Orleans and Hurricane Katrina. Businesses in New Orleans were faced with the need to address a hurricane, flooding, and loss of communication almost simultaneously.

Storms can be extremely costly. Table 8.1 ranks, by cost, ten of the worst hurricanes from 1900 to 2005, according to the National Hurricane Center.

TABLE 8.1   Top 10 Most Costly Hurricanes

Event	Year	Cost
Katrina	2005	$100 billion
Andrew	1991	$30 billion
Charley	2004	$14 billion
Hugo	1989	$14 billion
Agnes	1972	$12 billion
Rita	2005	$10 billion
Camille	1969	$7.5 billion
Frederic	1979	$7 billion
Jeanne	2004	$6.9 billion
Floyd	1999	$6.5 billion

Exposures occur not just from natural events, but they can also be man-made. They are sometimes accidental, but they might also be deliberate. They can come from any direction: Outsiders or insiders might threaten the physical security of the organization. In most business environments, insiders pose a bigger threat to the organization than do outsiders. Why? Because typically, committing a crime requires three elements: means, opportunity, and motive. Although outsiders might have a motive, the means and opportunity might be hard for them to obtain. Compare this to the trusted insider, who most likely has the means and opportunity and lacks only a motive. Basically, insiders have two of the three things needed for an attack. The following list looks at some of these potential man-made events.

▶ **Unauthorized entry**—Controlling who enters a facility, when they enter, and what they have access to is critical to the security of an organization.

▶ **Vandalism or damage**—Since the Vandals sacked Rome in 455 A.D., the term *vandalism* has been synonymous with the willful destruction of the property of others.

▶ **Theft**—Theft of company assets can range from mildly annoying to extremely damaging. Your CEO's laptop might be stolen from the airport. In this case, is the real loss the laptop or the plans for next year's new product release?

Identity Theft Is a Growing Problem   Current and past U.S. military veterans came close to learning the value of theft of personal identification when it was revealed that personal details of as many as 26.5 million veterans had been lost by means of a stolen laptop. Although the laptop and data were eventually recovered, it does not negate the breach of confidentiality or the fact that stronger security controls had not been used.

- **Access to sensitive information**—This exposure is linked directly to the loss of confidentiality. Information has value, and the loss of sensitive information can be extremely expensive. As an example, a trusted insider might place a keystroke logger on a co-worker's computer to find out more about a sensitive project that is being considered.

- **Alteration of equipment setting or information**—If an employee can access a system or change a setting, he can bypass access controls and any useful audit information can be altered or destroyed. As an example, a quick visit to the Cisco site provides you with the information needed to reset passwords and gain entry into any Cisco device.

- **Disclosure of information**—This category of exposure covers all threats that involve the deliberate or accidental disclosure of sensitive information. The privacy of information is affected because information is exposed without authorization. As an example, the insider that collected information by means of keystroke logging might offer it to a competitor for a large amount of money.

- **Abuse of resources**—This exposure can include any use of a resource that is not authorized by policy and procedure. This can include playing time-consuming computer games, using computer accounts for work not authorized for that account, and sending chain letters or other items for personal profit or illegal purposes.

- **Blackmail**—This is the act of threatening to perform a damaging action or make public sensitive information about a person or company unless certain demands are met.

- **Embezzlement**—This is the fraudulent appropriation of money or services from the organization.

- **Destruction**—This threat can come from insiders or outsiders and can include vandalism and damage. The destruction of physical assets can cost organizations huge sums of money.

Top Losses Reported by Organizations   FBI statistics compiled in 2005 noted that the top three losses by organizations were due to computer viruses, unauthorized access, and theft of proprietary information. As an example, even the FBI faces this problem—in the last three years, the FBI has lost or suffered the theft of 61 laptops holding extremely sensitive information (http://www.itbusinessedge.com/item/?ci=24214).

Potential threats to physical security can come from all angles, and it's important to consider all the ways in which an organization can suffer from undue exposure. Discarded media is one of these exposures. A malicious individual needs only to sift through an organization's trash to potentially find many types of useful information. This activity is known as *dumpster diving*. Figure 8.1 illustrates what the results of dumpster diving can yield.

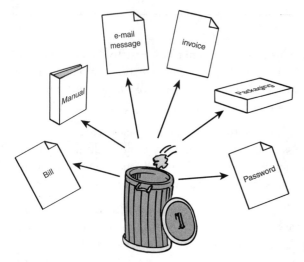

FIGURE 8.1 Dumpster diving.

Dumpster diving can reveal usernames, passwords, account numbers, and even enough information for identity theft. To prevent this type of activity, good policies should be implemented detailing what can and cannot be thrown away. Paper shredders should also be located throughout the facility so that employees can properly dispose of sensitive information. Many of these shredders can also shred DVDs and CDs. If this feature is not built in, organizations should purchase separate media shredding equipment. Hard drives and floppies also need to be properly disposed of. For these types of durable media, overwriting and degaussing are the preferred techniques:

▶ **Drive wiping**—This is the act of overwriting all information on the drive. As an example, DoD.5200.28-STD (7) specifies overwriting the drive with a special digital pattern through seven passes. Drive wiping allows the drive to be reused.

▶ **Degaussing**—This process is used to permanently destroy the contents of the hard drive or magnetic media. Degaussing works by means of a powerful magnet that uses its field strength to penetrate the housing of the hard drives and reverse the polarity of the magnetic particles on the hard disk platters. After a drive has been degaussed, it cannot be reused. Next to physical destruction, degaussing is the most secure way to ensure that the drive cannot be reused.

The two types of shredders are strip-cut and cross-cut:

▶ **Strip-cut shredder**—Slices the paper into long, thin strips. Strip-cut shredders generally handle a higher volume of paper with lower maintenance requirements. This type of shredder is cheap but doesn't shred well enough to prevent reassembly of the shredded document.

▶ **Cross-cut**—Provides more security by cutting paper vertically and horizontally into confetti. Although this type of shredder is more expensive, the shredded documents are much more difficult to reconstruct or reassemble. Some organizations pay for vendors to come on-site and shred their sensitive documents while an employee or monitor watches. These vendors might also handle disposal.

Challenge

This chapter emphasizes the importance of proper disposal of information and media. This challenge exercise has you look at several types of media and list the best form of disposal.

1. From the following table, determine the devices upon which your data exists.

Item	Shredding/Physical Destruction	Degaussing	Wiping
Post-it notes			
CDs/DVDs			
Floppy disks			
Paper documents			
Hard drives			
Hard drives with highly sensitive information			
Thumb drives			

2. When you have completed the table, compare it with the next one.

(continues)

(continued)

Item	Shredding/Physical Destruction	Degaussing	Wiping
Post-it notes	✓		
CDs/DVDs	✓		
Floppy disks	✓		✓
Paper documents	✓		
Hard drives		✓	
Hard drives with highly sensitive information	✓		
Thumb drives	✓		

3. Although your answers might vary, what is listed in this table is considered best practice.

Possible Perpetrators

Remember earlier in the chapter when the concept of *means, opportunity,* and *motive (MOM)* was introduced? If you apply this model to insiders and outsiders, who comes up as the greater risk? Insiders do: They possess two of the three items needed to commit a crime—means and opportunity. Outsiders typically have motive but not means or opportunity. Insiders are even more of a risk today because of advances in technology. Malicious insiders have many tools at their disposal, such as key chain–size hard drives, steganography, encryption, and wireless technology, that might make them harder to detect.

NOTE

Insider Attacks   The FBI and the Computer Security Institute conduct an annual FBI/CSI Computer Crime and Security Survey of U.S. corporations, government agencies, financial institutions, and universities. In 2005, the information security professionals who responded to this survey reported that disgruntled and dishonest employees represented almost 80% of the known attacks on their computer systems.

This doesn't mean that all exposures are malicious, of course. The most likely source of exposure is human error, accidents, or unintentional acts. People make mistakes, and without proper controls, this can have devastating effects. Table 8.2 shows some of the individuals who might be the source of an attack and their relationship to the organization.

TABLE 8.2 Perpetrators and Their Motives

Name	Relationship	Description
Disgruntled employees	Insiders	These employees are unhappy with their job or some situation at work.
Individuals threatened by disciplinary action	Insiders	If someone faces a threat of disciplinary action, they might seek to damage company property or disrupt operations.
Employees on strike	Insiders	Injury, financial loss, or sabotage can occur during strikes or other labor issues.
Individuals with financial problems	Insiders/outsiders	The need for money drives individuals into sometimes desperate behavior.
Employees notified of termination	Insiders	Individuals being terminated might seek to lash out at the company. This drives home the need for good termination policies.
Interested third parties	Outsiders	Individuals from other companies and government spies might want to gain access to company information or confidential data.
Former employees	Outsiders	These outsiders hold a unique position because they have knowledge of standard operating procedures used by the company. They might also have keys, passwords, or other means of re-entry.
Drug users	Insiders/outsiders	Drug addiction drives individuals to get money however possible.
Organized crime	Insiders/outsiders	Organized crime has a long history of blackmail and coercion.

Organizations can be attacked in many different ways. Unfortunately, not all exposures are mistakes—many are purposeful and are usually the most damaging. A determined perpetrator can target a company for a low-tech social-engineering attack or dumpster diving, or might attempt physical entry. Depending on their motives, attackers can do a huge amount of damage if they are successful. Let's look now at physical controls to see how to better protect an organization.

Physical Security Controls

A need for physical security has always existed. In the ancient history of man, castles were built for the safety and protection of the inhabitants. Even in the United States, the Anasazi Indians built their homes in the sides of cliffs to protect them from attack. In the modern world, physical security controls are designed to protect the organization from unauthorized access. These controls support the concept of confidentiality, integrity, and availability. As with any other control, these work best when layered. This offers the maximum amount of protection to slow intruders or make their target so unattractive that they move on. Physical security controls have three primary goals:

STEP BY STEP

8.1 Building Layered Control to Deter Attackers

1. Deter the attacker by using controls such as security lighting, No Trespassing signs, and armed guards.

2. Delay the attacker by using fences, gates, locks, access controls, and mantraps. Each of the techniques slows the attacker and makes the task more difficult.

3. Detect the attacker by using controls such as closed-circuit TV (CCTV) and alarms.

Let's continue this discussion by looking at some different types of controls, such as exterior, interior, and personal controls.

Exterior Controls

The first line in the defense-in-depth model is the design and placement of exterior controls. These controls prevent unauthorized individuals from gaining access to the facility. If you are involved in the design of a new facility, you might have the ability to ensure that many of these controls are added during design. That's not always the case, however: Often you are tasked with examining an existing facility. In both new and old facilities, the goal should be to look for controls that have been designed so that the breach of any one defensive layer will not compromise the physical security of the organization. Perimeter security controls can be any physical barrier, such as a wall, card-controlled entry, or a staffed reception desk. Perimeter security requires examination of the following:

- ▶ Natural boundaries at the location

- ▶ Fences or walls around the site

- ▶ Gates, access doors, the delivery dock, and entry points

- ▶ The design of the outer walls of a building

- ▶ Lighting and exterior design of the complex

Fences, Gates, and Bollards

Fences are one of the first layers of defense and one of the key components of perimeter security. When it is of the proper design and height, fencing can delay an intruder and also work as a psychological barrier. Just think about the Berlin Wall. This monument to the Cold War was quite effective in preventing East Germans from escaping to the west. Before its fall in 1989, most individuals that escaped to the west did so by hiding in trunks of cars or by bribing guards. The wall worked as a strong physical as well as psychological barrier. Does the height or gauge of wire used in the fence matter? Yes, taller fences with thicker gauge wire work better at deterring determined intruders, as outlined in Table 8.3. and Table 8.4.

TABLE 8.3 Fence Mesh and Gauge

Type	Security	Mesh	Gauge
A	Extreme high security	3/8 inch	11 gauge
B	Very high security	1 inch	9 gauge
C	High security	1 inch	11 gauge
D	Greater security	2 inch	6 gauge
E	Normal fencing	2 inch	9 gauge

TABLE 8.4 Fence Height and Purpose

Height	Security	Description
3–4 feet	Very little security	Will deter only casual trespassers.
6–7 feet	Moderate security	Too tall to easily climb.
8 feet or greater	High security	Of sufficient height to deter determined intruders. Topping with three strands of razor wire gives the fence even greater security.

Organizations that require very high security might consider using a perimeter intrusion and detection assessment system (PIDAS). This special fencing system works somewhat like an intrusion-detection system, in that it has sensors to detect anyone climbing or cutting the fence.

NOTE

Deterrence by Design The design of the physical environment and proper layout of access controls can increase security in many ways. An entire discipline actually was built around this concept, known as crime prevention through environmental design (CPTED); see http://www.cpted.net/.

Although fences are a good start, more physical controls, such as proper gates, can help. Gates act as a chokepoint to control the ingress and egress of employees and visitors into and out of the facility. Just as with fences, standards govern the strength of gates and the security of their design, as detailed in UL Standard 325.

Not only people need to be restricted on the grounds of a facility—vehicles must also be controlled. One method of controlling vehicles is to use *bollards*. Made of concrete or steel, bollards are used to block vehicular traffic. You might have noticed them in front of the doors of the facility or even at the local mall; sometimes they even look like large flower pots. Regardless of their shape, they are designed for one purpose: to prevent cars and trucks from ramming into a building and smashing doors. Recently designed bollards have electronic sensors to detect collisions and notify building inhabitants that someone has rammed the facility.

Although fences are considered the first line of defense, bollards are a close second because they further protect employees and the facility from common smash-and-grab techniques and terrorist car bombings.

> **EXAM ALERT**
>
> **Auditing Physical Controls**   Exam candidates must understand that some physical controls cannot be tested. As an example, you most likely will not set off a fire extinguisher, but you can make sure that the fire extinguisher has been serviced regularly and refilled as regulations recommend. Auditing physical controls requires mainly observation. While touring a facility, visually observe the safeguards discussed throughout this chapter and note their presence or absence.

Other Exterior Concerns

A few other exterior controls can further secure the facility:

▶ **Using dogs for guard duty**—Breeds such as German shepherds and chows have been used for centuries to guard facilities and assets. Dogs can be trained and are loyal, obedient, and steadfast, yet they are sometimes unpredictable and could bite or harm the wrong person. Because of these factors, dogs are usually restricted to exterior premises control and should be used with caution.

▶ **Adopting a low-key design**—The last thing an organization that handles sensitive information or high-value assets wants to do is to advertise its presence to attackers or others that might target the facility. The building or department should be discreetly identified. Server rooms, computer rooms, and other sensitive areas should not be easily visible and should contain no windows.

▶ **Controlling points of entrance**—Just as gates are used to control how individuals can enter and leave the property, doors should be used to control access into the building itself. All unnecessary entry points to the grounds and the facility should be eliminated.

▶ **Using adequate lighting**—Lighting is great perimeter protection. Far too much criminal activity happens at night or in poorly lit areas. Outside lighting discourages prowlers and thieves. Failure to adequately light parking lots and other high-traffic areas also could lead to lawsuits if an employee or visitor is attacked in a poorly lit area. Effective lighting means that the system is designed to put the light where it is needed in the proper wattage. More light isn't necessarily better: Too much light causes overlighting and glare.

What else can be done? Warning signs or notices should be posted to deter trespassing. A final review of the grounds area should be conducted to make sure that nothing has been missed. This includes securing any opening that is 96 square inches or larger within 18 feet of the ground, such as manholes and tunnels, gates leading to the basement, elevator shafts, ventilation openings, and skylights. Even the roof, basement, and walls of a building might contain vulnerable points of potential entry and should, therefore, be assessed. When these activities have been completed, you can move on to analyzing interior controls.

Interior Controls

Maybe you've heard the phrase "security starts at the front door." This applicable statement is of utmost importance to keep unauthorized individuals out of the facility or areas where they do not belong. This means you provide only the minimum level of access required for authorized employees and restrict unauthorized individuals so they have no access. Interior controls include the following:

▶ Doors

▶ Windows

▶ Receptionists or security guards

▶ Walls

▶ Locks

▶ Access control

Doors, Windows, and Walls

The weakest point of a structure is usually the first to be attacked. This is an important item to consider because, I assure you, a criminal will. The door itself is an easy target.

Doors must be of sufficient strength to protect critical assets. The interior doors at your house might be hollow core, but that is not of sufficient strength for a server room or other critical asset; these doors should have a solid core. Doors also have fire ratings and should be of the same specification as the walls to which they are attached. In addition, you should look closely at the placement of the hinges. Most doors open out, for safety reasons, but hinges need to be protected. Also, if the ceiling above the door has a plenum, the attacker might be able to climb over the door into the room via the plenum. For assets such as a server room, hinges should be on the inside of the door. The door should also have a strong strike plate and sturdy frame as shown in Figure 8.2; otherwise, an attacker can simply place a car jack into the frame and pry it open.

FIGURE 8.2 A strike plate helps prevent the bypassing of locked doors.

A great solid-core door is of little use if someone can simply remove the hinges to gain entry. Doors come in various configurations:

▶ Personal doors

▶ Industrial doors

▶ Vehicle access doors

▶ Bulletproof doors

▶ Vault doors

A final note about doors involves when to use electric locks. These locks can operate in one of two ways when power fails:

▶ **Fail safe**—These doors fail in the locked position if power is cut. Although this means that the facility is secure, it also means that employees might not be able to get out of the facility.

▶ **Fail soft**—Locks of this type fail open. Employees can easily leave if power is disrupted, but intruders can also easily enter.

Windows are a common point of entry for thieves, burglars, and others seeking access; they are actually much more of a problem than doors because they are usually designed with aesthetics, not security, in mind. The Romans were the first to use glass windows, and ever since, we have valued them as a way to let light in while providing a view. That view does come with a cost. Interior and exterior windows should be fixed in place and should be shatter proof. If critical operations are taking place in areas with windows, the windows should be either opaque or translucent. It's also a good idea to use sensors on the windows that can trip an alarm in case of breakage or damage.

Strong windows are not enough; walls are another important consideration. A reinforced wall can keep a determined attacker from entering an area through a way other than the defined doors. Walls should also be designed to slow the spread of fires to protect employees. If the floor is raised, as is the practice in a server room, you will want to verify that antistatic measures have been put in place. Many buildings use false ceilings. Areas such as server rooms should have walls that go all the way up to the roof; there should be no way someone can lift a ceiling panel and crawl from one room to another.

Locks and Access Control

Mechanical locks are one of the most effective and widely used forms of access control. Nothing provides as great of a level of protection for so little cost. Locks have been used for at least 4,000 years. The Egyptians used locks made of wood. Lock design improved during the 1700s, when *warded* and *tumbler* locks began to be used. These are the two most common types of locks used even today.

The warded lock, the most basically designed mechanical lock still in use, uses a series of wards that a key must match up to. This is the cheapest type of mechanical lock and also the easiest to pick. You can find these at any local hardware store, but they should not be used to protect a valuable asset.

Tumbler locks are considered more advanced because they contain more parts and are harder to pick. Linus Yale patented the modern tumbler lock in 1848. When the right key is inserted into the cylinder of a tumbler lock, the pins are lifted to the right height so that the device can open or close. The correct key has the proper number of notches and raised areas that allow the pins to be shifted into the proper position. The pins are spring-loaded so that when the key is removed, the pins return to the locked position. Figure 8.3 shows an example of a tumbler lock.

Another common form of lock is a *tubular* lock. Tubular locks are also known as Ace locks and are considered very secure because they are harder to pick. Tubular locks require a round key, as the lock itself has the pins arranged in a circular pattern. These are used for computers, vending machines, and other high-security devices.

When examining locks, just remember that you get what you pay for. More expensive locks are usually better made. The quality of a lock is determined by its grade. Table 8.5 describes the three grades of locks.

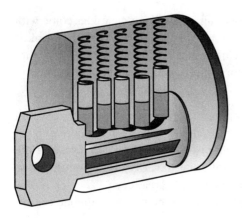

FIGURE 8.3 Tumbler lock.

TABLE 8.5 Lock Grades

Quality	Description
Grade 3	Consumer locks of the weakest design
Grade 2	Light-duty commercial locks or heavy-duty residential locks
Grade 1	Commercial locks of the highest security

Different types of locks provide different levels of protection. The American National Standards Institute (ANSI) defines the strength and durability of locks. As an example, Grade 3 locks are designed to function for 200,000 cycles, a Grade 2 lock must function for 400,000 cycles, and a Grade 1 lock must function for 800,000 cycles. Higher-grade locks are designed to withstand much more usage, are less likely to fail sooner, or wear so that they can be easily bypassed. Thus, it's important to select the appropriate lock to obtain the required level of security.

One way to bypass a lock is to pick it. This is usually not a criminal's preferred method. Breaking a window, prying a doorframe, or even knocking a hole in sheetrock might all be faster methods to gain access. Individuals who pick locks do so because it is a stealthy way to bypass security controls and might make it harder for victims to figure out that they have been compromised. These basic components are used to pick locks:

▶ **Tension wrenches**—These are not much more than a small angled flathead screwdriver. They come in various thicknesses and sizes

▶ **Picks**—As the name implies, these are similar to a dentist pick. Picks are small, angled, and pointed

Together, these tools can be used to pick a lock. One of the easiest techniques to learn is *scrubbing*, which is accomplished by applying tension to the lock with the tension wrench and then quickly scraping the pins. Some of the pins are placed in a mechanical bind and stuck in the unlocked position.

> **TIP**
>
> **Control Physical Access**   Company keys should be stamped "Do Not Duplicate."

> **NOTE**
>
> **Bump Keys Present New Danger**   Bump keys, or "999" keys, are keys that have been cut to the deepest allowable position. They present a new threat, as they can be used to gain unauthorized access. These special keys gained prominence after a 2005 Dutch TV special that highlighted the fact that many locks were vulnerable. Attackers place the bump key into the lock and give it a quick tap. A vulnerability in many locks drives the pins upward and allows the lock to open. For more information about this threat, take a look at http://stadium.weblogsinc.com/engadget/videos/lockdown/bumping_040206.pdf.

Personnel Controls

Organizations can have a large number of individuals moving about the facility during the working day. These individuals are usually a mix of people, including employees, suppliers, salesmen, contractors, and even the folks who stock the vending machines in the break room. Personnel controls limit the access and freedom of these individuals, and also provide a means of audit. Organizations must have a way to hold individuals accountable for their actions and activities.

Guards

Guards are a very basic type of protection. Guards have one very basic skill that sets them apart from computerized gear: discernment. Guards have the ability to make a judgment call, to look at something and know that it is just not right. Computerized premises-control equipment has actually increased the need for guards because someone must manage all these systems. Guards also can play a dual role by answering the phone, taking on the role of a receptionist and escorting visitors while in the facility. If guards are being used at a facility you are visiting, look closely to see how they are used because the principle of defense-in-depth can also be applied here. Guards are most useful with locked doors used in conjunction with closed-circuit TV (CCTV) systems. The CCTV systems can be actively monitored or recorded and watched later. CCTV systems don't prevent security breaches; they just alert the guard to a potential problem as it is occurring or afterward.

Guards do have some disadvantages—after all, they are only human. Guards are capable of poor judgment and can make mistakes. Therefore, if an organization hires guards from an external vendor, they should be bonded to protect the agency from loss.

Whether or not a guard is in place, the movement of visitors throughout the facility should be controlled. Anyone entering the building, including friends, visitors, vendors, contractors, and even maintenance personnel, should be escorted. Mantraps or a deadman door can control access into or out of the facility; these usually are found at the entryways of high security areas and require the outer door to be closed before authentication can take place and the inner door is opened. This is really just a system of doors that are arranged so that when one opens, the other remains locked.

Identification

ID badges are a simple method of identification. Policy should dictate that all the organization's employees must wear and display them. Table 8.6 lists the most common types of ID badges.

TABLE 8.6   Basic Identification Types

Type of Card	Attribute
Active electronic	Can transmit electronic data
Passive electronic	Has RFID embedded and can be used to track the location of the user
Electronic circuit	Has an electronic circuit embedded
Magnetic stripe	Has a stripe of magnetic material
Magnetic strip	Contains rows of copper strips
Optical coded	Contains a laser-burned pattern of encoded dots
Photo card	Contains a facial photograph of the card holder

Badges can range from the rather simple photo ID badge to the more sophisticated electronic ID badge. The cards described in Table 8.6, such as those with active electronics or electronic circuits, are really a type of smart card that might require the user to insert them into a card slot; others might require only that the user get the card close to the access-control device.

Intrusion Detection

Physical *intrusion-detection systems* (IDS) can also monitor the movement of individuals. These systems are particularly useful for detecting unauthorized physical access and can be designed to trigger from many types of sensors. These sensors can be placed around windows, attached to doors, or placed in pressure mats to trigger when someone steps on them. Three common types exist:

> ▶ **Photoelectric**—Uses infrared light

> ▶ **Motion detectors**—Triggered from audio, wave pattern, or capacitance

> ▶ **Pressure sensitive**—Sensitive to weight

The disadvantages of physical IDS is that these systems can produce a large number of false positives. They also require monitoring and response. When an alarm sounds, someone must respond and ascertain whether the event was a true positive.

EXAM ALERT

Auditing Intrusion Detection When auditing a physical IDS, you should always verify that it has been properly tied to a backup power supply. This is a key control because, without acceptable backup power, someone can bypass the IDS by killing the power.

We have talked about a range of safeguards and controls throughout the last couple of sections. Your area of concern should not stop here. During an actual audit, you should ensure that these controls extend beyond the organization's facility. These controls should also be present at remote locations, shared sites, service provider facilities, or other third parties. The IT auditor should examine each of these if sensitive information or assets are stored there.

Environmental Protection Practices

Knowledge Statement

> ▶ Knowledge of environmental protection practices and devices (e.g., fire suppression, cooling systems, water sensors)

Electrical power is the lifeblood of computer systems. As an IT auditor, you must make sure that the data center and critical systems have the power they need and that it is clean and usable.

Power Anomalies

Power systems can suffer from a range of problems. Table 8.7 outlines the most common power system problems and their solutions.

TABLE 8.7 Common Power System Problems and Solutions

Power Condition	Solution
Blackout	Generator
Brownout	Uninterrupted power supply (UPS)
Surge	Surge protector
Spike	Surge protector
Noise	Power conditioner
Clean power	No solution needed

Even if you have taken measures to prevent these problems, you should be aware of others. Florescent lights can generate electrical problems, a phenomenon known as *radio frequency interference* (RFI). Power lines are also subject to line noise and can suffer from *electromagnetic interference* (EMI). Even electrical motors can cause EMI.

Power Protections

Keeping power to critical systems is an important task. One way to help ensure that the power keeps flowing is to use power leads from two substations. This might not always be possible, but it is feasible when you are selecting the location of your own facility. Power grids are usually divided along highways, so you might be able to place a facility within a short distance of two substations. If you can accomplish this, don't defeat the purpose by placing both cables on the same set of poles or in the same trench. The idea is to try to avoid any single point of failure.

Although electricity is a great thing, at times you might need to kill power quickly, especially if someone is accidentally electrocuted or if there is danger of flooding. National fire-protection code NFPA 70 (http://www.nfpa.org) requires that you have an emergency power-off (EPO) switch located near the exit door to kill power quickly, if needed. These big red buttons are easy to identify.

EXAM ALERT

Protecting Against False Alarms CISA candidates should know what are considered important preventive controls. As an example, the EPO switch should have a durable plastic cover installed over the switch to prevent anyone from accidentally activating it.

Uninterrupted power supplies (UPS) and *standby generators* are two other power-protection mechanisms. A UPS is a device with one or more lead acid batteries and a circuit board that can intelligently monitor power and sense if power is lost. If power is lost, the UPS can supply power for a limited amount of time so that the system can be shut down properly or a generator can be started. The most common types of power backup systems are as follows:

▶ **Online systems**—An online system uses AC power to charge a bank of DC batteries. These batteries are held in reserve until power fails. At that time, a power inverter converts the DC voltage back to AC for the computer systems to use. These systems are good for short-term power outages.

▶ **Standby system**—This type of system monitors the power line for failure. When a failure is sensed, backup power is switched on. These systems rely on generators or power subsystems to keep computers running for longer power outages.

▶ **Generator**—The generator is a longer-term device. When the UPS signals the generator, it can power up and assume power responsibilities. Most standby generators work on diesel fuel or natural gas:

  ▶ **Diesel fuel**—Should maintain at least 12 hours of fuel

  ▶ **Natural gas**—Should be suitable for areas that have a good supply of natural gas and are geologically stable

Heating, Ventilation, and Air Conditioning (HVAC)

Do you know what can be hotter than Houston in the summer? A room full of computers without proper HVAC. Plan for adequate power for the right locations. Rooms that have servers or banks of computers and IT gear need adequate cooling to protect the equipment. Electronic equipment is quite sensitive; temperatures above 110°F to 115°F can damage circuits. Most data centers are kept to temperatures of around 70°F.

High humidity can be a problem because it causes rust and corrosion. Low humidity increases the risk of static electricity, which could damage equipment. The ideal humidity for a data center is 35%–45%.

Ventilation is another important concern. Facilities should maintain positive pressurization and ventilation. This controls contamination by pushing air outside. This is especially important in case of fire because it assures that smoke will be pushed out of the facility instead of being pulled in.

The final issue with HVAC is access control. Control of who has access to the system and how they can be contacted is an import issue. The bombing of the World Trade Center and the anthrax scare of 2001 increased awareness of the role HVAC systems play in protecting the health and safety of employees. These systems must be controlled to protect organizations and their occupants from the threat of chemical and biological threats.

Fire Prevention, Detection, and Suppression

Each year, fires result in injuries, deaths, and business losses. Organizations can avoid such injuries and losses by being prepared and practicing good fire-prevention practices. A big part of prevention is making sure people are trained and know how to prevent possible fire hazards. Fires need three things: oxygen, heat, and fuel. With those components, fires can present a lethal threat and can be devastating. Employees should be trained to deal with fires. Holding random periodic fire drills is another important component. Employees should be instructed to go to a designated area outside the facility, in a safe zone. Supervisors or others should be in charge of the safe zones to ensure that everyone is present and accounted for. Employees should also badge in after the drill when everyone is re-entering the building. This is a perfect time for an outsider to sneak in as a "tailgater" behind other employees streaming back into the building.

The Value of Physical Security

Sometimes we overlook the real importance of physical security. The director of security for Morgan Stanley, located in the south World Trade Tower, never had that problem. Rick Rescorla was born in England but dreamed of being an American, so much so that he volunteered for the Vietnam War.

Rescorla had a proven history of heroism. During the Vietnam War, he did his best to protect the safety of the soldiers he was in charge of. These thoughts and actions carried over to the civilian world, where he was a constant supporter of physical security and the need to protect employees and company assets. Although Rescorla was not always successful in his battles for greater security, the first World Trade Center bombing in 1993 served as a wakeup call and strengthened his hand when asking for greater support from senior management. He got it: additional drills, better evacuation lighting, and increased funds for security.

All this work paid off for Rescorla on September 11, 2001, when the north World Trade Tower was hit. He calmly instructed people to leave the facility. Before the day was over, he had personally escorted all 20 floors of Morgan Stanley employees out of the building to safety. Then he turned back and proceeded farther up the building to help others in the tower find their way out. Soon the South Tower collapsed. Rescorla was never found, but his efforts to lead 2,700 people to safety will not be forgotten.

Fire detectors can work in different ways. They can be activated by the following:

- **Heat**—A fixed temperature thermostat is usually set to trigger above 200°F or when the temperature rises quickly.

- **Smoke**—A smoke-activated sensor can be powered by a photoelectric optical detector or a radioactive smoke-detection device.

- **Flame**—A flame-activated sensor functions by sensing either ultraviolet radiation or the pulsation of the flame.

Fires are rated according to the types of materials that are burning. Whereas it might be acceptable to throw some water on smoldering paper, it would not be a good idea to try that with a grease fire. Table 8.8 lists four common fire types and their corresponding suppression methods.

TABLE 8.8 Fire-Suppression Methods

Class	Suppression Method
Class A	Paper or wood fires should be suppressed with water or soda acid.
Class B	Gasoline or oil fires should be suppressed by using CO_2, soda acid, or FM200.
Class C	Electronic or computer fires should be suppressed with CO_2 or Halon.
Class D	Fires caused by combustible metals should be suppressed by applying dry powder or using special techniques.

EXAM ALERT

Minimum Protection Levels CISA candidates need to know the minimum protection standards for data centers. As an example, data center walls should have at least a two-hour fire rating.

Water Sprinklers

Water sprinklers are an effective means of extinguishing Class A fires. Water is easy to work with, is widely available, and is nontoxic. The disadvantage of using sprinkler systems is that water is damaging to electronics. Any time the data center is adjacent to any water pipe, water detector sensors should be adequately placed to give fair warning of a potential flood. When water is used in the computer room, water detectors should be used. These should be under the raised floor and near drains, to quickly detect problems.

Four variations of sprinkler systems are available:

▶ **Dry pipe**—As the name implies, this sprinkler system maintains no standing water. When activated, air flows out of the system and water flows in. The benefit of this type of system is that it reduces the risk of accidental flooding and gives some time to cover or turn off electrical equipment.

▶ **Wet pipe**—Wet pipe systems are widely used and ready for activation; this system is charged and full of water. The next time you are staying in a hotel, take a look around and you will probably see this type of system. They typically use some type of fusible link that allows discharge when the link breaks or melts.

▶ **Preaction**—This is a combination system. Pipes are initially dry and do not fill with water until a predetermined temperature is reached. Even then, the system will not activate until a secondary mechanism triggers. The secondary mechanism might be some type of fusible link, as used in a wet pipe system.

▶ **Deluge**—This is similar to a dry pipe system, except that when the system is triggered, there is no holding back the water: A large volume of water will cover a large area quickly.

Halon

Halon was originally used in computer rooms for fire suppression. For years, it was considered a preferred fire-suppression system because it mixes easily with air, doesn't harm computer equipment, and, when dissipates, leaves no solid or liquid residue. Halon is found in two configurations:

▶ **Halon 1211**—Used in portable extinguishers and stored as a liquid

▶ **Halon 1301**—Used in fixed flooding systems and stored as a gaseous agent

The downside is that Halon is 3–10 times more damaging to the ozone layer than chlorofluorocarbons (CFCs). Because of this, the Montreal Protocol of 1987 designated Halon as an ozone-depleting substance. Halon also is toxic if subject to high temperatures of 900°F or more because it degrades into hydrogen fluoride, hydrogen bromide, and bromine. People should not breathe this toxic compound.

Existing Halon systems should be replaced. Some common EPA-approved replacements include the following:

▶ FM-200

▶ NAF-S-3

▶ Argon

Physical Authentication

Task

▶ Evaluate the design, implementation, and monitoring of physical access controls to ensure that information assets are adequately safeguarded.

Knowledge Statement

▶ Knowledge of physical security systems and practices (e.g., biometrics, access cards, cipher locks, tokens)

Controlling access into a facility or within various parts of the organization is a good security practice. Employees should be restricted to only the areas of the facility that they need access to for the completion of their daily tasks.

Authentication Methods

Authentication ensures that the correct person is granted access. This is accomplished in three basic ways:

▶ **Something You Know**—Passwords, PIN numbers.

▶ **Something You Have**—USB tokens, smart cards, magnetic strip cards. Figure 8.4 depicts a smart card.

▶ **Something You Are**—Based on what you are, such as a fingerprint, retina scan, or voice print.

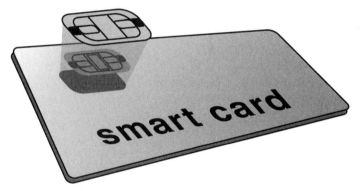

FIGURE 8.4 Generic smart card.

Biometrics

Biometric systems have made a lot of progress in the last decade; events such as 9/11 have increased the acceptance of biometric systems. Many different types of biometric systems exist, as described in this list (shown in order of best response times and lowest error rates):

1. **Palm scan**—System that analyzes characteristics associated with the palm, such as the creases and ridges of a user's palm.

2. **Hand geometry**—Another biometric system that uses the unique geometry of a user's fingers and hand to determine the user's identity. It is one of the oldest biometric techniques.

3. **Iris recognition**—A very accurate eye-recognition system, with more than 400 points of reference. It matches the person's blood vessels on the back of the eye.

4. **Retina pattern**—This system requires the user to remove any glasses and stare at a specific point for 10–15 seconds.

5. **Fingerprint**—System that is widely used for access control to facilities and items such as laptops. It works by distinguishing 30–40 details about the peaks, valleys, and ridges of the user's fingerprint.

6. **Facial scan**—System that requires the user to place his or her face about 2 to 5 feet from the camera.

7. **Voice recognition**—System that uses voice analysis for identification and authentication. Its main advantage is that it can be used for telephone applications.

Biometric systems have varying levels of accuracy. For example, fingerprint-scanning systems base their accuracy on an analysis of minutiae. These are the ridge endings and bifurcations found on the fingertips, as shown in Figure 8.5. Although the number of minutiae varies from finger to finger, the information can be stored electronically in file sizes that usually range from 250 to 1,000 bytes. When a user logs in, the stored file containing the minutiae is compared to the individual's finger being scanned.

FIGURE 8.5 Fingerprint recognition.

The accuracy of biometric devices is measured by the percentage of *Type 1* and *Type 2* errors they produce. Type 1 errors, *false rejection rate* (FRR), are a measurement of the percentage of individuals who should have gotten in but were not allowed access. Type 2 errors, *false acceptance rate* (FAR), are a measurement of the percentage of individuals who gained access but should not have been allowed in. When these two values are combined, the accuracy of the system is established. The point at which the FRR and FAR meet is known as the *equal error rate* (EER).

Although many items should be considered when deploying a biometric authentication system, this is one of the key accuracy factors—the lower the EER, the more accurate the system. Another attribute of biometric systems is that you cannot easily loan a fingerprint, retina, or hand to someone else. However, studies have demonstrated that these systems can be bypassed by using not much more than fake fingerprints made with gelatin in a clay mold. You can read more about this ingenious attack at http://www.puttyworld.com/thinputdeffi.html.

NOTE

Backup Authentication   If biometrics is being used, the auditor should verify that backup authentication methods are available in case the biometric system fails.

Policies and Procedures

Knowledge Statements

▶ Knowledge of data classification schemes (e.g., public, confidential, private, and sensitive data)

▶ Knowledge of the processes and procedures used to store, retrieve, transport, and dispose of confidential information assets

We have seen that the physical realm is an important area of concern because of the many areas of potential exposure. We also have looked at various types of controls to protect the facility, to control the access of individuals, and to identify and authenticate who goes where in the organization. The key to making all these controls work is policy; the best intentions in the world are of little use without the backing of policy. Establishing security policies, guidelines, and procedures is a critical step in securing the physical infrastructure and its information. Policies encompass much more than just physical security. Policies also address administrative and technical concerns. The lack of well-designed viable security polices and documents is one of the biggest vulnerabilities many organizations have. Building a policy framework is not easy. According to www.complianceandprivacy.com, 60% of companies do not have an information security policy. After a policy is defined, the next challenge is to implement it and get employees to follow it. The following sections discuss the types of security policies, how to define appropriate policies, how to deploy policies, and the lifecycle of security policies.

Types of Policies

Policies come in many shapes and sizes. With so many types of policies, how can you keep track of them all? *National Institute of Standards and Technology* (NIST) documentation classifies policies in three broad categories:

- ▶ **Management**—These policies define security roles and responsibilities within an organization. They also define how policy is created, revised, and retired.

- ▶ **Operational**—These policies deal with operational aspects of the organization, including physical security and employee training and awareness.

- ▶ **Technical**—These policies address all things technical. These are the policies that IT employees are familiar with. These types of policies cover such things as identification and authentication and account management.

Within these categories of policies are many different individual policies. Combined, these policies should control every aspect of security within an organization. Policies are not technology specific. This type of control is left for lower-level documents, such as procedures.

Purpose of Policies

Policies play a very specific role in the document structure. Policy must flow from the top. If management does not support it, it will fail. On a broad level, policies should do six things for an organization:

1. Protect confidential, proprietary, and sensitive information from unauthorized disclosure, modification, theft, or destruction

2. Define appropriate and inappropriate activities of employees

3. Reduce or eliminate legal liability to employees and outsiders

4. Prevent waste of company IT resources

5. Comply with federal, state, local, and regulatory requirements

6. Demonstrate due diligence and due care

Most of these six items deal with preventing or reducing risk. Therefore, some type of risk assessment is usually performed before policies are created. Nothing happens in a void.

Defining Policies

Before drafting an actual policy, a clear objective must be decided. Organizations also must determine who the policy applies to and who is responsible for the policy. These three key sections are as follows:

1. **Purpose**—Articulates why the policy was created, its purpose, and what the organization will gain from its creation. Policies can be created because of regulatory requirements, to be informative, or to advise on certain required activities or behaviors.

2. **Scope**—Specifies who the policy applies to. It might address all users who telecommute, those who have computer access, or only those who have access to the server room.

3. **Responsibility**—Defines who is responsible. Someone must be in charge of the policy to verify that it has been properly implemented and that employees are aware of its requirements and have received adequate training.

When the draft policy is developed, it must be approved by upper management and evaluated to ascertain that the objectives that drove the policy development were met or exceeded.

> **NOTE**
>
> **Change Management** Auditors involved in this process should make sure that the policy has been designed so that it can be updated and changed as needed. As with everything else in the world, policies require periodic change.

Deploying and Implementing Policies

After polices have been created, they must be deployed and made operational. Employee awareness and employee buy-in are needed to make this step successful. Employees must be made aware that the policies exist and should be provided training as to the purpose and meaning of specific policies.

Auditors are not always involved in the development process and many times examine the role of policies only after they have been deployed. In this situation, the auditor should look for indications of potential problems. These can include the following:

▶ Policies and procedures that are out-of-date and have not been updated

▶ Policies that do not comply with the law

▶ The lack of a review process for current policies and procedures

▶ The lack of documented policies and procedures

▶ Reliance on key personnel for instructions and guidance instead of the policy or procedure

▶ Undefined process that lacks policies and procedures

> **EXAM ALERT**
>
> **Compliance Verification** Auditors typically verify compliance by conducting interviews with employees, observing information-processing methods, and reviewing procedures, manuals, and documents.

Physical Asset and Information Control

All organizations encounter a lot of paper documents. These might contain information that is rather trivial or might hold the company's most valuable secrets. Information must be protected while in storage and also in transit. The information owners are ultimately responsible for determining how assets and resources are protected.

> **EXAM ALERT**
>
> **Document Transportation**   IT auditors should examine how organizations store and transport written documents. One area of concern is interoffice communication. Regulations such as HIPAA have increased the need for secure distribution. Document-distribution carts should be secured to prevent unauthorized access. An example of this type of inter-office communication cart can be found at http://www.filingtoday.com/Mailroom_Mail_Room_HIPAA_Lock_Top_Carts_Systems_REI.html.

The primary means of establishing value is establishing data classification levels so that sufficient controls can ensure their confidentiality. Two widely used systems have been adopted to protect information:

▶ **Government classification system**—Focused on secrecy

▶ **Commercial classification system**—Focused on integrity

Let's look at each one in a little more detail. The *governmental information classification system* developed by the Department of Defense (DoD) is most concerned with protecting the confidentiality of information. Therefore, it is divided into categories of Unclassified, Confidential, Secret, and Top Secret, as described in Table 8.9.

TABLE 8.9   DoD Classification System

Classification	Description
Top Secret	Disclosure would cause grave damage to national security. This information requires the highest level of control.
Secret	Disclosure would be expected to cause serious damage to national security and could divulge significant scientific or technological developments.
Confidential	Disclosure could cause damage to national security and should be safeguarded against disclosure.
Unclassified	Information is not sensitive and need not be protected. Its loss or disclosure would not cause damage.

The *commercial information classification system* is categorized as public, sensitive, private, and confidential, as shown in Table 8.10.

TABLE 8.10 Commercial Classification System

Classification	Description
Confidential	This is the most sensitive rating, for information that keeps a company competitive. Not only is this information for internal use only, but its release or alteration could seriously affect or damage the corporation.
Private	This category of restricted information is considered personal in nature and might include medical records or human resource information.
Sensitive	This information requires controls to prevent its release to unauthorized parties. Damage could result from its loss of confidentiality or its loss of integrity.
Public	Similar to unclassified information, its disclosure or release would cause no damage to the corporation.

NOTE

Choosing the Right Classification System   The classification methods described in Table 8.10 are just examples of data classification. The amount of classification levels, the requirements for each level, and the controls associated with each level should be analyzed specifically at every organization that is working on implementing such a system.

Regardless of the system being used, the role of an IT auditor is to see that the system was well developed and is being followed. A process must evaluate the value of information and determine its value and an approved method of storing documentation must de developed. After establishing a data classification schema, one method of classification is as follows:

1. Identify the administrator or custodian who will be in charge of maintaining the data.

2. Specify the criteria that will be used to identify how the data will be classified and at what layer of sensitivity.

3. The data owner must indicate and acknowledge the classification of the data.

4. Specify and document any exceptions that are allowed to the classification policy.

5. Indicate the security controls that will be implemented to protect each classification level.

6. Specify the end-of-life (EOF) procedures for declassifying the information and procedures for transferring custody of the information to another entity.

7. Integrate these issues into an employee-awareness program so that individuals understand and acknowledge the classification controls.

The information-classification process is of critical importance because it forces organizations to ask themselves what would happen if specific information was released and how its release would damage or affect the organization; possible legal requirements such as data retention should also be considered.

REVIEW BREAK

Physical security is like logical security, in that it benefits from defense-in-depth. Notice how each of the following physical security controls offers a different type of control.

Item	Usage	Attributes
Lock	Controls access	Ward, tumbler, and combination
CCTV	Personal control	Can be monitored in real time or recorded and viewed later
Guard	Personal control	Capable of discernment
Fence	Exterior control	Should deter a determined intruder at 8 feet high
Deadman door	Interior control	Prevents successful unauthorized individuals from entering secured areas
Shredder	Preventative control	Prevents successful dumpster diving
Access control	Personal control	Can use passwords, pin numbers, control smart cards, tokens, or biometrics

Chapter Summary

In this chapter, you learned about physical security. Physical security is as important as logical security and should be examined closely during an IT audit or assessment. Physical security might been seen as something that only prevents unauthorized access, but its usefulness cannot be overstated. Physical controls do not just involve the protection of property; they also protect employees and equipment. Items such as smoke detectors, fire alarms, and fire-suppression systems all add to security, as does lighting. They protect employees and can aid in evacuation. During the 1993 World Trade Tower attack, it took nearly four hours for people to evacuate the dark, smoky, poorly lit stairwells

Physical security works best when set up as defense-in-depth, layering one security mechanism on top of another. Therefore, you need locked servers located in a controlled access room, protected by a solid-core door and walls of the same strength. The facility should also be secure, with items such as CCTV cameras and controlled access such as mantraps. Together these layers make it much harder for someone to penetrate. Even the exterior of the facility can be made more secure by adding fences, gates, and possibly guards.

Finally, the chapter reviewed policies, procedures, and the classification of information. Documents are not just in electronic form; paper documents should be classified so that employees know their value and can take measures to protect them against theft or duplication. Without policies, there is no controlling mechanism in place. Policies reinforce physical security and provide control. Policies detail what management expects and provide a general roadmap on how these items will be achieved. Policies also show management's commitment to support employees and what types of controls are put in place to protect sensitive information. Policies outline acceptable and unacceptable behavior and can be used to enhance physical, logical, and administrative controls.

Key Terms

- ▶ Authentication
- ▶ Authorization
- ▶ Biometrics
- ▶ Bollards
- ▶ Closed-circuit TV (CCTV)
- ▶ Combination lock
- ▶ Commercial information classification system

- Crossover error rate (CER)
- Deadman door
- Destruction
- Device lock
- Dumpster diving
- False acceptance rate (FAR)
- False rejection rate (FRR)
- Fire detection
- Fire prevention
- Fire suppression
- Governmental information classification system
- Identification
- Man-made threat
- Mantrap
- Paper shredder
- Piggybacking
- Shoulder surfing
- Social engineering
- Tailgating
- Theft
- Tumbler lock
- Turnstile
- Vandalism
- Warded lock

Apply Your Knowledge

This chapter stressed the importance of physical security. Logical controls are of little good if someone can just walk in, sit down, and start accessing computer networks and data.

Exercises

8.1 Physical Security Checklist

In this exercise, you examine common concerns of physical security.

Estimated Time: 30 Minutes

1. Download the physical security checklist at http://www.callio.com/expertise/tmpldesc.asp?domid=7&id=34.

2. Complete the checklist using your organization as an example.

3. Examine the list. Do you feel that your organization is taking physical security seriously? Could more be done?

Exam Questions

1. The IS auditor is examining the authentication system used and has been asked to make a recommendation on how to improve it. Which of the following choices is generally considered the most effective form of two-factor authentication?

   ○ **A.** Token and pin

   ○ **B.** Token and photo ID card

   ○ **C.** Pin and password

   ○ **D.** Fingerprint and hand geometry

2. Which of the following is the first step in the data-classification process after establishing a data classification schema?

   ○ **A.** Reviewing security controls

   ○ **B.** Reviewing existing security policies

   ○ **C.** Determining data sensitivity

   ○ **D.** Identifying the custodian

3. Various types of locks have been developed for security. Which type of programmable lock uses a keypad for entering a pin number or password?

- ○ **A.** Cipher lock
- ○ **B.** Device lock
- ○ **C.** Warded lock
- ○ **D.** Tumbler lock

4. The equal error rate (EER) is used by which of the following?

- ○ **A.** Locks
- ○ **B.** Physical risk assessment
- ○ **C.** Biometrics
- ○ **D.** Firewalls

5. Which of the following best describes a system used to detect physical attackers?

- ○ **A.** Fences
- ○ **B.** Lights
- ○ **C.** Closed-circuit TV (CCTV)
- ○ **D.** Locks

6. You have been asked to examine a biometrics system that will be used for a high-security area. With this in mind, which of the following is the most important rating to examine?

- ○ **A.** The false rejection rate (FRR)
- ○ **B.** Finding a biometric system with a low equal error rate (EER)
- ○ **C.** The speed of the biometric system
- ○ **D.** The false acceptance rate (FAR)

7. This system is usually not tested and is verified by reviewing documentation.

- ○ **A.** Smoke detectors
- ○ **B.** Generators
- ○ **C.** Fire-suppression systems
- ○ **D.** Emergency evacuation plans

8. Which of the following is the best replacement for Halon?

  ○ **A.** Low-pressure water mists

  ○ **B.** FM-200

  ○ **C.** NAT-4000

  ○ **D.** Hydrogen bromide

9. Which of the following is the classification of a gasoline or oil fire?

  ○ **A.** Class A

  ○ **B.** Class B

  ○ **C.** Class C

  ○ **D.** Class D

10. Which of the following best describes a physical control that would control the flow of employees into the facility and allow security to hold those who fail authorization?

  ○ **A.** A turnstile

  ○ **B.** A deadman door

  ○ **C.** A piggyback

  ○ **D.** Biometric authentication

Answers to Exam Questions

1. **A**. A token and pin is the only two-factor authentication method shown. Answers B, C, and D all represent single-factor authentication methods. Therefore answers B, C, and D are incorrect.

2. **D**. The first step is to identify the administrator or custodian. Next, it is important to specify the criteria that will be used to identify how the data will be classified. The data owner must acknowledge the classification of the data, followed by any exceptions that are allowed to the classification policy. The security controls that will be implemented to protect each classification level should be indicated next. The end-of-life (EOF) procedures for declassifying the information and procedures for transferring custody of the information to another entity should be specified. The final step is integration.

3. **A**. A cipher lock is one in which a keypad is used for entering a pin number or passwords. These are commonly used on secured doors to control access. Answer B is incorrect because a device lock is used to secure a piece of equipment such as a laptop. Answer C is incorrect because a warded lock is a basic low-end padlock that can be easily picked. Answer D is incorrect because a tumbler lock is an improved version of a warded lock. Tumblers make it harder for the wrong key to open the wrong lock.

4. **C.** The equal error rate is a biometric measurement of the point at which the FAR and the FRR intersect. When these two values are combined, the accuracy of the system is established. The lower the EER, the more accurate the biometric system. Locks, risk assessment, and firewalls do not use EER ratings; therefore, answers A, B, and D are incorrect.

5. **C.** CCTV is a good example of a system used to detect physical attacks. Answer A is incorrect because fences are used to deter or delay intruders; answers B and D are incorrect because lights and locks also deter and delay intruders.

6. **D.** The FAR provides a way to measure how many people who should not have access could be able to gain entry into a high-security area. Although answers A, B, and C are all important, they are not the most important issue in this situation.

7. **C**. Fire-suppression systems are usually not tested because of the high cost involved. They are verified by reviewing documentation. Answers A, B, and D are incorrect because these systems are tested at least once yearly.

8. **B**. FM-200 is the preferred replacement for Halon because it does not damage equipment, as water mists would. Answers A, C, and D are incorrect because water is damaging, NAT-4000 is not used for fire suppression, and hydrogen bromide is a byproduct of Halon when exposed to high temperatures.

9. **B**. A gas or oil fire is considered Class B. Class A covers common combustibles, Class C covers electrical fires, and Class D covers metals. Therefore answers A, C, and D are incorrect.

10. **B.** A deadman door is a set of two doors. The idea is that only one person can enter at a time; the outer door must shut before the inner door will open. Answer A is incorrect because a turnstile controls the flow of human traffic and is similar to a one-way gate. Answer C is incorrect because piggybacking is the act of riding in on someone's coat tails. Answer D is incorrect because biometric authentication would not prevent more than one person at a time from entering.

Need to Know More?

▶ Physical Security Audit Information Available from ASIS International: http://www. asisonline.org/

▶ Physical Security Audit Checklist: http://tinyurl.com/35or2b

▶ High-Availability Power: http://www.powerquality.com/mag/power_high_availability_ electrical/

▶ How Locks Work: http://home.howstuffworks.com/lock-picking.htm

▶ Lock Picking: http://www.gregmiller.net/locks/

▶ All About Halon: http://en.wikipedia.org/wiki/Halon

▶ Fire Suppression Without Halon: http://tinyurl.com/3a5nfg

▶ Building an Information Classification System: http://tinyurl.com/2vxgsr

▶ Data Classification the Easy Way: http://www.security-manual.com/classify.htm

PART V

Business Continuity and Disaster Recovery

Chapter 9 Business Continuity and Disaster Recovery

CHAPTER NINE

Business Continuity and Disaster Recovery

This chapter helps you prepare for the Certified Information Systems Auditor (CISA) exam by covering the following ISACA objectives, which include understanding the role and importance of business continuity and disaster recovery. This includes items such as the following:

Tasks

Evaluate the adequacy of backup and restoration provisions to ensure the availability of information required to resume processing.

Evaluate the organization's disaster recovery plan to ensure that it enables the recovery of IT processing capabilities in the event of a disaster.

Evaluate the organization's business continuity plan to ensure its ability to continue essential business operations during the period of an IT disruption.

Knowledge Statements

Knowledge of data backup, storage, maintenance, retention and restoration processes, and practices

Knowledge of regulatory, legal, contractual, and insurance concerns related to business continuity and disaster recovery

Knowledge of business impact analysis (BIA)

Knowledge of the development and maintenance of the business continuity and disaster recovery plans

Knowledge of business continuity and disaster recovery testing approaches and methods

Knowledge of human resources management practices as related to business continuity and disaster recovery (e.g., evacuation planning, response teams)

Knowledge of processes used to invoke the business continuity and disaster recovery plans

Knowledge of types of alternate processing sites and methods used to monitor the contractual agreements (e.g., hot sites, warm sites, cold sites)

Outline

Study Strategies

This chapter addresses information you need to know about business continuity and disaster recovery. An organization can have controls in place to manage risk and ensure that business processes are properly controlled, yet not be prepared for disasters. It is not a matter of whether a disaster will occur, but when. The objective of this chapter is to ensure that, as a CISA, you understand and can provide assurance that an organization's policies sufficiently guard against disruptions. The CISA is tasked with verifying that the business continuity and disaster recovery process will ensure timely resumption of IT services while minimizing the impact to the business. The following are the primary topics a CISA candidate should review for the exam:

▶ Understand the threats that natural and man-made disasters represent

▶ Know the BCP process in terms of how ISACA interprets it

▶ Restate the importance of business continuity and disaster recovery, and the role an IT auditor plays in reducing this threat

▶ Understand the most common methods for testing disaster recovery plans

▶ Describe hardware and software alternatives for business continuity

Introduction

This chapter focuses on an organization's ability to recover from natural or man-made disasters and return to normal operations. Unfortunately, this is often an overlooked area of an IT audit. The need to develop plans to deal with such disasters is critical, as is the need to test such plans to make sure they are viable. Notable recent events such as 9/11 and Hurricane Katrina have highlighted the need to be adequately prepared. After both of these events, individuals reported that companies seriously underestimated how long it would take to restore operations. It has also been noted that many companies had not updated their plans as the company grew, changed, or modified existing processes. Some companies suffered significant vital record problems because of flaws in their backup and offsite storage programs, while others had no workstation recovery plans for end users. Even after such calamitous events, most U.S. companies still spend an average of only 3.7% of the IT budget on disaster recovery planning, while best practice calls for 6%. These low expenditures can have many reasons such as the fact that only a small percentage of businesses are required by regulation to have a disaster recovery plan. Another is that disaster recovery must compete for limited funds. Companies might be lulled into thinking that these funds might be best spent for more immediate needs. Some businesses might simply underestimate the risk and hope that adverse events don't happen to them. Disaster recovery planning requires a shift of thinking from reactive to proactive.

Disaster Recovery

Knowledge Statement

▶ Knowledge of regulatory, legal, contractual, and insurance concerns related to business continuity and disaster recovery

A disaster is any sudden, unplanned, calamitous event that brings about great damage or loss. Businesses face special challenges because they have a responsibility to shareholders and employees to protect life and guard company assets. In the realm of business, a disaster can be seen as any event that creates an inability to support critical business functions for an undetermined period of time.

Disasters and Disruptive Events

Many of us would prefer not to plan for disasters. Many might see it as an unpleasant exercise or something that we would prefer to ignore. Sadly, we all must deal with disasters and incidents. They are dynamic by nature. For example, mainframes face a different set of threats than distributed systems, just as computers connected to modems (or wired network connections) face a different set of threats than wireless networked computers. This means that management must be dynamic and be able to change with time. Threats can be man-made, technical, or natural; however, regardless of the source, they have the potential to cause an incident. Incidents might or might not cause disruptions to normal operations. What is needed is a way to measure these incidents and quantify their damage. Table 9.1 lists the incident classification per ISACA.

TABLE 9.1   Incident Classification

Level	Description
Crisis	A crisis is considered a major problem. It is of sufficient impact that it adversely affects the organization's ability to continue business functions.
Major	A major incident is of sufficient strength to negatively impact one or more departments, or might even affect external clients.
Minor	Although these events are noticeable, they cause little or no damage.
Negligible	These detectable events cause no damage or have no longer-term effect.

NOTE

Disruptive incidents such as a crisis or major or minor events should be tracked and analyzed so that corrective actions can be taken to prevent these events from occurring in the future.

Good incident response and a method to measure the disruption to the organization enable the company to reduce the potential impact of these situations. This gives organizations a structured method for developing procedures that provide management with sufficient information to develop an appropriate course of action. With these procedures in place, the organization can maintain or restore business continuity, defend against future attacks, and even prosecute violators when possible.

Reputation and Its Value

What comes to mind when you hear the word *reputation*? I always think of this quote by Benjamin Franklin: "It takes many good deeds to build a good reputation, and only one bad one to lose it." If you are wondering what this has to do with disaster recovery, consider the following brand names:

▶ **Enron**—A symbol of corporate fraud and corruption

▶ **Apple**—An industry leader of innovative products such as the iPod and iPhone

▶ **Arthur Andersen**—A firm that voluntarily surrendered its licenses in 2002 over its handling of the auditing of Enron

▶ **Dom Perignon**—A famous, high-quality, and expensive champagne

▶ **ValuJet**—A once-fast-growing airline until a deadly crash in the Florida Everglades in 1996

▶ **Rolls Royce**—Known for high-quality hand-made automobiles

▶ **Yugo**—A cheaply made car that was released in the United States in the mid-1980s

▶ **Ruth's Chris Steak House**—An upscale eatery known for serving high-quality steaks that are seared at 1800°

▶ **Food Lion**—Received a large amount of bad press in the 1990s over alleged unsanitary food practices.

As you read through these names, you probably had different thoughts as you looked at each name on the list. Some of these companies have worked for years to gain a level of respect and positive reputation. Catastrophes don't just happen. Most occur because of human error or as the result of a series of overlooked mistakes. Will a mistake be fatal to your organization? Reputations can be easily damaged. That is why disaster recovery is so important: The very future of the organization might rest on it. Damaging rumors can easily start, and it is important to have protocols in place for dealing with these incidents, accidents, and catastrophes. Negative public opinion can be costly. It is important to have a properly trained spokesperson to speak and represent the organization. Meeting with the media during a crisis is not an easy task or something that should be done without preparation. The appointed spokesperson should interface with senior management and legal counsel before making any public statement.

Preparing for these events should include creating communiqués that address each possible incident in a generic fashion. This gives the responsible parties a framework to work with in case a real disaster occurs. Liability should not be assumed; the spokesperson should simply state that an investigation has begun.

> **NOTE**
>
> A good example of a public relations fiasco is Coca-Cola's handling of its "New Coke" product. The company spent millions on blind taste tests, yet no one asked consumers, "Would you buy this product?" Sony is another company that suffered damage to its brand name when it denied the existence of its XCP rootkit. In that incident, the media giant inadvertently violated users' desktop security in an ill-conceived effort to enforce CD music antipiracy controls.

BCP in the Real World

The business continuity plan (BCP) is developed to prevent interruptions to normal business. If these events cannot be prevented, the goals of the plan are to minimize the outage and reduce the potential damage that such disruptions might cost the organization. Therefore, the BCP should also be designed to help minimize the cost associated with the disruptive events and mitigate the risks associated with these disruptive events. Disasters can be natural events; storms, floods, and so on; man-made events; computer viruses, malicious code, and so on; technical events; equipment failure, programming errors, and so on. Figure 9.1 diagrams the hierarchy of these threats.

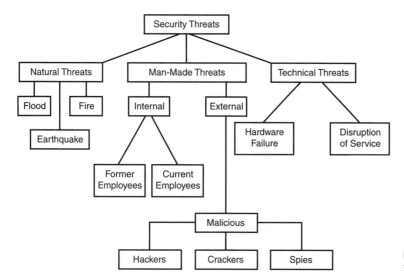

FIGURE 9.1 Security threats and their sources.

ISACA and the BCP Process

One of the best sources of information about the BCP process is the Disaster Recovery Institute International (DRII), which you can find online at http://www.drii.org. The process that DRII defines for BCP is much broader in scope than what ISACA defines. DRII breaks down the disaster recovery process into ten domains:

- ▶ Project Initiation and Management
- ▶ Risk Evaluation and Control
- ▶ Business Impact Analysis
- ▶ Developing Business Continuity Management Strategies

- Emergency Response and Operations
- Developing and Implementing Business Continuity Plans
- Awareness and Training Programs
- Exercising and Maintaining Business Continuity Plans
- Crisis Communications
- Coordination with External Agencies

The BCP process as defined by ISACA has a much narrower scope and focuses on the following seven steps, each of which is discussed in greater detail in the following sections:

1. Project management and initiation
2. Business impact analysis
3. Recovery strategy
4. Plan design and development
5. Training and awareness
6. Implementation and testing
7. Monitoring and maintenance

Step 1: Project Management and Initiation

Before the BCP process can begin, management must be on board. Management is ultimately responsible and must be actively involved in the process. Management sets the budget, determines the team leader, and gets the process started. The BCP team leader determines who will be on the BCP team. The team's responsibilities include the following:

- Identifying regulatory and legal requirements
- Identifying all possible threats and risks
- Estimating the possibilities of these threats and their loss potential and ranking them determined by the likelihood of the event occuring
- Performing a business impact analysis (BIA)
- Outlining which departments, systems, and processes must be up and running before any others
- Developing procedures and steps in resuming business after a disaster
- Assigning tasks to individuals that they would perform during a crisis situation
- Documenting, communicating to employees, and performing training and drills

One of the first steps the team is tasked with is meeting with senior management. The purpose is to define goals and objectives, discuss a project schedule, and discuss the overall goals of the BCP process. This should give everyone present some idea of the scope of the final BCP policy.

It's important for everyone involved to understand that the BCP is the most important *corrective control* the organization will have an opportunity to shape. Although the BCP is primarily corrective, it also has the following elements:

▶ **Preventive**—Controls to identify critical assets and develop ways to prevent outages

▶ **Detective**—Controls to alert the organization quickly in case of outages or problems

▶ **Corrective**—Controls to return to normal operations as quickly as possible

Step 2: Business Impact Analysis

Knowledge Statement

▶ Knowledge of business impact analysis (BIA)

Chance and uncertainty are part of the world we live in. We cannot predict what tomorrow will bring or whether a disaster will occur—but this doesn't mean that we cannot plan for it. As an example, the city of Tampa, Florida, is in an area prone to hurricanes. Just because the possibility of a hurricane in winter in Tampa is extremely low doesn't mean that planning can't take place to reduce the potential negative impact. This is what the BIA is about. Its purpose is to think through all possible disasters that could take place, assess the risk, quantify the impact, determine the loss, and develop a plan to deal with the incidents that seem most likely to occur.

As a result, the BIA should present a clear picture of what is needed to continue operations if a disaster occurs. The individuals responsible for the BIA must look at the organization from many different angles and use information from a variety of inputs. For the BIA to be successful, the BIA team must know what key business processes are. Questions the team must ask when determining critical processes might include the following:

▶ **Does the process support health and safety?**—Items such as the loss of an air traffic control system at a major airport or the loss of power in a hospital operating room could be devastating to those involved and result in the loss of life.

▶ **Does the loss of the process have a negative impact on income?**—As an example, a company such as eBay would find the loss of Internet connectivity devastating, whereas a small nonprofit organization might be able to live without connectivity for days.

▶ **Does the loss of the process violate legal or statutory requirements?**—As an example, a coal-powered electrical power plant might be using scrubbers to clean the air before emissions are released. Loss of these scrubbers might violate federal law and result in huge regulatory fines.

▶ **How does the loss of the process affect users?**—Returning to the example electrical power plant, it is easy to see how problems with the steam-generation process would shut down power generation and leave many residential and business customers without power. This loss of power in the Alaskan winter or in the Houston summer would have a large impact.

As you might be starting to realize, performing the BIA is no easy task. It requires not only the knowledge of business processes, but also a thorough understanding of the organization itself. This includes IT resources, individual business units, and the interrelationship of each of these pieces. This task requires the support of senior management and the cooperation of IT personnel, business unit managers, and end users. The general steps of the BIA are as follows:

1. Determine data-gathering techniques.

2. Gather business impact analysis data.

3. Identify critical business functions and resources.

4. Verify completeness of data.

5. Establish recovery time for operations.

6. Define recovery alternatives and costs.

> **NOTE**
>
> Many BIA programs look no further than the traditional network. They focus on mainframe systems and LAN-based distributed systems. It is important that the BIA also look at systems and information that might normally be overlooked, such as information stored on end-user systems that are not backed up and laptops used by the sales force or management.

The BIA typically includes both quantitative and qualitative components:

▶ *Quantitative analysis* deals with numbers and dollar amounts. It attempts to assign a monetary value to the elements of risk assessment and to place dollar amounts on the potential impact, including both loss of income and expenses. Quantitative impacts can include all associated costs, including these:

  ▶ Lost productivity

  ▶ Delayed or canceled orders

- ▶ Cost of repair

- ▶ Value of the damaged equipment or lost data

- ▶ Cost of rental equipment

- ▶ Cost of emergency services

- ▶ Cost to replace the equipment or reload data

- ▶ *Qualitative assessment* is scenario driven and does not attempt to assign dollar values to components of the risk analysis. A qualitative assessment ranks the seriousness of the impact into grades or classes, such as low, medium, and high. These are usually associated with items to which no dollar amount can be easily assigned:

  - ▶ **Low**—Minor inconvenience. Customers might not notice.

  - ▶ **Medium**—Some loss of service. Might result in negative press or cause customers to lose some confidence in the organization.

  - ▶ **High**—Will result in loss of goodwill between the company and a client or employee. Negative press also reduces the outlook for future products and services.

Although different approaches for calculating loss exist, one of the most popular methods of acquiring data is the questionnaire. The team develops a questionnaire for senior management and end users, and might hand it out or use it during an interview process. Figure 9.2 provides an example of a typical BIA questionnaire.

The questionnaire can even be used in a round-table setting. This method of performing information gathering requires the BIA team to bring the required key individuals into a meeting and discuss as a group what impact specific types of disruptions would have on the organization. Auditors play a key role because they might be asked to contribute information such as past transaction volumes or the impact to the business if specific systems were unavailable.

Reviewing the results of this information is the next step of the BIA process. During this step, the BIA team should ask questions such as these:

- ▶ **Are the systems identified critical?**—All departments like to think of themselves as critical, but that is usually not the case. Some departments can be offline longer than others.

- ▶ **What is the required recovery time for critical resources?**—If the resource is critical, costs will mount the longer the resource is offline. Depending on the service and the time of interruption, these times will vary.

BIA Questionnaire

Item	Description	Conclusions
Introduction		
Unit Name		
Date of Interview		
Contact		
Description of		
Business Unit Function		
Financial Impacts		
Revenue Loss Impact		
Expense Impact		
Operational Impact		
Business Interruption Impact		
Loss of Confidence		
Loss of Customers		
Loss of Market Share		
Technology Dependence		
System Function		
System Interdependences		
Existing BCP Controls		
Other BIA Issues		

FIGURE 9.2 BIA questionnaire.

All this information might seem a little overwhelming; however, it is needed because at the core of the BIA are two critical items:

▶ **Recovery point objective (RPO)**—The RPO defines how current the data must be or how much data an organization can afford to lose. The greater the RPO, the more tolerant the process is to interruption.

▶ **Recovery time objective (RTO)**—The RTO specifies the maximum elapsed time to recover an application at an alternate site. The greater the RTO, the longer the process can take to be restored.

The lower the time requirements are, the higher the cost will be to reduce loss or restore the system as quickly as possible. For example, most banks have a very low RPO because they cannot afford to lose any processed information. Figure 9.3 presents an overview of how RPO and RTO are related.

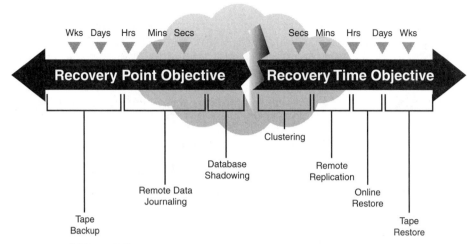

FIGURE 9.3 RPO and RTO.

TIP

The RTO specifies the maximum elapsed time to recover an application at an alternate site. The greater the RTO, the longer the process can take to be restored.

These items must be considered in addition to RTO and RPO:

▶ **Maximum acceptable outage**—This value is the time that systems can be offline before causing damage. This value is required in creating RTOs and is also known as maximum tolerable downtime (MTD).

▶ **Service delivery objective (SDO)**—This defines the level of service provided by alternate processes while primary processing is offline. This value should be determined by examining the minimum business need.

▶ **Maximum tolerable outages**—This defines the maximum amount of time the organization can provide services at the alternate site. This value can be determined by items such as contractual values.

▶ **Core processing**—These activities are specifically required for critical process and produce revenue.

▶ **Supporting processes**—These activities are required to support the minimum services needed to generate revenue.

▶ **Discretionary processes**—These include all other processes that are not part of the core or supporting processes, and that are not required for any critical processes or functions.

Criticality Analysis

How do you classify systems and resources according to their value or order of importance? You determine the estimated loss if a disruption occurred and calculate the likelihood that the disruption will occur. The quantitative method for this process involves the following three steps:

1. **Estimate potential losses (SLE)**—This step involves determining the single loss expectancy (SLE). SLE is calculated as follows:

   Single Loss Expectancy = Asset Value × Exposure Factor

   Items to consider when calculating the SLE include the physical destruction of manmade events, the loss of data, and threats that might cause a delay or disruption in processing. The exposure factor is the measure or percent of damage that a realized threat would have on a specific asset.

2. **Conduct a threat analysis (ARO)**—The purpose of a threat analysis is to determine the likelihood that an unwanted event will happen. The goal is to estimate the annual rate of occurrence (ARO). Simply stated, how many times is this expected to happen in one year?

3. **Determine annual loss expectancy (ALE)**—This third and final step of the quantitative assessment seeks to combine the potential loss and rate/year to determine the magnitude of the risk. This is expressed as annual loss expectancy (ALE). ALE is calculated as follows:

   Annualized Loss Expectancy (ALE) =

   Single Loss Expectancy (SLE) × Annualized Rate of Occurrence (ARO)

As an example, suppose that the potential loss due to a hurricane on a business based in Tampa, Florida, is $1 million. By examining previous weather patterns and observing historical trends, there has been an average of one hurricane of serious magnitude to hit the city every 10 years, which translates to 1/10, or 0.1% per year. This means the assessed risk that the organization will face a serious disruption is ($1 million × 0.1= $100,000.00) per year. That value is the annualized loss expectancy and, on average, is the amount per year that the disruption will cost the organization. Placing dollar amounts on such risks can aid senior management in determining what processes are most important and should be brought online first. Qualitatively, these items might be categorized not by dollar amount, but by a risk-ranking scale. Per ISACA, the scale shown in Table 9.2 is used to classify systems according to their importance to the organization.

TABLE 9.2 System Classification

Classification	Description
Critical	These extremely important functions cannot be performed with duplicate systems or processes. These functions are extremely intolerant to disruptions, so any disruption is very costly.
Vital	Although these functions are important, they can be performed by a backup manual process—but not for a long period of time. These systems can tolerate disruptions for typically five days or less.
Sensitive	Although these tasks are important, they can be performed manually at a reasonable cost. However, this is inconvenient and requires additional resources or manpower.
Noncritical	These services are not critical and can be interrupted. They can be restored later with little or no negative effects.

After addressing all these questions, the BCP team can start to develop recommendations and look at some potential recovery strategies. The BCP team should report these findings to senior management as a prioritized list of key business resources and the order in which restoration should be processed. The report should also offer potential recovery scenarios.

Before presenting the report to senior management, however, the team should distribute it to the various department heads. These individuals were interviewed, and the plan affects them and their departments; therefore, they should be given the opportunity to review it and note any discrepancies. The information in the BIA must be correct and accurate because all future decisions will be based upon its findings. Now let's move to the next step, recovery strategies.

> **NOTE**
>
> Interdependencies can make criticality analysis very complex. For example, you might have two assets that on their own are noncritical, but in certain contexts or situations they become critical!

Step 3: Recovery Strategy

At this point, the team has completed both the project initiation and the BIA. Now it must determine the most cost-effective recovery mechanisms to be implemented based on the critical processes and threats determined during the BIA. An effective recovery strategy should apply preventive, detective, and corrective controls to meet the following objectives:

- ▶ Remove identified threats
- ▶ Reduce the likelihood of identified risks
- ▶ Reduce the impact of identified risks

The recovery strategies should specify the best way to recover systems and processes in case of interruption. Operations can be interrupted in several different ways:

- **Data interruptions**—Caused by the loss of data. Solutions to data interruptions include backup, offsite storage, and remote journaling.

- **Operational interruptions**—Caused by the loss of equipment. Solutions to this type of interruption include hot sites, redundant equipment, RAID, and BPS.

- **Facility and supply interruptions**—Caused by interruptions due to fire, loss of inventory, transportation problems, HVAC problems, and telecommunications. Solutions to this type of interruption include redundant communication and transporting systems.

- **Business interruptions**—Caused by interruptions due to loss of personnel, strikes, critical equipment, supplies, and office space. Solutions to this type of interruption include redundant sites, alternate locations, and temporary staff.

The selection of a recovery strategy is based on several factors, including cost, criticality of the systems or process, and the time required to recover. To determine the best recovery strategy, follow these steps:

1. Document all costs for each possible alternative.

2. Obtain cost estimates for any outside services that might be needed.

3. Develop written agreements with the chosen vendor for such services.

4. Evaluate what resumption strategies are possible if there is a complete loss of the facility.

5. Document your findings and report your chosen recovery strategies to management for feedback and approval.

Normally, any IT system that runs a mission-critical application needs a recovery strategy. There are many to choose from; the right choice is based on the impact to the organization of the loss of the system or process. Recovery strategies include the following:

- Continuous processing

- Standby processing

- Standby database shadowing

- Remote data journaling

- Electronic vaulting

- Mobile site

▶ Hot site

▶ Warm site

▶ Cold site

▶ Reciprocal agreements

Each of these options are discussed later in the chapter, when recovery alternatives are reviewed. To get a better idea of how each of these options compares to the cost of implementation, take a moment to review Figure 9.4. At this point, it is important to realize that there must be a balance between the level of service needed and the recovery method.

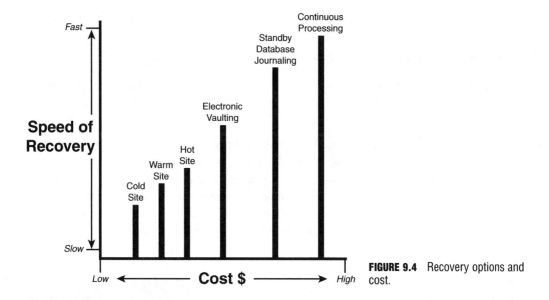

FIGURE 9.4 Recovery options and cost.

NOTE

Recovery strategies should be based on the disruptive cost versus the recovery costs. Finding a balance between the two offers recovery at the minimized cost.

Step 4: Plan Design and Development

Knowledge Statement

▶ Knowledge of the development and maintenance of the business continuity and disaster recovery plans

In the plan design and development phase, the team prepares and documents a detailed plan for recovering critical business systems. This plan should be based on information gathered during the project initiation, the BIA, and the recovery strategies phase. The plan should be a guide for implementation. The plan should address factors and variables such as these:

- Selecting critical functions and priorities for restoration

- Determining support systems critical functions need

- Estimating potential disasters and calculating the minimum resources needed to recover from the catastrophe

- Determining the procedures for declaring a disaster and under what circumstances this will occur

- Identifying individuals responsible for each function in the plan

- Choosing recovery strategies and determining what systems and equipment will be needed to accomplish the recovery

- Determining who will manage the restoration and testing process

- Calculating what type of funding and fiscal management is needed to accomplish these goals

The plan should be written in easy-to-understand language that uses common terminology that everyone will understand. The plan should detail how the organization will interface with external groups such as customers, shareholders, the media, and community, region, and state emergency services groups during a disaster. Important teams should be formed so that training can be performed. The final step of the phase is to combine all this information into the BCP plan and then interface it with the organization's other emergency plans.

EXAM ALERT

Copies of the BCP plan should be kept both on-site and off-site.

Step 5: Training and Awareness

The goal of training and awareness is to make sure all employees know what to do in case of an emergency. Studies have shown that training improves response time and helps employees be better prepared. Employees need to know where to call or how to maintain contact with the organization if a disaster occurs. Therefore, the organization should design and develop training programs to make sure each employee knows what to do and how to do it. Training can include a range of specific programs, such as CPR, fire drills, crisis management, emergency procedures, and so on. Employees assigned to specific tasks should be trained to carry out needed procedures. Cross-training of team members should occur, if possible, so that team members are familiar with a variety of recovery roles and responsibilities. Some people might not be able to lead under the pressure of crisis command; others might not be able to report to work. Table 9.3 describes some of the key groups involved in the BCP process and their responsibilities.

TABLE 9.3   BCP Process Responsibilities

Person or Department	Responsibility
Senior management	Project initiation, ultimate responsibility, overall approval and support
Midmanagement or business unit managers	Identification and prioritization of critical systems
BCP committee and team members	Planning, day-to-day management, implementation, and testing of the plan
Functional business units	Plan implementation, corporation, and testing
IT audit	BCP plan review, test results evaluation, off-site storage facilities, alternate processing contracts, and insurance coverage

EXAM ALERT

The number one priority of any BCP or DRP is to protect the safety of employees.

I Am in Control Here!

It is important to understand that, during a disaster, people will sometimes panic or act irrationally. Employees will be looking for leadership, and there will be a need for a clearly defined structure of command and control. The U.S. government operates in much the same way. For a good example of how not to handle an emergency situation, one must look no further than the 1981 shooting of President Reagan. In case of a president's incapacitation, there is a clear line of succession. After Reagan was shot, Secretary of State Alexander Haig appeared at a press conference and declared, "I'm in control here." This caused a greater level of panic and confusion because the Secretary of State is not in charge when the President is incapacitated; this was seen by many as an attempt to exceed his authority.

Step 6: Implementation and Testing

Knowledge Statements

▶ Knowledge of business continuity and disaster recovery testing approaches and methods

▶ Knowledge of human resources management practices as related to business continuity and disaster recovery (e.g., evacuation planning, response teams)

▶ Knowledge of processes used to invoke the business continuity and disaster recovery plans

The BCP team has now reached the implementation and testing phase. This is where the previously agreed-upon steps are implemented. No demonstrated recovery exists until the plan has been tested. Before examining the ways in which the testing can occur, look at some of the teams that are involved in the process:

▶ **Incident response team**—Team developed as a central clearinghouse for all incidents.

▶ **Emergency response team**—The first responders for the organization. They are tasked with evacuating personnel and saving lives.

▶ **Emergency management team**—Executives and line managers that are financially and legally responsible. They must also handle the media and public relations.

▶ **Damage assessment team**—The estimators. They must determine the damage and estimate the recovery time.

▶ **Salvage team**—Those responsible for reconstructing damaged facilities. This includes cleaning up, recovering assets, creating documentation for insurance filings or legal actions, and restoring paper documents and electronic media.

▶ **Communications team**—Those responsible for installing communications (data, voice, phone, fax, radio) at the recovery site.

▶ **Security team**—Those who manage the security of the organization during the time of crisis. They must maintain order after a disaster.

▶ **Emergency operations team**—Individuals who reside at the alternative site and manage systems operations. They are primarily operators and supervisors who are familiar with system operations.

▶ **Transportation team**—Team responsible for notifying employees that a disaster has occurred. They are also in charge of providing transportation, scheduling, and lodging for those who will be needed at the alternative site.

▶ **Coordination team**—Team tasked with managing operations at different remote sites and coordinating the recovery efforts.

▶ **Finance team**—Team that provides budgetary control for recovery and accurate accounting of costs.

▶ **Administrative support team**—Team that provides administrative support and also handles payroll functions and accounting.

▶ **Supplies team**—Team that coordinates with key vendors to maintain needed supplies.

▶ **Relocation team**—Team in charge of managing the process of moving from the alternative site to the restored original location.

▶ **Recovery test team**—Individuals deployed to test the BCP/DRP plans and determine their effectiveness.

Did you notice that the last team listed is the recovery test team? These are the individuals who test the BCP plan; this should be done at least once a year. Without testing the plan, there is no guarantee that it will work. Testing helps bring more theoretical plans into reality. To build confidence, the BCP team should start with easier parts of the plan and build to more complex items. The initial tests should focus on items that support core processing and should be scheduled during a time that causes minimal disruption to normal business operations. Tests should be observed by an auditor who can witness the process and record accurate test times. Having an auditor is not the only requirement: Key individuals who would be responsible in a real disaster must play a role in the testing process. The actual testing methods vary among organizations and range from simple to complex. Regardless of the method or types of testing performed, the idea is to learn from the practice and improve the process each time a problem is discovered. As a CISA candidate, you should be aware of the three different types of BCP testing as defined by the ISACA:

▶ Paper tests

▶ Preparedness tests

▶ Full operation tests

The following sections describe these basic testing methods in more detail.

EXAM ALERT

ISACA defines three types of BCP tests: paper tests, preparedness tests, and full operation tests.

Paper Tests

The most basic method of BCP testing is the *paper test*. Although it is not considered a replacement for a real test, this is a good start. A paper test is an exercise that can be performed by sending copies of the plan to different department managers and business unit managers for review. Each person the plan is sent to can review it to make sure nothing has been overlooked, and that everything that is being asked of them is possible.

A paper test can also be performed by having the members of the team come together and discuss the BCP plan. This is sometimes known as *walk-through testing*. The plans are laid out across the table so that attendees have a chance to see how an actual emergency would be handled. By reviewing the plan in this way, some errors or problems should become apparent. Under either method, sending the plan around or meeting to review the plan, the next step is usually a preparedness test.

Preparedness Tests

A *preparedness test* is a simulation in which team members go through an exercise that reenacts an actual outage or disaster. This type of test is typically used to test a portion of the plan. The preparedness test consumes time and money because it is an actual test that measures the team's response to situations that might someday occur. This type of testing provides a means of incrementally improving the plan.

TIP

During preparedness tests, team leaders might want to adopt the phrase *exercise* because the term *test* denotes passing or failing. Adding this type of additional pressure on team members can be detrimental to the goals of continual improvement. As an example, during one disaster recovery test I was involved in, the backup media was to be returned from the offsite location to the primary site. When the truck arrived with the media, it was discovered that the tapes had not been properly secured. The tapes were scattered around the bed of the truck. Even though the test could not continue, it was not a failure as it uncovered a weakness in the existing procedure.

Full Operation Tests

The *full operation test* is as close to the actual service disruption as you can get. The team should have performed paper tests and preparedness tests before attempting this level of interruption. This test is the most detailed, time consuming, and thorough of all discussed. A full interruption test mimics a real disaster, and all steps are performed to start up backup operations. This involves all the individuals who would be involved in a real emergency, including internal and external organizations. Goals of the full operation test include the following:

- ▶ Verifying the business continuity plan
- ▶ Evaluating the level of preparedness of the personnel involved
- ▶ Measuring the capability of the backup site to operate as planned
- ▶ Assessing the ability to retrieve vital records and information
- ▶ Evaluating the functionality of equipment
- ▶ Measuring overall preparedness for an actual disaster

EXAM ALERT

The disaster recovery and continuity plan should be tested at least once yearly. Environments change; each time the plan is tested, more improvements might be uncovered.

Step 7: Monitoring and Maintenance

When the testing process is complete, individuals tend to feel their job is done. If someone is not made responsible for this process, the best plans in the world can start to become outdated in six months or less. Don't be surprised to find out that no one really wants to take on the task of documenting procedures and processes. The responsibility of performing periodic tests and maintaining the plan should be assigned to a specific person. The plan's maintenance can be streamlined by incorporating change-management procedures to address issues that might affect the BCP plan.

A few additional items must be done to finish the BCP plan. The primary remaining item is to put controls in place to maintain the current level of business continuity and disaster recovery. This is best accomplished by implementing change-management procedures. If changes are required to the approved plans, you will then have a documented structured way to accomplish this. A centralized command and control structure will ease this burden. Life is not static; neither should be the organization's BCP plans

Recovery Alternatives

Knowledge Statement

▶ Knowledge of types of alternate processing sites and methods used to monitor the contractual agreements (e.g., hot sites, warm sites, cold sites)

Recovery alternatives are the choices the organization has to restore critical systems and the data in those systems. Recovery alternatives can include the following:

▶ Alternate processing sites

▶ Hardware recovery

▶ Software recovery

▶ Telecommunications recovery

▶ Backup and restoration

The goal is to find the recovery alternative that balances the cost of downtime, the criticality of the system, and the likelihood of occurrence. As an example, if you have an RTO of less than 12 hours and the resource you are trying to recover is a mainframe computer, a cold-site facility would never work. Why? Because you can't buy a mainframe, install it, and get the cold site up and running in less than 12 hours. Therefore, although cost is important, so are criticality and the time to recover. The total outage time that the organization can endure is referred to as *maximum tolerable downtime* (MTD). Table 9.4 shows some MTDs used by many organizations.

TABLE 9.4 Required Recovery Times

Item	Required Recovery Time
Critical	Minutes to hours
Urgent	24 hours
Important	72 hours
Normal	7 days
Nonessential	30 days

Alternate Processing Sites

For disasters that have the potential to affect the primary facility, plans must be made for a backup process or an alternate site. Some organizations might opt for a *redundant processing site*. Redundant sites are equipped and configured just like the primary site. They are owned by the organization, and their cost is high. After all, the company has spent a large amount of funds to build and equip a complete, duplicate site. Although the cost might seem high, it must be noted that organizations that choose this option have done so because they have a very short (if any) RPO. A loss of services for even a very short period of time would cost the organization millions. The organization also might be subjected to regulations that require it to maintain redundant processing. Before choosing a location for a redundant site, it must be verified that the site is not subject to the same types of disasters as the primary site. Regular testing is also important to verify that the redundant site still meets the organization's needs and that it can handle the workload to meet minimum processing requirements.

Mobile sites are another alternate processing alternative. Mobile sites are usually tractor-trailer rigs that have been converted into data-processing centers. They contain all the necessary equipment and can be transported to a business location quickly. These can be chained together to provide space for data processing and can provide communication capabilities. Used by the military and large insurance agencies, they are a good choice in areas where no recovery facilities exist. Other types of recovery alternatives include *subscription services* such as hot sites, warm sites, and cold sites.

The *hot site* facility is ready to go. It is fully configured and is equipped with the same system as the production network. It can be made operational within just a few hours. A hot site merely needs staff, data files, and procedural documentation. Hot sites are a high-cost recovery option, but they can be justified when a short recovery time is required. Because a hot site is typically a subscription-based service, a range of fees are associated with it, including a monthly cost, subscription fees, testing costs, and usage or activation fees. Contracts for hot sites need to be closely examined; some might charge extremely high activation fees to prevent users from utilizing the facility for anything less than a true disaster.

Regardless of what fees are involved, the hot site needs to be periodically tested. These tests should evaluate processing abilities as well as security. The physical security of the hot site should be at the same level or greater than the primary site. Finally, it is important to remember that the hot site is intended for short-term usage only. As a subscriber service, other companies might be competing for the same resource. The organization should have a plan to recover primary services quickly or move to a secondary location.

EXAM ALERT

Hot sites should not be externally identifiable because this increases the risk of sabotage and other potential disruptions.

For a slightly less expensive alternative, an organization can choose a *warm site*. A warm site has data equipment and cables, and is partially configured. It could be made operational in anywhere from a few hours to a few days. The assumption with a warm site is that computer equipment and software can be procured in case of a disaster. Although the warm site might have some computer equipment installed, it is typically of lower processing power than at the primary site. The costs associated with a warm site are similar to those of a hot site but are slightly lower. The warm site is the most popular subscription alternative.

For organizations that are looking for a cheaper alternative and that have determined that they can tolerate a longer outage, a *cold site* might be the right choice. A cold site is basically an empty room with only rudimentary electrical, power, and computing capability. It might have a raised floor and some racks, but it is nowhere near ready for use. It might take several weeks to a month to get the site operational. A common misconception with cold sites is that the organization will be able to get the required equipment after a disaster. This might not be true. For a large disaster, such as what was experienced with Katrina, there could be a run on equipment so that vendors simply cannot meet demand. Backorders could push out the operation dates of the cold site to much longer than planned. Cold sites offer the least of the three subscription services discussed. Table 9.5 shows some example functions and their recovery times.

EXAM ALERT

Cold sites are a good choice for the recovery of noncritical services.

TABLE 9.5 Example Functions and Recovery Times

Process	Recovery Time	Recovery Strategy
Database	15 minutes to 1 hour	Database shadowing at a redundant site
Applications	12–24 hours	Hot site
Help desk	24–48 hours	Hot site
Purchasing	24–48 hours	Hot site
Payroll	1–3 days	Redundant site
Asset inventory	5–7 days	Warm site
Non-essential services	30 days	Cold site
Used by companies that need to set up operations quickly in areas that have been hit by disasters, such as insurance companies, governmental agencies, military, and so on	Hours to a few days	Mobile site

Reciprocal agreements are less frequently used. In this method, two organizations pledge assistance to one another in the event of a disaster. These agreements are carried out by sharing space, computer facilities, and technology resources. On paper, this appears to be a cost-effective solution because the primary advantage is its low cost. However, reciprocal agreements have drawbacks. The parties to this agreement are trusting that the other organization will aid in the event of a disaster. However, the nonvictim might be hesitant to follow through if such a disaster occurs based on concerns such as the realization that the damaged party might want to remain on location for a long period of time or that their presence will degrade their own network services. Even concerns about the loss of competive advantage can drive this hesitation. The issue of confidentiality also arises: The damaged organization is placed in a vulnerable position and must rely on the other party with confidential information. Finally, if the parties to the agreement are near each other, there is always the danger that disaster could strike both parties and thereby render the agreement useless. The legal departments of both firms will need to look closely at such an agreement. ISACA recommends that organizations considering reciprocal agreements address the following issues before entering into such an agreement:

▶ What amount of time will be available at the host computer site?

▶ Will the host site's employees be available for help?

▶ What specific facilities and equipment will be available?

▶ How long can emergency operations continue at the host site?

▶ How frequently can tests be scheduled at the host site?

▶ What type of physical security is at the host site?

▶ What type of logical security is available at the host site?

▶ Is advance notice required for using the site? If so, how much?

▶ Are there any blocks of time or dates when the facility is not available?

EXAM ALERT

Although reciprocal agreements are not usually appropriate for organizations with large databases, some organizations, such as small banks, have been known to sign reciprocal agreements for the use of a shared hot site.

When reviewing alternative processing options, subscribers should look closely at any agreements and at the actual facility to make sure it meets the need of the organization. One common problem is oversubscription. If situations such as Hurricane Katrina occur, there could be more organizations demanding the subscription service than the vendor can supply. The subscription agreement might also dictate when the organization may inhabit the facility. Thus, even though an organization might be in the path of a deadly storm, it might not be able to move into the facility yet because the area has not been declared a disaster area. Procedures and documentation should also be kept at the off-site location, and even backup must be available. It's important to note that backup media should be kept in an area that is not subject to the same type of natural disaster. As an example, if the primary site is in the hurricane zone, the backup needs to be somewhere less prone to those conditions. If backup media is at another location, agreements should be in place to ensure that the media is moved to the alternate site so it is available for the recovery process. A final item is that organizations must also have prior financial arrangements to procure needed equipment, software, and supplies during a disaster. This might include emergency credit lines, credit cards, or agreements with hardware and software vendors.

Hardware Recovery

Recovery alternatives are just one of the items that must be considered to cope with a disaster. Hardware recovery is another. Remember that an effective recovery strategy involves more than just corrective measures; it is also about prevention. Hardware failures are one of the most common disruptions that can occur. This means that it is important to examine ways to minimize the likelihood of occurrence and to reduce the effect if it does occur. This process can be enhanced by making well-informed decisions when buying equipment. At purchase time, you should know two important numbers:

▶ **The mean time between failure (MTBF)**—The MTBF calculates the expected lifetime of a device. A higher MTBF means the equipment should last longer.

▶ **The mean time to repair (MTTR)**—The MTTR estimates how long it would take to repair the equipment and get it back into use. For MTTR, lower numbers mean the equipment takes less time to repair and can be returned to service sooner.

For critical equipment, the organization might consider a *service level agreement* (SLA), a contract with the hardware vendor that provides a certain level of protection. For a fee, the vendor agrees to repair or replace the equipment within the contracted time.

Fault tolerance can be used at the server or the drive level. At the server level is *clustering*, which is technology that groups several servers together yet allows them to be viewed logically as a single server. Users see the cluster as one unit, although it is actually many. The advantage is that if one server in the cluster fails, the remaining active servers will pick up the load and continue operation. Fault tolerance on the drive level is achieved primarily with *Redundant Array of Inexpensive Disks (RAID)*, which is used for hardware fault tolerance and/or performance improvements. This is achieved by breaking up the data and writing it to multiple disks. To applications and other devices, RAID appears as a single drive. Most RAID systems have *hot-swappable disks*, which means that the drives can be removed or added while the computer systems are running. If the RAID system uses parity and is fault tolerant, the parity date is used to rebuild the newly replaced drive. Another RAID technique is *striping*, which simply means that the data is divided and written over several drives. Although write performance remains almost constant, read performance drastically increases. RAID has humble beginnings that date back to the 1980s at the University of California. According to ISACA, the most common levels of RAID used today include these:

▶ RAID 0

▶ RAID 3

▶ RAID 5

RAID level descriptions are as follows:

▶ **Level 0**—Striped Disk Array without Fault Tolerance: Provides data striping and improves performance, but provides no redundancy.

▶ **Level 1**—Mirroring and Duplexing: Disk mirroring duplicates the information on one disk to another. It provides twice the read transaction rate of single disks and the same write transaction rate as single disks, yet effectively cuts disk space in half.

▶ **Level 2**—Error-Correcting Coding: ECC is rarely used because of the extensive computing resources needed. It stripes data at the bit level instead of the block level.

▶ **Level 3**—Parallel Transfer with Parity: Uses byte-level striping with a dedicated disk. Although it provides fault tolerance, it is rarely used.

▶ **Level 4**—Shared Parity Drive: Similar to RAID 3, but provides block-level striping with a parity disk. If a data disk fails, the parity data is used to create a replacement disk. Its primary disadvantage is that the parity disk can create write bottlenecks.

▶ **Level 5**—Block Interleaved Distributed Parity: Provides data striping of both data and parity. Level 5 has good performance and fault tolerance. It is a popular implementation of RAID.

▶ **Level 6**—Independent Data Disks with Double Parity: Level 6 provides high fault tolerance with block-level striping and parity data distributed across all disks.

▶ **Level 10**—A Stripe of Mirrors: This level of RAID is known to have very high reliability. IT requires a minimum of four drives.

▶ **Level 0+1**—A Mirror of Stripes: This mode of RAID is not one of the original RAID levels. RAID 0+1 uses RAID 0 to stripe data and creates a RAID 1 mirror. It provides high data rates.

One final drive-level solution worth mentioning is *Just a Bunch of Disks (JBOD)*. It is similar to RAID 0 but offers few of the advantages. What it does offer is the capability to combine two or more disks of various sizes into one large partition. It also has an advantage over RAID 0: In case of drive failure, only the data on the affected drive is lost; the data on surviving drives remains readable. This means that JBOD has disaster recovery advantages. JBOD does not carry the performance benefits associated with RAID 0. With our discussion of hardware recovery complete, let's move on to discuss software-recovery options.

Software and Data Recovery

Knowledge Statement

▶ Knowledge of data backup, storage, maintenance, retention and restoration processes, and practices

Because data processing is essential to most organizations, having the software and data needed to continue this operation is critical to the recovery process. The objectives are to back up critical software and data, and be able to restore these quickly. Policy should dictate when backups are performed, when the media is stored, who has access to the media, and what its reuse or rotation policy is. Backup media can include tape reels, tape cartridges, removable hard drives, disks, and cassettes. The organization must determine how often backups should be performed and what type of backup should be performed. These operations will vary depending on the cost of the media, the speed of the restoration needed, and the time allocated for backups. Typically, the following four backup methods are used:

▶ **Full backup**—All data is backed up. No data files are skipped or bypassed. All items are copied to one tape, set of tapes, or backup medium. If restoration is needed, only one tape or set of tapes is needed. A full backup requires the most time and space on the storage medium but takes the least time to restore.

▶ **Differential backup**—A full backup is done typically once a week, and a daily differential backup is done only to those files that have changed since the last full backup. If you need to restore, you need the last full backup and the most recent differential backup. This method takes less time per backup but longer to restore because both the full and differential backups are needed.

▶ **Incremental backup**—This method backs up only those files that have been modified since the previous incremental backup. An incremental backup requires additional backup media because the last full backup, the last incremental backup, and any additional incremental backups are required to restore the media.

▶ **Continuous backup**—Some backup applications perform a *continuous backup* that keeps a database of backup information. These systems are useful because if a restoration is needed, the application can provide a full restore, a point-in-time restore, or a restore based on a selected list of files.

Although tape and optical systems still have the majority of market share for backup systems, hardware alternatives are making inroads. One of these technologies is Massive Array of Inactive Disks (MAID). MAID offers a hardware storage option for the storage of data and applications, and was designed to reduce the operational costs and improve long-term reliability of disk-based archives and backups. MAID is similar to RAID, except that it provides power management and advanced disk monitoring. The MAID system powers down inactive drives, reduces heat output, reduces electrical consumption, and increases the drive's life expectancy. This represents real progress to concerns of using hard disks to back up data. Storage Area Networks (SANs) are another alternative. SANs are designed as a subnetwork of high-speed, shared storage devices. When software- and data-recovery methods have been determined, the next item is to look at backup and data-restoration provisions.

Backup and Restoration

Task

▶ Evaluate the adequacy of backup and restoration provisions to ensure the availability of information required to resume processing.

Knowledge Statement

▶ Knowledge of data backup, storage, maintenance, retention and restoration processes, and practices

Where the backup media is stored can have a real impact on how quickly data can be restored and brought back online. The media should be stored in more than one physical location, to reduce the possibility of loss. A tape librarian should manage these remote sites by maintaining the site, controlling access, rotating media, and protecting this valuable asset. Unauthorized access to the media is a huge risk because it could impact the organization's ability to provide uninterrupted service. Encryption can help mitigate this risk. Transportation to and from the remote site is also an important concern. Items of importance include these:

► Secure transportation to and from the site must be maintained.

► Delivery vehicles must be bonded.

► Backup media must be handled, loaded, and unloaded in an appropriate way.

► Drivers must be trained on the proper procedures to pick up, handle, and deliver backup media.

► Access to the backup facility should be 24×7 in case of emergency.

Off-site storage should be contracted with a known firm that has control of the facility and is responsible for its maintenance. Physical and environmental controls should be equal or better than those of the organization's facility. A letter of agreement should specify who has access to the media and who is authorized to drop off or pick up media. There should also be an agreement on response time that is to be met in times of disaster. *On-site storage* should be maintained to ensure the capability to recover critical files quickly. Backup media should be secured and kept in an environmentally controlled facility that has physical control sufficient to protect such a critical asset. This area should be fireproof, with controlled access so that anyone depositing or removing media is logged. Although most backup media is rather robust, it will not last forever and will fail over time. This means that tape rotation is another important part of backup and restoration. Backup media must be periodically tested. Backups will be of little use if you find during a disaster that they have malfunctioned and no longer work. Common media-rotation strategies include the following:

► **Simple**—A simple backup-rotation scheme is to use one tape for every day of the week and then repeat the next week. One tape can be for Mondays, one for Tuesdays, and so on. You would add a set of new tapes each month and then archive the monthly sets. After a predetermined number of months, you would put the oldest tapes back into use.

► **Grandfather-father-son**—This rotation method includes four tapes for weekly backups, one tape for monthly backups, and four tapes for daily backups. It is called grandfather-father-son because the scheme establishes a kind of hierarchy. Grandfathers are the one monthly backup, fathers are the four weekly backups, and sons are the four daily backups.

▶ **Tower of Hanoi**—This tape-rotation scheme is named after a mathematical puzzle. It involves using five sets of tapes, each set labeled A through E. Set A is used every other day; set B is used on the first non-A backup day and is used every fourth day; set C is used on the first non-A or non-B backup day and is used every eighth day; set D is used on the first non-A, non-B, or non-C day and is used every 16th day; and set E alternates with set D.

NOTE

Encryption and Backups—An organization's backups are a complete mirror of the organization's data. Although most backups are password-protected, this really offers only limited protection. If attackers have possession of the backup media, they are not under any time constraints. This gives them ample time to crack passwords and access the data. Encryption can offer an additional layer of protection and help protect the confidentiality of the data.

SANs are an alternative to tape backup. SANs support disk mirroring, backup and restore, archival and retrieval of archived data, and data migration from one storage device to another. SANs can be implemented locally or can use storage at a redundant facility. If this is beyond the organization's budget, it can opt for *electronic vaulting*, the transfer of data by electronic means to a backup site, as opposed to the physical shipment. With electronic vaulting, organizations contract with a vaulting provider. The organization typically loads a software agent onto systems to be backed up, and the vaulting service accesses these systems to copy the selected files. If large amounts of data are to be moved, this can slow WAN service. Another backup alternative is *standby database shadowing*. A standby database is an exact duplicate of a database maintained on a remote server. In case of disaster, it is ready to go. Changes are applied from the primary database to the standby database to keep records synchronized.

What about situations when backup is not the problem? What if the software developer goes bankrupt or is no longer in business? How is the organization supposed to maintain or update the needed code? These concerns can be addressed by a *software escrow* agreement. Software escrow allows the organization to maintain access to the source code of an application if the vendor goes bankrupt. Although the organization can modify the software for continued use, it can't steal the design or sell the code on the open market. This is simply one way of protecting you in case things go wrong and the vendor is no longer in business.

Telecommunications Recovery

Telecommunications recovery should play a key role in recovery. After all, the telecommunication network is a critical asset and should be given a high priority for recovery. Although these communications networks can be susceptible to the same threats as data centers, they also face some unique threats. Protection methods include redundant WAN links, bandwidth on demand, and dial backup. Whatever the choice, the organization should verify capacity requirements and acceptable outage times. The primary methods for network protection include the following:

▶ **Redundancy**—This involves exceeding what is required or needed. Redundancy can be added by providing extra capacity, providing multiple routes, using dynamic routing protocols, and using failover devices to allow for continued operations.

▶ **Diverse routing**—This is the practice of routing traffic through different cable facilities. Organizations can obtain both diverse routing and alternate routing, yet the cost is not cheap. Most of these systems use facilities that are buried. These systems usually emerge through the basement and can sometimes share space with other mechanical equipment. This adds risk. Many cities have aging infrastructures, which is another probable point of failure.

▶ **Alternate routing**—This is the ability to use another transmission line if the regular line is busy or unavailable. This can include using a dial-up connection in place of a dedicated connection, a cell phone instead of a land line, or microwave communication in place of a fiber connection.

▶ **Long-haul diversity**—This is the practice of having different long-distance communication carriers. This recovery facility option helps ensure that service is maintained; auditors should verify that it is present.

▶ **Last-mile protection**—This is a good choice for recovery facilities, in that it provides a second local loop connection and can add to security even more if an alternate carrier is used.

▶ **Voice communication recovery**—Many organizations are highly dependent on voice communications. Some of these organizations have started making the switch to VoIP because of the cost savings. Some land lines should be maintained to provide recovery capability.

> **NOTE**
>
> Recovery strategies have historically focused on computing resources and data. Networks are susceptible to many of the same problems, yet many times they are not properly backed up. This can be a real problem because there is a heavy reliance on networks to deliver data when needed.

Verification of Disaster Recovery and Business Continuity Process

Tasks

▶ Evaluate the organization's disaster recovery plan to ensure that it enables the recovery of IT processing in the event of a disaster.

▶ Evaluate the organization's business continuity plan to ensure its ability to continue essential business operations during the period of an IT disruption.

As an IT auditor, you will be tasked with understanding and evaluating DR/BCP strategy. The auditor should review the plan and make sure that it is current and up-to-date. The auditor also will want to examine last year's test to verify the results and look for any problem areas. The business continuity coordinator is responsible for maintaining previous tests. Upon examination, the auditor should confirm that the test met targeted goals or minimum standards. The auditor will also want to inspect the off-site storage facility and review its security, policies, and configuration. This should include a detailed inventory that checks data files, applications, system software, system documentation, operational documents, consumables, supplies, and a copy of the BCP plan.

Contracts and alternative processing agreements should also be reviewed. Any off-site processing facilities should be audited, and the owners should have a reference check. All agreements should be made in writing. The off-site facility should meet the same security standards as the primary facility and should have environmental controls such as raised floors, HVAC controls, fire prevention and detection, filtered power, and uninterruptible power supplies. If the location is a shared site, the rules that determine who has access and when they have access should be examined. Another area of concern is the BCP plan itself. The auditor must make sure the plan is written in easy-to-understand language and that users have been trained. This can be confirmed by interviewing employees.

Finally, insurance should be reviewed. The auditor will want to examine the level and types of insurance the organization has purchased. Insurance can be obtained for each of the following items:

▶ IS equipment

▶ Data centers

▶ Software recovery

▶ Business interruption

▶ Documents, records, and important papers

▶ Errors and omissions

▶ Media transportation

Insurance is not without its drawbacks, which include high premiums, delayed claim payout, denied claims, and problems proving financial loss. Finally, most policies pay for only a percentage of actual loss and do not pay for lost income, increased operating expenses, or consequential loss.

REVIEW BREAK

The business continuity process follows a structured path that includes the following steps:

1. **Project management and initiation**—Management identifies a need for the BCP and appoints a team leader.

2. **Business impact analysis**—The team determines various risks and determines a threat level based on qualitative or quantitative assessment.

3. **Recovery strategy**—Based on identified threats, the team determines what is needed to recover from identified disasters.

4. **Plan design and development**—The team designs a plan and develops a procedure to recover from disasters determined in the BIA.

5. **Training and awareness**—The team trains employees and makes sure all employees are aware of BCP policies and procedures.

6. **Implementation and testing**—No recovery is guaranteed until the plan has been tested. Tests can be paper-based tests or complete real interruption tests.

7. **Monitoring and maintenance**—Changes to the network and systems require plans to be periodically updated.

Chapter Summary

This chapter discussed the process of business continuity planning. This process is the act of preparing for the worst possible events that could happen to the organization. Not uncommonly, many organizations give it low priority for a host of reasons, including cost, people's inability to quantify some potential threats, and the belief that they can somehow escape these events.

Initiation is the first step. This requires that senior management establish business continuity as a priority. Developing and carrying out a successful business continuity plan takes much work and effort, and should be done in a modular format. The business impact analysis is the next step. Although auditors are unlikely to be directly involved in this process, they can be of help here in providing data on the impact to the business if specific systems are unavailable. The goal of the business impact analysis is to determine which processes need to come on first, second, third, and so on. Each step of the business continuity process builds on the last; this requires the BCP team members to know the business and have worked with other departments and management to determine critical processes.

Recovery strategies must also be determined. As an example, in case of loss of power, will a generator be used, or might the process continue at another location that has power? With these decisions made, a written plan must be developed that locks into policy whatever choices have been decided upon.When the plan is implemented, the process is still not complete because the team must test the plan. During the test, an IS auditor should be present to observe the results. No demonstrated recovery exists until the plan has been tested. Common test methods include paper tests, preparedness tests, and full operation tests. To make sure these plans and procedures do not grow old or become obsolete, disaster recovery should become part of the decision-making process so that when changes are made, issues that may affect the policies can be updated. Business continuity and disaster recovery plans can also be added to job responsibilities and to yearly performance reviews.

Key Terms

- ▶ Business impact analysis
- ▶ Cold site
- ▶ Corrective control
- ▶ Data communications
- ▶ Database

- ▶ Hot site

- ▶ JBOD

- ▶ Local area network (LAN)

- ▶ MAID

- ▶ Mobile site

- ▶ Network

- ▶ Off-site storage

- ▶ Open Shortest Path First

- ▶ Paper test

- ▶ Protocol

- ▶ Recovery point objective

- ▶ Recovery testing

- ▶ Recovery time objective

- ▶ Redundant Array of Inexpensive Disks

- ▶ Resilience

- ▶ Risk

- ▶ Software

- ▶ Storage Area Network (SAN)

- ▶ Telecommunications

- ▶ Transaction

- ▶ Uninterruptible power supply

Apply Your Knowledge

This chapter documented the importance of business continuity and disaster recovery. This "Apply Your Knowledge" section has you review some of the items an IS auditor would need to review.

The exercise has you examine a hypothetical organization and list possible audit items.

Exercises

9.1 Business Impact and Risk

Estimated Time: 10 Minutes

Review the following profile and then answer the following questions.

Kerney, Cleveland, and Glass Law Firm

Driving Concern

> This high-flying law firm located in the Washington, D.C., area has serviced a who's who of individuals inside and outside the beltway. The firm recently suffered a major network outage after a key server failed and it was determined that the backup media was corrupt. Management has existing BCP plans but could not contact the person in charge of backups during this late-night problem. They are now worried that the plans are not adequate.

Overview

> The firm has two offices: one in the D.C. area and the other on the West Coast. The firm handles many confidential documents, often of high monetary value. The firm is always looking for ways to free up the partners from administrative tasks so that they can have more billable hours. Partners access their data from wireless LANs and remotely through a corporate VPN.

> The two offices are connected by a T1 leased line. Only the D.C. office has a connection to the Internet. The West Coast office connects to the Internet through the D.C. office. The wireless network supports Windows servers in the D.C. office. Partners also carry notebook computers that contain many confidential documents needed at client sites. No encryption is used, and there is no insurance to protect against downtime or disruptions.

1. Which of the following items should you perform if you were asked to audit the law firm's BCP plans?

    Verify that the business continuity plan provides for the recovery of all systems? Yes/No

    Require that you or another auditor is present during a test of the BCP plan? Yes/No

    Verify that the notification directory is being maintained and is current? Yes/No

    Verify that the IS department is responsible for declaring a disaster if such a situation repeated itself? Yes/No

    Suggest that the law firm increase its recovery time objective? Yes/No

    Determine the most critical finding? Lack of insurance/Loss of data

2. Examine the list from item 1 and compare your answers with the following:

    Verify that the business continuity plan provides for the recovery of all systems? Yes/**No** (Typically, only 50% of information is critical.)

    Require that you or another auditor is present during a test of the BCP plan? **Yes**/No (The auditor should be present to make sure the test meets required targets.)

Verify that the notification directory is being maintained and is current? **Yes**/No (Without a notification system, there is no easy way to contact employees or for them to check in case of disaster.)

Verify that the IS department is responsible for declaring a disaster if such a situation repeated itself? Yes/**No** (Senior management should designate someone for that task.)

Suggest that the law firm increase its recovery time objective? Yes/**No** (This would increase recovery time, not decrease it.)

Determine the most critical finding? Lack of insurance/**Loss of data** (The most vital asset for an organization is its data.)

Exam Questions

1. Tape backup should be used as a recovery strategy when:

    ○ **A.** The RPO is high.

    ○ **B.** The RPO is low.

    ○ **C.** The RTO is low.

    ○ **D.** Fault tolerance is low.

2. Which of the following is the best reason to use a hot site?

    ○ **A.** It can be used for long-term processing.

    ○ **B.** It is not a subscription service.

    ○ **C.** There is no additional cost for usage or periodic testing.

    ○ **D.** It is ready for service.

3. Which of the following describes the greatest advantage of JBOD?

    ○ **A.** In case of drive failure, only the data on the affected drive is lost.

    ○ **B.** It is superior to disk mirroring.

    ○ **C.** It offers greater performance gains than RAID.

    ○ **D.** Compared to RAID, it offers greater fault tolerance.

4. Which of the following processes is most critical in terms of revenue generation?

    ○ **A.** Discretionary

    ○ **B.** Supporting

    ○ **C.** Core

    ○ **D.** Critical

5. How often should BCP plans be updated?

   ○ **A.** Every 5 years

   ○ **B.** Every year or as required

   ○ **C.** Every 6 months

   ○ **D.** Upon any change or modification

6. When maintaining data backups at off-site locations, which of the following is the most important control concern?

   ○ **A.** That the storage site is as secure as the primary site

   ○ **B.** That a suitable tape-rotation plan is in use

   ○ **C.** That backup media is tested regularly

   ○ **D.** That copies of current critical information are kept off-site

7. The most important purpose of the BIA is which of the following?

   ○ **A.** Identify countermeasures

   ○ **B.** Prioritize critical systems

   ○ **C.** Develop recovery strategies

   ○ **D.** Determine potential test strategies

8. Which of the following is not a valid BCP test type?

   ○ **A.** Paper test

   ○ **B.** Structured walk-through

   ○ **C.** Full operation

   ○ **D.** Preparedness test

9. Which of the following is the practice of routing traffic through different cable facilities?

   ○ **A.** Alternate routing

   ○ **B.** Long-haul diversity

   ○ **C.** Diverse routing

   ○ **D.** Last-mile protection

10. When classifying critical systems, which category describes the following description: "These functions are important and can be performed by a backup manual process, but not for a long period of time."

- ○ **A.** Vital
- ○ **B.** Sensitive
- ○ **C.** Critical
- ○ **D.** Demand driven

Answers to Exam Questions

1. **B.** The recovery point objective is the earliest point in time at which recovery can occur. If RPO is low, tape backup or another solution is acceptable. Answer A is incorrect because a high RPO would require mirroring or other type of timely recovery method. Answer C is incorrect because a low RTO would mean that little time is available for recovery. Answer D is incorrect because a low fault tolerance indicates that little time is available for unavailable services.

2. **D.** Although hot sites are an expensive alternative, they are ready for service. Answer A is incorrect because they cannot be used for long-term processing. Answer B is incorrect because a hot site is a subscription service. Answer C is incorrect because there are additional fees; the organization must pay a variety of fees for usage, testing, and access.

3. **A.** JBOD allows users to combine multiple drives into one large drive. JBOD's only advantage is that, in case of drive failure, only the data on the affected drive is lost. Answers B, C, and D are incorrect because JBOD is not superior to disk mirroring, is not faster than RAID, and offers no fault tolerance.

4. **C.** Critical processes that produce revenue are considered a core activity. Answer A is incorrect because discretionary process are considered nonessential. Answer B is incorrect because supporting processes require only minimum BCP services. Answer D does not specify a process; *critical* is a term used to describe how important the service or process is.

5. **D.** BCP planning is an ongoing process that should be revisited each time there is a change to the environment. Therefore, answers A, B, and C are incorrect.

6. **D.** The most critical concern is keeping the copies of critical information current at an off-site location. Answers A, B, and C are important but are not the *most* important.

7. **B.** The BIA is an important part of the BCP process. The purpose of the BIA is to document the impact of outages, identify critical systems, prioritize critical systems, analyze outage impact, and determine recovery times needed to keep critical systems running. Answers A, C, and D are incorrect because they do not specify steps performed during the BIA.

8. **B.** There is no BCP test known as a structured walk-through. Valid types are listed in answers A, C, and D: paper tests, full operation test, and preparedness test.

9. **C.** Diverse routing is the practice of routing traffic through different cable facilities. Answer A is incorrect because alternate routing is the ability to use another transmission line if the regular line is busy or unavailable. Answer B is incorrect because long-haul diversity is the practice of having different long-distance communication carriers. Answer D is incorrect because last-mile protection provides a second local loop connection.

10. **A.** *Vital* meets the description of functions that are important and can be performed by a backup manual process, but not for a long period of time. Answer B is incorrect because it describes tasks that are important but can be performed manually at a reasonable cost. Answer C is incorrect because *critical* refers to extremely important functions. Answer D is incorrect because *demand driven* does not describe a valid functional label.

Need to Know More?

▶ Five Steps to Risk Assessment: http://tinyurl.com/2tn5tx

▶ Business Continuity Planning Model: http://www.drj.com/new2dr/model/bcmodel.htm

▶ BCP Good Practice Guidelines: http://www.thebci.org/gpg.htm

▶ Contingency Planning: http://tinyurl.com/2n2b99

▶ SLAs: http://www.disasterrecoveryworld.com/sla.htm

▶ Business Impact Analysis: http://tinyurl.com/2ornyb

▶ Exploring Backup Alternatives: http://www.ameinfo.com/39672.html

▶ Auditing BCP Plans: http://tinyurl.com/2l2mqf

PART VI

Final Preparation

Fast Facts

Practice Exam

Practice Exam Answers

Fast Facts

Certified Information Systems Auditor (CISA)

The fast facts listed in this chapter are designed as a refresher for some of the key knowledge areas required to pass the Certified Information Systems Auditor (CISA) certification exam. If you can spend an hour before your exam reading through this information, you will have a solid understanding of the key information required to succeed in each major area of the exam. You should be able to review the information presented here in less than an hour.

This summary cannot serve as a substitute for all the material supplied in this book. However, its key points should refresh your memory on critical topics. In addition to the information in this chapter, remember to review the glossary terms because they are intentionally not covered here.

ISACA (Information Systems Audit and Control Association) uses the job practice areas that are addressed in this book. The fast facts are arranged by these six job practice areas:

- ▶ IS Audit Process (approximately 10% of exam)

- ▶ IT Governance (approximately 15% of exam)

- ▶ Systems and Infrastructure Lifecycle Management (approximately 16% of exam)

- ▶ IT Service Delivery and Support (approximately 14% of exam)

- ▶ Protection of Information Assets (approximately 31% of exam)

- ▶ Business Continuity and Disaster Recovery (approximately 14% of exam)

1.0: IS Audit Process

Standards are agreed-upon principles of protocol. ISACA standards are designed and developed by the ISACA standards board, which meets twice a year to develop ISACA standards to help advance the IS auditing profession. The term *standard* is used here to describe the category of guidance document, as shown in Table 1.

TABLE 1   Guidance Document Description

Title	Description
Standards	These documents specify requirements that are considered mandatory.
Guidelines	These documents provide guidance and require professional judgment.
Procedures	These documents provide examples of activities and procedures an auditor can use to maintain standards.

The following are some common categories of risks:

▶ **Audit risk**—The risk that an auditor will accept

▶ **Control risk**—The risk that might not be detected by a system of internal controls

▶ **Business risk**—The risk that will affect the business's functional goals

▶ **Continuity risk**—The risk the business faces that it might not be able to recover from a disaster

▶ **Detection risk**—The risk that an improper test is performed that will not detect a material error

▶ **Material risk**—An unacceptable risk

▶ **Inherent risk**—The risk of a material misstatement in the unaudited information assumed in the absence of internal control procedures

▶ **Security risk**—The risk that unauthorized access to data will result in the exposure or loss of integrity of the data

Risk mitigation addresses how risks will be handled. Risks can be avoided, reduced, accepted, or transferred, as described in more detail here:

▶ **Avoid risk**—Avoiding risk can seem like a simple alternative. You simply don't perform the activity that allows the risk to be present. In reality, many activities cannot be avoided. Even when something can be avoided, an opportunity cost might be involved, so avoiding the risk can also avoid the opportunity for profit.

▸ **Reduce risk**—Reducing risk is one of the most common methods of dealing with a risk. An example of risk reduction could be installing a firewall or implementing a new internal accounting control.

▸ **Accept risk**—Risk acceptance means that the organization knows about the risk yet makes a conscious decision to accept the risk. Accepting risk means that the company is retaining the potential costs that are associated with the risk. As an example, a business might be thinking about building an e-commerce website but has determined that there will be an added risk. However, along with the risk is the potential to make greater revenues.

▸ **Transfer risk**—To transfer risk is to place the risk in someone else's hands. The best example of risk transference is insurance. Although there are benefits to the approach, there are also some drawbacks. Chief among these is that insurance is an ongoing expense. In addition, it is time-consuming and costly to document and settle relatively small losses. Finally, even small payouts by the insurance company can have an adverse effect on future insurance costs.

Management can use internal controls to exercise authority and effectively manage the organization. Controls typically start with high-level policy and are applied to all areas of the company. Controls filter down the organizational structure by means of policy and procedure. These procedures can be divided into two categories—general control and information system control; these are compared and contrasted in Table 2.

TABLE 2   Control Procedures

General Control Procedures	Information System Control Procedures
Internal accounting controls used to safeguard financial records	Procedures that provide reasonable assurance for the control of database administration
Operational controls that focus on day-to-day activities	Business continuity and disaster-recovery procedures that provide reasonable assurance that the organization is secure against disasters
Administrative controls designed for corporate compliance	System-development methodologies and change-control procedures have been implemented to protect the organization and maintain compliance
Procedures that safeguard access and use of organizational resources	Procedures that provide reasonable assurance for the control of access to data and programs
Logical security policies designed to support proper transactions	Procedures that provide reasonable assurance to control and manage data processing operations
Logical security policies designed to support transactional audit trails	Procedures that provide reasonable assurance for the control of networks and communications
Security policies that address the physical control of data centers	Physical access-control procedures developed to provide assurance for the organization's safety

Internal controls can be preventive, detective, or corrective, as described more fully in Table 3.

TABLE 3   Control Categories

Class	Function	Example
Preventive	Prevents problems before they occur	Access-control software that uses passwords, tokens, and/or biometrics
	Attempts to predict problems	Intrusion-prevention systems
		User registration process
Detective	Senses and detects problems as they occur	Internal audit functions
	Attempts to detect problems	Hashing algorithms
		Variance reports
		Intrusion-detection systems
Corrective	Reduces impact of a threat	Backup procedures
	Attempts to minimize the impact of a problem	Backup power supplies
		Intrusion-detection systems

Sampling is the process of selecting items from a population of interest. When sampling is required, the most appropriate method for the auditor is to pull samples in an automated method. The following are the different types of sampling:

▶ **Attribute sampling**—Attribute sampling is used primarily for compliance testing. It records deviations by measuring the rate of occurrence that a sample has a certain attribute.

▶ **Variable sampling**—Variable sampling is used primarily for substantive testing. It measures characteristics of the sample population, such as dollar amounts or other units of measurement.

Attribute sampling is the primary sampling method used for compliance testing.

While strong internal controls, separation of duties, procedures, recordkeeping, and a structure of responsibility can reduce the frequency of fraud, it can still occur. Auditors should not overlook any of the following items, which are fraud indicators:

▶ No clear lines of authority

▶ Lack of documents and records

▶ Lack of independent checks and balances

▶ Inadequate or nonexistent separation of duties

▶ Few internal controls

2.0: IT Governance

The primary role of an auditor in IT governance is to provide guidance and recommendations to senior management. The first step of this process is to review the following:

- **Learn the organization**—Know the company's goals and objectives. Start by reviewing the mission statement.

- **Review the IT strategic plan**—Strategic plans provide details for the next three to five years.

- **Analyze organizational charts**—Become familiar with the roles and responsibility of individuals within the company.

- **Study job descriptions**—Job descriptions detail the level of responsibility and accountability for employees' actions.

- **Evaluate existing policies and procedures**—These documents detail the approved activities of employees.

The policy process can be driven from the top or from the bottom of the organization:

- In top-down policy development, policies are pushed down from the top of the company. The advantage of a top-down policy development approach is that it ensures that policy is aligned with the strategy of the company. What it lacks is speed; this process requires a substantial amount of time to implement.

- Bottom-up policy development addresses the concerns of operational employees: It starts with their input and concerns, and builds on known risk. This is faster than a top-down approach, but it does not always map well with high-level strategy.

Direct observation is the best way to identify problems between procedure and activity. As an example, if a policy specifies a lockout policy but direct observation reveals that a no-lockout policy has been implemented, an auditor can then interview the process owner to find out why.

Standards, policies, and procedures all lay out important administrative controls. Table 4 highlights their relationship to the goal of the organization.

TABLE 4 Documentation/Level of Control

Level/Document	Policy	Standard	Procedure
Strategic	✓		
Tactical		✓	
Operational			✓

Table 5 shows sample quantitative risk assessment results.

The steps for quantitative risk assessment are as follows:

1. **Determine the exposure factor**—This is a subjective potential percentage of loss to a specific asset if a specific threat is realized. This is usually in the form of a percentage, similar to how weather reports predict the likelihood of weather conditions.

2. **Calculate the single loss expectancy (SLE)**—The SLE value is a dollar figure that represents the organization's loss from a single loss or the loss of this particular information asset. SLE is calculated as follows:

   Single Loss Expectancy = Asset Value × Exposure Factor

   Items to consider when calculating the SLE include the physical destruction or theft of assets, loss of data, theft of information, and threats that might delay processing.

3. **Assign a value for the annualized rate of occurrence (ARO)**—The ARO represents the estimated frequency at which a given threat is expected to occur. Simply stated, how many times is this expected to happen in one year?

4. **Assign a value for the annualized loss expectancy (ALE)**—The ALE is an annual expected financial loss to an organization's information asset because of a particular threat occurring within that same calendar year. ALE is calculated as follows:

   Annualized Loss Expectancy (ALE) =

   Single Loss Expectancy (SLE) × Annualized Rate of Occurrence (ARO)

   The ALE is typically the value that senior management needs to assess to prioritize resources and determine what threats should receive the most attention.

5. **Analyze the risk to the organization**—The final step is to evaluate the data and decide to accept, reject, or transfer the risk.

TABLE 5 Sample Assessment Results

Asset	Risk	Asset Value	EF	SLE	Annualized Frequency	ALE
Customer database	Loss of consumer data due to no backup	$118,000	78.06%	$92,121	.25	$23,030
E-commerce website	Hacked	$22,500	35.50%	$8,000	.45	$3,600
Domain controller	Power supply failure	$16,500	27.27%	$4,500	.25	$1,125

ISO 9001 certification requires an organization to perform a deficiency assessment or gap analysis. This allows the company to identify shortcomings that must be addressed to obtain certification.

Some basic common controls should be used during the hiring process:

- Background checks
- Education checks
- Reference checks
- Confidentiality agreements
- Noncompete agreements
- Conflict of interest agreements

After they're hired, employees should be provided with an employee handbook that details employees' code of conduct, acceptable use of company assets, and employee responsibilities to the company. Per ISACA, the handbook should address the following issues:

- Security practices, policies, and procedures
- Employee package of benefits
- Paid holiday and vacation policy
- Work schedule and overtime policy
- Moonlighting and outside employment
- Employee evaluations
- Disaster response and emergency procedures
- Disciplinary action process for noncompliance

The Capability Maturity Model (CMM) has five maturity levels, shown in Table 6.

TABLE 6 Capability Maturity Model

Maturity Level	Name	Description
1	Initial	This is an ad-hoc process with no assurance of repeatability.
2	Repeatable	Change control and quality assurance are in place and controlled by management, although a formal process is not defined.
3	Defined	Defined process and procedures are in place and used. Qualitative process improvement is in place.
4	Managed	Qualitative data is collected and analyzed. A process-improvement program is used.
5	Optimized	Continuous process improvement is in place and has been budgeted for.

Control Objectives for Information and Related Technology (*CobiT*) was designed for performance management and IT management, and is considered a system of best practices. CobiT was created by ISACA and the IT Governance Institute (ITGI) in 1992. It is designed around 34 key processes, which address the following:

- Performance concerns

- IT control profiling

- Awareness

- Benchmarking

3.0: Systems and Infrastructure Lifecycle Management

Projects are constrained by their scope, time, and cost. Therefore, one must consider the following:

- **Scope**—How much work is defined? What do the sponsor and the customer expect from this project?

- **Time**—How long is this project scheduled to run? Does it have a defined schedule?

- **Cost**—How much money is this project expected to cost? Has the sponsor approved it?

Projects must take on an organizational form. Table 7 shows the primary types of project organizational forms.

TABLE 7   Project Organizational Types

Name	Description
Pure project	The project manager holds formal authority.
	Team might also have a dedicated project work area.
Influence	The project manager has no real authority, and the functional manager remains in charge.
Weak matrix	The project manager has little or no authority and is part of the functional organization.
Balanced matrix	The project manager has some functional authority and shares management duties with functional managers.
Strong matrix	In this more expensive model, members are assigned to dedicated tasks. The advantage is that this offers a greater level of authority.

Critical path methodology (CPM) determines what activities are critical and identifies the dependencies between the various tasks. CPM is accomplished by doing the following:

▶ Compiling a list of each task required to complete the project

▶ Determining the time that each task will take from start to finish

▶ Examining the dependencies between each task

Table 8 describes each phase of the system development lifecycle (SDLC).

TABLE 8   SDLC Overview

SDLC Step	Description
Feasibility	Benefits are determined at this phase of the SDLC.
Requirements	The purpose of the project must be defined. What user need will this project meet?
Design	Based on the requirements and user input, a specification should be developed. At this point, the auditor must verify that all required controls are in the design.
Development	Developers begin to write code, and verification and testing occur.
Implementation	Final user testing occurs, and the application is placed into operation.
Post-implementation	A formal review should evaluate the adequacy of the system. A cost-benefit analysis and review can be performed to determine the value of the project and to improve future projects.

An entity relationship diagram (ERD) helps map the requirements and define the relationship between elements. The basic components of an ERD are an entity and relationship. An entity is very much like a database, in that it is a grouping of like data elements. An entity has specific attributes, which are called the entity's primary key. Entities are drawn as a rectangular box with an identifying name. Relationships describe how entities are related to each other and are defined as a diamond.

In computer programming, it is important to test software to make sure it meets all requirements. Test classifications are divided into the following categories:

▶ **Unit testing**—Examines an individual program or module

▶ **Interface testing**—Examines hardware or software to evaluate how well data can be passed from one entity to another

▶ **System testing**—Consists of a series of tests, which can include recovery testing, security testing, stress testing, volume testing, regression testing, and performance testing

▶ **Final acceptance testing**—Usually performed at the implementation phase, after the project staff has satisfied all other tests and when the application is ready to be deployed

Table 9 lists some other types of tests used for requirement verification.

TABLE 9   Testing Types

Test Type	Description
Alpha test	The first and earliest version of an application, followed by a beta version. Both are considered prerelease.
Pilot test	Used as an evaluation to verify the application's functionality.
White-box test	Verifies inner program logic; is cost-prohibitive on a large application or system.
Black-box test	Integrity-based testing; looks at inputs and outputs.
Function test	Validates the program against a checklist of requirements.
Regression test	Used after a system or software change to verify that inputs and outputs are correct.
Parallel test	Used to verify a new or changed system by feeding data into a new and unchanged system and comparing the results.
Sociability test	Verifies that the system can operate in its target environment.

Changeover techniques include the following:

▶ **Parallel operation**—Both the old and new systems are run at the same time. Results between the two systems can be compared. Fine-tuning can also be performed on the new system as needed. As confidence in the new system improves, the old system can be shut down. The primary disadvantage of this method is that both systems must be maintained for a period of time.

▶ **Phased changeover**—If the system is large, a phased changeover might be possible. With this method, systems are upgraded one piece at a time.

▶ **Hard changeover**—This method establishes a date when users will be forced to change over. The advantage of the hard changeover is that it forces all users to change at once. However, this introduces a level of risk into the environment because things can go wrong.

The SDLC is not the only development methodology used today. As an auditor, you must be knowledgeable of other development methods and have a basic understanding of their operation.

▶ **Incremental development**—This method defines an approach that develops systems in stages so that development is performed one step at a time. A minimal working system can be deployed while subsequent releases build on functionally or scope.

▶ **Waterfall**—This well-defined linear model assumes that requirements will remain stable.

▶ **Spiral development**—The spiral model was developed based on the experience of the waterfall model. The spiral model is based on the concept that software development is evolutionary. It begins by creating a series of prototypes to develop a solution. As the project continues it spirals out, becoming more detailed. Each step passes through planning, requirements, risks, and development phases.

▶ **Prototyping**—The prototyping model reduces the time required to deploy applications. Prototyping uses high-level code to quickly turn design requirements into application screens and reports that the users can review. User feedback is used to fine-tune the application and improve it. Top-down testing works well with prototyping. Although prototyping clarifies user requirements, it can result in overly optimistic project timelines. Also, because change happens quickly, it might not be properly documented, which is a real concern for the auditor.

▶ **Rapid application development (RAD)**—RAD uses an evolving prototype and requires heavy user involvement. Per ISACA, RAD requires well-trained development teams that use integrated power tools for modeling and prototyping. With the RAD model, strict limits are placed on development time. RAD has four unique stages, which include concept, functional design, development, and deployment.

▶ **Extreme programming (XP)**—The XP development model requires that teams include business managers, programmers, and end users. These teams are responsible for developing useable applications in short periods of time. Issues with XP include that teams are responsible not only for coding, but also for writing the tests used to verify the code. Lack of documentation is another concern. XP does not scale well for large projects.

▶ **Scrum**—Scrum is an iterative development method in which repetitions are referred to as sprints and typically last 30 days. Scrum is typically used with object-oriented technology, requires strong leadership, and requires the team to meet each day for a short time. The idea is to move planning and directing tasks from the project manager to the team. The project manager's main task is to work on removing any obstacles from the team's path.

Table 10 provides an overview of input/output, processing, and output controls.

TABLE 10   Business Process Controls

Input/Output Controls	Processing Controls	Output Controls
Input authorization	Processing	Logging
Batch controls	Validation	Security signatures
	Editing	Report distribution
		Balancing and reconciliation

Table 11 lists the control techniques used to protect the integrity of the data.

TABLE 11   Processing Control Techniques

Processing Control	Description
Manual recalculations	Some transactions might be recalculated to ensure that processing is operating correctly.
Editing	This program instruction controls input or processing of data to verify its validity.
Run-to-run totals	This ensures the validity of data through various stages of processing.
Programming controls	These software-based controls flag problems and initiate corrective action.
Reasonableness verification	This ensures the reasonableness of data. For example, someone might try to process a negative amount through a payment system.
Limit checks	These checks set bounds on what are reasonable amounts. For example, someone might attempt to order 565 flat-screen TVs.
Reconciliation of file totals	This refers to the act of balancing debits, credits, and totals between two systems. Reconciliation should be performed periodically to verify accuracy and completeness of data.
Exception reports	This type of report should be generated when transactions appear to be incorrect.

Table 12 describes edit controls.

TABLE 12   Processing Edit Controls

Validation Edit	Description
Sequence check	Sequence numbers are used to make sure that all data falls within a given range. For example, checks are numbered sequentially. If the day's first check that was issued was number 120 and the day's last check was number 144, all checks issued that day should fall between those numbers, and none should be missing.
Limit check	Data to be processed should not exceed a predetermined limit. For example, the weekly sale item might be limited to five per customer. Sales over that amount should trigger an alert.
Range check	A range check ensures that a date is within a predetermined range. For example, a range check might verify that the date is after 01/01/2000 and before 01/01/2010.
Validity check	This type of check is used to check the validity of a data. For example, orders to be processed today should be dated with today's date.
Reasonableness check	This check verifies the reasonableness of the data. For example, if an order is usually for no more than 20 items yet this order is for 2,000 items, an alert should be generated.
Table look-ups	This check verifies that the data matches the data in a lookup table.
Existence check	An existence check verifies that all required data is entered.
Key verification	Key verification requires a second employee to reenter the data. There must be a match before the data can be processed.

TABLE 12 *Continued*

Validation Edit	Description
Check digit	A check digit is used to verify accuracy. A check digit is a sum of a value appended to the data.
Completeness check	This check ensures that all required data has been added and that no fields contain null values.
Duplicate check	This check ensures that a data item is not a duplicate. For example, before payment is made, accounts payable must verify that invoice number 833 for $1,612 has not already been paid.
Logical relationship check	This type of edit check verifies logic; if one condition is true, additional items must also be true. For example, if the data shows that an applicant is old enough to vote, logic dictates that the person must have been born before 1989.

Per ISACA, output controls should address the following:

▶ Logging and storage of sensitive negotiable and critical forms

▶ Negotiable instruments, forms, and signatures that are computer generated

▶ Distribution control

▶ Balancing and reconciliation of control totals

▶ Output errors (logged and reviewed)

▶ Retention records that specify how long output data should be stored or maintained

When working with applications, auditors should observe and test the items in Table 13.

TABLE 13 Observation and Test

Observation/Test	Details
Separation of duties	Auditors should verify separation of duties, which provides control by limiting ability of each employee. As an example, operators should not also have the ability to review work or clear the audit log.
Input authorization	Auditors should review records to verify who is authorized to access applications. If supervisor override is used frequently, this might signal problems.
Balancing	Auditors should verify that run-to-run totals are reconciled on a timely basis.
Report distribution	Auditors should review report distribution logs to see who has access and whether the reports are properly controlled.
Error correction and control	Auditors should review past error corrections and verify that they are viewed and addressed in a timely manner.
Access control and authorization	Auditors should verify that access is limited to individuals who have a clearly demonstrated need. Testing can be performed to ensure that access controls are in place as specified.

Continuous online auditing also increases security. Overall, five techniques are used, as described in Table 14.

TABLE 14   Continuous Audit Techniques

Name	Description	Level of Complexity	Attribute
Systems control audit review file and embedded audit modules (SCARF/EAM)	The application must contain embedded audit software to act as a monitoring agent	◆◆◆◆◆	Cannot be used to interrupt regular processing
Integrated test facilities	Live and dummy data is fed into the system. The results of the dummy data are compared to precalculated results.	◆◆◆◆	Should not be used with test data
Continuous and intermittent simulation (CIS)	CIS simulates the transaction run. If data meets certain criteria, the simulator logs the transaction; otherwise, processing continues.	◆◆◆	Requires examination of transactions that meet specific criteria
Snapshots	This technique tags transactions and then takes snapshots as the data is moved from input to output.	◆◆◆	Requires an audit trail
Audit hooks	This technique uses embedded hooks that act as red flags if certain conditions are met.	◆◆	Detects items that meet specific criteria

4.0: IT Service Delivery and Support

The auditor should know to review the problem log to verify that problems are being resolved. Auditors must also check to see that problems are being handled by the most appropriate department or individual.

Sufficient controls should be in place to prevent nonproduction code from inadvertently being executed in the production environment. Ensuring that these requirements are met is a complicated task that can be made easier by verifying that the program library system has certain capabilities:

▶ **Integrity**—Each piece of source code should be assigned a unique ID and version number. Security should be maintained through password-controlled directories, encryption, and regular backups. Periodic security audits should be performed.

▶ **Update**—Any changes or modification to source code should be tracked, and an audit trail should be produced.

▶ **Reporting**—Controls should be in place to report changes to code or any modification.

▶ **Interface**—Library management systems need to interface with the OS, access-control system, audit, and access-control mechanisms.

Source code comparison is one way to verify code. However, it is important to be aware that source code comparison has its limitations. As an example, it cannot detect a change in source code that has been changed and restored between checks. Compiled code must also be examined.

Release management is the discipline within software management of controlling the release of software to end users. Releases can be divided into one of several categories:

▶ **Emergency fix**—These are updates that need to be done quickly. These are sometimes referred to as a patch. An emergency fix is designed to fix a small number of known problems. This can be dangerous because it might introduce additional errors into the program.

▶ **Minor release**—Minor releases contain small enhancements or fixes that supersede an emergency fix. Minor releases improve performance, reliability, or security.

▶ **Major release**—Major releases supersede minor releases and emergency fixes. They are designed to provide a significant improvement to the program. Major releases are usually scheduled to be released at predetermined times, such as quarterly, biannually, or yearly.

CPUs have two primary components, the control unit and the arithmetic logic unit. The arithmetic logic unit is where computations are performed and can be described as the brain of the CPU. The control unit handles the sequence of operations for the CPU and is also responsible for the retrieval of instructions and data. CPUs also have different types of registers to hold data and instructions.

CPUs can be classified in one of several categories, based on its functionality:

▶ **Multiprogramming**—The CPU can interleave two or more programs for execution at any one time.

▶ **Multitasking**—The CPU can perform one or more tasks or subtasks at a time.

▶ **Multiprocessor**—The computer has support for more than one CPU. As an example, Windows 95 does not support a multiprocessor, but Windows Longhorn does.

ROM is typically used to load and store firmware. ROM is considered nonvolatile, in that it retains information even if power is removed. Some common types of ROM include the following:

▶ Erasable Programmable Read-Only Memory (EPROM)

▶ Electrically Erasable Programmable Read-Only Memory (EEPROM)

▶ Flash memory

▶ Programmable logic devices (PLD)

Computers can be categorized by the role they play in the organization, their amount of processing power, and their architecture or design. Table 15 outlines the common computer types.

TABLE 15 Computer Types

Computer Type	Description
Server	Computers that share resources such as applications, files, or web content with other computers and clients on a network. Servers are typically dedicated to one task, such as a web server, file server, or DHCP server.
Supercomputer	Large, expensive computers that have great processing power. An example is the Cray supercomputer. Supercomputers can cost billions of dollars and have extremely vast capabilities. This category of computer can also include clusters, such as the Beowulf system.
Mainframe	Large general-purpose computers that at one time were the predominant type of computer. Mainframes are usually used in a centralized design and typically have their own proprietary operating systems.
Client	Desktops found throughout organizations based on microprocessor technology. Client systems allow users to perform many activities, such as word processing and spreadsheet activities, locally. Client systems typically use either the Microsoft or Linux operating systems.
Laptop	Lightweight and easily transportable. Laptops are similar to desktops but have built-in battery supplies and allow workers to make their computer mobile. One major problem is theft. Laptop computers should use encryption to protect confidential information from loss or exposure.
PDAs/handhelds	Small computing devices such as Blackberrys, Palm Pilots, and cell phones. These devices have some computing power, along with the ability to check email, perform scheduling, and make and receive phone calls. Thet and loss are also problems for these devices.

Most networks also consist of some common hardware elements, which are discussed in more depth in Chapter 6 but are summarized here in Table 16.

TABLE 16   Common Hardware Elements Used for IT Delivery

Name	Description
Firewall	A specialized device that inspects traffic traveling into and out of the organization's network. Also used between internal segments, such as finance and HR.
Intrusion-detection system	A detective device that sniffs network or host traffic and inspects it for malicious content.
Router	Devices used to link physically separate networks.
Switch	Data-link devices used to increase performance and reduce traffic collisions.
Load balancer	Distributed traffic among several different devices. Commonly used for distributing web traffic on large domains.
Hub	A physical-layer device used for connectivity. As such, traffic on hubs is susceptible to collisions.

Capacity management requires analyzing current utilization, past performance, and capacity changes. Table 17 lists capacity-management issues.

TABLE 17   Capacity-Management Issues

Item	Indicator
CPU utilization	High usage indicates a needed processor or computer upgrade.
Computer storage	Lack of space indicates the need for additional hard disk storage.
Network bandwidth	Low bandwidth might indicate the need for a network upgrade to Gigabit or better control over traffic, music streaming, P2P, and so on.
Terminal utilization	High utilization might indicate the need for additional terminals.
Total number of users	Additional users usually indicate the need for more terminals or computers.
Application usage	High application usage requires the inspection of licensing agreements.
Service level agreements	Monitoring should be preformed to verify that the organization is getting the bandwidth for which the organization is paying. Growth requires a review of existing service level agreements.

Programs can be hard-coded instruction or firmware, or can be executed by a higher-layer process. Regardless of the format, code must be translated into a language that the computer will understand. The three most common methods of conversion are as follows:

▶ **Assembler**—An assembler is a program that translates assembly language into machine language.

▶ **Compiler**—A compiler translates a high-level language into machine language.

▶ **Interpreter**—An interpreter does not assemble or compile; it takes an alternate approach and translates the program line by line. Interpreters fetch and execute.

The five generations of computer languages are as follows:

- ▶ Generation One: Machine language
- ▶ Generation Two: Assembly language
- ▶ Generation Three: High-level language, such as FORTRAN
- ▶ Generation Four: Very high-level language, such as Structured Query Language
- ▶ Generation Five: Natural language, such as Prolog or LISP

Databases are widely used. If you are not familiar with databases, you might not be familiar with the following terms:

- ▶ **Aggregation**—The process of combining several low-sensitivity items to produce a higher-sensitivity data item.
- ▶ **Attribute**—A single data item related to a database object.
- ▶ **Field**—The smallest unit of data within a database.
- ▶ **Foreign key**—An attribute in one table whose value matches the primary key in another table.
- ▶ **Granularity**—The control one has over the view someone has of the database. Highly granular databases can restrict certain fields or rows from unauthorized individuals.
- ▶ **Relation**—Data that is represented by a collection of tables.

Per ISACA, three primary types of database structures exist:

- ▶ Hierarchical database-management systems (HDMS)
- ▶ Network database-management systems (NDMS)
- ▶ Relational database-management systems (RDMS)

During transactions, controls can be put in place. These are sometimes referred to as the *acid test*, which is defined as follows:

- ▶ **A**tomicity—Results of a transaction are either all or nothing.
- ▶ **C**onsistency—Transactions are processed only if they meet system-defined integrity constraints.
- ▶ **I**solation—The results of a transaction are invisible to all other transactions until the original transaction is complete.
- ▶ **D**urability—Once complete, the results of the transaction are permanent.

The ISO is recognized for its development of the OSI model. The ISO set the worldwide standards for its work in developing a common approach to networking. The seven layers of the OSI model are application, presentation, session, transport, network, data link, and physical.

Networks can use a variety of topologies. The topology is the physical design of the network. Topologies include bus, star, ring, and mesh, as summarized in Table 18.

TABLE 18   Description and Features of Various Topologies

Topology	Feature	Advantage	Disadvantage
Bus	A single length of cable is used.	The design is simple.	The design is hard to expand. One break can disable the entire segment.
Star	Devices all connect to a central wiring point.	Expansion does not disrupt other systems.	More cable is required.
		A cable failure affects only one device.	A hub or switch is required.
Ring	Devices are connected in a loop.	The design is easy to trouble-shoot and fault- tolerant if dual rings are used.	Network expansion creates a disruption.
Mesh	All points have redundant connections.	Multiple links provide greater fault tolerance.	The design is expensive to implement.
		Expansion requires little or no disruption.	

Table 19 provides an overview of the primary types of network equipment.

TABLE 19   Network Equipment

Equipment	OSI Layer	Description
Gateway	OSI Layer 4 or higher	Gateways operate at the transport layer and above. Gateways translate each source-layer protocol into the appropriate destination-layer protocol. As an example, an application-layer gateway is found at Layer 7.
Router	OSI Layer 3	Routers connect distant sites connected by a WAN, improve performance by limiting physical broadcast domains, and ease network management by segmenting devices into smaller subnets, rather than one large network.
Switch	OSI Layer 2	Switches are hardware-based and provide logical segmentation by observing the source and destination physical address of each data frame. Many switches can provide *network virtual LANs* (VLANs), which separate various ports on a switch and segment traffic much like a Layer 3 router would.
Bridge	OSI Layer 2	Bridges connect two separate collision domains and provide physical segmentation. Bridges are software based and do not block broadcast traffic.

(continues)

TABLE 19 *Continued*

Equipment	OSI Layer	Description
Hub	OSI Layer 1	Hubs connect individual devices and provide physical connectivity so that devices can share data. Hubs amplify and regenerate the electrical signals. They are similar to a repeater, except that hubs have multiple ports.
Repeater	OSI Layer 1	Repeaters are designed only to boost signal strength and remove noise. They are designed to overcome cable distance limitations.

5.0: Protection of Information Assets

Privacy of personal information is a very important issue. Companies need to address this concern early by developing a company-wide policy based on a privacy impact analysis (PIA). The PIA should evaluate privacy risks and ensure that appropriate privacy controls exist.

The discretionary access control (DAC) model is so titled because access control is left to the owner's discretion. DAC allows the owner to activate security controls as necessary. An analogy of DAC can be seen in a peer-to-peer network.

A mandatory access control (MAC) model is static and based on a predetermined list of access privileges; therefore, in a MAC-based system, access is determined by the system rather than the user. Organizations that handle highly sensitive data, such as the U.S. Department of Defense, the National Security Administration, the Central Intelligence Agency, and the Federal Bureau of Investigation, typically use the MAC model.

Three authentication methods exist:

▶ **Authentication by knowledge**—What a user knows

▶ **Authentication by ownership**—What a user has

▶ **Authentication by characteristic**—What a person is and does

Biometric systems are an example of authentication by characteristic, whether it is by a physiological trait, such as a fingerprint or retina scan, or by behavioral characteristic, such as keystroke or signature pattern. Some common biometric types include the following:

▶ Fingerprint

▶ Hand geometry

▶ Palm scan

▶ Voice pattern

- ▶ Retina pattern/scan

- ▶ Iris pattern/recognition

- ▶ Signature dynamics

- ▶ Facial recognition

- ▶ Keystroke dynamics

Important concerns for the IS auditor when examining biometric systems include the following:

- ▶ **False reject rate (FRR)**—The FRR is the percentage of legitimate users who are denied access. This is also known as Type I errors.

- ▶ **False accept rate (FAR)**—This measurement is the percentage of users who are allowed access and who are not authorized users. This is also known as Type II errors.

- ▶ **Equal error rate (EER)**—A measurement that indicates the point at which FRR equals FAR. Low numbers indicate that the system has greater accuracy.

Passive attacks do not inject traffic into the network or attempt other types of active activities. Sniffing, done with a network sniffer or analyzer, is a good example of a passive attack.

Active attacks inject traffic, modify systems, and seek to change settings to gain access or escalate privilege of the network or system. The least technical active attack is social engineering.

What if passive or active attacks don't work? The attacker might decide to launch a *denial-of-service* (DoS) attack. Some common DoS attacks include the following:

- ▶ **Ping of death**—Uses an oversized IP packet.

- ▶ **Smurf**—Sends a message to the broadcast of a subnet or network so that every node on the network produces one or more response packets.

- ▶ **Syn flood**—Manipulates the standard three-way handshake used by TCP.

- ▶ **Trinoo**—Launches UDP flood attacks from various channels on a network.

- ▶ **Botnets**—Botnets are another tool used for DDoS attacks. A *botnet* is a collection of computers hijacked during virus and worm attacks that are now under the control of a remote attacker. Botnets can be used to launch a variety of TCP and UDP flood attacks.

Firewalls have gone through what are considered generational improvements. The five generations of firewalls include the following:

▶ **Packet filtering**—These are considered the first generation of firewalls. Packet filtering can be performed by routers and is the lowest form of packet inspection. Packet filters cannot keep track of status and make a pass or drop decision on items such as port, protocol, and IP address.

▶ **Stateful inspection**—Stateful-inspection firewalls provide the same functionality as packet filters, but they can track the status of the session. Therefore, if a type of reply is presented to the firewall, it can actually look to see if this reply is in response to a valid request.

▶ **Proxy**—A proxy is referred to as a circuit-level firewall because it resides between a client and the Internet. A proxy stands in place of each party. It increases security by presenting a single IP address to the Internet and prevents direct access to an internal client.

▶ **Dynamic packet filtering**—This generation of firewalls addresses the challenges of dynamic ports. As an example, when an FTP client communicates to an FTP server, a dynamically assigned port is used to transfer files and data. Historically, a firewall administrator might have left a wide range of high-order ports open for this activity. Dynamic packet filtering allows an open port to be generated as needed and then closed when the communication is completed.

▶ **Kernel proxy**—In this fifth and most advanced type of firewall, a kernel proxy builds a virtual stack to examine each packet at each layer to ensure integrity. Not only is a kernel proxy fast, but it also can perform address translation.

Intrusion-detection systems (IDS) play a critical role in the protection of the IT infrastructure. *Intrusion detection* involves monitoring network traffic, detecting attempts to gain unauthorized access to a system or resource, and notifying the appropriate individuals so that counteractions can be taken.

IDS systems can be divided into two broad categories:

▶ Network-based intrusion-detection systems (NIDs)

▶ Host-based intrusion-detection systems (HIDs)

IDS detection methods include the following:

▶ **Statistical**—This IDS detection method requires the administrator to use profiles of authorized activities or place them into the IDS so that it understands normal activity. A considerable amount of time is needed to make sure the IDS produce few false negatives. These systems trigger when individuals deviate from specified behavior.

▶ **Signature**—This IDS detection method requires the administrator to load a database of known attacks. As soon as the signatures are loaded into the IDS, it can begin to guard the network. These systems cannot guard against new attacks that have not yet been loaded into the IDS.

▶ **Neural**—This IDS detection method requires the administrator to place the IDS in learning mode so that it understands normal patterns of activity. It functions much like a statistical IDS. These systems can be fooled because the attack makes very small incremental changes.

Symmetric encryption uses a single shared secret key for encryption and decryption. Symmetric algorithms include the following:

▶ **Data Encryption Standard (DES)**—The most common symmetric algorithm used.

▶ **Blowfish**—A general-purpose symmetric algorithm intended as a replacement for the DES; it has been replaced by AES and Twofish.

▶ **Rijndael**—A block cipher that the U.S. government adopted as the Advanced Encryption Standard (AES) to replace DES.

▶ **RC4**—Rivest Cipher 4, a stream-based cipher

▶ **RC5**—Rivest Cipher 5, a block-based cipher

▶ **SAFER**—Secure and Fast Encryption Routine, a block-based cipher

Per ISACA requirements, CISA candidates should have a basic understanding of *public key infrastructure* (PKI). PKI is a framework that consists of hardware, software, and policies that manage, create, store, and distribute keys and digital certificates. The components of the PKI framework include the following:

▶ **Certificate authority (CA)**—The CA is a person or group that issues certificates to authorized users. The CA creates and signs the certificate, to guarantee the authenticity of the certificate.

▶ **The Certificate Revocation List (CRL)**—The CA maintains the CRL list. The list is signed to verify its accuracy and used to report problems with certificates. When requesting a digital certificate, anyone can check the CRL to verify the certificate's integrity.

▶ **The Registration authority (RA)**—The RA reduces the load on the CA. The RA cannot generate a certificate, but it can accept requests, verify an owner's identity, and pass along the information to the CA for certificate generation.

▶ **Certificate server**—The certificate server maintains the database of stored certificates.

▶ **X.509 standard**—This is the accepted standard for digital certificates.

Physical security controls have three primary goals:

▶ **Deter**—Security lighting and armed guards are two examples of methods used to deter intruders.

▶ **Delay**—Fences, gates, locks, access controls, and mantraps are some of the techniques that can be used to delay intruders.

▶ **Detect**—Closed-circuit TV (CCTV) and alarms are two examples of systems used to detect intruders.

Power systems can suffer from a range of problems. Table 20 shows the most common ones and their solutions.

TABLE 20   Network Equipment

Power Condition	Solution
Blackout	Generator
Brownout	Uninterrupted power supply (UPS)
Surge	Surge protector
Spike	Surge protector
Noise	Power conditioner
Clean power	No solution needed

Halon was originally used in computer rooms for fire suppression. Halon mixes easily with air, doesn't harm computer equipment, and, when dissipated, leaves no solid or liquid residue. The downside is that Halon is 3 to 10 times more damaging to the ozone layer than CFCs. The Montreal Protocol of 1987 designated Halon as an ozone-depleting substance. The most common replacement is FM-200.

6.0: Business Continuity and Disaster Recovery

Per ISACA, incidents can be classified as shown in Table 21.

TABLE 21   Incident Classification

Level	Description
Crisis	A crisis is considered a major problem. It is of sufficient impact to adversely affect the organization's ability to continue business functions.
Major	A major incident can cause a negative impact on one or more departments and might even affect external clients.
Minor	Although noticeable, these events result in little or no damage.
Negligible	These detectable events cause no damage and have no longer-term effect.

The business continuity plan (BCP) process as defined by ISACA focuses on the following seven steps.

1. Project management and initiation

2. Business impact analysis

3. Recovery strategy

4. Plan design and development

5. Training and awareness

6. Implementation and testing

7. Monitoring and maintenance

Questions auditors must ask when determining what processes are critical can include the following:

▶ **Does the process support health and safety?**—Items such as the loss of an air traffic control system at a major airport or the loss of power in a hospital operating room could be devastating to those involved and result in the loss of life.

▶ **Does the loss of the process have a negative impact on income?**—As an example, a company such as eBay would find the loss of Internet connectivity devastating, whereas a small nonprofit organization might be able to live without connectivity for days.

▶ **Does the loss of the process violate legal or statutory requirements?**—As an example, a coal-powered electrical power plant might use scrubbers to clean the air before emissions are released. Loss of these scrubbers might violate federal law and result in huge regulatory fines.

▶ **Does the loss of the process affect a large number of users?**—Returning to our example electrical power plant, it is easy to see how problems with the steam-generation process would shut down power generation and leave many residential and business customers without power.

The general steps of the business impact analysis (BIA) include the following:

1. Determine data-gathering techniques

2. Gather business impact analysis data

3. Identify critical business functions and resources

4. Verify completeness of data

5. Establish recovery time for operations

6. Define recovery alternatives and costs

At the core of the BIA are two critical items:

▶ The *recovery point objective (RPO)* defines how current the data must be or how much data an organization can afford to lose. The greater the RPO, the more tolerant the process is to interruption.

▶ The *recovery time objective (RTO)* specifies the maximum elapsed time to recover an application at an alternate site. The greater the RTO, the longer the process can take to be restored.

For both RPO and RTO, the lower the time requirements are, the higher the cost will be to reduce loss or restore the system as quickly as possible.

Per ISACA, the scale shown in Table 22 classifies systems according to their importance to the organization.

TABLE 22 Priority Ranking

Classification	Description
Critical	These extremely important functions cannot be performed with duplicate systems or processes. These functions are extremely intolerant to disruptions, so any disruption is very costly.
Vital	Although these functions are important, they can be performed by a backup manual process—but only for a short period of time. These systems can tolerate disruptions of typically five days or less.
Sensitive	Although these tasks are important, they can be performed manually at a reasonable cost. However, this is an inconvenience and will require additional resources or manpower.
Noncritical	These services are not critical and can be interrupted. They then can be restored later, with little or no negative effects.

ISACA defines three types of BCP tests:

▶ The most basic disaster-recovery test is the *paper test*. Although it is not considered a replacement for a real test, it is a good start. A paper test is an exercise that can be performed by sending copies of the plan to different department managers and business unit managers for review to make sure nothing is overlooked or to remove something that was added.

▶ A *preparedness test* is a simulation in which team members go through an exercise that reenacts an actual outage or disaster. This type of test is typically used to test a portion of the plan. The preparedness test consumes time and money because it is an actual test that measures the team's response to situations that might someday occur. This type of testing provides a means of incrementally improving the plan.

▶ The *full operational test* is as close to the actual service disruption as you can get. The team should have preformed paper tests and preparedness tests before attempting this level of interruption. This test is the most detailed, time-consuming, and thorough of all discussed. A full interruption test mimics a real disaster, and all steps are performed to startup backup operations. It involves all individuals who would be involved in a real emergency, including internal and external organizations.

No demonstrated recovery exists until a test is performed.

Practice Exam

Certified Information Systems Auditor (CISA)

This exam consists of 135 questions that reflect the material covered in this book. The questions represent the types of questions you should expect to see on the Certified Information Systems Auditor exam; however, they are not intended to match exactly what is on the exam. The exam requires candidates to use higher learning skills, working through more than just knowledge questions.

Some of the questions require that you deduce the best possible answer. In other cases, you are asked to identify the best course of action to take in a given situation. Some questions are considered enhanced in that you will be required to examine a figure, graphic, or other item to properly answer the question. You must read the questions carefully and thoroughly before you attempt to answer them. It is strongly recommended that you treat this exam as if it were the actual exam. The actual exam has 200 questions with a four-hour time limit. This means that you should spend no more than two hours and 42 minutes on this practice exam. When you take it, time yourself, read carefully, and answer all the questions to the best of your ability. It also worth noting that passing the exam requires the candidate to be familiar with a voluminous list of terms. Although the candidate is expected to know what the acronyms stand for, most will be spelled out on the actual exam.

The answers to all the questions appear in the "Answers to Practice Exam Questions" chapter, next in the book. Check your letter answers against those in the answer key, and then read the explanations provided. If you answer incorrectly, you should return to the appropriate chapter in the book to review the material.

Practice Exam Questions

1. Which type of sampling is best when dealing with population characteristics such as dollar amounts and weights?

   - A. Attribute sampling
   - B. Variable sampling
   - C. Stop-and-go sampling
   - D. Discovery sampling

2. Which of the following sampling techniques is generally applied to compliance testing?

   - A. Attribute sampling
   - B. Variable sampling
   - C. Stop-and-go sampling
   - D. Discovery sampling

3. To guarantee the confidentiality of client information, an auditor should do which of the following when reviewing such information?

   - A. Contact the CEO or CFO and request what sensitive information can and cannot be disclosed to authorities
   - B. Assume full responsibility for the audit archive and stored data
   - C. Leave all sensitive information at the owners' facility
   - D. Not back up any of his or her work papers

4. Which of the following best describes materiality?

   - A. An audit technique used to evaluate the need to perform an audit
   - B. The principle that individuals, organizations, and the community are responsible for their actions and might be required to explain them
   - C. The auditor's independence and freedom from conflict of interest
   - D. An auditing concept that examines the importance of an item of information in regard to the impact or effect on the entity being audited

Practice Exam

5. Which of the following sampling technique is best to use to prevent excessive sampling?

- A. Attribute sampling
- B. Variable sampling
- C. Stop-and-go sampling
- D. Discovery sampling

6. Which of the following descriptions best defines auditor independence?

- A. The auditor has high regard for the company and holds several hundred shares of the company's stock
- B. The auditor has a history of independence and even though the auditor has a niece that is employed by the company, he has stated that this is not a concern
- C. The auditor has previously given advice to the organization's design staff while employed as the auditor
- D. The auditor is objective, not associated with the organization, and free of any connections to the client

7. Which of the following meets the description "the primary objective is to leverage the internal audit function by placing responsibility of control and monitoring onto the functional areas"?

- A. Integrated auditing
- B. Control self-assessment
- C. Automated work papers
- D. Continuous auditing

8. Which of the following sampling techniques would be best to use if the expected discovery rate is extremely low?

- A. Attribute sampling
- B. Variable sampling
- C. Stop-and-go sampling
- D. Discovery sampling

9. Which of the following offers how-to information?

- A. Standards
- B. Policy
- C. Guidelines
- D. Procedures

10. The type of risk that might not be detected by a system of internal controls is defined as which of the following?

    A. Control risk

    B. Audit risk

    C. Detection risk

    D. Inherent risk

11. Which of the following items makes computer-assisted audit techniques (CAAT) important to an auditor?

    A. A large amount of information is obtained by using specific techniques to analyze systems.

    B. An assistant or untrained professional with no specialized training can utilize CAAT tools, which frees up the auditor to participate in other activities.

    C. CAAT requires more human involvement in the analysis than multifunction audit utilities.

    D. CAAT requires the auditor to reduce the sampling rate and provides a more narrow audit coverage.

12. The risk that a material error will occur because of weak controls or no controls is known as which of the following?

    A. Control risk

    B. Audit risk

    C. Detection risk

    D. Inherent risk

13. You have been asked to audit a series of controls. Using Figure E.1 as your reference, what type of control have you been asked to examine?

    A. Amount total

    B. Hash total

    C. Item total

    D. Data checksum

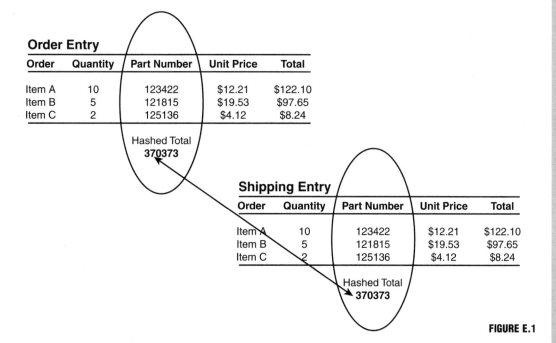

FIGURE E.1

14. Which of the following is the best tool to extract data that is relevant to the audit?

     ○   **A.** Integrated auditing

     ○   **B.** Generalized audit software

     ○   **C.** Automated work papers

     ○   **D.** Continuous auditing

15. You have been asked to perform an audit of the disaster-recovery procedures. As part of this process, you must use statistical sampling techniques to inventory all backup tapes. Which of the following descriptions best defines what you have been asked to do?

     ○   **A.** Continuous audit

     ○   **B.** Integrated audit

     ○   **C.** Compliance audit

     ○   **D.** Substantive audit

16. According to ISACA, which of the following is the fourth step in the risk-based audit approach?

  A. Gather information and plan

  B. Perform compliance tests

  C. Perform substantive tests

  D. Determine internal controls

17. Which general control procedure most closely maps to the information systems control procedure that specifies, "Operational controls that are focused on day-to-day activities"?

  A. Business continuity and disaster-recovery procedures that provide reasonable assurance that the organization is secure against disasters

  B. Procedures that provide reasonable assurance for the control of database administration

  C. System-development methodologies and change-control procedures that have been implemented to protect the organization and maintain compliance

  D. Procedures that provide reasonable assurance to control and manage data-processing operations

18. Which of the following is the best example of a detective control?

  A. Access-control software that uses passwords, tokens, and/or biometrics

  B. Intrusion-prevention systems

  C. Backup procedures used to archive data

  D. Variance reports

19. Which of the following is not one of the four common elements needed to determine whether fraud is present?

  A. An error in judgment

  B. Knowledge that the statement was false

  C. Reliance on the false statement

  D. Resulting damages or losses

20. You have been asked to implement a continuous auditing program. With this in mind, which of the following should you first identify?

- **A.** Applications with high payback potential
- **B.** The format and location of input and output files
- **C.** Areas of high risk within the organization
- **D.** Targets with reasonable thresholds

21. Which of the following should be the first step for organizations wanting to develop an information security program?

- **A.** Upgrade access-control software to a biometric or token system
- **B.** Approve a corporate information security policy statement
- **C.** Ask internal auditors to perform a comprehensive review
- **D.** Develop a set of information security standards

22. Which of the following is primarily tasked with ensuring that the IT department is properly aligned with the goals of the business?

- **A.** Chief executive officer
- **B.** Board of directors
- **C.** IT steering committee
- **D.** Audit committee

23. The balanced score card differs from historic measurement schemes, in that it looks at more than what?

- **A.** Financial results
- **B.** Customer satisfaction
- **C.** Internal process efficiency
- **D.** Innovation capacity

24. Which of the following is the purpose of enterprise architecture (EA)?

- **A.** Ensure that internal and external strategy are aligned
- **B.** Map the IT infrastructure of the organization
- **C.** Map the IT infrastructure of the organization and ensure that its design maps to the organization's strategy
- **D.** Ensure that business strategy and IT investments are aligned

25. Which of the following types of planning entails an outlook of greater than three years?

    ○ **A.** Daily planning

    ○ **B.** Long-term planning

    ○ **C.** Operational planning

    ⊗ **D.** Strategic planning

26. A new IT auditor has been asked to examine some processing, editing, and validation controls. Can you help define the control shown in Figure E.2?

    ○ **A.** Validity check

    ○ **B.** Reasonableness check

    ⊗ **C.** Existence check

    ○ **D.** Range check

```
Please review the fields marked with a red asterisk (*) for missing or incorrect
information. When finished, click on the button at the bottom of the page to
continue.

☑ I acknowledge affirmatively that I understand that the requested software is subject to export
controls under the Export Administration Act and that I may only export or re-export the software
under the laws, restrictions and regulations of the U.S. Bureau of Export Administration or foreign
agencies or authorities.


Name and Address:

* First Name              * Last Name
Mike                      Gregg
* Company

* Address 1

Address 2

* City                    * State/Province (U.S. and Canada Only)
                          Not applicable
* Zip/Postal Code         * Country
                          United States
* E-mail
```

FIGURE E.2

27. Senior management needs to select a strategy to determine who will pay for the information system's services. Which of the following payment methods is known as a "pay as you go" system?

    ○ **A.** Single cost

    ○ **B.** Shared cost

    ⊗ **C.** Chargeback

    ○ **D.** Sponsor pays

28. Which of the following is the best method to identify problems between procedure and activity?

   ○ **A.** Policy review

   ✗ **B.** Direct observation

   ○ **C.** Procedure review

   ○ **D.** Interview

29. You are working with a risk-assessment team that is having a hard time calculating the potential financial loss to the company's brand name that could result from a risk. What should the team do next?

   ○ **A.** Calculate the return on investment (ROI)

   ○ **B.** Determine the single loss expectancy (SLE)

   ✗ **C.** Use a qualitative approach

   ○ **D.** Review actuary tables

30. What operation-migration strategy has the highest possible level of risk?

   ○ **A.** Parallel

   ✗ **B.** Hard

   ○ **C.** Phased

   ○ **D.** Intermittent

31. Many organizations require employees to rotate to different positions. Why?

   ○ **A.** Help deliver effective and efficient services

   ○ **B.** Provide effective cross-training

   ✗ **C.** Reduce the opportunity for fraud or improper or illegal acts

   ○ **D.** Increase employee satisfaction

32. The balanced score card looks at four metrics. Which of the following is not one of those metrics?

   ⊙ **A.** External operations

   ○ **B.** The customer

   ✗ **C.** Innovation and learning

   ○ **D.** Financial data

33. You have been assigned to a software-development project that has 80 linked modules and is being developed for a system that handles several million transactions per year. The primary screen of the application has data items that carry up to 20 data attributes. You have been asked to work with the audit staff to determine a true estimate of the development effort. Which of the following is the best technique to determine the size of the project?

- ○ **A.** White-boxing
- ○ **B.** Black-boxing
- **C.** Function point analysis
- **D.** Source lines of code

34. Which of the following is the preferred tool for estimating project time when a degree of uncertainty exists?

- **A.** Program Evaluation and Review Technique (PERT)
- ○ **B.** Source lines of code (SLOC)
- ○ **C.** Gantt
- ○ **D.** Constructive Cost Model (COCOMO)

35. Which of the following techniques is used to determine what activities are critical and what the dependencies are among the various tasks?

- ○ **A.** Compiling a list of each task required to complete the project
- ○ **B.** COCOMO
- **C.** Critical path methodology (CPM)
- ○ **D.** Program Evaluation and Review Technique (PERT)

36. Which of the following is considered a traditional system development lifecycle model?

- **A.** The waterfall model
- ○ **B.** The spiral development model
- ○ **C.** The prototyping model
- ○ **D.** Incremental development

37. You have been assigned as an auditor to a new software project. The team members are currently defining user needs and then mapping how the proposed solution meets the need. At what phase of the SDLC are they?

    A. Feasibility

    B. Requirements

    C. Design

    D. Development

38. Which of the following is not a valid output control?

    A. Logging

    B. Batch controls

    C. Security signatures

    D. Report distribution

39. The following question references Figure E.3. Item A refers to which of the following?

    A. Foreign key

    B. Tuple

    C. Attribute

    D. Primary key

Table A

	Customer	Location	Phone Number	Sales Rep
	Bank One	Houston	555-1234	Jim Barnes
	Compass Bank	Dallas	555-2346	George Mays
	Texas Gulf Bank	Galveston	555-8412	Alan Simpson
	First Bank	Austin	555-0973	Ted Knight

Item C

Item A

Item D

Item B

Table B

Sales Ranking	Customer	Dollar Sales
1	First Bank	$54,125
2	Compass Bank	$44,136
3	Bank One	$16,124
4	Texas Gulf Bank	$8,012

FIGURE E.3

40. You have been asked to suggest a control that could be used to determine whether a credit card transaction is legitimate or potentially from a stolen credit card. Which of the following would be the best tool for this need?

   ○ **A.** Decision support systems

   ✗ **B.** Expert systems

   ○ **C.** Intrusion-prevention systems

   ◉ **D.** Data-mining techniques

41. You have been asked to suggest a control that can be used to verify that batch data is complete and was transferred accurately between two applications. What should you suggest?

   ◉ **A.** A control total

   ✗ **B.** Check digit

   ○ **C.** Completeness check

   ○ **D.** Limit check

42. Which of the following types of programming language is used to develop decision support systems?

   ○ **A.** 2GL

   ○ **B.** 3GL

   ◉ **C.** 4GL

   ✗ **D.** 5GL

43. You have been asked to work with a new project manager. The project team has just started work on the payback analysis. Which of the following is the best answer to identify the phase of the system development lifecycle of the project?

   ◉ **A.** Feasibility

   ✗ **B.** Requirements

   ○ **C.** Design

   ○ **D.** Development

44. In many ways, IS operations is a service organization because it provides services to its users. As such, how should an auditor recommend that the percentage of help-desk or response calls answered within a given time be measured?

   ○ **A.** Uptime agreements

   ✗ **B.** Time service factor

   ○ **C.** Abandon rate

   ○ **D.** First call resolution

45. What is the correct term for items that can occur without human interaction?

- A. Lights out
- B. Automated processing
- C. "Follow the sun" operations
- D. Autopilot operations

46. Which of the following is an example of a 2GL language?

- A. SQL
- B. Assembly
- C. FORTRAN
- D. Prolog

47. When discussing web services, which of the following best describes a proxy server?

- A. Reduces load for the client system
- B. Improves direct access to the Internet
- C. Provides an interface to access the private domain
- D. Provides high-level security services

48. Regarding cohesion and coupling, which is best?

- A. High cohesion, high coupling
- B. High cohesion, low coupling
- C. Low cohesion, low coupling
- D. Low cohesion, high coupling

49. Bluetooth class 1 meets which of the following specifications?

- A. Up to 5 m of range and .5 mW of power
- B. Up to 10 m of range and 1 mW of power
- C. Up to 20 m of range and 2.5 mW of power
- D. Up to 100 m of range and 100 mW of power

50. When discussing electronic data interface (EDI), which of the following terms best describes the device that transmits and receives electronic documents between trading partners?

   ○ **A.** Value Added Network (VAN)

   ○ **B.** X12

   ⊗ **C.** Communications handler

   ○ **D.** Electronic Data Interchange For Administration Commerce And Transport (EDIFACT)

51. Which type of network is used to connect multiple servers to a centralized pool of disk storage?

   ○ **A.** PAN

   ○ **B.** LAN

   ⊗ **C.** SAN

   ○ **D.** MAN

52. The following question references Figure E.4. Item C refers to which of the following?

   ○ **A.** Foreign key

   ○ **B.** Tuple

   ⊗ **C.** Attribute

   ○ **D.** Primary key

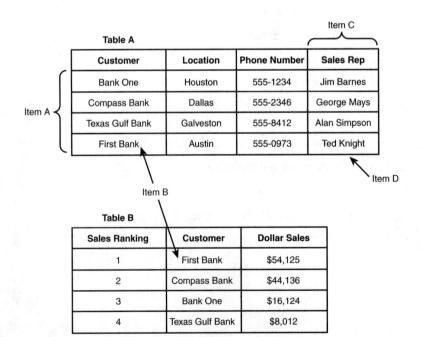

FIGURE E.4

53. Which layer of the OSI model is responsible for packet routing?

- A. Application
- B. Transport
- C. Session
- D. Network

54. Which of the following types of testing is usually performed at the implementation phase, when the project staff is satisfied with all other tests and the application is ready to be deployed?

- A. Final acceptance testing
- B. System testing
- C. Interface testing
- D. Unit testing

55. Which of the following devices can be on the edge of networks for basic packet filtering?

- A. Bridge
- B. Switch
- C. Router
- D. VLAN

56. MAC addresses are most closely associated with which layer of the OSI model?

- A. Data link
- B. Network
- C. Session
- D. Physical

57. The IP address of 128.12.3.15 is considered to be which of the following?

- A. Class A
- B. Class B
- C. Class C
- D. Class D

58. Which of the following statements is most correct? RIP is considered...

    A. A routing protocol

    B. A routable protocol

    C. A distance-vector routing protocol

    D. A link-state routing protocol

59. Which of the following test types is used after a change to verify that inputs and outputs are correct?

    A. Regression testing

    B. System testing

    C. Interface testing

    D. Pilot testing

60. Which of the following is an example of a 5GL language?

    A. SQL

    B. Assembly

    C. FORTRAN

    D. Prolog

61. Which of the following types of network topologies is hard to expand, with one break possibly disabling the entire segment?

    A. Bus

    B. Star

    C. Token Ring

    D. Mesh

62. What is the most important reason to use plenum-grade cable?

    A. Increased network security

    B. Less attenuation

    C. Less cross-talk

    D. Fire-retardant coating

63. Which of the following copper cable network configurations is considered the most secure from eavesdropping or interception?

    ○ **A.** A switched VLAN using multimode fiber cable

    ○ **B.** A Token Ring network using Cat 5 cabling

    ○ **C.** A switched network that uses Cat 5e shielded cable

    ○ **D.** A bus network using 10BASE2 cabling

64. Which of the following is an iterative development method in which repetitions are referred to as sprints and typically last 30 days?

    ○ **A.** Scrum

    ○ **B.** Extreme programming

    ○ **C.** RAD

    ○ **D.** Spiral

65. Which type of database is shown in Figure E.5?

    ○ **A.** Relational

    ○ **B.** Network

    ○ **C.** Hierarchical

    ○ **D.** Floating flat

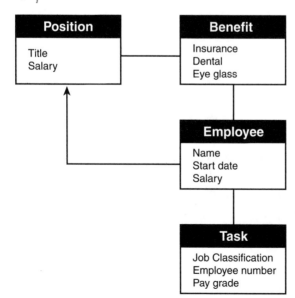

FIGURE E.5

66. As a new auditor, you have been asked to review network operations. Which of the following weaknesses should you consider the most serious?

　○　**A.** Data files can be amended or changed by supervisors.

　✗　**B.** Data files can be lost during power outages because of poor backup.

　○　**C.** Sensitive data files can be read by managers.

　○　**D.** Copies of confidential reports can be printed by anyone.

67. Which of the following is the best example of a control mechanism to be used to control component failure or errors?

　○　**A.** Redundant WAN links

　✗　**B.** Just a Bunch of Disks/Drives (JBOD)

　○　**C.** RAID 0

　○　**D.** RAID 1

68. Which of the following is the best technique for an auditor to verify firewall settings?

　○　**A.** Interview the network administrator

　✗　**B.** Review the firewall configuration

　○　**C.** Review the firewall log for recent attacks

　○　**D.** Review the firewall procedure

69. Which of the following is not a circuit-switching technology?

　○　**A.** DSL

　✗　**B.** POTS

　○　**C.** T1

　○　**D.** ATM

70. Which of the following uses a process to standardize code modules to allow for cross-platform operation and program integration?

　○　**A.** Component-based development (CBD)

　○　**B.** Web-based application development (WBAD)

　✗　**C.** Object-oriented systems development (OOSD)

　○　**D.** Data-oriented system development (DOSD)

71. Data warehouses are used to store historic data of an organization. As such, which of the following is the most accurate way to describe data warehouses?

    A. Subject oriented
    ○ B. Object oriented
    ○ C. Access oriented
    ○ D. Control oriented

72. Which of the following access-control models allows the user to control access?

    ○ A. Mandatory access control (MAC)
    B. Discretionary access control (DAC)
    ○ C. Role-based access control (RBAC)
    ○ D. Access control list (ACL)

73. While auditing the identification and authentication system, you want to discuss the best method you reviewed. Which of the following is considered the strongest?

    ○ A. Passwords
    ○ B. Tokens
    C. Two-factor authentication
    ○ D. Biometrics

74. If asked to explain the equal error rate (EER) to another auditor, what would you say?

    ○ A. The EER is used to determine the clipping level used for password lockout.
    B. The EER is a measurement that indicates the point at which FRR equals FAR.
    ○ C. The EER is a rating used for password tokens.
    ○ D. The EER is a rating used to measure the percentage of biometric users who are allowed access and who are not authorized users.

75. You have been asked to head up the audit of a business application system. What is one of the first tasks you should perform?

    ○ A. Interview users
    B. Review process flowcharts
    ○ C. Evaluate controls
    ○ D. Determine critical areas

76. Closed-circuit TV (CCTV) systems are considered what type of control?

- ○ **A.** Corrective
- ⊗ **B.** Detective
- ○ **C.** Preventive
- ○ **D.** Delayed

77. According to ISACA, the second step in the business continuity planning (BCP) process is which of the following?

- ○ **A.** Project management and initiation
- ○ **B.** Plan design and development
- ⊗ **C.** Recovery strategy
- ○ **D.** Business impact analysis

78. You have been asked to review the documentation for a planned database. Which type of database is represented by Figure E.6?

- ○ **A.** Relational
- ⊗ **B.** Network
- ○ **C.** Hierarchical
- ○ **D.** Floating flat

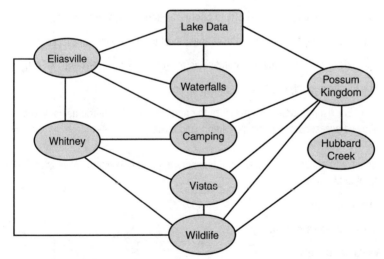

FIGURE E.6

79. Which of the following issues ticket-granting tickets?

    A. The Kerberos authentication service

    ○ **B.** The RADIUS authentication service

    ○ **C.** The Kerberos ticket-granting service

    ○ **D.** The RADIUS ticket-granting service

80. Which of the following is the most important corrective control that an organization has the capability to shape?

    ○ **A.** Audit plan

    ○ **B.** Security assessment

    C. Business continuity plan

    ○ **D.** Network topology

81. Which one of the following is not considered an application system testing technique?

    ○ **A.** Snapshots

    B. Mapping

    C. Integrated test facilities

    ○ **D.** Base case system evaluation

82. Which of the following statements regarding recovery is correct?

    A. The greater the recovery point objective (RPO), the more tolerant the process is to interruption.

    ○ **B.** The less the recovery time objective (RTO), the longer the process can take to be restored.

    ○ **C.** The less the RPO, the more tolerant the process is to interruption.

    ○ **D.** The greater the RTO, the less time the process can take to be restored.

83. Which of the following best defines the service delivery objective (SDO)?

    ○ **A.** Defines the maximum amount of time the organization can provide services at the alternate site

    B. Defines the level of service provided by alternate processes

    C. Defines the time that systems can be offline before causing damage

    ○ **D.** Defines how long the process can take to be restored

84. During which step of the business continuity planning (BCP) process is a risk assessment performed?

   ◯ **A.** Project management and initiation

   ◯ **B.** Plan design and development

   ◯ **C.** Recovery strategy

   ✗ **D.** Business impact analysis

85. When auditing security for a data center, the auditor should look for which of the following as the best example of long-term power protection?

   ✗ **A.** Standby generator

   ◯ **B.** Uninterrupted power supply

   ◯ **C.** Surge protector

   ◯ **D.** Filtered power supply

86. Which of the following would be considered the most complex continuous audit technique?

   ✗ **A.** Continuous and intermittent simulation (CIS)

   ◯ **B.** Snapshots

   ◯ **C.** Audit hooks

   ◉ **D.** Integrated test facilities

87. Which of the following is not a replacement for Halon?

   ◯ **A.** FM-200

   ◯ **B.** NAF-S-3

   ✗ **C.** FM-100

   ◯ **D.** Argon

88. When discussing biometrics, what do Type 1 errors measure?

   ◯ **A.** The point at which the false rejection rate (FRR) equals the false acceptance rate (FAR)

   ◯ **B.** The accuracy of the biometric system

   ✗ **C.** The percentage of illegitimate users who are given access

   ◉ **D.** The percentage of legitimate users who are denied access

89. Class A fires are comprised of which of the following?

- ○ **A.** Electronic equipment
- ✗ **B.** Paper
- ○ **C.** Oil
- ○ **D.** Metal

90. You are performing an audit of an organization's physical security controls, specifically, emergency controls. When doors that use relays or electric locks are said to fail soft, what does that mean?

- ✗ **A.** Locks of this type fail open.
- ○ **B.** Locks of this type are easy to pick.
- ○ **C.** Locks of this type fail closed.
- ○ **D.** Locks of this type are hard to pick.

91. Which type of database is represented by Figure E.7?

- ○ **A.** Relational
- ○ **B.** Network
- ✗ **C.** Hierarchical
- ○ **D.** Floating flat

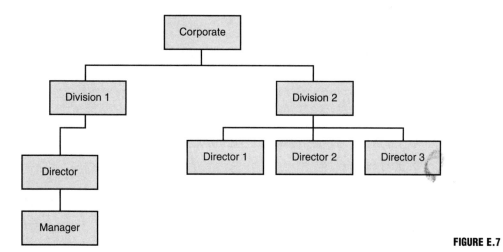

FIGURE E.7

92. Systems control audit review file and embedded audit modules (SCARF/EAM) is an example of which of the following?

    ○ **A.** Output controls

    ⊗ **B.** Continuous online auditing

    ○ **C.** Input controls

    ○ **D.** Processing controls

93. Which type of access rights control model is widely used by the DoD, NSA, CIA, and FBI?

    ○ **A.** MAC

    ○ **B.** DAC

    ⊗ **C.** RBAC

    ○ **D.** ACL

94. Why is the protection of processing integrity important?

    ○ **A.** To maintain availability to users so they have the availability to copy and use data without delay

    ○ **B.** To protect data from unauthorized access while in transit

    ⊗ **C.** To prevent output controls from becoming tainted

    ○ **D.** To maintain data encryption on portable devices so that data can be relocated to another facility while being encrypted

95. A privacy impact analysis (PIA) is tied to several items. Which of the following is not one of those items?

    ○ **A.** Technology

    ○ **B.** Processes

    ⊗ **C.** People

    ○ **D.** Documents

96. Which of the following is ultimately responsible for the security practices of the organization?

    ○ **A.** Security advisory group

    ○ **B.** Chief security officer

    ⊗ **C.** Executive management

    ○ **D.** Security auditor

97. Which of the following guarantees that all foreign keys reference existing primary keys?

    ○ **A.** Relational integrity

    ○ **B.** Referential integrity

    ○ **C.** Entity integrity

    ○ **D.** Tracing and tagging

98. Which of the following would a company extend to allow network access to a business partner?

    ○ **A.** Internet

    ○ **B.** Intranet

    ○ **C.** Extranet

    ○ **D.** VLAN

99. What term is used to describe the delay that information will experience from the source to the destination?

    ○ **A.** Echo

    ○ **B.** Latency

    ○ **C.** Delay

    ○ **D.** Congestion

100. You have been asked to describe what security feature can be found in the wireless standard 802.11a. How will you respond?

    ○ **A.** Wi-Fi Protected Access (WPA)

    ○ **B.** Wired Equivalent Privacy (WEP)

    ○ **C.** Temporal Key Integrity Protocol (TKIP)

    ○ **D.** Wi-Fi Protected Access 2 (WPA2)

101. Which of the following is not a packet-switching technology?

    ○ **A.** X.25

    ○ **B.** ISDN

    ○ **C.** Frame Rely

    ○ **D.** ATM

102. Transport-layer security (TLS) can best be described as being found between which two layers of the OSI model?

   ○ **A.** Layers 2 and 3

   ○ **B.** Layers 3 and 4

   ○ **C.** Layers 4 and 5

   ○ **D.** Layers 5 and 6

103. Which of the following descriptions highlights the importance of domain name service (DNS)?

   ○ **A.** Address of a domain server

   ○ **B.** Resolves fully qualified domain names to IP addresses

   ○ **C.** Resolves known IP address for unknown Internet addresses

   ○ **D.** Resolves IP and MAC addresses needed for delivery of Internet data

104. Using Figure E.8 as a reference, which of the following best describes a 10BASE5 network design?

   ○ **A.** Item A

   ○ **B.** Item B

   ○ **C.** Item C

   ○ **D.** Item D

Item A

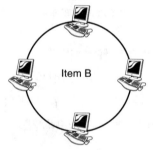

Item B

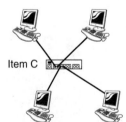

Item C

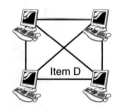

Item D

FIGURE E.8

105. You have been asked to describe a program that can be classified as terminal-emulation software. Which of the following would you mention?

    ○ **A.** Telnet

    ○ **B.** FTP

    ○ **C.** SNMP

    ○ **D.** SMTP

106. Which of the following services operates on ports 20 and 21?

    ○ **A.** Telnet

    ○ **B.** FTP

    ○ **C.** SMTP

    ○ **D.** DHCP

107. Which layer of the OSI model is responsible for reliable data delivery?

    ○ **A.** Data link

    ○ **B.** Session

    ○ **C.** Transport

    ○ **D.** Network

108. An objective of the implementation phase of a newly installed system can include which of the following?

    ○ **A.** Conducting a certification test

    ○ **B.** Determining user requirements

    ○ **C.** Assessing the project to see if expected benefits were achieved

    ○ **D.** Reviewing the designed audit trails

109. Which of the following is the best example of a processing control?

    ○ **A.** Exception reports

    ○ **B.** Sequence check

    ○ **C.** Key verification

    ○ **D.** Logical relationship check

110. Which of the following devices is most closely related to the data link layer?

    ○ **A.** Hub

    ○ **B.** Repeater

    ○ **C.** Bridge

    ○ **D.** Router

111. Which of the following provide the capability to ensure the validity of data through various stages of processing?

    ○ **A.** Manual recalculations

    ○ **B.** Programming controls

    ○ **C.** Run-to-run totals

    ○ **D.** Reasonableness verification

112. You overheard the database administrator discussing normalizing some tables. What is the purpose of this activity?

    ○ **A.** Decrease redundancy

    ○ **B.** Increase redundancy

    ○ **C.** Decrease application malfunction

    ○ **D.** Increase accuracy

113. Which of the following is not included in a PERT chart?

    ○ **A.** The most optimistic time the task can be completed in

    ○ **B.** The most cost-effective scenario for the task

    ○ **C.** The worst-case scenario or longest time the task can take

    ○ **D.** The most likely time the task will be completed in

114. Verifications such as existence checks can best be described as:

    ○ **A.** A processing control that is considered preventive

    ○ **B.** A validation edit control that is considered preventive

    ○ **C.** A processing control that is considered detective

    ○ **D.** A validation edit control that is considered detective

115. Referential integrity is used to prevent which of the following?

    ◯ **A.** Attribute errors

    ◯ **B.** Relational errors

    ◯ **C.** Dangling tuples

    ◯ **D.** Integrity constraints

116. Which of the following best describes the difference between accreditation and certification?

    ◯ **A.** Certification is initiated after the accreditation of the system to ensure that the system meets required standards.

    ◯ **B.** Certification is initiated before accreditation to ensure that quality personnel are using the new designed systems.

    ◯ **C.** Accreditation is issued after certification. Accreditation is a management function, while certification is a technical function.

    ◯ **D.** Production and management might see accreditation and certification as basically one and the same.

117. You have been asked to review the organization's planned firewall design. As such, which of the following best describes the topology shown in Figure E.9?

    ◯ **A.** Packet filter

    ◯ **B.** Screened subnet

    ◯ **C.** Screened host

    ◯ **D.** Dual-homed host

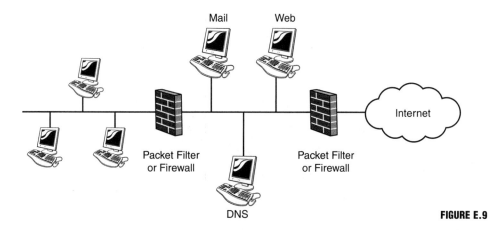

DNS

FIGURE E.9

118. Which of the following database designs is considered a lattice structure because each record can have multiple parent and child records? Although this design can work well in stable environments, it can be extremely complex.

 ○ **A.** The hierarchical database-management systems

 ○ **B.** The relational database-management systems

 ○ **C.** The network database-management systems

 ○ **D.** The structured database-management systems

119. Which of the following is not used when calculating function point analysis?

 ○ **A.** Number of user inquires

 ○ **B.** Number of files

 ○ **C.** Number of user inputs

 ○ **D.** Number of expected users

120. Which of the following is an example of an interpreted programming language?

 ○ **A.** FORTRAN

 ○ **B.** Assembly

 ○ **C.** Basic

 ○ **D.** Java

121. Which of the following is an example of a 4GL language?

 ○ **A.** SQL

 ○ **B.** Assembly

 ○ **C.** FORTRAN

 ○ **D.** Prolog

122. Which of the following database takes the form of a parent/child structure?

 ○ **A.** The hierarchical database-management systems

 ○ **B.** The relational database-management systems

 ○ **C.** The network database-management systems

 ○ **D.** The structured database-management systems

123. You have been asked to explain rings of protection and how the concept applies to the supervisory mode of the operating system (OS). Which of the following is the best description?

   ○ **A.** System utilities should run in supervisor mode.

   ○ **B.** Supervisor state allows the execution of all instructions, including privileged instructions.

   ○ **C.** Supervisory mode is used to block access to the security kernel.

   ○ **D.** Rings are arranged in a hierarchy from least privileged to the most privileged as the most trusted usually has the highest ring number

124. You have been asked to design a control. The organization would like to limit what check numbers are used. Specfically, they would like to be able to flag a check numbered 318 if the day's first check had the number 120 and the day's last check was number 144. What type of validation check does the department require?

   ○ **A.** Limit check

   ○ **B.** Range check

   ○ **C.** Validity check

   ○ **D.** Sequence check

125. Which of the following descriptions best describes a delay window?

   ○ **A.** The time between when an event occurs and when the audit record is reviewed

   ○ **B.** The time between when an incident occurs and when it is addressed

   ○ **C.** The time between when an event occurs and when the audit record is recorded

   ○ **D.** The difference between a threshold and a trigger

126. You have been asked to review a console log. What type of information should you expect to find?

   ○ **A.** Names and passwords of system users

   ○ **B.** Application access and backup times

   ○ **C.** System errors

   ○ **D.** Errors from data edits

127. During a software change process, auditors might be asked to verify existing source code at some point. What is the most effective tool for auditors to compare old and new software for unreported changes?

○ **A.** Function point analysis (FPA)

○ **B.** Manual review of the software

○ **C.** Variation tools

○ **D.** Source code comparison software

128. Which of the following is not a valid processing control?

○ **A.** Authorization

○ **B.** Processing

○ **C.** Validation

○ **D.** Editing

129. Which of the following is not part of the project-management triangle?

○ **A.** Scope

○ **B.** Time

○ **C.** Resources

○ **D.** Cost

130. Using Figure E.10 as a reference, place the four recovery time objectives in their proper order.

○ **A.** Items A, B, C, D

○ **B.** Items B, C, D, A

○ **C.** Items D, A, C, B

○ **D.** Items C, B, D, A

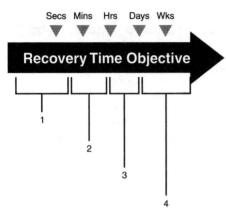

FIGURE E.10

131. When dealing with project-management issues, which of the following is ultimately responsible and must ensure that stakeholders' needs are met?

○ **A.** Stakeholders

○ **B.** Project steering committee

○ **C.** Project manager

○ **D.** Quality assurance

132. Projects must take on an organizational form. These organizational forms or frameworks can be either loosely structured or very rigid. Which project form matches the description "The project manager has no real authority, and the functional manager remains in charge"?

○ **A.** Weak matrix

○ **B.** Pure project

○ **C.** Balanced matrix

○ **D.** Influence

133. Which of the following is the best description of the Constructive Cost Model (COCOMO)?

   ○ **A.** COCOMO is a model that forecasts the cost and schedule of software development, including the number of persons and months required for the development.

   ○ **B.** COCOMO is a model that forecasts network costs associated with hardware, the physical medium, and trained personnel.

   ○ **C.** COCOMO is a forecast model that estimates the time involved in producing a product and shipping to the end user.

   ○ **D.** COCOMO is a model that forecasts the construction of additional companies associated with organizational growth.

134. Which of the following software-estimating methods does not work as well in modern development programs because additional factors that are not considered will affect the overall cost?

   ○ **A.** Facilited Risk Assessment Process (FRAP)

   ○ **B.** Gantt

   ○ **C.** Function point analysis (FPA)

   ○ **D.** Source lines of code (SLOC)

135. Which of the following is the best example of a quantitative risk-assessment technique?

   ○ **A.** The Delphi technique

   ○ **B.** Facilitated risk-assessment process

   ○ **C.** Actuarial tables

   ○ **D.** Risk rating of high, medium, or low

Answers to Practice Exam Questions

Answers at a Glance to Practice Exam

1. B	28. B	55. C	82. A	109. A
2. A	29. C	56. A	83. B	110. C
3. C	30. B	57. B	84. D	111. C
4. D	31. C	58. C	85. A	112. A
5. C	32. A	59. A	86. D	113. B
6. D	33. C	60. D	87. C	114. B
7. B	34. A	61. A	88. D	115. C
8. D	35. C	62. D	89. B	116. C
9. D	36. A	63. C	90. A	117. B
10. A	37. B	64. A	91. C	118. C
11. A	38. B	65. A	92. B	119. D
12. D	39. D	66. D	93. A	120. C
13. B	40. D	67. D	94. B	121. A
14. B	41. A	68. B	95. D	122. A
15. D	42. C	69. D	96. C	123. B
16. C	43. A	70. B	97. B	124. D
17. D	44. B	71. A	98. C	125. B
18. D	45. A	72. B	99. B	126. C
19. A	46. B	73. C	100. B	127. D
20. C	47. C	74. B	101. B	128. A
21. B	48. B	75. B	102. C	129. C
22. C	49. D	76. B	103. B	130. B
23. A	50. C	77. D	104. A	131. B
24. D	51. C	78. B	105. A	132. D
25. D	52. C	79. A	106. B	133. A
26. C	53. D	80. C	107. C	134. D
27. C	54. A	81. C	108. A	135. C

Answers with Explanations

1. B. Variable sampling is best when dealing with population characteristics such as dollar amounts and weights. Variable sampling provides conclusions related to deviations from the norm. Answer A is incorrect because attribute sampling is generally applied to compliance testing. Answer C is incorrect because stop-and-go sampling is used to prevent excessive sampling and allows an audit to be stopped quickly. Answer D is incorrect because discovery sampling is used to seek out or discover fraud. For more information, see Chapter 1.

2. A. Attribute sampling is generally applied to compliance testing. Answer B is incorrect because variable sampling is best when dealing with population characteristics such as dollar amounts and weights. Answer C is incorrect because stop-and-go sampling is used to prevent excessive sampling and allows an audit to be stopped quickly. Answer D is incorrect because discovery sampling is used to seek out or discover fraud. For more information, see Chapter 1.

3. C. It is best if sensitive information is not removed from the owners' property. Answer A is incorrect because legal counsel should be contacted concerning the confidentiality and laws concerning disclosure to authorities. Answer B is incorrect because all records and the safe retention of the records are the sole responsibility of the client. Answer D is incorrect because although backing up all your work is very important, it is not the primary guarantee of confidentiality. For more information, see Chapter 1.

4. D. Materiality is the auditing concept that examines the importance of an item of information in regard to the impact or effect on the entity being audited. Answer A is incorrect because it does not properly describe materiality. Materiality is not the evaluation for the need of an audit. Answer B is incorrect because it describes accountability. Answer C is incorrect because it describes independence. For more information, see Chapter 1.

5. C. Stop-and-go sampling prevents excessive sampling and allows an audit to be stopped quickly. Answer A is incorrect because attribute sampling is generally applied to compliance testing. Answer B is incorrect because variable sampling is best when dealing with population characteristics such as dollar amounts and weights. Answer D is incorrect because discovery sampling is used to seek out or discover fraud. For more information, see Chapter 1.

6. D. Answer D is correct because no professional relationship between the external auditor and client must exist, and the auditor must not be financially interested in the organization. Answers A, B, and C are incorrect because auditors cannot be independent if their interest involves any financial or personal outcomes to the client. Objectivity is required of an auditor. Giving design or control advice can result in a serious conflict. For more information, see Chapter 1.

7. B. Control self-assessment can be described as a process that ensures that stakeholders, employees, and others are part of the audit process. The primary objective of the control self-assessment process is to leverage the internal audit function by placing responsibility of control and monitoring on the functional areas. Answer A is incorrect because integrated auditing describes a technique used to apply audit disciplines to assess key controls over operations and processes. Answer C is incorrect because automated work papers are software packages designed to automate the auditor's daily tasks. Answer D is incorrect because continuous auditing uses embedded audit controls to reduce the amount of time between items to be audited and the collection and reporting of evidence. For more information, see Chapter 1.

8. D. Discovery sampling can be used when the expected discovery rate is very low. Discovery sampling can also be used to uncover fraud. Answer A is incorrect because attribute sampling is generally applied to compliance testing. Answer B is incorrect because variable sampling is best when dealing with population characteristics such as dollar amounts and weights. Answer C is incorrect because stop-and-go sampling is used to prevent excessive sampling and allows an audit to be stopped quickly. For more information, see Chapter 1.

9. D. Procedures offer how-to information. Answers A, B, and C are incorrect because standards are mandatory, policies provide a high level of control, and guidelines provide guidance. For more information, see Chapter 1.

10. A. A control risk is the risk that might not be detected by a system of internal controls. Answer B is incorrect because the audit risk is the risk an auditor will accept. Answer C is incorrect because the detection risk is the risk that an improper test is performed that will not detect a material error. Answer D is incorrect because inherent risk is the risk that a material error will occur because of weak or no controls. For more information, see Chapter 1.

11. A. CAAT tests are specialized tests that can evaluate system configurations, analyze network traffic, count software licenses, and inspect password conformity, to name only a few. These tests are much more accurate and precise than when performed manually. Answers B, C and D are incorrect because CAAT tools require specialized training to perform and are much more detailed and faster for compiling evidence. For more information, see Chapter 1.

12. D. An inherent risk is the risk that a material error will occur because of weak controls or no controls. Answer A is incorrect because a control risk is the risk that might not be detected by a system of internal controls. Answer B is incorrect because the audit risk is the risk an auditor will accept. Answer C is incorrect because the detection risk is the risk that an improper test is performed that will not detect a material error. For more information, see Chapter 1.

13. B. Hash totals are generated by choosing a selected number of fields in a series of transactions. These values are computed again at a later time to see if the numbers match. An incorrect value indicates that something has been lost, entered incorrectly, or corrupted somehow. Answer A is incorrect because total dollar amounts verify that each item totals up to the correct batched total amount. Answer C is incorrect because item total counts verify that the total counts match. Answer D is incorrect because a data checksum is a value sent along with the contents of a packet. For more information, see Chapter 4.

14. B. Generalized audit software is the best tool to extract data that is relevant to the audit. Answer A is incorrect because integrated auditing describes a technique used to apply audit disciplines to assess key controls over operations and processes. Answer C is incorrect because automated work papers are software packages designed to automate the auditor's daily tasks. Answer D is incorrect because continuous auditing uses embedded audit controls to reduce the amount of time between items to be audited and the collection and reporting of evidence. For more information, see Chapter 1.

15. D. Statistical samples are examples of substantive audits. During this type of audit, the auditor must determine how closely the sample should represent the population. Answers A, B, and C are incorrect because they do not describe statistical techniques. For more information, see Chapter 1.

16. **C.** ISACA lists the steps as: 1) Gather information and plan, 2) determine internal controls and review their functionality, 3) perform compliance tests, 4) perform substantive tests, and 5) conclude the audit. For more information, see Chapter 1.

17. **D.** Procedures that provide reasonable assurance to control and manage data processing operations map to logical security policies designed to support proper transactions. Answer A is incorrect because business continuity and disaster-recovery procedures provide reasonable assurance that the organization is secure against disasters. Answer B is incorrect because procedures that provide reasonable assurance for the control of database administration map to internal accounting controls used to safeguard financial records. Answer C is incorrect because system-development methodologies and change-control procedures implemented to protect the organization and maintain compliance map to administrative controls designed for corporate compliance. For more information, see Chapter 1.

18. **D.** Examples of detective controls include internal audit functions, hashing algorithms, and variance reports. Answers A and B are incorrect because they are examples of preventive controls. Answer C is incorrect because it is an example of a corrective control. For more information, see Chapter 1.

19. **A.** For fraud to be present, four items must exist. These include a material false statement, knowledge that the statement was false, reliance on the false statement, and resulting damages or losses. For more information, see Chapter 1.

20. **C.** The first step in continuous monitoring is to identify areas of high risk within the organization. Next, an assessment of potential impact of applications with high payback can be identified. Then tests can be performed to determine reasonable thresholds. With targeted thresholds determined, the development and format of monitoring programs can be defined. For more information, see Chapter 1.

21. **B.** The first step in the process should be to develop a policy statement. Changes to access control, internal review by auditors, and policy standards should not occur until this first step is completed. Therefore answers A, C, and D are incorrect. For more information, see Chapter 2.

22. **C.** Referred to as an IT steering committee or an IT strategy committee, this committee is tasked with ensuring that the IT department is properly aligned with the goals of the business. This is accomplished by using the committee as a conduit to move information and objectives from senior business management to IT management. The committee consists of members of high-level management from within the company. For more information, see Chapter 2.

23. **A.** Traditionally, financial results have been the sole indicator of performance. In the early 1990s, Robert Kaplen and David Norton developed a new method named the *balanced score card*. The balanced score card differs from historic measurement schemes, in that it looks at more than just the financial perspective. It balances this perspective by gathering input from four perspectives, including the customer, internal operations, innovation and learning, and financial data. Answers B, C, and D are incorrect. For more information, see Chapter 2.

24. D. The primary purpose of using EA is to ensure that business strategy and IT investments are aligned. Enterprise architecture (EA) is the practice within information technology of organizing and documenting a company's IT assets so that planning, management, and expansion can be enhanced. Answers A, B, and C do not adequately define EA. For more information, see Chapter 2.

25. D. A company that is involved in planning activities three to five years out is involved in strategic planning. Organizations need sufficient time to evolve long-term strategic goals and to map them to the organization. Answers A, B, and C are incorrect because those types of planning phases look at a closer time completion window of one to three years for long-term planning and one year or less for operational planning. For more information, see Chapter 2.

26. C. An existence check verifies that all required data is entered. Answers A, B, and D are incorrect because a validity check verifies the validity of the information. A reasonableness check verifies the reasonableness of the data. For example, if an order is usually for no more than 20 items and the order is for 2,000 items, an alert would be generated. A range check verifies that the entered range is valid. As an example, an item ordered column should not denote a negative amount. For more information, see Chapter 4.

27. C. The chargeback system is known as a "pay as you go" system. As such, individual departments are directly charged for the services they use. Answers A, B, and D are incorrect. A single-cost system is not considered a "pay as you go" system. Shared-cost systems share costs among all departments of the organization. This method is relatively easy to implement and for accounting to handle. A sponsor pays system works by having the project sponsors pay all costs. For more information, see Chapter 2.

28. B. Direct observation is the best way to identify problems between procedure and activity. Therefore answers A, C, and D are incorrect. For more information, see Chapter 2.

29. C. Risk analysis can be performed in one of two basic methods. The first of these is quantitative risk assessment, which deals with dollar amounts. It attempts to assign a cost (monetary value) to the elements of risk assessment and the assets and threats of a risk analysis. Next is a qualitative risk assessment, which ranks threats by nondollar values and is based more on scenario, intuition, and gut feeling. If a team is having a hard time determining a potential dollar loss to something such as a brand name, the team should use a qualitative approach. Answers A, B, and D are incorrect because they all deal with quantitative methods. For more information, see Chapter 2.

30. B. A hard change requires the old system to be shut down at a specific date. The new system then will be brought online and powered up. This can be very risky because the new system might not operate properly, just as the old system might not restart easily if it is needed. There's considerable risk in productivity and the potential of loss of revenue, which could cripple an organization. Answers A, C, and D are incorrect because a parallel operation involves operating both the old and new systems simultaneously to compare differences in the systems. Phased or pilot operations involve bringing the new system up one interval or phase at a time to test reliability and functionality. For more information, see Chapter 9.

31. C. Rotation of assignment can be useful because it requires more than one person to perform a specific task. A side effect of this might be to provide backup in case an employee is not available, but its primary purpose is to reduce fraud or misuse by giving the company the means of rotating people to prevent an individual from having too much control over an area. Therefore, answers A, B, and D are incorrect. For more information, see Chapter 2.

32. A. The balanced score card balances its perspective by gathering input from four perspectives, including the customer, internal operations, innovation and learning, and financial data. Answers B, C, and D are incorrect. For more information, see Chapter 2.

33. C. FPA is based on the number of inputs, outputs, interfaces, files, and queries. FPA can be used to budget application development costs, estimate productivity after project completion, and determine annual maintenance costs. Answers A, B, and D are incorrect. Both black-box and white-box techniques are not used to estimate software development size. Source lines of code can be used but does not give an accurate picture and is considered a dated technique. For more information, see Chapter 3.

34. A. Program Evaluation and Review Technique (PERT) is the preferred tool for estimating time when a degree of uncertainty exists. PERT uses a critical path method that applies a weighted average duration estimate. PERT uses a three-point time estimate to develop best, worst, and most likely time estimates. Answers B, C, and D are incorrect. SLOC refers to the size of software. The Gantt chart was developed in the early 1900s as a tool to schedule activities and monitor progress. The COCOMO model specifically deals with software development and the cost, time, and effort in the software-development cycle. For more information, see Chapter 3.

35. C. Critical path methodology (CPM) is used to determine what activities are critical and what the dependencies are among the various tasks. CPM is accomplished by compiling a list of each task required to complete the project, determining the time that each task will take from start to finish, and examining the dependencies among the tasks. For more information, see Chapter 3.

36. A. The waterfall model is considered a traditional system development lifecycle model. The advantage of this model is that it is well known and extremely stable when used if requirements are not expected to change and the architecture is well known. Answer B is incorrect because the spiral model is based on the concept that software development is evolutionary. The spiral model begins by creating a series of prototypes to develop a solution. Answer C is incorrect because prototyping uses high-level code to quickly turn design requirements into application screens and reports that the users can review. Answer D is incorrect because the incremental model defines an approach that develops systems in stages so that development is performed one step at a time. For more information, see Chapter 3.

37. B. During the requirements phase of the system development lifecycle (SDLC), team members are responsible for fully defining the need and then mapping how the proposed solution meets the need. Answer A is incorrect because during the feasibility phase, a payback analysis must be performed. Answer C is incorrect because during the design phase, the design is finalized and test plans are developed. Answer D is incorrect because during the development phase, developers become deeply involved in their work. For more information, see Chapter 3.

38. B. Output controls include logging, security signatures, report distribution, and balancing and rec-onciliation. Batch controls are an example of an input control. For more information, see Chapter 4.

39. D. Item A references the primary key. The primary key of a relational table uniquely identifies each record in the table. Answers A, B, and C are incorrect because they do not reference primary keys. For more information, see Chapter 4.

40. D. Data mining makes it possible to query very large databases to satisfy a hypothesis, such as whether a credit card is stolen or legitimate. Answer A is incorrect because decision support sys-tems (DSS) are used to solve common problems that managers face. Answer B is incorrect because expert systems are used to solve complex problems. Answer C is incorrect because intru-sion-prevention systems are used to detect and prevent attacks or outbreaks of malware. For more information, see Chapter 4.

41. A. Control totals can be used as a recalculation control and offer an easy way to implement an audit trail. Answer B is incorrect because a check digit is used to verify accuracy. A check digit is a sum of a value appended to the data. Answer C is incorrect because a completeness check is used to ensure that all required data has been added and that no fields contain null values. Answer D is incorrect because a limit check is used to set bounds on what are reasonable amounts. For more information, see Chapter 4.

42. C. Decision support systems (DSS) are used to solve problems that managers face. DSS uses models and mathematical techniques. They are usually designed by fourth-generation program-ming (4GL) tools. This makes the systems flexible and adaptable, yet these tools are not always as efficient as lower-level programming tools might be. Answers A, B, and D are incorrect. For more information, see Chapter 4.

43. A. A payback analysis must be performed during the feasibility phase. Answer B is incorrect because during the requirements phase of the system development lifecycle (SDLC), team mem-bers are responsible for fully defining the need and then mapping how the proposed solution meets the need. Answer C is incorrect because during the design phase, the design is finalized and test plans are developed. Answer D is incorrect because during the development phase, developers become deeply involved in their work. For more information, see Chapter 3.

44. B. Time service factor is the percentage of help-desk or response calls answered within a given time. Answer A is incorrect because uptime agreements are one of the most well-known types of SLAs, detailing the agreed-on amount of uptime. Answer C is incorrect because the abandon rate is the number of callers who hang up while waiting for a service representative to answer. Answer D is incorrect because first call resolution is the number of resolutions that are made on the first call and that do not require the user to call the help desk to follow up or seek additional measures for resolution. For more information, see Chapter 5.

45. A. Lights-out operations are those that can take place without human interaction. These can include job scheduling, report generation, report balancing, and backup. Answers B, C, and D are incorrect because they do not describe lights-out operations. For more information, see Chapter 5.

46. B. Assembly is an example of a 2GL language. Answer A is incorrect because SQL is an example of a 4GL language. Answer C is incorrect because FORTRAN is an example of a 3GL language. Answer D is incorrect because Prolog is an example of a 5GL language. For more information, see Chapter 5.

47. C. Proxies provide several services, including load balancing and caching. Most important, the proxy stands in place of the real client and acts as an interface to the private domain, thereby preventing direct access. Answer A is incorrect because the proxy is not used to reduce the load of a client. Answer B is incorrect because proxies prevent direct access. Answer D is incorrect because although proxy servers provide some level of security, they do not allow high-level security such as an application or kernel firewall. For more information, see Chapter 5.

48. B. Programmers should strive to develop modules that have high cohesion and low coupling. Cohesion addresses the fact that a module can perform a single task with little input from other modules. Coupling is the measurement of the interconnection between modules. Low coupling means that a change to one module should not affect another. For more information, see Chapter 3.

49. D. Class 1 Bluetooth supports up to 100 m of range and 100 mW of power. Answer A is not a valid selection, answer B specifies Bluetooth class 3, and answer C specifies Bluetooth class 2. For more information, see Chapter 6.

50. C. EDI systems are used to transfer data between different companies using private networks or the Internet. Communications handlers are the devices responsible for transmitting and receiving data. Answers A, B, and D are incorrect. VANs are the networks or communications networks used to move information. X12 is a common EDI communication protocol. EDIFACT is an international EDI standard. For more information, see Chapter 6.

51. C. SANs are storage area networks that are used to connect multiple servers to a centralized pool of disk storage. SANs improve system administration by allowing centralized storage instead of having to manage hundreds of servers, each with their own disks. PANs are personal area networks. LANs are local area networks, and MANs are metropolitan area networks. For more information, see Chapter 6.

52. C. Item C defines an attribute. An attribute is a component of a databases; in this case, the attribute references the sales rep field. Answers A, B, and D are incorrect because they do not describe an attribute. For more information, see Chapter 4.

53. D. The OSI model defines networking into a seven-layer process. Within the OSI model, the data is passed down from layer to layer. It begins at the application layer and ends at the physical layer. The network layer is tied to routers and routing, and is responsible for the movement of data from network A to network B. The network layer is the home of the *Internet Protocol* (IP). Answers A, B, and C are incorrect. For more information, see Chapter 6.

54. A. Final acceptance testing is usually performed at the implementation phase, when the project staff is satisfied with all other tests and the application is ready to be deployed. Answer B is incorrect because system testing is a series of tests that can include recovery testing, security testing, stress testing, volume testing, and performance testing. Answer C is incorrect because interface testing examines hardware or software to evaluate how well data can be passed from one entity to another. Answer D is incorrect because unit testing examines an individual program or module. For more information, see Chapter 3.

55. C. A router is an OSI Layer 3 device that also can work as a packet filter through the use of access control lists (ACLs). Answers A, B, and D are incorrect because they do not meet that criteria. For more information, see Chapter 6.

56. A. The data link layer is most closely associated with MAC addresses. MAC addresses are 48-bit hardware addresses that identify the specific physical device. Answer B is incorrect because the network layer is associated with IP addresses. Answers C and D are not associated with MAC addresses. For more information, see Chapter 6.

57. B. Class A addresses range from 1 to 126. Class B addresses range from 128 to 191. Class C addresses range from 192 to 223. Class D addresses are considered multicast addresses. Therefore, an address of 128.12.3.15 is a Class B address. For more information, see Chapter 6.

58. C. Routing Information Protocol (RIP) is the most common distance-vector routing protocol in use. Although RIP is a routing protocol, answer A is not the most specific; therefore, it is incorrect. Answer B is incorrect because RIP is not a routable protocol. An example of a routable protocol is IP. Answer D is incorrect because RIP is not a link-state routing protocol. For more information, see Chapter 6.

59. A. Regression is used after a change to verify that inputs and outputs are correct. Answer B is incorrect because system testing is a series of tests that can include recovery testing, security testing, stress testing, volume testing, and performance testing. Answer C is incorrect because interface testing examines hardware or software to evaluate how well data can be passed from one entity to another. Answer D is incorrect because pilot testing is used as an evaluation to verify functionality of the application. For more information, see Chapter 3.

60. D. Prolog is an example of a 5GL language. Answer A is incorrect because SQL is an example of a 4GL language. Answer B is incorrect because Assembly is an example of a 2GL language. Answer C is incorrect because FORTRAN is an example of a 3GL language. For more information, see Chapter 5.

61. A. A bus network is hard to expand, and one break can disable the entire segment. This is not true of star, ring, or mesh topologies. For more information, see Chapter 6.

62. D. The only valid answer is fire-retardant coating. Guarding the health and safety of employees is always a concern. Therefore, plenum-grade cable is designed for use in the crawl spaces of a building. Plenum-grade cable does not give off toxic gasses and smoke as it burns. For more information, see Chapter 6.

63. C. The switched network using Cat 5e cabling is the most secure. It would require an attacker to use ARP poisoning or flooding to be able to see all of the traffic. Although fiber might be more secure overall, it is not a copper cable standard. For more information, see Chapter 6.

64. **A.** Scrum is typically used with object-oriented technology, requires strong leadership, and requires the team to meet each day for a short meeting. Scrum is an iterative development method in which repetitions are referred to as sprints and typically last 30 days. Answer B is incorrect because extreme programming (XP) requires that teams include business managers, programmers, and end users. These teams are responsible for developing useable applications in short periods of time. Answer C is incorrect because RAD uses an evolving prototype and requires heavy user involvement. Answer D is incorrect because the spiral model is based on the concept that software development is evolutionary. The spiral model begins by creating a series of prototypes to develop a solution. As the project continues, it spirals out, becoming more detailed. For more information, see Chapter 3.

65. **A.** Figure E.5 describes a relational database. A relational database is considered a collection of tables that are linked by their primary keys. Answers B, C, and D are incorrect because a network or hierarchical database is not shown. Floating flat is not a valid database type. For more information, see Chapter 5.

66. **D.** The printing of confidential reports represents a real risk because although an operator might not be able to directly read this information, he or she can print it and remove it from the facility. Although answers A, B, and C, are important they are not the most important concern. For more information, see Chapter 6.

67. **D.** Adding RAID 1 is the best example of how to protect against loss from component loss or errors. JBOD offers no fault tolerance, and redundant WAN links would provide protection against loss of connectivity but would not protect against component failures such as hard drives. RAID 0 offers improvement in speed, but no fault tolerance. For more information, see Chapter 6.

68. **B.** Reviewing the configuration would offer the best evidence of how the firewall is actually configured. Answers A, C, and D do not offer as strong audit evidence and, therefore, are incorrect. For more information, see Chapter 6.

69. **D.** ATM is a packet-switching technology; DSL, POTS, and T1 are all examples of circuit-switching technologies. For more information, see Chapter 6.

70. **B.** Web-based application development (WBAD) uses a process to standardize code modules to allow for cross-platform operation and program integration. WBAD offers the capability of standardized integration through the uses of application development technologies such as Extensible Markup Language (XLM). Answer A is incorrect because component-based development (CBD) uses a process of enabling objects to communicate with each other. Answer C is incorrect because OOSD uses a process of solution specifications and models in which items are grouped as objects. Answer D is incorrect because data-oriented system development (DOSD) uses a process that examines software requirements by focusing on data and its structure. For more information, see Chapter 3.

71. **A.** Data warehouses are subject oriented, integrate data from the various operational systems, and are typically loaded from these systems at regular intervals. Answers B, C, and D are incorrect. For more information, see Chapter 4.

72. **B.** The discretionary access control (DAC) model is titled because access control is left to the owner's discretion. DAC allows owners to activate security controls as they see fit. Answer A is incorrect because the mandatory access control (MAC) model is static and based on a predetermined list of access privileges. Answer C is incorrect because role-based access control (RBAC) allows a user to have certain preestablished rights to objects. These rights are assigned to users based on their roles in the organization. Answer D is incorrect because an access control list (ACL) is used by a router for packet filtering. For more information, see Chapter 7.

73. **C.** Two-factor authentication is considered the strongest because it combines two single factor methods, such as biometrics and tokens. Therefore, answers A, B, and D are incorrect. For more information, see Chapter 7.

74. **B.** The EER is a measurement that indicates the point at which FRR equals FAR. Its primary usage is in measuring the overall effectiveness of a biometric device. For more information, see Chapter 7.

75. **B.** Flowcharts are one of the first things an auditor should examine when evaluating business application systems. Answers A, C, and D are incorrect. Although interviewing users, evaluating controls, and determining critical areas are important, they are not the first item that should be completed. For more information, see Chapter 4.

76. **B.** Closed-circuit TV (CCTV) systems don't prevent security breaches; they just alert the guard to a potential problem after it occurs. Therefore, these are considered a detective control. Answers A, C, and D are incorrect. For more information, see Chapter 8.

77. **D.** According to ISACA, the BCP steps include: 1) project management and initiation, 2) business impact analysis, 3) recovery strategy, 4) plan design and development, 5) training and awareness, 6) implementation and testing, and 7) monitoring and maintenance. For more information, see Chapter 9.

78. **B.** Figure E.6 describes a network database. A network database was developed to be more flexible than a hierarchical database. The network database model is considered a lattice structure because each record can have multiple parent and child records. Although this design can work well in stable environments, it can be extremely complex. Answers A, C, and D are incorrect because a relational or hierarchical database is not shown, and floating flat is not a valid database type. For more information, see Chapter 5.

79. **A.** The Kerberos authentication service issues ticket-granting tickets (TGTs) that are good for admission to the ticket-granting service (TGS). Answers B, C, and D are incorrect. The Kerberos ticket-granting service receives tickets created to authenticate specific target services. There is no valid RADIUS authentication service or ticket-granting service. For more information, see Chapter 7.

80. **C.** It's important for everyone involved to understand that the BCP is the most important corrective control that the organization has an opportunity to shape. Therefore answers A, B, and D are incorrect. For more information, see Chapter 9.

81. **C.** Application system testing techniques include snapshots, mapping, and base case system evaluation. Integrated test facilities are an example of a continuous online auditing technique. For more information, see Chapter 4.

82. **A.** The RPO defines how current the data must be or how much data an organization can afford to lose. The greater the RPO, the more tolerant the process is to interruption. The RTO specifies the maximum elapsed time to recover an application at an alternate site. The greater the RTO, the longer the process can take to be restored. For more information, see Chapter 9.

83. **B.** The service delivery objective (SDO) defines the level of service provided by alternate processes while primary processing is offline. Answer A is incorrect because it defines the maximum tolerable outage. Answer C is incorrect because it defines the maximum acceptable outage. Answer D is incorrect because it defines the recovery time objective (RTO). For more information, see Chapter 9.

84. **D.** A risk assessment is performed during the business impact analysis phase. According to ISACA, the BCP steps include: 1) project management and initiation, 2) business impact analysis, 3) recovery strategy, 4) plan design and development, 5) training and awareness, 6) implementation and testing, and 7) monitoring and maintenance. For more information, see Chapter 9.

85. **A.** The generator is a longer-term device. When the UPS signals the generator, it can power up and assume power responsibilities. Most standby generators work on diesel fuel or natural gas. For more information, see Chapter 8.

86. **D.** Integrated test facilities are considered the most complex type of continuous audit technique, followed by continuous and intermittent simulation (CIS), snapshots, and audit hooks. For more information, see Chapter 4.

87. **C.** FM-100 is not a replacement for Halon. Valid replacements include FM-200, NAF-S-3, and argon. For more information, see Chapter 8.

88. **D.** Type 1 errors are also known as the false rejection rate (FRR); they measure the percentage of legitimate users who are denied access. Answer A defines the equal error rate (EER). Answer B also defines the EER. Answer C defines Type 2 errors. For more information, see Chapter 7.

89. **B.** Class A fires are comprised of paper or wood. Answers A, C, and D are incorrect. For more information, see Chapter 8.

90. **A.** Locks of this type fail open. Employees can easily leave if power is disrupted, but intruders can also easily enter. Answers B, C, and D are incorrect. For more information, see Chapter 8.

91. **C.** Figure E.7 describes a hierarchical database. A hierarchical database takes the form of a parent-child structure. These are considered 1:N (one to many) mappings. Each record can have only one owner, so hierarchical databases often can't be used to relate to structures in the real world; however, they are easy to implement, modify, and search. Answers A, B, and D are incorrect because a relational or network database is not shown, and floating flat is not a valid database type. For more information, see Chapter 5.

92. **B.** Continuous online auditing gives auditors the tools needed to perform ongoing monitoring. Continuous online auditing produces audit results at either real-time intervals or after a short period of time. This method actually can reduce costs because the need for conventional audits might be reduced or eliminated. Therefore answers A, C, and D are incorrect. For more information, see Chapter 4.

93. **A.** A mandatory access control (MAC) model is static and based on a predetermined list of access privileges; therefore, in a MAC-based system, access is determined by the system rather than the user. The MAC model is typically used by organizations that handle highly sensitive data, such as the DoD, NSA, CIA, and FBI. Systems based on the MAC model use sensitivity labels and are prohibitive in nature, just as anything that is not explicitly allowed is also denied. Therefore answers B, C, and D are incorrect. For more information, see Chapter 7.

94. **B.** All data must be protected from unauthorized access by initiating internal and output controls to protect confidentiality and data assets. Answers A, C, and D are incorrect because users should not be allowed to copy any data without proper authorization by management. Furthermore, internal controls need to be as restrictive as all output controls for data control. For more information, see Chapter 7.

95. **D.** A privacy impact analysis (PIA) should determine the risks and effects of collecting, maintaining, and distributing personal information in electronic-based systems. A PIA is tied to technology, processes, and people. For more information, see Chapter 7.

96. **C.** Executive management is ultimately responsible for the security practices of the organization. Answers A, B, and D are incorrect. The security advisory group is responsible for reviewing security issues with the chief security officer and also is responsible for reviewing security plans and procedures. The chief security officer is responsible for the day-to-day security of the organization and its critical assets. The security auditor is responsible for examining the organization's security procedures and mechanisms. For more information, see Chapter 7.

97. **B.** Referential integrity guarantees that all foreign keys reference existing primary keys. Answer A is incorrect because relational integrity ensures that validation routines exist to test data before it is entered into a database and that any modification can be detected. Answer C is incorrect because entity integrity ensures that each tuple contains a primary key. Answer D is incorrect because tagging is used to mark selected transactions, while tracing allows these tagged transactions to be monitored. For more information, see Chapter 4.

98. **C.** The extranet is an extension of the organization's private network that uses the public telecommunication system to securely share part of a business's information or operations with suppliers or business partners. Therefore, answers A, B, and D are incorrect. For more information, see Chapter 6.

99. **B.** Latency is the delay that information will experience from the source to the destination. Latency can be caused because data must travel great distances or because of high volumes of network traffic and inadequate bandwidth. Latency is commonly measured with the ping command. For more information, see Chapter 6.

100. **B.** Both 802.11a and 802.11b use the Wired Equivalent Privacy (WEP) protocol. 802.11g devices use WPA, and 802.11i devices use WPA2 and TKIP. For more information, see Chapter 6.

101. **B.** ISDN is considered a circuit-switching technology, while X.25, Frame Rely, and ATM are all considered packet-switching technologies. For more information, see Chapter 6.

102. C. Layers 4 and 5 correspond to the transport and session layer. Between these two layers, services such as TLS are located. Answer A is incorrect because Layers 2 and 3 are the data link and network layers. Answer B is incorrect because Layers 3 and 4 are the network and transport layers. Answer D is incorrect because Layers 5 and 6 are the session and presentation layers. For more information, see Chapter 6.

103. B. DNS is used to resolve domain names to IP addresses. Answer A is incorrect because providing the address of a domain server is not the primary purpose of DNS. Answer C is incorrect because determination of an IP address is not the most correct answer. DNS performs a resolution of FQDN to IP address. Answer D is incorrect because ARP resolves IP addresses to MAC addresses. For more information, see Chapter 6.

104. A. A 10BASE5 network uses a bus topology. Answers B, C, and D are incorrect because they describe a ring, star, and mesh topology. For more information, see Chapter 6.

105. A. Terminal-emulation software (TES) is a category of network service that allows users to access remote hosts. These hosts then appear as local devices. An example of TES is Telnet, which allows a client at one site to establish a session with a host at another site. Answer B is incorrect because FTP is the File Transfer Protocol. Answer C is incorrect because SNMP is the Simple Network Management Protocol and is used for network management. Answer D is incorrect because SMTP is the Simple Mail Transfer Protocol and is used for electronic mail. For more information, see Chapter 6.

106. B. File Transfer Protocol (FTP) operates on ports 20 and 21. Telnet operates on port 23. SMTP operates on port 25, and DHCP operates on ports 67 and 68. For more information, see Chapter 6.

107. C. The transport layer is responsible for reliable data delivery. Protocols such as TCP that are found at this layer feature flow-control, session-startup, and session-shutdown procedures to provide for reliable delivery of data. The data link layer is not the correct answer because this layer deals with physical frames. The session layer does not directly provide this functionality. The network layer is responsible for routing data packets. For more information, see Chapter 6.

108. A. Conducting certification tests is part of the implementation phase. Answers B, C, and D are incorrect. Determining user requirements is part of the user requirements phase. Assessing the project to see if expected benefits were achieved is part of the post implementation phase. Reviewing audit trails is part of the design phase. For more information, see Chapter 3.

109. A. An exception report is a processing control that should be generated when transactions appear to be incorrect. Answers B, C and D are incorrect because they all describe processing edit controls. For more information, see Chapter 4.

110. C. The data link layer is responsible for formatting and organizing the data before sending it to the physical layer. Layer 2 devices include bridges and switches. Hubs and repeaters are found at the physical layer, whereas routers are found at the network layer. For more information, see Chapter 6.

111. C. Run-to-run totals provide the capability to ensure the validity of data through various stages of processing. Answer A is incorrect because manual recalculations are used to ensure that processing is operating correctly. Answer B is incorrect because programming controls are software based and are used to flag problems and initiate corrective action. Answer D is incorrect because reasonableness verification is used to ensure the reasonableness of data. For more information, see Chapter 4.

112. A. Normalization is the process of optimizing a relational database to minimize redundancy. This process reduces repeating data and decreases the potential for anomalies during data operations. Answers B, C, and D are incorrect. For more information, see Chapter 3.

113. B. A PERT chart is used to depict the most cost-effective scenario for the task. Each chart begins with the first task that branches out to a connecting line that contains three estimates: The most optimistic time the task can be completed in, the most likely time the task will be completed in, and the worst-case scenario or longest time the task can take. For more information, see Chapter 3.

114. B. Verifications such as existence checks can best be described as a validation edit control that is considered preventive. Answers A, C, and D are therefore incorrect. For more information, see Chapter 4.

115. C. Every tuple in a table that references a foreign key should be a tuple in the foreign table that is referenced. This ensures referential integrity and prevents dangling tuples. Answers A, B, and D are incorrect and are simply misleading. For more information, see Chapter 5.

116. C. Certification tests a system's internal controls for correct functionality against a known reference. Certification is a technical review of the system. Before systems are placed into operation, they must undergo certification. When certification testing is complete, management will review the compiled results and decide on the location and use of the system. This is known as accreditation; it is management's decision of acceptance. For more information, see Chapter 3.

117. B. The screened subnet sets up a type of DMZ. Screened subnet and DMZs are the basis for most modern network designs. Answer A is incorrect because a packet filter sets up a single-tier packet filter design and has one packet-filtering router installed between the trusted and untrusted networks. Answer C is incorrect because the screened host adds a router. The router is typically configured to see only one host computer on the intranet network. Users on the intranet must connect to the Internet through this host computer, and external users cannot directly access other computers on the intranet. Answer D is incorrect because dual-homed hosts are comprised of a bastion host that has two network interfaces. For more information, see Chapter 6.

118. C. The network database-management systems were created in 1971 and are based on mathematical set theory. This type of database was developed to be more flexible than a hierarchical database. The network database model is considered a lattice structure because each record can have multiple parent and child records. Although this design can work well in stable environments it can be extremely complex. Therefore answers A, B, and D are incorrect. For more information, see Chapter 5.

119. **D.** FPA does not examine the number of expected users. Five functional point values exist: number of user inputs, number of user outputs, number of user inquires, number of files, and number of external interfaces. For more information, see Chapter 3.

120. **C.** Basic is an example of an interpreted programming language. An interpreted language does not assemble or compile the program; it takes an alternate approach by translating the program line by line. Interpreters fetch and execute. Answers A, B, and D are examples of compiled programs. For more information, see Chapter 5.

121. **A.** SQL is an example of a 4GL language. Answer B is incorrect because Assembly is an example of a 2GL language. Answer C is incorrect because FORTRAN is an example of a 3GL language. Answer D is incorrect because Prolog is an example of a 5GL language. For more information, see Chapter 5.

122. **A.** With hierarchical database-management systems, the database takes the form of a parent/child structure. These are considered 1:N (one to many) mappings. Each record can have only one owner, so hierarchical databases often can't be used to relate to structures in the real world; however, they are easy to implement, modify, and search. Therefore, answers B, C, and D are incorrect. For more information, see Chapter 5.

123. **B.** Supervisor state allows the execution of all instructions, including privileged instructions. Any user allowed to run programs in supervisory mode can bypass any kind of security mechanisms and gain complete control of the system. Answers A, C, and D are incorrect. System utilities that run in supervisory mode should be strictly controlled. Supervisory mode is used to gain access to the kernel, not block it. Rings are arranged in a hierarchy from most privileged, lowest numbered ring to least privileged, highest numbered ring. For more information, see Chapter 5.

124. **D.** Sequence numbers are used to make sure that all data falls within a given range. Answer A is incorrect because a limit check is used to verify that the data to be processed does not exceed a predetermined limit. Answer B is incorrect because a range check is used to ensure that a date is within a predetermined range. Answer C is incorrect because a validity check is used to check the validity of a data. For more information, see Chapter 4.

125. **B.** The time between when a incident occurs and when it is addressed is called the delay window. Incident handling should look at ways to reduce the delay window to as small of a value as possible. For more information, see Chapter 5.

126. **C.** System errors are the type of information you would expect to find in a console log. You would not find names and passwords, backup times, or data edit errors. Therefore, answers A, B, and D are incorrect. For more information, see Chapter 5.

127. **D.** Auditors might be asked to verify existing source code at some point. If so, the auditor might want to use source code comparison software. This software enables the auditor to compare a previously obtained copy of the source code to a current copy. The software runs a comparison and can identify any changes. Answer A is incorrect because function point analysis is used to determine the complexity of a software build project. Answer B is incorrect because although a manual review might work, it would be unrealistic for large software projects. Answer C is incorrect because variation tools are not used to measure software changes. For more information, see Chapter 5.

128. A. Processing controls include processing, validation, and editing controls. Authorization is an example of an input control. For more information, see Chapter 4.

129. C. Projects are constrained by their scope, time, and cost. Many approaches and standards exist for meeting this triple constraint. The most well-known is PMBOK. Resources are not part of this triangle. For more information, see Chapter 3.

130. B. The proper order is clustering, remote replication, online restore, and tape restore. Answers A, C, and D are incorrect. For more information, see Chapter 9.

131. B. The project steering committee is ultimately responsible and must ensure that stakeholders' needs are met. Answer A is incorrect because stakeholders are anyone involved or affected by the project activities. Answer C is incorrect because the project manager is responsible for day-to-day management of the project team. Answer D is incorrect because quality assurance is responsible for reviewing the activities of the project-management team and ensuring that output meets quality standards. For more information, see Chapter 3.

132. D. In the influence project management style, the project manager has no real authority and the functional manager remains in charge. Answer A is incorrect because the weak matrix style is characterized by a project manager who has little or no authority and is part of the functional organization. Answer B is incorrect because in a pure project, the project manager has formal authority. Answer C is incorrect because a balanced matrix is characterized by a project manager who has some functional authority and management duties that are shared with functional managers. For more information, see Chapter 2.

133. A. COCOMO specifically deals with software development and the cost, time, and effort in the software-development cycle. Answers B, C and D are incorrect because COCOMO is not associated with hardware, consumer products, or construction. For more information, see Chapter 3.

134. D. Traditional software sizing has been done by counting source lines of code (SLOC). This method does not work as well in modern development programs because additional factors will affect the overall cost. This method determines cost solely on length of code. Answer A is incorrect because FRAP is a risk-assessment method. Answer B is incorrect because Gantt is a project-management technique. Answer C is incorrect because FPA is a newer software cost method that the ISO has approved as a standard to estimate the complexity of software. For more information, see Chapter 3.

135. C. Actuarial tables display statistical values that can be used to determine the probability of risks. These tables are based on mathematical models that examine the cause of specific events and the timing of the events. Actuarial tables can be used in quantitative risk-assessment calculations. Answers A, C, and D are incorrect because the Delphi technique, facilitated risk-assessment process (FRAP), and risk ratings such as high, medium, or low are all examples of qualitative risk-assessment techniques. For more information, see Chapter 2.

Glossary

Numbers

802.11 standard   A legacy set of wireless LAN standards developed by working group 11 of the IEEE LAN/MAN Standards Committee. 802.11 is known for its use of WEP and RC4.

802.11i standard   This is one of the replacements for 802.11. It uses WPA and Advanced Encryption Standard (AES) as a replacement for RC4 encryption.

A

acceptable use policy (AUP)   A policy that defines what employees, contractors, and third parties are authorized to do on the organization's IT infrastructure and its assets. AUPs are common for access to IT resources, systems, applications, Internet access, email access, and so on.

access control list (ACL)   A table or list stored by a router to control access to and from a network by helping the device determine whether to forward or to drop packets that are entering or exiting it.

access creep   The result of an employee moving from one position to another within an organization without losing privileges from the old position, while at the same time gaining additional access in the new position. Thus, over time, the employee builds up much more access than he or she should have.

access point spoofing   This form of man-in-the-middle attack works by pretending to be a legitimate access point for the purpose of tricking a user into passing traffic, by using the fake connection to have the traffic captured and analyzed.

accountability   The traceability of actions performed on a system to a specific system entity or user.

accreditation   Management's formal acceptance of a system or application.

ACID test   Test that addresses atomicity, consistency, isolation, and durability. Programmers involved in database management use the ACID test to determine whether a database-management system has been properly designed to handle transactions.

active fingerprint   An active method of identifying the OS of a targeted computer or device that involves injecting traffic into the network and then sniffing the response.

activity blocker   Similar to an activity monitor, it not only alerts the user to unusual or dangerous computer operations, but it also can block the user's activity.

Address Resolution Protocol (ARP)   Protocol used to map a known IP address to an unknown physical address.

ad-hoc mode   Refers to wireless LAN communication. An individual computer is in a wireless ad-hoc operation mode if the user can communicate directly with other client units. No access point is required. Ad-hoc operation mode is ideal for smaller networks of no more than two to four computers. It is not usually used in the business world because of the potential security risks.

adware   A software program that automatically forces pop-up windows of Internet marketing messages to users' browsers on their workstation devices. Adware is different from spyware; it does not examine a user's individual browser usage and does not exploit such information on the user's browser.

algorithm   A mathematical procedure used for solving a problem. It is commonly used in cryptography.

annualized loss expectancy (ALE)   An annual expected financial loss to an organization's IT asset because of a particular threat being realized within that same calendar year.

anomaly detection   A type of intrusion detection that looks at behavior that is not normal with standard activity. These unusual patterns are identified as suspicious.

ANSI X12   Developed by ANSI to standardize the electronic data interchange (EDI) transactions within North America.

appenders   A type of virus infection that places the virus code at the end of an infected file.

applet   A small Java program that can be embedded in an HTML page. Applets differ from full-fledged Java applications, in that they are not allowed to access certain resources on the local computer, such as files and serial devices (modems, printers, and so on), and are prohibited from communicating with most other computers across a network. The current rule is that an applet can make an Internet connection only to the computer from which the applet was sent.

application   A software program designed to perform a specific task or group of tasks, such as word processing, communications, or database management.

application controls   Category of controls used to verify the accuracy and completeness of records made by manual or automated processes. Controls used for applications include encryption, batch totals, and data input validation.

application layer   Highest layer of the seven-layer OSI model. The application layer is used as an interface to applications or communications protocols.

application programming   The process of developing, updating, and maintaining programs.

application programming interface (API)   A set of system-level routines that can be used in an application program for tasks such as basic input/output and file management. In a graphics-oriented operating environment such as Microsoft Windows, high-level support for video graphics output is part of the Windows graphical API.

arithmetic logic unit (ALU)   A device used for logical and arithmetic operations within a computer.

artificial intelligence   Computer software that can mimic the learning capability of a human, such as reasoning and learning.

ASCII (American Standard Code for Information Interchange)   A standard code for transmitting data, consisting of 128 letters, numerals, symbols, and special codes, each of which is represented by a unique binary number. An ASCII word typically is 8 bits of binary data.

assembler   A program that converts the assembly language of a computer program into the machine language of the computer.

assessment   An evaluation and/or valuation of IT assets based on predefined measurement or evaluation criteria. This does not typically require an accounting or auditing firm to conduct an assessment, such as a risk or vulnerability assessment.

asset   Anything of value that an individual or business owns or possesses.

asymmetric algorithm   Though keys are related, an asymmetric key algorithm uses a pair of different cryptographic keys to encrypt and decrypt data.

asymmetric encryption   In cryptography, an asymmetric key algorithm uses a pair of cryptographic keys to encrypt and decrypt. The two keys are related mathematically; a message encrypted by the algorithm using one key can be decrypted by the same algorithm using the other. In a sense, one key "locks" a lock (encryption), but a different key is required to unlock it (decryption).

Asynchronous Transfer Mode (ATM) Communication technology that uses high-bandwidth, low-delay transport technology and multiplexing techniques. Through dedicated media connections, it provides simultaneous transport of voice, video, and data signals more than 50 times faster than current technology. ATM might be used in phone and computer networks of the future.

asynchronous transmission   The method whereby data is sent and received 1 byte at a time.

attenuation   Occurs with any signal and can be described as a weakening of the signal that increase as the signal travels farther from the source.

attribute sampling   Technique used in auditing that selects certain samples that have specific attributes or characteristics.

audit   Term that typically accompanies an accounting or auditing firm. It refers to a specific and formal methodology and definition on how an investigation should be conducted, with specific reporting elements and metrics being examined. An example is a financial audit conducted according to the Public Accounting and Auditing Guidelines and Procedures.

audit evidence   The auditor gathers information in the course of performing an audit. Once collected, all information is used to meet the audit's objectives.

audit objective   The purpose of the audit, or what the audit expects to achieve.

audit program   A listing of audit procedures to be performed to complete an audit.

audit risk   The risk that the auditor will fail to draw attention to a material misstatement, deficiency, abuse, or other unacceptable matter in an audit.

audit trail   A set of records that collectively provide documentary evidence of processing used to aid in tracing from original transactions forward to related records and reports, and/or backward from records and reports to their component source transactions.

authentication   A method used to enable one to identify an individual. Authentication verifies the identity and legitimacy of the individual who wants to access the system and its resources. Common authentication methods include passwords, tokens, and biometric systems.

authorization   The process of granting or denying access to a network resource based on the user's credentials.

availability   Ensures that the system is responsible for delivering, storing, and processing data, as well as being available and accessible to individuals who are authorized to use its resources.

B

back door   Type of software that allows access to a computer without using conventional security procedures. Back doors are often associated with either hardcoded user/passwords in a vendor product left over from debugging, or with Trojans and other forms of malware.

backup   Copies of programs, databases, other files, and so on are made with the purpose of restoring information in case it is lost, for instance, because of a computer failure, a natural disaster, or a virus infection.

balanced score card   A method developed by Robert Kaplan and David Norton to measure the organization's performance in meeting goals tied to the company's mission statement and strategy.

bandwidth   The range of frequencies, expressed in hertz (Hz), that can pass over a given transmission channel. The bandwidth determines the rate at which information can be transmitted through the circuit.

bar code   A series of bars and spaces that are encoded to represent characters. Bar codes are designed to be machine readable.

base test case   Data created for testing purposes. Used to validate production application systems and to perform ongoing testing to verify the accuracy of the system.

baseband   The name given to a transmission method in which the entire bandwidth (the rate at which information travels through a network connection) is used to transmit just one signal.

baseline   A consistent or established base used to establish a minimum acceptable level of security.

batch control   The application of sequential automation and control to repetitive processes.

batch processing   The performing of a group of computer tasks at the same time.

Bayesian filter   A technique used to detect spam. Bayesian filters give a score to each message based on the words and numbers in a message. They are often employed by antispam software to filter spam based on probabilities. Messages with high scores are flagged as spam and can be discarded, deleted, or placed in a folder for review.

benchmark   A standard test or measurement to compare the performance of similar components or systems.

binary code   A sequence of 0s and 1s used by computer systems as the basis of communication.

biometrics   A method of verifying an individual's identity for authentication by analyzing a unique physical attribute of that individual's fingerprint, retinal scan, or palm print.

black-box testing   Type of testing that occurs when the auditor has little or no knowledge of the organization's network structure.

block cipher   An encryption scheme in which the data is divided into fixed-size blocks, with each encrypted independently from the others.

Blowfish   A symmetric block encryption designed in 1993. It is similar to Twofish, which was designed to meet the specifications for AES.

Blu-ray Disc   Designed as a replacement for DVDs. Blu-ray is a high-density optical disk that can hold audio, video, or data.

Bluejacking   The act of sending unsolicited messages, pictures, or information to a Bluetooth user.

Bluesnarfing   The act of stealing information from a wireless device by using a Bluetooth connection.

Bluetooth   An open standard for short-range wireless communication of data and voice between both mobile and stationary devices that comes in several configurations, the strongest of which is rated for 100 meters. Used in cell phones, PDAs, laptops, and other devices.

bollard   Usually placed in the path of doorways, a heavy round post used to prevent automobiles from ramming buildings or breaching physical security.

bottom-up testing   Testing that works up from the bottom starting with code, then modules, programs, and all the way to systems. The advantage of bottom-up testing is that it can be started as soon as modules are complete. This approach also allows errors in modules to be discovered early.

bridge   A Layer 2 device for passing signals between two LANs or two segments of a LAN.

broadband   A wired or wireless transmission medium capable of supporting a wide range of frequencies, typically from audio up to video frequencies. It can carry multiple signals by dividing the total capacity of the medium into multiple, independent bandwidth channels, with each channel operating on only a specific range of frequencies.

broadcast   A type of transmission used on local and wide area networks in which all devices are sent the information from one host.

brute-force attack   A method of breaking a cipher or encrypted value by trying a large number of possibilities. Brute-force attacks function by working through all possible values. The feasibility of brute-force attacks depends on the key length and strength of the cipher and the processing power available to the attacker. This type of attack can also be targeted against user/password credentials at a login.

buffer   An amount of memory reserved for the temporary storage of data.

buffer overflow   In computer programming, this occurs when a software application somehow writes data beyond the allocated end of a buffer in memory. Buffer overflow is usually caused by software bugs and improper syntax and programming, thus opening or exposing the application to malicious code injections or other targeted attack commands.

bus   A common shared channel among multiple computer devices.

bus LAN configuration   A LAN network design that was developed to connect computers used for 10BASE-5 and 10BASE-2 computer networks. All computers and devices are connected along a common bus or single communication line so that transmissions by one device are received by all.

business case   A document developed to establish the merits and desirability of a project. This is the information necessary to enable approval, authorization, and policy-making bodies to assess a project proposal and reach a reasoned decision, as well as justify the commitment of resources to a project.

business continuity planning (BCP)   A system or methodology used to create a plan on how an organization will resume its partially or completely interrupted critical functions within a predetermined time after the occurrence of a disaster or disruption. The goal is to keep critical functions operational.

business impact analysis (BIA)   A component of the business continuity plan. The BIA looks at all the components that an organization is reliant upon for continued functionality. Its goal is to distinguish which are the most crucial and require a greater allocation of funds in the wake of a disaster.

business process reengineering (BPR) The activity by which an enterprise rethinks and reexamines its goals and how it achieves them, followed by a disciplined approach of business process redesign to achieve dramatic improvements in critical, contemporary measures of performance, such as cost, quality, service, and speed.

business risk The possibility or uncertainty of not meeting business goals or objectives.

bypass label processing (BLP) Used to bypass security and access-control systems and allow the user to read a computer file.

C

Capability Maturity Model A structured model that was designed by Carnegie Melon's Software Engineering Institute to improve and optimize the software development lifecycle.

Carrier Sense Multiple Access/Collision Avoidance (CSMA/CA) The access method used by local area networking technologies, such as the Ethernet.

Carrier Sense Multiple Access/Collision Detection (CSMA/CD) The access method used by local area networking technologies, such as Token Ring.

catastrophe A calamity or misfortune that causes the destruction of a facility and data.

central processing unit (CPU) One of the central components of a system, the CPU carries out the vast majority of the calculations performed by a computer. It can be thought of as the "brain" of a computer. The CPU is like a manager or boss, telling what the other components of the system should be doing at a given moment.

certificate A digital certificate is a file that uniquely identifies its owner. A certificate contains owner identity information and its owner's public key. Certificates are created by the certificate authority.

certificate authority (CA) Used in the PKI infrastructure to issue certificates and report status information and Certificate Revocation Lists.

certificate practice statement (CPS) Provides a detailed explanation of how the certificate authority manages the certificates it issues and associated services such as key management. The CPS acts as a contact between the CA and users, describing the obligations and legal limitations, and setting the foundation for future audits.

Certificate Revocation List (CRL) The CRL is the certification authority's listing of invalid certificates, such as compromised, revoked, or superceded certificates. CRL is used during the digital signature verification process to check the validity of the certificate from which the public verification key is extracted.

certification The technical review of the system or application.

Challenge Handshake Authentication Protocol (CHAP) A secure method for connecting to a system. CHAP functions as follows: 1) When the authentication request is made, the server sends a challenge message to the requestor. The requestor responds with a value obtained by using a one-way hash. 2) The server then checks the response by comparing the received hash to the one calculated locally by the server. 3) If the values match, authentication is acknowledged; otherwise, the connection is terminated.

channel service unit/digital service unit (CSU/DSU) A telecommunications device used to terminate telephone company equipment, such as a T1, and prepare data for router interface at the customer's premises.

check digit An extra digit generated by some mathematical process that is placed after a string of numbers to ensure that they have been correctly input, or to validate numbers as a means of checking against errors in transcription.

cipher text Plain text or clear text is what you have before encryption; cipher text is the encrypted result that is scrambled into an unreadable form.

client/server Describes the relationship between two computer programs in which one program, the client, makes a service request from another program, the server, which fulfills the request. Clients rely on servers for resources, such as files, devices, and even processing power.

clipping level The point at which an alarm threshold or trigger occurs.

closed-circuit television (CCTV) A system comprised of video transmitters that can feed one or more receivers the captured video. Mostly used in banks, casinos, shopping centers, airports, or anywhere that physical security can be enhanced by monitoring events. Placements in these facilities are typically at locations where people enter or leave the facility and where critical transactions occur.

closed system Typically used in context of availability of source code in that a system that is not "open" is considered a proprietary system. Open systems employ modular designs, are widely supported, and facilitate multivendor and multitechnology integration.

CNAMES CNAMES, or conical names, are used in DNS and are considered an alias or nickname.

coaxial cable A cable composed of an insulated central conducting wire wrapped in another cylindrical conductor (the shield). The whole thing is usually wrapped in another insulating layer and an outer protective layer. A coaxial cable has great capacity to carry vast quantities of information. It is typically used in high-speed data and CATV applications.

CobiT An acronym for Control Objectives for Information and Related Technology. CobiT is a framework that was designed by ISACA to aid in information security best practices.

cohesion The extent to which a system or subsystem performs a single function.

cold site A site that contains no computing-related equipment except for environmental support, such as air conditioners and power outlets, and a security system made ready for installing computer equipment.

collision When discussed in the realm of cryptography, describes when a hashing algorithm, such as MD5, creates the same value for two or more different files.

combination lock A lock that can be opened by turning dials in a predetermined sequence.

committed information rate (CIR)   Used when describing the data rate guaranteed by a Frame Relay data communications circuit.

compact disc (CD)   A means of storing video, audio, and data on an optical disk. CDs were originally designed for digital audio music.

compensating control   An internal control designed to reduce risk or weakness in an existing control.

compiler   A computer program that translates a computer program written in one computer language (called the source language) into an equivalent program written in another computer language (called the object, output, or target language).

completely connected (mesh) configuration   Type of network configuration designed so that all devices are connected to all others with many redundant interconnections between network devices.

completeness check   A type of verification that no fields are missing in a form.

compliance testing   A set of tests designed to obtain evidence on the effectiveness of the internal controls and their operation during the audit period.

comprehensive audit   An in-depth audit of financial records that examines internal controls of departments and/or company functions.

computer-aided software engineering (CASE)   The use of software tools to assist in the development and maintenance of software. Tools used in this way are known as CASE tools.

computer emergency response team (CERT)   An organization developed to provide incident-response services to victims of attacks, publish alerts concerning vulnerabilities and threats, and offer other information to help improve an organization's ability to respond to computer and network security issues.

concurrency control   In computer science—or, more specifically, in the field of databases—a method used to ensure that database transactions are executed in a safe manner (that is, without data loss). Concurrency control is especially applicable to database-management systems, which must ensure that transactions are executed safely and that they follow the ACID rules.

confidentiality   Data or information that is not made available or disclosed to unauthorized persons.

confidentiality agreement   An agreement that employees, contractors, or third-party users must read and sign before being granted access rights and privileges to the organization's IT infrastructure and assets. These agreements typically specify that the parties cannot divulge confidential information they become aware of during the course of the engagement.

console log   A report of computer system activity that details specific events and is recorded automatically.

contingency planning   The process of how to prepare to deal with calamities and non-calamitous situations before they occur, thus minimizing effects.

continuity   The state or quality of being continuous or unbroken, without interruption and with a succession of parts intimately united.

control risk   The tendency of the internal control system to lose effectiveness over time and to expose or fail to prevent the exposure of the assets under control.

control unit   The part of the central processing unit (CPU) that is responsible for the execution of software, allocation of internal memory, and transfer of operations between the arithmetic-logic, internal storage, and output sections of the computer.

controlled self-assessment (CSA)   A process that makes management and work teams directly responsible for the management and assessment of internal controls.

corporate governance   The method by which a corporation is directed, administered, or controlled. It includes the laws and customs affecting that direction, as well as the goals for which it is governed. (How objectives of an organization are set, the means of attaining such objectives, how performance-monitoring guidelines are determined, and ways to emphasize the importance of using resources efficiently are significant issues within the makeup of such method.)

corrective controls   Internal controls designed to resolve problems soon after they arise.

coupling   The extent of the complexity of interconnections with other modules.

covert channel   An unintended communication path that allows a process to transfer information in such a way that violates a system's security policy.

cracker   A term derived from "criminal hacker," someone who acts in an illegal manner. This term was developed to distinguish malicious individuals from the classic definition of "hacker."

criminal law   Laws pertaining to crimes against the state or those considered detrimental to society. These violations of criminal statues are punishable by law and can include monitory penalties and jail time.

critical path methodology (CPM)   Determines what activities are critical and what the dependencies are among the various tasks.

criticality   The quality, state, degree, or measurement of the highest importance.

cryptographic key   A value that is used in the cryptographic process of encryption or decryption.

customer relationship management (CRM)   Entails all aspects of interaction that a company has with its customers. It includes methodologies, software, and usually Internet capabilities that help an organization manage customer relationships in an organized way.

D

data communications   The transmission or sharing of data between computers via an electronic medium.

data custodian   Role delegated by the data owner that has the responsibility of maintaining and protecting the organization's data.

data dictionary   A catalog of all data held in a database, or a list of items giving data names and structures.

Data Encryption Standard (DES)   A symmetric encryption standard that is based on a 64-bit block. DES processes 64 bits of plain text at a time to output 64-bit blocks of cipher text. DES uses a 56-bit key and has four modes of operation. Because DES has been broken, 3DES is more commonly used. 3DES uses two or three keys and uses 48 rounds of transposition.

data leakage   Any type of computer information loss. This can involve removal of information by CD, floppy, or USB thumb drive, or any other method that allows the removal or leakage of information by stealing computer reports, data, or tapes.

data owner   Usually a member of senior management of an organization who is ultimately responsible for ensuring the protection and use of the organization's data.

data security   The science and study of methods of protecting data in computer and communications systems against unauthorized disclosure, transfer, modification, or destruction, whether accidental or intentional.

data structure   A logical relationship among data elements that is designed to support specific data-manipulation functions.

database   A collection of data that is organized and stored on a computer and can be searched and retrieved by a computer program.

database administrator (DBA)   A person (or group of people) responsible for the maintenance activities of a database, including backup and recovery, performance, and design.

database-management system (DBMS)   An integrated set of computer programs that provide the capabilities needed to establish, modify, make available, and maintain the integrity of a database.

deadman door   Two sets of doors: It allows one person to enter the first door; then after it is closed, the second door is allowed to open. Deadman doors are used to control access. Also known as a mantrap.

decentralized computing   The act of distributing computing activities and computer processing to different locations.

decision support system (DSS)   A now-superseded term for a software application that analyzes business data and presents it so that users can make business decisions more easily.

decryption   The process of converting encrypted content into its original form, often the process of converting cipher text to plain text. Decryption is the opposite of encryption.

defense-in-depth   The process of multilayered security. The layers can be administrative, technical, or logical.

demilitarized zone (DMZ)   The middle ground between a trusted internal network and an untrusted, external network. Services that internal and external users must use, such as HTTP, are typically placed there.

denial of service (DoS)   Occurs when an attacker consumes the resources on your computer for things it was not intended to do, thus preventing normal access to network resources and applications for legitimate purposes.

destruction   Destroying data or information so that it is deprived from the legitimate user.

detection risk   The risk that audit procedures will lead to a conclusion that material error does not exist, when, in fact, such error does exist.

detective control   Controls to identify and correct undesirable events that have occurred.

device lock   Lock used to secure laptops and other devices from theft.

dial back   Can be used for personal identification. A procedure established for positively identifying a terminal that is dialing into a computer system. It works by disconnecting the calling terminal and reestablishing the connection by the computer system dialing the telephone number of the calling terminal.

dictionary attack   A type of cryptographic attack in which the attacker uses a word list or dictionary list to try to crack an encrypted password. A newer technique is to use a time memory tradeoff, such as in rainbow tables.

digital certificate   Usually issued by trusted third parties and contains the name of a user or server, a digital signature, a public key, and other elements used in authentication and encryption. X.509 is the most common type.

digital signature   An electronic signature that can authenticate the identity of the sender of a message. A digital signature is usually created by encrypting the user's private key and is decrypted with the corresponding public key.

digital watermark   A technique that adds hidden copyright information to a document, picture, or sound file.

direct-sequence spread spectrum (DSS)   A technique used to scramble the signal of wireless devices.

disaster   A natural or man-made event that includes fire, flood, storm, or equipment failure and that negatively affects an industry or facility.

disaster tolerance   Refers to the amount of time that an organization can accept the unavailability of IT facilities and services.

discovery sampling   A sampling plan for locating at least one deviation, provided that the deviation occurs in the population with a specified frequency.

discretionary access control (DAC)   An access policy that allows the resource owner to determine access.

diskless workstation   A thin client that has no hard drive or local operating system. The system boots from a centralized server and stores files on a network file server.

distributed denial of service (DDoS)   Similar to DoS, except that the attack is launched from multiple and distributed agent IP devices. DDoS is harder to defend against because it originates from many different devices; thus, it is harder to identify the true attacker. This is also difficult because it is hard to distinguish legitimate traffic from malicious traffic.

domain name system (or service or server) (DNS)   A hierarchy of Internet servers that translate alphanumeric domain names into IP addresses, and vice versa. Because domain names are alphanumeric, it is easier to remember these names than IP addresses.

downloading   Transferring information from one computer to another computer and storing it there.

downtime report   A record that tracks the amount of time that a computer or device is not operating because of a hardware or software failure.

dropper   A program designed to drop a virus to the infected computer and then execute it on the user's system.

due care   The standard of conduct taken by a reasonable and prudent person. When you see the term *due care*, think of the first letter of each word and remember "do correct" because due care is about the actions that you take to reduce risk and keep it at that level.

due diligence   The execution of due care over time. When you see the term *due diligence*, think of the first letter of each word and remember "do detect" because due diligence is about finding the threats an organization faces. This is accomplished by using standards, best practices, and checklists.

dumb terminal   A computer workstation or terminal that consists of a keyboard and screen, but with no processor of its own. It sends and receives its data to and from a large central computer or server.

dumpster diving   The practice of rummaging through the trash of a potential target or victim to gain useful information.

Dynamic Host Configuration Protocol (DHCP)   The process of dynamically assigning an IP address to a host device.

E

eavesdropping   The unauthorized capture and reading of network traffic.

echo request and echo reply   The technical name for a ping. The first part of an ICMP ping message, officially a Type 8. The second part of an ICMP ping message, officially a Type 0.

edit controls   Manual or automated process to check for and allow the correction of data errors before processing. Edit controls detect errors in the input portion of information.

editing   To review for possible errors and make final changes, if necessary, to information in a database.

EGDAR database   The Electronic Data Gathering, Analysis, and Retrieval System used by the Securities and Exchange Commission to store public company filings.

Electronic Code Book (ECB)   A symmetric block cipher that is a form of DES. ECB is considered the weakest form of DES. When used, the same plain-text input will result in the same encrypted text output.

electronic data interchange (EDI)   The exchange of business information or transaction documents between computers of two organizations. This can be accomplished by direct computer-to-computer transfer of transaction information contained in standard business format without paper or human intervention.

electronic funds transfer (EFI)   The transfer of money or funds between accounts initiated through an electronic terminal, automated teller machine, computer, telephone, or magnetic tape rather than using conventional paper-based payment methods.

electronic serial number   Used to identify a specific cell phone when turned on and requesting to join a cell network.

email bomb   A hacker technique that floods the email account of the victim with useless emails.

email/interpersonal messaging   Instant messages, usually text, sent from one person to another, or to a group of people, via computer.

embedded audit module   An integral part of an application system that is designed to identify and report specific transactions or other information based on predetermined criteria. Identification of reportable items occurs as part of real-time processing. Reporting might be real-time online, or might use store-and-forward methods.

encapsulation (objects)   As used by layered protocols, a technique that applies to a layer adding header information to the protocol data unit (PDU) from the layer above. Basically, this refers to the ability to cover and seal an object.

encryption   The science of turning plain text into cipher text.

encryption key   A sequence of characters used by an encryption algorithm to encrypt plain text into cipher text.

end-user computing   The use or development of information systems by the principal users of the systems' outputs or by their staffs.

end-user licensing agreement (EULA)   The software license that software vendors create to protect and limit their liability, as well as hold the purchaser liable for illegal pirating of the software application. The EULA typically includes language that protects the software manufacturer from software bugs and flaws, and limits the liability of the vendor.

enterprise architecture   A blueprint that defines the business structure and operation of the organization.

enterprise resource planning (ERP)   ERP systems are software systems used for operational planning and administration, and for optimizing internal business processes. The best-known supplier of these systems is SAP.

enterprise vulnerability management   The overall responsibility and management of vulnerabilities within an organization and how that management of vulnerabilities will be achieved through the dissemination of duties throughout the IT organization.

entity relationship diagram (ERD)   Helps map the requirements and define the relationship between elements.

equal error rate (EER)   A comparison measurement for different biometric devices and technologies to measure their accuracy. The CER is the point at which FAR and FRR are equal, or cross over. The lower the CER, the more accurate the biometric system.

Ethernet   A network protocol defining a specific implementation of the physical and data link layers in the OSI model (IEEE 802.3). Ethernet is a local area network that uses a bus topology and provides reliable high-speed communications (maximum of 100 million bps) in a limited geographic area (such as an office complex or university complex).

ethical hack   A term used to describe a type of hack done to help a company or individual identify potential threats on the IT infrastructure or network. Ethical hackers must obey rules of engagement, do no harm, and stay within legal boundaries. Also referred to as penetration testing.

ethical hacker   A security professional who legally attempts to break into a computer system or network to find its vulnerabilities.

evasion   The act of performing activities to avoid detection.

evidence   Gathered by an auditor during the course of an audit. The information gathered stands as proof that can support conclusions of an audit report.

exception report   A report that uses data selection based on a very specific set of circumstances to identify process exceptions. Reports that identify items with negative on-hand quantities or locations with more than one item stored in them are examples of exception reports.

exclusive-OR (XOR)   Exclusive disjunction (usual symbol xor) is a logical operator that results in "true" if one, but not both, of the operands is "true."

expert system   An expert system is a class of computer programs developed by researchers in artificial intelligence during the 1970s and applied commercially throughout the 1980s. In essence, they are programs made up of a set of rules that analyze information (usually supplied by the user of the system) about a specific class of problems, as well as provide analysis of the problem(s), and, depending upon their design, a recommended course of user action to implement corrections.

exploit   The actual tool or code one can use to take advantage of a system vulnerability.

exposure factor   A value calculated by determining the percentage of loss to a specific asset due to a specific threat.

Extended Binary Coded Decimal Interchange Code (EBCDIC)   An IBM-developed 8-bit binary code that can represent 256 characters. It allows control codes and graphics to be represented in a logical format. EBCDIC was created to represent data in particular types of data processing and communications terminal devices.

Extensible Authentication Protocol   A method of authentication that can support multiple authentication methods, such as tokens, smart cards, certificates, and one-time passwords. Some common variants include LEAP and EAP-RADIUS.

Extensible Markup Language (XML)   An emerging standard or system for defining, validating, or sharing document formats and data distributed on the Web. XML enables authors to create customized tags that can help them efficiently achieve their goals.

extranet   A private network that uses Internet protocols and the public telecommunication system to securely share part of a business's information or operations with suppliers, vendors, partners, customers, or other businesses. An extranet can be viewed as part of a company's intranet that is extended to users outside the company. An extranet requires security and privacy.

F

fail safe   In the logical sense, the process of discovering a system error, terminating the process, and preventing the system from being compromised.

false acceptance rate (FAR)   Measurement that evaluates the likelihood that a biometric access-control system will wrongly accept an unauthorized user.

false authorization rate See *false acceptance rate*.

false rejection rate (FRR) Measurement that evaluates the likelihood that a biometric access-control system will reject a legitimate user.

feasibility study A phase of an SDLC methodology that researches the feasibility and adequacy of resources for the development or acquisition of a system solution for a user's need.

fiber-optic cable A medium for transmission comprised of many glass fibers. Light-emitting diodes or lasers send light through the fiber to a detector that converts the light back to an electrical signal for interpretation. Advantages include huge bandwidth, immunity to electromagnetic interference, and the ability to traverse long distances with minimal signal degradation.

field In a database, the part of a record reserved for a particular type of data; for example, in a library catalog, author, title, ISBN, and subject headings would all be fields.

file Data stored as a named unit on a data storage medium. Examples include a program, a document, and a database.

file allocation table (FAT) A table or list maintained by an operating system to keep track of the status of various segments of disk space used for file storage.

file server A high-capacity disk storage device or a computer that each computer on a network can use or access and retrieve files that can be shared among attached computers. Such computer programs can be set up to accept (or not accept) different programs running on other computers, to access the files of that computer.

financial audit The examination of financial records and reports of a company to verify that the figures in the financial reports are relevant, accurate, and complete.

finger On some UNIX systems, finger identifies who is logged on and active, and sometimes to provide personal information about that individual.

firewall Security system in hardware or software form that manages and controls both network connectivity and network services. Firewalls act as chokepoints for traffic entering and leaving the network, and prevent unrestricted access. Firewalls can be stateful or stateless.

firmware A computer program or software stored permanently in PROM or ROM, or semipermanently in EPROM. Software is "burned in" on the memory device so that it is nonvolatile (will not be lost when power is shut off).

first in, first out (FIFO) A method of data and information storage in which the data stored for the longest time is retrieved first.

flooding The process of overloading the network or target application with traffic so that no legitimate traffic or activity can occur.

fourth-generation language (4GL) Programming languages that are easier to use than lower-level languages such as BASIC, Assembly, or FORTRAN. 4GL languages such as SQL and Python are also known as nonprocedural, natural, or very high-level languages.

Frame Relay   A type of packet-switching technology that transmits data faster than the X.25 standard. Frame Relay does not perform error correction at each computer in the network. Instead, it simply discards any messages with errors. It is up to the application software at the source and destination to perform error correction and to control for loss of messages.

frequency-hopping spread spectrum (FHSS) One of the basic modulation techniques used in spread spectrum signal transmission. FHSS is another technique used to make wireless communication harder to intercept and more resistant to interference.

function point analysis (FPA)   An ISO-approved method as a standard to estimate the complexity of software.

G

gap analysis   The analysis of the differences between two states, often to determine how to get from point A to point B, thus aiming to look for ways to bridge the gap.

gateway   A device that allows for the translation and management of communication between networks that use different protocols or designs. Can also be deployed in a security context to control sensitive traffic.

generalized audit software (GAS)   A computer program or series of programs designed to perform certain automated functions. These functions include reading computer files, selecting data, manipulating data, sorting data, summarizing data, performing calculations, selecting samples, and printing reports or letters in a format specified by the IS auditor. This technique includes software acquired or written for audit purposes and software embedded in production.

gentle scan   A type of vulnerability scan that does not present a risk to the operating network infrastructure. Tools such as Nessus have the option of running a gentle scan or running a scan with dangerous plug-ins.

geographical information system (GIS)   A computer system that combines database-management system functionality with information about location. In this way, it can capture, manage, integrate, manipulate, analyze, and display data that is spatially referenced to the earth's surface.

gold standard   Generally regarded as practices and procedures that are considered the very best.

governance   The planning, influencing, and conducting of the policy and affairs of an organization (in our case, the organization refers to a project).

gray-box testing   Testing that occurs with only partial knowledge of the network, or that is performed to see what internal users have access to. Testers might also have access to some code.

guidelines   Much like standards, these are recommendations; they are not hard-and-fast rules.

H

hardware   The physical equipment of a computer system, including the central processing unit, data-storage devices, terminals, and printers.

hardware keystroke logger   A form of key logger that is a hardware device such as DIN5, PS2, or USB. When placed on the system, it is hard to detect without doing a physical inspection. It can be plugged into the keyboard connector or be built into the keyboard.

hash   A mathematical algorithm used to ensure that a transmitted message has not been tampered with. The sender generates a hash of the message, encrypts it, and sends it with the message itself. The recipient then decrypts both the message and the hash, produces another hash from the received message, and compares the two hashes. If they are the same, there is a very high probability that the message was transmitted intact.

hashing algorithm   Verifies the integrity of data and messages. A well-designed hashing algorithm examines every bit of the data while it is being condensed; even a slight change to the data results in a large change in the message hash. Hashing is considered a one-way process.

help desk   A support system designed to assist end users with technical and functional questions and problems. Also serves as technical support for hardware and software. Help desks are staffed by people who can either solve the problem directly or forward the problem to someone else. Help-desk software provides the means to log problems and track them until solved. It also gives management information regarding support activities.

heuristic filter   An IDS/IPS and antispam filter technology that uses criteria based on a centralized rule database.

heuristic scanning   A form of virus scanning that looks at irregular activity by programs. For example, a heuristic scanner will flag a word-processing program that has attempted to format the hard drive, which is not normal activity.

hierarchical database   Database that is organized in a tree structure, in which each record has one owner. Navigation to individual records takes place through predetermined access paths.

honey pot   An Internet-attached server that acts as a decoy, luring in potential hackers to study their activities and monitor how they are able to break into a system. This can be deployed internally as well, to provide targets for attackers who get by perimeter defenses.

hot site   A commercial disaster-recovery service that enables an organization to sustain its computing and network capabilities in the event of a massive equipment failure. A hot site provides the equipment and office facilities needed for the organization to continue its operations.

hub   A device used for physical connectivity in networks. It provides connectivity, amplification, and signal regeneration.

Hypertext Markup Language (HTML)   A coding technique used to create documents and web pages for the World Wide Web.

I

IANA   A primary governing body for Internet networking. IANA oversees three key aspects of the Internet: top-level domains (TLDs), IP address allocation, and port number assignments. IANA is tasked with preserving the central coordinating functions of the Internet for the public.

identity theft   An attack in which an individual's personal, confidential, banking, or financial identity is stolen and compromised by another individual or individuals. Use of a social security number without the individual's consent or permission could result in identity theft.

impact   Best defined as an attempt to identify the extent of the consequences if a given event occurs.

impact assessment   A study of the potential future effects of a development project on current projects and resources. The resulting document should list the pros and cons of pursuing a specific course of action.

independence   The state or quality of being free from subjection or the influence, control, or guidance of individuals, things, or situations. Applied to auditors and examining officials and their respective organizations who must maintain neutrality and exercise objectivity so that opinions, judgments, conclusions, and recommendations on examined allegations are impartial and are viewed as impartial by disinterested third parties.

Indexed Sequential Access Method (ISAM)
A combination or compromise between indexed blocks of data arranged sequentially within each block; used for storing data for fast retrieval.

information-processing facility (IPF)   The areas where information is processed, usually the computer room and support areas.

Information Technology Security Evaluation Criteria (ITSEC)   A European standard that was developed in the 1980s to evaluate the confidentiality, integrity, and availability of an entire system.

infrastructure mode   A form of wireless networking in which wireless stations communicate with each other by first going through an access point.

inherent risk   The susceptibility of an audit area to error, which could be material, individual, or in combination with other errors, assuming that there are no related internal controls.

initial sequence number   A number defined during a TCP startup session.

input controls   Computer controls designed to provide reasonable assurance that transactions are properly authorized before processed by the computer; that transactions are accurately converted to machine-readable form and recorded in the computer; that data files and transactions are not lost, added, duplicated or improperly changed; and that incorrect transactions are rejected, corrected, and, if necessary, resubmitted on a timely basis.

insecure computing habits   The bad habits that employees, contractors, and third-party users have accumulated over the years can be attributed to the organization's lack of security-awareness training, lack of security controls, and lack of any security policies or acceptable use policies (AUPs).

Integrated Services Digital Network (ISDN)
A system that provides simultaneous voice
and high-speed data transmission through a
single channel to the user's premises. ISDN
is an international standard for end-to-end
digital transmission of voice, data, and
signaling.

integrity   One of the three items considered
part of the security triad; the others are confidentiality and availability. It is used to verify the accuracy and completeness of an item
and that it has not been tampered with.

Internet   An interconnected system of networks that connects computers around the
world via the TCP/IP protocol.

Internet Assigned Numbers Authority (IANA)
An organization dedicated to preserving the
central coordinating functions of the global
Internet for the public good. Used by hackers and security specialists to track down
domain owners and their contact details.

Internet Control Message Protocol (ICMP)
Part of TCP/IP that supports diagnostics
and error control. Ping is a type of ICMP
message.

Internet Engineering Task Force (IETF)   A
large open, international community of network designers, operators, vendors, and
researchers concerned with the evolution of
the Internet architecture and the smooth
operation of the Internet. It is open to any
interested individual. The IETF is the pro-
tocol-engineering and development arm of
the Internet.

Internet packet spoofing (IP spoofing)   A
technique used to gain unauthorized access
to computers or in denial of service attacks.
Newer routers and firewall arrangements
can offer protection against IP spoofing.

Internet Protocol (IP)   One of the key protocols of TCP/IP. The IP protocol is found at
Layer 3 (network layer) of the OSI model.

intrusion detection   A key component of
security that includes prevention, detection,
and response. It is used to detect anomalies
or known patterns of attack.

intrusion-detection system (IDS)   A network-monitoring device typically installed at
Internet ingress/egress points. An IDS
inspects inbound and outbound network
activity and identifies suspicious patterns
that could indicate a network or system
attack from someone attempting to break
into or compromise a system.

IPsec   Short for IP security. An IETF standard used to secure TCP/IP traffic by
means of encapsulation. It can be
implemented to provide integrity and
confidentiality.

irregularities   Intentional violations of
established management policy, or deliberate misstatements, or omissions of information concerning the area under audit or the
organization as a whole.

ISO 17799   A comprehensive security standard that is divided into 10 sections. It is
considered a leading standard and a code
of practice for information security
management.

IT   Information technology.

IT asset   Information technology assets
such as hardware, software, or data.

IT asset criticality   The act of assigning a
criticality factor or importance value (critical, major, or minor) to an IT asset.

IT asset valuation   The act of assigning a monetary value to an IT asset.

IT infrastructure   A general term used to encompass all information technology assets (hardware, software, data), components, systems, applications, and resources.

IT security architecture and framework   A document that defines the policies, standards, procedures, and guidelines for information security.

J

JBOD   Just a Bunch of Disks, a technique that is somewhat like RAID, in that two or more hard drives are combined into one storage array. However, JBOD offers none of the fault tolerance advantages of RAID.

K

key-exchange protocol   A protocol used to exchange secret keys for the facilitation of encrypted communication. Diffie-Hellman is an example of a key-exchange protocol.

kilo lines of code (KLOC)   A technique used to determine the cost of software development that is based solely on length of code.

L

last in, first out (LIFO)   A data-processing method that applies to buffers. The last item in the buffer is the first to be removed.

latency   The delay that it takes one packet to travel from one node to another.

librarian   The individual in the corporation who is responsible for storing, safeguarding, and maintaining data, programs, and computer information.

limit check   Test of specified amount fields against stipulated high or low limits of acceptability. When both high and low values are used, the test can be called a range check.

limitation of liability and remedies   A legal term that limits the organization in the amount of financial liability and remedies it is legally responsible for.

local area network (LAN)   A group of wired or wireless computers and associated devices that share a common communications line and typically share the resources of a single processor or server within a small geographic area (for example, within an office building).

log   In computing, the log is equivalent to the history log of ships. The log is an automatic system that records significant events. The files that contain these records are called log files. Generally, the log is a file; what is written on it is a record.

log on   The process of identifying yourself to your computer or an online service; the initial identification procedure to gain access to a system as a legitimate user. The usual requirements are a valid username (or user ID) and password.

logic bomb   One of the most dangerous types of malware, in that it waits for a predetermined event or an amount of time to execute its payload. Typically a disgruntled employee/insider attack.

M

MAC filtering   A method of controlling access on a wired or wireless network by denying access to a device in which the MAC address does not match one on a preapproved list.

macro infector   A type of computer virus that infects macro files. The "I love you" virus and Melissa virus are examples of macro viruses.

MAID   Massive Array of Inactive Disks. A large array of hard drives that are kept inactive until needed.

man-in-the-middle attack   A type of attack in which the attacker can read, insert, and change information that is being passed between two parties without either party knowing that the information has been compromised.

man-made threat   Threat caused by humans, such as hacker attack, terrorism, or destruction of property.

management information system (MIS)   An organized approach to gathering data from inside and outside the company, and processing it by computer to produce current, accurate, and informative reports for decision makers. It provides management with much-needed information on a regular basis.

mandatory access control (MAC)   A means of restricting access to objects based on the sensitivity (as represented by a label) of the information contained in the objects and the formal authorization (such as clearance) of subjects to access information of such sensitivity.

mantrap   See deadman door.

master boot record infector   A virus that infects a master boot record.

materiality   An expression of the relative significance or importance of a particular matter in the context of the organization as a whole.

MD5   A hashing algorithm that produces a 128-bit output.

Media Access Control (MAC)   The hard-coded address of the physical-layer device that is attached to the network. All network interface controllers must have a hard-coded and unique MAC address. The MAC address is 48 bits long.

message switching   A strategy that enables communication channels to be used simultaneously by more than one node. At each transfer point in the connection, incoming data is stored in its entirety and then forwarded to the next point. This process continues until the data reaches its destination.

methodology   A set of documented procedures used for performing activities in a consistent, accountable, and repeatable manner.

middleware   Software that "glues together" two or more types of software (for example, two applications, their operating systems, and the network on which everything works) by translating information between them and exchanging this information over a network without both interacting applications being aware of the middleware.

minimum acceptable level of risk   The stake in the ground that an organization defines for the seven areas of information security responsibility. Depending on the goals and objectives for maintaining confidentiality, integrity, and availability of the IT infrastructure and its assets, the minimum level of acceptable risk dictates the amount of information security.

mobile site   Portable data-processing facility transported by trailers to be quickly moved to a business location. Typically used by insurance companies and the military, these facilities provide a ready-conditioned information-processing facility that can contain servers, desktop computers, communications equipment, and even microwave and satellite data links.

modem   A device used to connect a computer to an analog phone line. Modems use the process of modulation.

modulation   Used by modems to convert a digital computer signal into an analog telecommunications signal.

Moore's law   The belief that processing power of computers will double about every 18 months.

multicast   The process of sending a computer packet to a group of recipients.

multipartite virus   A virus that attempts to attack both the boot sector and executable files.

N

NetBus   A back-door Trojan along the lines of back orifice 2000 (BOK2) that gives an attacker total control of the victim's computer.

Network Address Translation (NAT)   A method of connecting multiple computers to the Internet using one IP address so that many private addresses are being converted to a single public address. Addressed in RFC 1918.

network administrator   The individual responsible for the installation, management, and control of a network. When problems with the network arise, this is the person to call.

network operations center (NOC)   An organization's help desk or interface to its end users, where questions, trouble calls, and trouble tickets are generated.

NIST 800-42   Document that provides guidance on network security testing. It deals mainly with techniques and tools used to secure systems connected to the Internet.

noise   Any unwanted signal, such as static, that interferes with the clarity of data being transmitted, thus creating the possibility that the receiver will receive a misconstrued message.

nonattribution   The act of not providing a reference to a source of information.

nonrepudiation   A system or method put into place to ensure that an individual cannot deny his own actions and prevents the reply of network traffic.

normalization   The process of reducing a complex data structure into its simplest, most stable structure. In general, the process entails removing redundant attributes, keys, and relationships from a conceptual data model.

NSA IAM The National Security Agency (NSA) Information Security Assessment Methodology (IAM), a systematic process used by government agencies and private organizations to assess security vulnerabilities.

nslookup A standard UNIX, Linux, and Windows tool for querying name servers.

null session A Windows feature through which anonymous logon users can list domain user names, account information, and enumerate share names.

O

objectivity An independent mental attitude that requires internal auditors to perform audits in such a manner that they have an honest belief in their work product and that no significant quality compromises are made. The auditor's objectivity depends on the organizational status of the internal audit function, whether the internal auditor has direct access and reports regularly to the board, the audit committee, and more. Therefore, objectivity requires that internal auditors not subordinate their judgment on audit matters to that of others.

off-site storage A storage facility that is not located at the organization's primary facility. The idea behind off-site storage is to protect information and limit damage that might occur at the primary facility. Off-site storage facilities are used to store computer media, backup data, and files.

one-time pad An encryption mechanism that can be used only once and that is, theoretically, unbreakable. One-time pads function by combining plain text with a random pad that is the same length as the plain text.

Open Shortest Path First (OSPF) A routing protocol that determines the best path for routing IP traffic over a TCP/IP network. It uses less router-to router update traffic than the RIP protocol that it has been designed to replace.

open source Based on the GNU General Public License. Although several "flavors" of GPL exist, this generally works by means of software that is open source and is released under an open-source license or to the public domain. The source code can be seen and modified.

operating system (OS) identification The practice of identifying the operating system of a networked device by using passive or active techniques.

operational control Day-to-day controls that are used for normal daily operation of the organization. Operational controls ensure that normal operational objectives are achieved.

outsourcing A contract arrangement between a third party and the organization for services such as web hosting, application development, or data processing.

P

packet A block of data sent over the network that transmits the identities of the sending and receiving stations, for error control. Also known as a packed data unit (PDU).

packet filter A form of stateless inspection performed by some firewalls and routers.

packet switching   A data-transmission method that divides messages into standard-sized packets for greater efficiency of routing and transporting them through a network.

paper shredder   A hardware device used for destroying paper and documents, to prevent dumpster diving. Many modern shredders support CD/DVD destruction as well.

paper test   A type of disaster-recovery test that reviews the steps of the test without actually performing the steps. This type of disaster-recovery test is usually used to help team members review the proposed plan and become familiar with the test and its objectives.

parallel testing   A mode of testing in which a stream of data is fed into two systems to allow processing by both so that the results can be compared.

parity check   A type of error check of control by means of an added digit (a 0 or a 1). The digit is added to an individual data item to indicate whether the sum of that data item's bit is odd or even. It can detect error when the parity bit disagrees with the sum of the other bits.

passive OS fingerprint   A passive method of identifying the operating system (OS) of a targeted computer or device. No traffic or packets are injected into the network; attackers simply listen and analyze existing traffic.

Password Authentication Protocol (PAP)   A form of authentication in which clear-text usernames and passwords are passed.

pattern matching   A method of identifying malicious traffic that is used by IDS systems. Also called signature matching, it works by matching traffic against signatures stored in a database.

penetration test   A method of evaluating the security of a network or computer system by simulating an attack by a malicious hacker. The goal is to accomplish this without doing harm and with the owner's consent.

personal area network (PAN)   When discussing Bluetooth devices, refers to the connection that can be made between Bluetooth and the various devices. PANs are used for short-range communication.

personal digital assistant (PDA)   A handheld device that combines computing, telephone/fax, and networking features. A typical PDA can function as a cellular phone, fax sender, and personal organizer. Many PDAs incorporate handwriting and/or voice-recognition features. PDAs also are called palmtops, handheld computers, and pocket computers.

phishing   The act of misleading or conning an individual into releasing and providing (personal and confidential) information to an attacker masquerading as a legitimate individual or business. Spear phishing occurs when attackers go after a particular business, type of person, clients, and so on.

phreaker   Individual who hacks phone systems or phone-related equipment. Phreakers predate computer hackers.

piggybacking   A method of gaining unauthorized access into a facility by following an authorized employee through a controlled access point or door. Piggybacking is also known as tailgating.

ping sweep   The process of sending ping requests to a series of devices or to the entire range of networked devices, with the objective being to see what responds. Pings are often blocked by network devices or OS configuration tweaks.

point-of-sale (PoS) system   Systems that enable the capture of data at the time and place of transaction. PoS terminals can include using optical scanners with bar codes or magnetic card readers with credit cards. PoS systems might be online to a central computer or might use standalone terminals or microcomputers that hold the transactions until the end of a specified period, when they are sent to the main computer for batch processing.

policy   A high-level document that dictates management's intentions regarding security.

polymorphic virus   A virus that is capable of change and self-mutation.

POP   Post Office Protocol, a commonly implemented method of delivering email from the mail server to the client machine. Other methods include IMAP and Microsoft Exchange.

port   Defined by IANA and used by protocols and applications. Port numbers are divided into three ranges: well-known ports, registered ports, and dynamic and/or private ports. Well-known ports are ports 0–1023. Registered ports are ports 1024–49151. Dynamic and/or private ports are ports 49152–65535.

port knocking   A defensive technique that requires users of a particular service to access a sequence of ports in a given order before the service will accept their connection. Some port knocking will not have the service listening until the proper sequence of knocks happens.

port redirection   The process of redirecting one protocol from an existing port to another.

prepender   A virus type that adds the virus code to the beginning of existing executables.

pretexting   Collecting information about a person under false pretenses.

preventative controls   Controls that reduce risk and are used to prevent undesirable events from occurring.

principle of deny all   A process of securing logical or physical assets by first denying all access and then allowing access only on a case-by-case basis.

privacy impact analysis   The process of reviewing the information held by the corporation and assessing the damage that would result if sensitive or personal information were lost, stolen, or divulged.

probability   The likelihood of an event happening.

problem-escalation procedure   The procedure that details the process of increasing the priority of a problem from junior to senior staff, and ultimately to higher levels of management if resolution is not achieved.

procedure   A detailed, in-depth, step-by-step document that lays out exactly what is to be done and how it is to be accomplished.

Program Evaluation and Review Technique (PERT)   A planning and control tool representing, in diagram form, the network of tasks required to complete a project, establishing sequential dependencies and relationships among the tasks.

promiscuous mode   The act of changing the network adapter from its normal mode of examining traffic that matches only its address to examining all traffic. Promiscuous mode allows a network device to intercept and read all network packets that arrive at its interface in their entirety.

protocol   A set of formalized rules that describe how data is transmitted over a network. Low-level protocols define the electrical and physical standard, while high-level protocols deal with formatting of data. TCP and IP are examples of high-level LAN protocols.

prototyping   The process of quickly putting together a working model (a prototype) to test various aspects of the design, illustrate ideas or features, and gather early user feedback. Prototyping is often treated as an integral part of the development process, where it is believed to reduce project risk and cost.

public key encryption   An encryption scheme that uses two keys. In an email transaction, the public key encrypts the data, and a corresponding private key decrypts the data. Because the private key is never transmitted or publicized, the encryption scheme is extremely secure. For digital signatures, the process is reversed; the sender uses the private key to create the digital signature, which anyone who has access to the corresponding public key can read.

public key infrastructure (PKI)   Infrastructure used to facilitate e-commerce and build trust. PKI consists of hardware, software, people, policies, and procedures; it is used to create, manage, store, distribute, and revoke public key certificates. PKI is based on public key cryptography.

Q

qualitative analysis   A weighted factor or nonmonetary evaluation and analysis based on a weighting or criticality factor valuation as part of the evaluation or analysis.

qualitative assessment   An analysis of risk that places the probability results into categories such as none, low, medium, and high.

qualitative risk assessment   A scenario–based assessment in which one scenario is examined and assessed for each critical or major threat to an IT asset.

quantitative analysis   A numerical evaluation and analysis based on monetary or dollar valuation as part of the evaluation or analysis.

quantitative risk assessment   A methodical, step-by-step calculation of asset valuation, exposure to threats, and the financial impact or loss if the threat is realized.

queue   Any group of items, such as computer jobs or messages, waiting for service.

R

radio frequency identification (RFID) A set of components that include a reader and a small device referred to as a tag. The tag can be used to hold information for inventory, management, tracking, or other purposes. RFID provides a method to transmit and receive data over short range from one point to another.

RADIUS Remote Authentication Dial-In User Service. A client/server protocol and software that allows remote-access servers to communicate. Used in wireless systems such as 802.1x.

RAM resident infection A type of virus that spreads through RAM.

record A collection of data items or fields treated as one unit.

recovery point objective (RPO) The point in time to which data must be restored to resume processing transactions. RPO is the basis on which a data-protection strategy is developed.

recovery testing Testing aimed at verifying the system's capability to recover from varying degrees of failure.

recovery time objective (RTO) During the execution of disaster recovery or business continuity plans, the time goal for the reestablishment and recovery of a business function or resource.

Redundant Array of Independent Disks (RAID) A type of fault tolerance and performance improvement for disk drives that use two or more drives in combination. Also known as Redundant Array of Inexpensive Disks.

registration authority (RA) Entity responsible for the identification and authentication of the PKI certificate. The RA is not responsible for signing or issuing certificates. The most common form of certificate is the X.509 standard.

regression testing Retesting of a previously tested program following modification to ensure that faults have not been introduced or uncovered as a result of the changes made.

remote procedure call (RPC) A protocol that allows a computer program running on one host to cause code to be executed on another host without the programmer needing to explicitly code for this. When the code in question is written using object-oriented principles, RPC is sometimes referred to as remote invocation or remote method invocation.

repeater A network device used to regenerate or replicate a signal. Repeaters are used in transmission systems to regenerate analog or digital signals distorted by transmission loss.

repository A central place where data is stored and maintained. A repository can be a place where multiple databases or files are located for distribution over a network, or it can be a location that is directly accessible to the user without having to travel across a network.

request for proposal (RFP) A document that asks vendors to propose a hardware and system software that will meet the requirements of a new system.

required vacations A security control used to uncover misuse or illegal activity by requiring employees to use their vacation.

requirements definition An assessment of the needs that a system is to fulfill, including why the system is needed, what features will service or satisfy the need, and how the system is to be constructed.

resilience The capability of a system to maintain or regain normal function and development following a disturbance.

reverse engineering The process of taking a software program apart and analyzing its workings in detail, usually to construct a new device or program that does the same thing without actually copying anything from the original.

Rijndael A symmetric encryption algorithm chosen to be the Advanced Encryption Standard (AES).

ring topology A topology used by Token Ring and FDDI networks in which all devices are connected in a ring. Data packets in a ring topology are sent in a deterministic fashion from sender and receiver to the next device in the ring.

RIP Routing Information Protocol. A well-known distance-vector protocol that determines the best route by hop count. The original version, RIP 1, has security issues and as such was revised. RIP 2 has been revised but still has some security issues.

risk The exposure or potential for loss or damage to IT assets within that IT infrastructure.

risk acceptance An informed decision to suffer the consequences of likely events.

risk assessment A process for evaluating the exposure or potential loss or damage to the IT and data assets for an organization.

risk avoidance A decision to take action to avoid a risk.

risk management The overall responsibility and management of risk within an organization. Risk management is the responsibility and dissemination of roles, responsibilities, and accountabilities for risk in an organization.

risk transference Shifting the responsibility or burden to another party or individual.

rogue access point An 802.11 access point that might be added by an unapproved employee or by an attacker set up to divert legitimate users so that their traffic can be sniffed or manipulated.

role-based access control A type of discretionary access control in which users are placed into groups to facilitate management. Banks and casinos typically use this type of access control.

rotation of assignment A security mechanism that moves employees from one job to another so that one person does not stay in one position forever. This makes it harder for an employee to hide malicious activity.

rounding down A method of computer fraud that involves rounding down dollar amounts so that small amounts of money are stolen. As an example, the value $1,199.50 might be rounded down to $1,199.00.

router   A device that determines the next network point to which a data packet should be forwarded en route toward its destination. The router is connected to at least two networks and determines which way to send each data packet based on its current understanding of the state of the networks it is connected to. Routers create or maintain a table of the available routes and use this information to determine the best route for a given data packet. Routing occurs at Layer 3 (network layer) of the OSI seven-layer model.

rule-based access control   A type of mandatory access control that matches objects to subjects. It dynamically assigns roles to subjects based on their attributes and a set of rules defined by a security policy.

S

scope creep   The uncontrolled change in the project's scope. It causes the assessment to drift away from its original scope and results in budget and schedule overruns.

script kiddie   The lowest form of cracker, a hanger-on in the technical sense, in that they look for easy targets or well-worn vulnerabilities.

Secure Sockets Layer (SSL)   Developed by Netscape for transmitting private documents via the Internet. It works by using a private key to encrypt data that is transferred over the SSL connection. It is widely used and accepted by Netscape and Internet Explorer. Very similar to transport layer security (TLS).

security breach or security incident   The result of an attacker exploiting a threat or vulnerability.

security bulletin   A memorandum or message from a software vendor or manufacturer documenting a known security defect in the software or application itself. Security bulletins are typically accompanied with instructions for loading a software patch to mitigate the security defect or software vulnerability.

security by obscurity   The controversial use of secrecy to ensure security—for example, changing the name of the administrator account.

security controls   Policies, standards, procedures, and guideline definitions for various security control areas or topics.

security countermeasure   A security hardware or software technology solution that is deployed to ensure the confidentiality, integrity, and availability of IT assets that need protection.

security defect   A security defect is usually an unidentified and undocumented deficiency in a product or piece of software that ultimately results in a security vulnerability being identified.

security incident response team (SIRT)   A team of professionals that usually encompasses human resources, legal, IT, and IT security representatives to appropriately respond to critical, major, and minor security breaches and security incidents that the organization encounters.

security kernel   A combination of software, hardware, and firmware that makes up the trusted computer base (TCB). The TCB mediates all access, must be verifiable as correct, and is protected from modification.

security testing   Techniques used to confirm the design and/or operational effectiveness of security controls implemented within a system. Examples include attack and penetration studies to determine whether adequate controls have been implemented to prevent breach-of-system controls and processes, and password strength testing by using tools such as "password crackers."

security workflow definitions   Given the defense-in-depth, layered approach to information security roles, tasks, responsibilities, and accountabilities, a security workflow definition is a flowchart that defines the communications, checks and balances, and domain of responsibility and accountability for the organization's IT and IT security staff.

separation of duties   Given the seven areas of information security responsibility, separation of duties defines the roles, tasks, responsibilities, and accountabilities for information security uniquely for the different duties of the IT staff and IT security staff.

service level agreement (SLA)   A contractual agreement between an organization and its service provider. SLAs define and protect the organization in regard to holding the service provider accountable for the requirements as defined in an SLA.

service set ID (SSID)   A sequence of up to 32 letters or numbers that is the ID, or name, of a wireless local area network and is used to differentiate networks.

session slicing   Used to avoid an IDS by sending parts of the request in different packets.

SHA-1   A hashing algorithm that produces a 160-bit output.

sheepdip   The process of scanning for viruses on a standalone computer.

shoulder surfing   The act of looking over someone's shoulder to steal a password.

signature scanning   Used by IDS and virus scanning. One of the most basic ways of scanning for computer viruses. It works by comparing suspect files and programs to signatures of known viruses stored in a database.

Simple Mail Transfer Protocol (SMTP)   The standard protocol used for Internet mail.

Simple Network Management Protocol (SNMP)   An application-layer protocol that facilitates the exchange of management information between network devices. SNMP offers cryptographic support in SNMPv3, but not in SNMPv1 or SNMPv2. Uses well-known community strings of public and private.

single loss expectancy (SLE)   A dollar-value figure that represents an organization's loss from a single loss or the loss of this particular IT asset.

site survey   The process of determining the optimum placement of wireless access points. The objective of the site survey is to create an accurate wireless system design/layout and budgetary quote.

smurf attack   A DDoS attack in which an attacker transmits large amounts of ICMP echo request (ping) packets to a targeted IP destination device using the targeted destination's IP source address. This is called spoofing the IP source address. IP routers and other IP devices that respond to broadcasts respond to the targeted IP device with ICMP echo replies, thus multiplying the amount of bogus traffic.

sniffer   A hardware or software device that can be used for legitimate analysis or to intercept and decode network traffic.

social engineering   The practice of tricking employees into revealing sensitive data about their computer system or infrastructure. This type of attack targets people and is the art of human manipulation. Even when systems are physically well protected, social-engineering attacks are possible.

software bug or software flaw   An error in software coding, implementation, or its design that can result in software vulnerability.

software vulnerability standard   A standard that accompanies an organization's vulnerability assessment and management policy. This standard typically defines the organization's vulnerability window definition and how the organization is to provide software vulnerability management and software patch management throughout the enterprise.

source code   A nonexecutable program written in a high-level language. A compiler or assembler must translate the source code into an object code (machine language) that the computer can understand.

source document   The forms used to record data that has been captured. A source document can be a piece of paper, a turnaround document, or an image displayed for online data input.

source lines of code (SLOC)   A software metric used to measure the amount of code in a software program. SLOC is typically used to estimate the amount of effort that will be required to develop a program, as well as to estimate productivity or effort after the software is produced.

spam   The use of any electronic communication's medium to send unsolicited messages in bulk. Spamming is a major irritation of the Internet era.

spoofing   The act of masking one's identity and pretending to be someone else or another device. Common spoofing methods include ARP, DNS, and IP. IS also implemented by email in what is described as phishing schemes. Caller ID can also be spoofed.

spyware   Any software application that covertly gathers information about a user's Internet usage and activity, and then exploits this information by sending adware and pop-up ads similar in nature to the user's Internet usage history.

stateful inspection   An advanced firewall architecture that works at the network layer and can keep track of packet activity. Unlike static packet filtering, which examines a packet based on the information in its header, stateful inspection tracks each connection traversing all interfaces of the firewall and confirms that they are valid. For example, it verifies that the DNS reply just received is actually in response to a DNS request.

statistical sampling   The selection of sample units from a population, and the measurement and/or recording of information on these units, to obtain estimates of population characteristics.

steganography   A cryptographic method of hiding the existence of a message. A commonly used form places information in pictures.

storage area network (SAN)   A high-speed subnetwork that interconnects different data-storage devices with associated data servers for a large network. SANs support disk mirroring, backup and restore, archival and retrieval of archived data, data migration from one storage device to another, and the sharing of data among different servers in a network.

stream cipher   Encrypts data typically 1 byte at a time.

Structured Query Language (SQL)   The standardized relational database language for querying, manipulating, and updating information in a relational database.

substantive testing   Tests of detailed activities and transactions, or analytical review tests, designed to obtain audit evidence on the completeness, accuracy, or existence of those activities or transactions during the audit period.

supply chain management (SCM) Intercompany planning control and monitoring of central functions such as procurement, production, and sales to increase their efficiency.

switch   Operating at Layer 2 of the OSI model, a switch is a network device that links several separate LANs and provides packet filtering among them. A LAN switch is a device with multiple ports, each of which can support an entire Ethernet or Token Ring LAN.

symmetric algorithm   Both parties use the same cryptographic key.

symmetric encryption   An encryption standard that requires all parties to have a copy of a shared key. A single key is used for both encryption and decryption.

SYN flood attack   A DDoS attack in which the attacker sends a succession of SYN packets with a spoof address to a targeted destination IP device, but does not send the last ACK packet to acknowledge and confirm receipt. This leaves half-open connections between the client and the server until all resources are absorbed, rendering the server or targeted IP destination device unavailable because of resource allocation to this attack.

synchronize sequence number   Initially passed to the other party at the start of the three-step startup. It is used to track the movement of data between parties. Every byte of data sent over a TCP connection has a sequence number.

synchronous transmission   A method of communication in which data is sent in blocks, without the need for start and stop bits between each byte. Synchronization is achieved by sending a clock signal along with the data and by sending special bit patterns to denote the start of each block.

system software   The software that controls the operations of a computer system. It is a group of programs instead of one program. The operating system controls the hardware in the computer and peripherals, manages memory and files and multitasking functions, and is the interface between application programs and the computer. Utility programs perform tasks such as format, check disk, and defragment disks.

system testing   Bringing together all the programs that a system comprises, for testing purposes. Programs are typically integrated in a top-down, incremental fashion.

systems criticality matrix (SCM)   Similar to the OICM, the SCM defines the organization's critical systems. This allows the organization to identify and focus its security mechanisms on the systems that are most critical to the organization's mission.

system development lifecycle (SDLC)   A method for developing information systems. It has five main stages: analysis, design, development, implementation, and evaluation. Each stage has several components; for example, the development stage includes programming (coding, including internal documentation, debugging, testing, and documenting) and acquiring equipment (selection, acquisition [purchase or lease], and testing).

T

TACACS   A TCP-based access-control protocol that provides authentication, authorization, and accountability.

TCB   Trusted computer base, all the protection mechanisms within a computer system. This includes hardware, firmware, and software that are responsible for enforcing a security policy.

TCP handshake   A three-step process computers go through when negotiating a connection with one another. The process is a target of attackers and others with malicious intent.

telecommunications   Systems that transport information over a distance, sending and receiving audio, video, and data signals through electronic means.

test data   Data that is run through a computer program to test the software. Test data can be used to test compliance with controls in the software.

threat   Any agent, condition, or circumstance that could potentially cause harm, loss, damage, or compromise to any IT asset or data asset.

throughput   The amount of data transferred from one place to another or processed in a specified amount of time. Data-transfer rates for disk drives and networks are measured in terms of throughput. Typically, throughputs are measured in kilobits per second, megabits per second, and gigabits per second.

Time to Live (TTL)   A counter within an IP packet that specifies the maximum number of hops that a packet can traverse. When a TTL is decremented to zero, a packet expires.

traceroute   A way of tracing hops or computers between the source and the target computer you are trying to reach. Gives the path the packets are taking.

Transient Electromagnetic Pulse Emanation Standard (TEMPEST)   A method of shielding equipment to prevent the capability of capturing and using stray electronic signals and reconstructing them into useful intelligence.

Transmission Control Protocol (TCP)   One of the main protocols of IP. TCP is used for reliability and guaranteed delivery of data.

Transmission Control Protocol/Internet Protocol (TCP/IP)   A collection of protocols used to provide the basis for Internet and World Wide Web services.

trap-door function   A one-way mathematical function based on discrete logarithms or the factoring of large prime numbers that describes how asymmetric algorithms function.

Trojan   A program that is a malicious piece of software. Typically, the user is tricked by some means into running the Trojan; otherwise, the malicious program would have never been accessed had the end user known about its true purpose.

Trusted Computer System Evaluation Criteria (TCSEC)   U.S. Department of Defense (DOD) Trusted Computer System Evaluation Criteria, also called the Orange Book. TCSEC is a system designed to evaluate standalone systems that places systems into one of four levels, A, B, C, or D. Each level has subcategories. Its basis of measurement is confidentiality.

tumbling   The process of rolling through various electronic serial numbers on a cell phone to attempt to find a valid set to use.

tunneling   A technology that enables one network to send its data via another network's connections. Tunneling works by encapsulating a network protocol within packets carried by the second network. For example, Microsoft's PPTP technology enables organizations to use the Internet to transmit data across a VPN. It does this by embedding its own network protocol within the TCP/IP packets carried by the Internet. Tunneling is also called encapsulation. Can also be used covertly, such as with STUNNEL and other programs.

turnstile   A one-way gate or access-control mechanism that is used to limit traffic and control the flow of people.

U

uninterruptible power supply (UPS) A device designed to provide a backup power supply during a power failure. Basically, a UPS is a battery backup system with an ultra-fast sensing device.

unit testing In computer programming, a method of testing the correctness of a particular module of source code.

Universal Serial Bus (USB) A specification standard for connecting peripherals to a computer. It can connect up to 127 devices to a computer and transfers data at a slower rate, a maximum of 12Mbps.

URL Uniform resource locator, the global address on the Internet and World Wide Web by which domain names are used to resolve IP addresses.

User Datagram Protocol (UDP) A connectionless protocol that provides very few error-recovery services, but offers a quick and direct way to send and receive datagrams.

utility programs A standard set of routines that assist in the operation of a computer system by performing some frequently required process, such as copying, sorting, or merging.

V

vandalism The willful destruction of property.

verification The process of confirming that data is correct and accurate before it is processed or entered.

Videocipher II Satellite Encryption System Encryption mechanism used to encrypt satellite video transmissions

virtual private network (VPN) A private network that uses a public network to connect remote sites and users.

virus A computer program with the capability to generate copies of itself and, thereby, spread. Viruses usually require the interaction of an individual and can have rather benign results, such as flashing a message to the screen, or rather malicious results that destroy data, systems, integrity, or availability.

virus hoax A chain letter designed to trick you into forwarding to many other people, warning of a virus that does not exist. The Good Times virus is an example.

voice mail A service that works like an answering machine and allows callers to leave a message. This message can be reviewed, copied, stored, annotated, and forwarded to one or many people.

voice over IP (VoIP) The capability to convert voice or fax calls into data packets for transmission over the Internet or other IP-based networks.

vulnerability The absence or weakness of a safeguard in an asset.

vulnerability assessment A methodical evaluation of an organization's IT weaknesses of infrastructure components and assets, and how those weaknesses can be mitigated through proper security controls and recommendations to remediate exposure to risks, threats, and vulnerabilities.

vulnerability management   The overall responsibility and management of vulnerabilities within an organization, and how that management of vulnerabilities will be achieved through dissemination of duties throughout the IT organization.

W

war chalking   The act of marking on the wall or sidewalk near a building to indicate that it has wireless access.

war dialing   The process of using a software program to automatically call thousands of telephone numbers to look for anyone who has a modem attached.

war driving   The process of driving around a neighborhood or area to identify wireless access points.

warm site   An alternative computer facility that is partially configured and can be made ready in a few days.

white-box testing   A security assessment or penetration test in which all aspects of the network are known. It can also be an assessment of a device or program while knowing the code, and so on.

WHOIS   An Internet utility that returns registration information about the domain name and IP address.

wide area network (WAN)   Network that spans the distance between buildings, cities, and even countries. WANs are LANs connected using wide area network services from telecommunications carriers; they typically use technologies such as standard

phone lines—called plain old telephone service (POTS) or public switched telephone network (PSTN)—Integrated Services Digital Network (ISDN), Frame Relay, Asynchronous Transfer Mode (ATM), or other high-speed services.

Wi-Fi Protected Access (WPA)   A security standard for wireless networks, designed to be more secure than WEP. Developed from the draft 802.11i standard. Replaced by WPA2.

Wired Equivalent Privacy (WEP)   Based on the RC4 encryption scheme. It was designed to provide the same level of security as that of a wired LAN. Because of 40-bit encryption and problems with the initialization vector, it was found to be insecure.

work breakdown structure (WBS)   Process oriented; shows what activities need to be completed in a hierarchical manner.

worm   A self-replicating sometimes polymorphic program that spreads by inserting copies of itself into other executable codes, programs, or documents. Worms typically flood a network with traffic and result in a denial of service.

wrapper   A type of program such as Whack-a-mole, that is used to bind a Trojan program to a legitimate program. The objective is to trick the user into running the wrapped program and installing the Trojan.

written authorization   One of the most important parts of the ethical hack. IT gives you permission to perform the tests that the client has agreed to.

Z

zone transfer   The mechanism DNS servers use to update each other by transferring resource records. This should be a controlled process between DNS servers, but hackers will attempt to perform a zone transfer to steal the organization's DNS information. This can be used to map the network devices.

Index

simple backup-rotation schemes, 433

simplex communication, 225

single sign-on, 307-309

site licensing, 230

size of software, estimating, 123-124

SLAs (service level agreements), 95-96, 199

SLE (single loss expectancy), calculating, 86, 416

SLOC (source lines of code), 123

SMTP (Simple Mail Transfer Protocol), 248

smurf attacks, 318

sniffers, 275

SNMP (Simple Network Management Protocol), 249, 275

sociability tests, 456

social engineering, 314

software
cost estimation, 122-123
licensing issues, 230
size estimation, 123-124
testing, 455-456

software development, 221
decompilers, 223
programming languages, 222
sandbox scheme, 222

software escrow, 434

software recovery, 431-432

source code, verifying, 460

sources of physical security breaches, 370-371

sourcing, 93
SLAs, 95-96

SOX (Sarbanes-Oxley Act), 25, 40

spiral application development model, 143, 457

sponsor payment method of security system funding, 74

spreading code, 270

sprints, 144

SSH (Secure Shell), 349

SSIDs (Service Set IDs), 269

SSL (Secure Sockets Layer), 349

standards, 28, 78
ISACA auditing standards, 28-29

standby database shadowing, 434

standby UPS systems, 383

standing data, 165

star topologies, 255

stateful inspection firewalls, 264, 321, 468

stateless connections, 249

stateless firewalls, 322

statistical IDS detection, 323, 468

statistical sampling, 46

steering committee, 70

stochastic events, 85

store-and-forward switching, 260

STP (shielded twisted-pair), 256

strategic planning, 26

stream cipher algorithm, 343

strip-cut shredders, 369

strong matrix organizational form, 119

study tips, 9-10

subnetworks, 250

substantive testing, 46

substantive tests, 28

supercomputers, 215

supervisory mode, 224

SURRE (Sufficient, Useable, Reliable, Relevant, Effective) rule, 47

switches, 217, 259-261

symmetric encryption, 341
AES, 344
DES, 343-344
private key encryption, 342-343

symmetric encryption algorithms, 469

syn floods, 319

system access
access creep, 301
discretionary access control, 301

layers of security controls, 299-300

mandatory access control, 302

role-based access control, 302-303

system testing, 137

System-control parameter, 165

systems development, auditing, 176-177

T

T-carriers, 268

TACACS, 310

tactical planning, 26

tape-management systems, 219

tasks, CPM, 127

TCP (Transmission Control Protocol), 246

TCP/IP model
application layer, 253-254
host-to-host layer, 252-253
internet layer, 250-252
network access layer, 250
versus OSI reference model, 249

technical support, 204, 206

telecommunications recovery, 434-435

TEMPEST, 314

TES (terminal-emulation software), 249

testing applications, 172-173

testing methodologies, 137

testing phase of BCP process, 421-423
full operation testing, 424
paper tests, 423
preparedness testing, 424

testing software, 456

tests (practice)
answers, 509-525
questions, 476-508

threat identification, 81

threats, 32. *See also* incident handling